GRAPEVINE

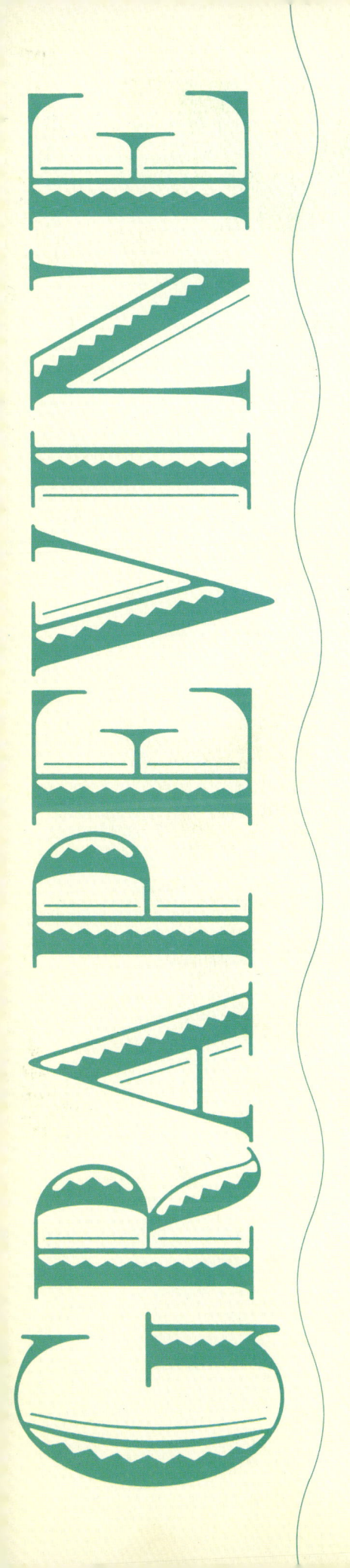

Teacher's Book 1

PETER VINEY AND KAREN VINEY

Oxford University Press 1990

Note on recorded material:
All presentation material is recorded except in Units 7, 11, 12, and 40.

☺ listening development activities

♪ songs

The recordings occur on the cassette in the order in which they appear in the Student's Book units.

Teachers are reminded that if they do not wish students to write in their books, answers should be written on a separate sheet of paper.

Oxford University Press
Walton Street, Oxford OX2 6DP

Oxford New York Toronto
Delhi Bombay Calcutta Madras Karachi
Petaling Jaya Singapore Hong Kong Tokyo
Nairobi Dar es Salaam Cape Town
Melbourne Auckland

and associated companies in
Berlin Ibadan

OXFORD and Oxford English are trade marks of Oxford University Press

First published 1990
Second impression 1990

ISBN 0 19 425382 1   Teacher's Book
ISBN 0 19 425381 3   Student's Book
ISBN 0 19 425383 X   Workbook (part A)
ISBN 0 19 425385 6   Workbook (part B)
ISBN 0 19 425384 8   Audio cassettes (x 2)

Video – VHS PAL (other formats available)
ISBN 0 19 458375 9   Video cassette 1
ISBN 0 19 458384 8   Video cassette 2
ISBN 0 19 458393 7   Video Activity Book

© Oxford University Press, 1990

All rights reserved. No part of this publication may be reproduced, stored in a retrieval system, or transmitted, in any form or by any means, electronic, mechanical, photocopying, recording, or otherwise, without the prior permission of Oxford University Press.

This book is sold subject to the condition that it shall not, by way of trade or otherwise, be lent, re-sold, hired out, or otherwise circulated without the publisher's prior consent in any form of binding or cover other than that in which it is published and without a similar condition including this condition being imposed on the subsequent purchaser.

Typeset by Tradespools Ltd., Frome, Somerset
Printed and bound in Hong Kong

To the teacher

Course components

The components of *Grapevine 1* are:

♦ **Student's Book,** with one double-page introductory unit, forty double-page main units, four 'Stories for pleasure', a Grammar summaries section, a Listening appendix, Irregular verbs list and a Vocabulary index.

♦ **Workbook,** in parts A and B, with 40 units corresponding to those in the Student's Book. Workbook 1 A corresponds to Student's Book Units 1–20, Workbook 1 B to Student's Book Units 21–40.

♦ **Teacher's Book,** interleaved with the pages from the Student's Book. It contains detailed lesson plans, including notes on the Workbooks. The Listening appendix, Irregular verbs list, Vocabulary index, and Grammar summaries section from the Student's Book are included as well as a key to the Workbook exercises.

♦ **Stereo audio cassette,** containing recordings of the dialogues, texts, songs, and listening material.

♦ An optional **video cassette**, with 8 video sketches for use with the introductory unit, and Units 5, 10, 15, 20, 25, 30, and 35.

♦ **Video Activity Book** with exploitation exercises, language summaries, transcripts, and a teacher's section including an introduction on video techniques and detailed notes on exploitation of each sketch.

The optional video component

♦ The course can be used equally effectively with or without the video component. There is nothing in the Student's Book to indicate that the introductory unit and Units 5, 10, 15, 20, 25, 30, and 35 have a video component.

♦ The Video Activity Book gives a full exploitation procedure for those teachers using the videos.

♦ The video sketches can be used:

1 For presentation instead of the audio cassette. They contain the same material as the audio cassette, but often have additional material as well.

2 In a later lesson, when the teacher can arrange access to video equipment, to review and extend the material used for the initial audio cassette presentation.

3 Together at the end of the course, as a rapid review of the syllabus.

The beginner level

Grapevine 1 is designed for beginners. It can be used with a very wide age and ability range. There is no continuing story, and the units are all independent of each other. With false beginners the material can be used selectively. The materials will be suitable for:

♦ **Zero beginners** – Students who have studied no English before. With these students we would suggest working carefully to the syllabus. We would also suggest using some exercises from the Workbooks in class. (See detailed teacher's notes for each lesson.)

♦ **Beginners** – Students who may have studied English at primary level, or older students who studied a little English several years earlier. Again we would suggest working to the progression of the syllabus.

♦ **False beginners** – Students who have studied a previous course, but who need to go through everything again. With these students it is possible to select units, and it is less important to stick rigidly to the progression of the syllabus. As each unit has a new and discrete story or topic, it will be easy to use the materials selectively. With these students the Workbooks can be done outside the class.

First principles

We believe that the following points are essential for a successful beginners' course:

♦ **A co-operative, non-judgemental atmosphere in the classroom**

Students must feel free to experiment with language without fear of ridicule or embarrassment.

♦ **An emphasis on communicative goals**

We remember seeing two students in a coffee bar. One sat with his textbook rehearsing what he was going to say. It took him ten minutes to pluck up the courage to go to the counter, and say *Excuse me, I would like a cup of coffee, please*. The second student went straight to the counter, nodded and smiled, and said *Coffee*. In terms of communication, the second student was much more successful. The dialogues have been designed with communicative effectiveness in mind.

◆ **Transparent teaching points**

We leave it up to the teacher to decide whether to introduce grammatical or functional descriptions of the language, and when to introduce them. However, each unit has a clear focus, and the teaching point should be transparent. If you wish to avoid describing the language (either structurally or functionally) you will be able to do so. The students should be able to deduce the point of the lesson. They are provided with full Grammar summaries at the end of the Student's Book.

◆ **A clear, carefully-ordered syllabus**

The syllabus has interwoven structural and functional elements. They have been designed to follow a clear and logical progression. We have tried to balance the immediate communicative needs with the long-term aims of knowledge of the grammatical system.

◆ **Vocabulary development strategies**

The importance of vocabulary has been greatly underrated in recent years. It seemed to be forgotten during the 1970s and early 1980s while arguments raged about structural and functional syllabus design. It is important to promote the students' abilities to cope with new and unfamiliar vocabulary items, and to refine their ability to make intelligent guesses. To this end we have made a pragmatic division of the vocabulary in *Grapevine 1* into three categories (Active, Passive, Classroom) and noted where 'redundant' vocabulary occurs in reading development work. (See also notes on The reference section, page 3.) Both the Student's Book and, in particular, the Workbooks contain reading and vocabulary development material. The Workbooks also contain many exercises designed to review vocabulary.

◆ **A balanced approach to skills development**

There should be a balance between the skills of listening, speaking, reading, and writing. We are convinced that the Student's Book material at beginner level should be biased towards listening and speaking, though reading and writing should also be steadily developed. The Workbooks concentrate more on reading and writing. Reading and listening development activities have been included throughout the course, which will enable students to develop their skills in reading and listening to 'roughly-tuned' materials. There are four 'Stories for pleasure', where the teacher can choose between using the stories for extensive reading, extensive listening, or intensive reading for revision.

◆ **Variety of classroom activity**

Lessons should not follow a predictable formula. There should be individual solo activities, teacher-centred activities, paired activities, group activities, and games and role plays which involve the whole class.

◆ **Varied and interesting contexts**

A variety of contexts keep up the students' interest level. Different types of context appeal to different people. On tape and video, students will hear a variety of accents and speaking styles. Humour has a vital role in language learning, and contexts have been designed to amuse and interest students.

◆ **Recognition of the broader educational context**

Language learning is not an isolated activity, but a part of a student's general development. Contexts and activities have been designed with this in mind.

◆ **Drills and repetition**

There is still a place for a mechanical element. The teaching notes suggest some mechanical activities, such as drills and repetition work. We believe that these help to instil confidence in the students. It should be noted that *everything* we suggest in the teacher's notes is optional. Although we believe that there is a role for mechanical activities (see notes on drills and repetition below), the course can be used successfully without them. Criticism of mechanical activities has led to courses without drills and repetition. As long as these activities are done at speed, are not laboured, are not continued to the point of boredom, and are seen as what they are—they are not communication, but a step on the road to eventual communication—they have a purpose in the language teacher's repertoire for the 21st century. In several units, drills and repetition work are included for beginners, but there is a note advising teachers of false beginners to skip some of them.

◆ **The teacher**

We have left the most important element until last. During lesson observation, we have seen the same material taught in a huge variety of styles. There is no '*Grapevine* style' of teaching, in spite of the very detailed plans we have given. One teacher may be extrovert and amusing, another may be quiet and sympathetic, a third may be highly organized and disciplined. You have to make the best of your own personality and beliefs. Books can give plans, but they can never show you how to relate to a number of individuals in a particular place on a particular day. Points to bear in mind are:

1 The ability to listen sympathetically and with interest to your students may be the most important teacher skill of all. You cannot be genuinely interested in all your students every day, but you can learn to pretend and demonstrate interest.

2 Clarity of classroom instruction is essential with beginners. We have done our best to make the printed instructions clear and consistent. It is just as important to be clear and consistent with oral instructions and explanations.

3 Don't set unrealistic goals. The course has a spiral progression. Everything will be covered again, and so it is unrealistic to expect perfect accuracy from students, in structure or pronunciation, the first time

around. To do so breaks the students' confidence and makes them too self-conscious to aim for communicative goals. Don't set unrealistic goals for yourself either. Don't try to do too much in a lesson. If something comes up which interests all the students, go with it. Leave space to allow yourself to be side-tracked.

4 Accuracy and fluency. There are times in the lesson for both. You can ask for reasonable accuracy in drills and controlled-question work. However, in role plays, discussions, and free-practice phases of the lesson the aim is not accuracy. It is communication.

5 Feedback. There is a place in the classroom for both confirmation and correction. Students need confirmation when they are performing effectively. Confirmation can be a nod, a smile, or a gesture. You needn't say *Yes, that's right*. If you use confirmation when things are going well, you may find that the most effective correction device is simply a lack of confirmation. When we are speaking in a foreign language we often realize we are making mistakes as we make them. Students should have the chance to *self-correct* before the teacher intervenes.

6 An open door.... We have never observed other teachers without learning something of value. One of the most appealing things about being a teacher is that when you are in class, you are in a private world with your students. The presence of an outsider in this situation is inhibiting: you don't feel free to make jokes; you find yourself teaching for the observer, not for the class. However, we can all benefit by watching our colleagues, and by having our colleagues watch us. It is worth trying to watch other teachers, and it is worth inviting other teachers to watch you. You may never learn to enjoy the experience, but we are sure that you will find it valuable.

The Teacher's Book

Lesson plans

The detailed lesson plans for each unit begin with a reference section, before going on to step-by-step notes for each phase of the lesson.

◆ **Timing**

Each double-page unit has been planned to take an average of one and a half hours in the classroom. In some situations this is the length of a language lesson, in other situations it is a 'double lesson' (two 45-minute periods).

However, the suggested timings will vary widely in different teaching situations. With good false beginners it would be reasonable to expect to cover a unit in one 45–50-minute lesson, and on an intensive course there would be advantages in doing so.

With zero beginners and pre-beginners it may take longer than one and a half hours to complete a lesson, especially if the Workbooks are being used in class. You will need to weigh the desire to exploit the materials thoroughly with the need to cover a given syllabus within the duration of this course. The course has cyclical review elements throughout, and the early units of *Grapevine 2* are designed to review the syllabus. (See the notes on 'unrealistic goals' on pages 2–3.) This means that students will have every chance to cover the teaching points again, so you should not need to labour for perfection on a given point before moving on.

◆ **The reference section**

The reference section at the beginning of each plan is divided into:

Teaching points – These summarize the structural and functional targets of the unit. (See the Grammar summaries appendix for more details.)

Grammar note – This appears in many units, and comments on the structures being covered.

Expressions – This section lists the formulas and fixed expressions used in the unit. This section is important. We have often used items in this section as formulas before teaching the structure later in the course. For example, students learn *I don't know* early in the course. It is extremely useful, and they are also familiarizing themselves with the form of 'simple present negatives' long before they meet the simple present as a structure.

Active vocabulary – This section includes structural terms, and is indexed at the back of the book in the Vocabulary index. Because a word is included in this section, it does not mean that students are expected to 'learn' it. We would expect students to become familiar with words by using them. Individual students may wish to sit and memorize words, but this should not be necessary.

Passive vocabulary – This list contains words occurring in texts and dialogues which are necessary for the context of a particular unit, but which students will not be expected to use or recall once the lesson has finished. As long as they understand them in context it is enough. Some words will appear as 'passive' vocabulary in an earlier unit, but will become 'active' vocabulary in a later unit. There is no suggestion that words in this section are less useful, less frequent, or less important than those in the active vocabulary section. Their place under passive vocabulary relates to their use in that particular unit. They are indicated by the letter 'P' in the Vocabulary index.

Classroom vocabulary – This list contains words which the teacher will need to use in the lesson, but which only (if at all) appear in print in the Student's Book in headings and instructions. They may also appear in the Workbooks. Many of these words are part of the language of classroom instruction. They may become part of the 'active' vocabulary in a later unit, in which case they will be listed again. They are indicated by the letter 'C' in the Vocabulary index.

Redundant vocabulary – Some sections are designed to develop reading skills, and therefore contain totally redundant words. These will not be taught, explained, or used in the lesson. They are words that we want students to 'read around'. They are not listed in the Vocabulary index.

Audio-visual aids – Extra vocabulary which may appear in the Workbooks, particularly in vocabulary-guessing exercises and reading-development material is not listed. This section lists the audio and video cassettes which relate to the unit, together with suggestions for other visual aids where appropriate. These are optional.

◆ **The step-by-step teaching notes**

The sections – The step-by-step notes are divided into clear sections. This makes it easier to plan breaks between the various parts of a unit, and makes the material easier to handle when it is shared between two teachers.

In the lesson plans we have used the following abbreviations:

T represents the teacher;
C represents the class in chorus;
S represents an individual student;
S1, S2, S3 represent three different individual students.

We hope that the plans are clear and self-evident. The notes below discuss techniques which are used in them. At this point in an introduction many readers are speed reading, or using the introduction to look up a particular point. *Please* read the notes below. They do not (and could not) cover everything which you might do in the classroom, but they do cover some techniques. We are *not* telling you how to teach the course; we are *not* saying that the suggestions below are the best way of teaching a lesson. We would claim that the procedure we suggest gives a thorough and competent route through the materials—but not the only one.

Techniques

◆ **Presenting recorded materials**

Whenever possible, recorded texts and dialogues should be presented on cassette. The cassette component has a variety of speakers, accents, and registers. It has been timed carefully to be towards the lower end of the normal native-speaker speed range. It is not artificially slowed or over-enunciated. It is, however, recorded in stereo, which greatly aids voice separation and clarity. Students need to hear a variety of voices. If they are confronted with natural pace from the beginning, they will accept English at its natural speed from then on.

Teachers can present dialogues themselves, yet—though it may be amusing for the students—teacher presentation removes both challenge and variety. There will be occasions when equipment is not working or power supplies fail, and then teachers will have to resort to acting out dialogues themselves.

When playing a cassette to a class, be careful not to distract them from the listening task. Don't use the time to write on the board, order your notes, or tidy your desk. Move out of eye contact with the class, and listen with them. We would *not* recommend using cassette players with variable-speed controls at any time during the course.

◆ **Repetition**

Choral repetition gives students a chance to get their tongues round the sound of English words without fear of embarrassment. In a large class, it gives everyone the chance to practise sounds before having to produce them individually.

Ask students to repeat chorally, then follow up the choral repetition by checking a few individuals. Pay attention to stress, rhythm, intonation, and catenation as well as pronunciation.

Wherever possible, get students to repeat after the recorded model initially. If it's acceptable, move on. If there are problems, get them to repeat after you, breaking up the sentence by backchaining (backward build-up) or frontchaining (forward build-up).

For example:

Backchaining
Target sentence: *Would you like a cup of tea?*
Stages: *Would you like a cup of tea? / tea? / cup of tea? / like a cup of tea? / Would you like a cup of tea?*

Frontchaining
Target sentence: *I'd like an apple juice.*
Stages: *I'd like an apple juice. / I / I'd like / I'd like an apple juice.*

In some units, selective repetition is suggested. This means repeating only the sentences which are part of the teaching points of the lesson, or which have particularly interesting stress and intonation patterns.

The recordings try to demonstrate the range of pronunciation among native speakers. We show RP (Received Pronunciation or 'BBC English') accents, but we also show American, Scottish, Irish, Welsh, Australian, Northern English, Western English, and many other accents. When students hear a variety of accents they work out the median for themselves. We feel that undue time spent in learning to reproduce the RP pronunciation of (for example) 'bath' [bɑːθ] may be wasted when you consider that most native speakers, including Americans and English people living in the middle and north of the country, say [bæθ].

Some people believe it is important to learn the basic sounds of English perfectly at the beginning of a course. They often get excellent results. However, we feel that over-attention to exact reproduction at the earliest stages leads to embarrassment. Some students genuinely have a 'poor ear' for foreign sounds, and they will need time to improve at their own pace. Remember that there is no such thing as English without an accent. We see nothing wrong in people guessing your nationality when you are speaking English, as long as you are clear and comprehensible.

◆ **Stress, rhythm, and intonation**

During repetition work, stress, rhythm, and intonation are as important as pronunciation. The recordings are designed to demonstrate these features of the language. We have avoided the use of stress and intonation diagrams, as they can often cause confusion for students and teachers alike, though occasionally simple arrows can be employed to denote rising or falling intonation. A cassette recording is the best way of noting stress, rhythm, and intonation. If you are happy with diagrams and gestures to demonstrate patterns, use them. If not, concentrate on the recordings.

◆ **Drills**

Drills are not communication, and we would not claim that they are. Drills do, however, give students confidence when the time comes to perform freely, and they maximize student speaking-time in a large class. With very small groups (fewer than 7 or 8 students) they may be less necessary, although we would still use them. We have deliberately chosen drills which are simple. They are always contextualized. They help to train students to make automatic connections, e.g. between *he* and *she* and *does* and *has*.

Drills operate at a mechanical level, and the mere ability to do a drill is not the aim of any unit in the course. Drills come early in lessons, and they should be short, contextualized, and done at speed.

The drills should usually be done chorally at first, then individuals should be checked.

There are only 6 or 8 prompts per drill. Even with very large classes, drills need not be extended beyond 6 or 8 prompts in the individual stage. If you do so, the drills will become boring.

We suggest the following procedure for doing a drill:

1 Get students to repeat the key sentence chorally (e.g. *I'd like a cup of coffee.*).
2 Demonstrate how the drill works with examples (two for simple substitution and response drills, three for more complex two/three slot substitutions). Do this by turning your head or body to show that there are two parts to the drill.
For example, say:
Teacher: *I*
Class: *I'd like a cup of coffee.*
Teacher: *He*
Class: *He'd like a cup of coffee.*
3 Do the drill chorally at speed, remembering that intonation and stress are as important as structure.
For example:
Teacher: *I*
Class: *I'd like a cup of coffee.*
Teacher: *He*
Class: *He'd like a cup of coffee.*
Teacher: *She*
Class: *She'd like a cup of coffee.*
etc.
4 Do the drill again, asking six or eight selected individuals. This is the most difficult part of the drill, and drills often become tedious and unchallenging because of the way this stage is handled. The key elements are:

a Students must be chosen <u>at random</u>, *never* round the class.
b The most important part of the individual phase is <u>thinking time</u>. Give the prompt, then pause long enough for everyone in the class to formulate the response mentally, then—and only then—choose an individual student at random to respond. In this way, though only six students may actually speak, everyone in the room has been through the process of working out the response.
c Even if you only give 6 prompts to a class of 40, you should occasionally ask the same student to respond twice in a drill. Then students realize that they cannot 'switch off' once they have spoken.

Example
T: *I* (pause, select S1)
S1: *I'd like a cup of coffee.*
T: *He* (pause, select S2)
S2: *He'd like a cup of coffee.*
T: *She* (pause, select S3)
S3: *She'd like a cup of coffee.*
T: *We* (pause, select S1 again)
S1: *We'd like a cup of coffee.*
T: *They* (pause, select S4)
S4: *They'd like a cup of coffee.*
T: *You* (pause, select S5)
S5: *You'd like a cup of coffee.*

◆ **Reading aloud**

Reading aloud is a very important skill for the teacher. At beginner level, we *never* ask students to read aloud in front of the class. Reading aloud presents a bad model; it's boring for the rest of the class; it's something native speakers do badly; and it's unnecessary for students to be able to do it unless they are studying for an exam which requires reading aloud. When students do paired reading of a dialogue, they will get sufficient practice in reading aloud without personal embarrassment, without boring other students, and without presenting a bad model.

◆ **Reading silently**

The natural way to read is silently. Students are asked to read texts and dialogues silently, usually after hearing them on tape and having repeated them either from the tape or after the teacher. Sometimes, particularly when a text is designed to enhance reading comprehension, or is explanatory, they are asked to read texts silently before any other work is done.

If students are allowed to ask you questions during a silent reading phase it breaks everyone else's concentration. They should be encouraged to note down problem words and to read on to the end of a text. Then, when everyone has finished reading, you can take questions.

◆ Paired reading

Students are asked to read dialogues aloud in pairs. This maximizes student speaking-time, and gives them a chance to move from the printed word to vocalization without the pressure of an audience.

In a two-part dialogue, this will mean going through the dialogue twice, reversing roles after the first reading. Sometimes paired reading will involve controlled substitutions from a list or exercise. When they are making free substitutions we would call it a role play (see below). With short, communicatively useful dialogues, it may be worth the teacher re-enacting the dialogue with a selected student. If you do this, it is sometimes a good idea to push the student into a role-playing situation by giving unexpected responses (having done it properly once or twice already). For example, the original dialogue may contain this sequence (from Unit 22):

A: *Have you got any tickets for Saturday?*
B: *Yes, we have. Where would you like to sit?*
A: *Can we have two seats at the back?*
B: *Yes, that's OK. Here you are …*

If you acted it out with a student at the front of the class, it might become:

S: *Have you got any tickets for Saturday?*
T: *What? Are you talking to me?*
S: *Yes. Have you got any tickets for Saturday?*
T: *I don't know.*
S: *Er … you don't know? Why?*
T: *It's not my job. I'm an electrician. There's a problem with the lights in the ticket office.*
S: *Well, when can I get tickets?*
T: *I don't know. Look, can you help me?*
S: *Um … yes, I can.*
T: *Hold this electric wire. Be careful, there's 10,000 volts in it …*

This is an elaborate example, but the same kind of thing can be done in small ways whenever you are practising a dialogue with a student. The unexpected forces them into using language outside a controlled situation.

◆ Questions

Questions have two purposes in the language classroom.

Comprehension questions are based on a text or dialogue, and are a form of controlled language practice. When asking comprehension questions, remember to give everyone in the class time to formulate the answer mentally before selecting an individual student to respond. (See the notes on 'thinking time' under **Drills** on page 5.)

Transfer questions are related to the students, and their own experiences, knowledge, or opinions.

In both question types, you should not insist on a fixed answer. If you do so, it becomes a 'question drill'. Answers like: *I don't know. / Maybe. / Yes. / No. / London. / Yesterday.* are all genuine answers, which native speakers might use in a given situation.

You can, of course, frame the question so that a particular type of answer becomes *more likely*. (Full question sequences are given in the step-by-step notes.)

Types of question include:

1. **Yes/No questions**. These questions elicit short responses, and are useful for reviewing the content of texts and dialogues, and also for setting up 'interactive questions' (see below). Yes/No questions are questions like: *Are you listening? / Have you got a pen? / Do you like tea? / Is he going to phone her? / Did she buy any meat?* etc.
The answers will tend to be like this: *Yes, I am. / No, I'm not. / Yes, I have. / No, She hasn't. / Yes, I do. / No, it doesn't. / Yes, we did. / No, they didn't.*

   The student's task is easier than the content of the questions, while the questions review the information given in a text or dialogue.

2. **Either/or questions**. These questions are artificial, in that they are designed to elicit a full response, and such questions are fairly rare in normal discourse. Examples are: *Has she got a red pen or has she got a blue pen? / Did he go to the bank, or did he go to the post office? / Are they in the kitchen, or are they in the living room?* The usual answer would be a complete sentence: *She's got a blue pen. / He went to the bank. / They're in the living room.*
   i.e. The students are producing complete sentences, which reproduce the original text.

3. **Wh- questions**. Wh- questions (or 'open questions') are questions like: *Where are they? / Who went to the bank? / What are they doing? / How many people are there? / Why is she going to drive to London?* Again, these tend to produce a full answer, though it might often be a truncated answer. It might elicit: *They're in the living room*, or it might elicit *The living room*. Students will usually give the full answer, as they wish to practise their English!

4. **Interactive questions**. These are prompts designed to get students to make questions. At the simplest level, you can say *Ask me / him / her / each other*. For example:

   T: *Do you like dancing?*
   S1: *No, I don't.*
   T: (points at S2) *Ask her.*
   S1: *Do you like dancing?*
   S2: *Yes, I do.*
   T: *Juan, do you like dancing?*
   S4: *Sometimes.*
   T: (indicates S5) *Ask me.*
   S5: *Do you like dancing?*
   T: *No, I don't. I've got two left feet! Ask each other.*
   (All students ask someone near them: it is informal pair work.)

Informal pair work is useful. Don't worry about careful pairing. *Ask each other* is only used for one or two questions, where it would not be worth setting up formal pairs.

You could vary the questions by adding prompts. For example:

T: *Do you like football?*
S1: *Yes, I do.*
T: *Ask him … 'tennis'.*
S1: *Do you like tennis?*
S2: *No, not much.*
T: *Ask her … 'volleyball'.*
S3: *Do you like volleyball?*
S4: *No, I don't. I hate volleyball! It's a stupid game.*

We often use slightly more complex interactive questions, such as: *Ask 'Where?' / Ask 'Who?' / Ask 'Why?' / Ask 'When?' / Ask 'How much?' / Ask 'What?' / Ask 'Whose?'* etc. These can be set up by deliberately provoking a negative response to a Yes/No question. For example:

T: *Did she go to the post office?*
S1: *No, she didn't.*
T: *Ask 'Where?'* (indicate S2)
S2: *Where did she go?* (teacher indicates S3 with a nod)
S3: *She went to the bank.*
T: *Ask 'When?'* (indicate S4)
S4: *When did she go there?* (teacher indicates S5)
S5: *Yesterday afternoon.*
T: *Ask 'Why?'* (indicate S6)
S6: *Why did she go to the bank?* (teacher indicates S2)
S2: *She needed some money.*

Note how much the students said, and how little the teacher said.

5 Tag questions. After we have introduced tag questions—*It's a nice day, isn't it? It isn't very nice, is it?*—in Unit 37, you can use tag questions during a question phase. These serve to check information, and to familiarize students with the form. They are only used with *is it?* and *isn't it?* at this level.

◆ **Recall activities**

Recall activities include 'correct these sentences' and 'free reproduction'.

Correct these sentences can usually be done chorally with the class. You can check one or two individuals. It should not be necessary to allow thinking time as in a drill. For example (from Unit 33):

Teacher: *He was wearing a short coat.*
Class: *No, he wasn't. He was wearing a long coat.*
or *He was wearing a long coat.*
Teacher: *Sorry?* (indicate S1)
S1: *He was wearing a long coat.*

Free reproduction – This is introduced simply by asking *What's happening? … What's going to happen? … What happened? …* Students retell the story.

◆ **Listening**

Nearly every unit involves listening practice, in that students hear the recording, and often do repetition work and drills before they ever see the text. However, by 'listening' we mean exercises designed to practise the listening skill.

There are listening exercises at intervals throughout the course. There is a transcript of the listening tape in the Listening appendix. If equipment fails, the teacher can read out the listening exercise from the appendix although the recording will always be preferable.

Listening material usually includes a redundant element, which need not—and should not—be explained or exploited. As the listening exercises vary in kind, full exploitation procedures are always given.

If 'listening comprehension' is involved, it is best to play the tape through before commencing the exercise. If 'listening for specific information' is involved, students may be able to do the exercise 'cold'. You should explain to students that completion of the set task is *all* that is required of them. They need understand no more than is necessary to do the exercise.

Types of listening exercise include:

Listening for specific information – We concentrate on this skill in the early units so that students become accustomed to approaching a complicated text or dialogue, with simple goals in mind. For example, in Units 2, 4, 6, 20, 29, 31.

One-task listening – Students listen to a fairly long text, with only one task in mind, e.g. working out the winners of a race in Unit 9, or working out who the speakers are talking about in Unit 13.

Following instructions – For example, tracing a route on a map in Unit 16.

Listening for register – For example, students are asked which person is being friendly in Unit 37.

Multiple choice comprehension – For example, in Unit 22.

Guessing from sound effects – For example, this is done with the main dialogue in Unit 35.

Listening for sound discrimination – In Unit 36 students listen to the main text again, marking verbs according to the pronunciation of their regular past endings. In Unit 38, they listen for the *'ll* sound.

Extensive listening for pleasure – This is an optional use of the four Stories for pleasure. You can choose whether to use these stories for reading development or listening development.

◆ **Reading development materials**

These are always approached through silent reading. There are reading development exercises in many units of the Student's Book, together with the four 'Stories for pleasure' (after units 15, 25, 30, and 35.) They occur throughout the workbooks, increasing gradually in frequency towards the end. Exercises include: reading for specific information, jigsaw reading, reading for gist, unscrambling, matching, multiple choice, cloze exercises, gap filling exercises and a series of game activities such as word squares, crosswords and word snakes.

See also the note on **Redundant vocabulary** on page 3.

◆ **Pair work**

In large and small classes, pair work is the only practical way of getting students to use English in a less controlled situation. For very short exchanges you will not need to set up pairs, you can simply say *Ask each other*. (See **Interactive questions** on page 6.)

For longer paired activities it is essential that students should be absolutely clear about the task expected of them in pairs. There are sometimes instructions on the student's page, and you should check that these have been clearly understood.

It is beneficial for students to work with different partners, and pair work can be organized in these ways:

1 Geographically. Students work with neighbours.
2 Streamed. Students work with partners at a similar level.
3 Strong with weak. Stronger students are deliberately paired with weaker ones.
   Every teacher knows that you often come to understand something fully by explaining it to someone else.
4 Friends. Students choose their own partners.
5 Male/Female. In mixed classes there are advantages in pairing males with females. With younger students, it aids discipline (they are less inclined to chatter together!) and helps social integration. With older students, it helps with roles in the many male/female dialogues.

There are advantages in all five types of organization. We would suggest using several of them at different times during a lesson.

In some pair-work activities students are asked to work alone, drawing up a list for example, before pair work commences. This means that no student is aware of the contents of his or her partner's list, thus creating an *information gap*. The questions asked are then genuine questions—you don't know the answer when you ask the question and you acquire information through your questions.

In other paired activities, students are asked to change partners, so that they can ask about the answers of their partner's previous partner. In simple terms, this encourages third-person questions and answers.

For the same reason, the teacher will often ask students about their partner's answers after a pair-work phase.

We have done pair work ourselves with groups of 200. We have seen it done with huge conference audiences—in one case with 2,000. It worked.

◆ **Group work**

The main disadvantage of group work at beginner level is the time that it takes to set up. It is not worth spending fifteen minutes to set up a two-minute activity. The first time that you do group work, setting-up time will seem over-long and perhaps unproductive. But if you are going to use group work frequently throughout a course, the time taken will later prove to be worthwhile.

With very large classes, the disadvantages will usually outweigh the advantages, and you may wish to stick to paired activities. Group work can be used for discussions, games, and role play. Group role plays require time for the characters to be worked out before they are started.

◆ **Role play**

In role plays, students are asked to adopt the role of a character in a dialogue or situation. They are asked to go through a known dialogue with free substitutions, or to improvize completely freely on a given situation. Students may feel constrained in a situation when they are being themselves. Acting out the role of another person can remove this feeling. There are times when students have to be free to experiment with their abilities in a simulated situation, and role play is an enjoyable and stimulating way of doing it.

What about correction? Role play is a *fluency* activity, not an *accuracy* activity. The teacher should only intervene where the student has failed to communicate. It is best not to make a note of mistakes during the activity. You may wish to comment if a student has repeatedly made the same error, but the comment should come after the activity has finished. If the mistake is important, you will remember it without notes.

◆ **Games**

Several games are suggested in the course. Some can be played with the whole class, some can be played in groups. It is up to you whether or not to introduce a competitive element. The class can be divided into teams, and scores can be kept.

Some teachers may wish to avoid a competitive element, and most of the games will work without it.

◆ **Songs**

Four songs appear in the course, three of them at the end of lessons. They are in Units 1, 13, 21, and 39. The song in Unit 21 is used as presentation material at the beginning of the lesson.

Songs help students to work on stress, rhythm, and catenation. They are not subject to strict structural control. The usual procedure is:

1 Listen.
2 Listen and read.
3 Listen, read, and sing.

Teachers who can't sing are often reluctant to use songs in the classroom. This is a pity, but both authors are poor singers who have happily used songs in class. You don't need to sing yourself. All the work can be done from the recordings.

An alternative approach to songs, if you dislike using music, or if the cassette player is missing or broken, is to use them as rhythmic chants in the classroom. This retains many of the virtues of song (stress, rhythm, and catenation practice). For further information on using chants rather than songs, see Carolyn Graham *Jazz Chants* (Oxford University Press, New York).

◆ **Discussion**

Possibilities for discussion are obviously limited at beginner level. Students should be encouraged to discuss subjects arising from the contexts, and it is surprising how well beginners can often do in a controlled discussion.

The greatest danger of discussion phases is that they can either become a lecture by the teacher, or be dominated by one or two students. One way round this is to get students to discuss in groups before moving to general class discussion. Role-play discussion (where students are given set roles to play) can remove student reluctance to express their own opinions, and, in our experience, role-play discussions often develop into genuine discussions. Of course, discussion is a *fluency* activity. (See the notes on correction under **Role play** on page 8.)

◆ **Transfer/application**

This phase usually begins with a few questions by the teacher about the students' own lives and experiences. Students are using English in a meaningful way, and transfer-question phases often become real discussions. We believe that lessons should be phased so that they end with real communication, whether it is role play, discussion, or transfer-question sessions.

Appendices

The Teacher's Book contains the following appendices from the Student's Book:

◆ **Irregular verbs** – A list of irregular verbs, including those presented in the course.

◆ **Listening appendix** – giving the full text of listening development materials.

◆ **Vocabulary index** – coded into three categories: Active vocabulary, Passive vocabulary, and Classroom vocabulary. (See page 3.)

◆ **Grammar summaries** – giving an overview of the syllabus, as well as being reference material.
The Grammar summaries section has been designed with the following points in mind:

Transparency for the student reader – We have avoided extensive use of metalanguage beyond the students' level at the point at which they first refer to the material.

Use of labels – We see no need for a student *at this early stage* to worry about labels like:
Subject pronoun / possessive adjective / indefinite article.
Nor do we see any need to use functional / notional labels beyond the level of work in the classroom.

It has always seemed strange to us to waste time and memory learning words like *interrogative* when the perfectly good (and useful) English word *question* covers the same thing.

We have included labels and simple language explanation in the grammar summaries where we felt some students and teachers might find it helpful. The use of such explanatory material is entirely optional and may be best referred to in revision when the whole course is completed.

Brevity and clarity – We have preferred to put as much information in one paradigm as we can, while remaining consistent with our goal of clarity.

Grammar in context – The paradigms show grammatical items in sentences wherever possible, not as isolated discrete items.

Repetition/recycling – Within the paradigms, previously-covered structures reappear in full in new paradigms which might demonstrate a new element.

The teacher in control – Most importantly, as nearly all of the small amount of grammatical terminology in this course appears in the Grammar summaries and not in the Student's Book unit itself, the teacher can decide how much to use with his or her class. If the course used grammatical terms extensively, it would control your style of teaching. Students can learn, have learned, and do learn English without resort to metalanguage. Some teachers find it useful, some have an open mind, some find it positively harmful. In this course—because of the amount and placing of grammatical terminology—it is entirely up to *you*, the teacher, to decide on its use, or non-use.

To sum up, we have taken a positive position on the use of grammar. Language teaching experiences swinging pendulums and changing fashions. Twenty years ago, there was far too much grammar in many classrooms. Ten years ago, at the height of interest in functional/notional syllabus design, there was often too little. As we write this, the popular trend seems to be towards overt grammatical explanation. So, you can add more labels to our paradigms, and it will seem dynamic—from the teacher in my class today. If, as we expect, future trends lead away from overt explanation, there will be nothing in the course to interfere with your chosen approach. What is presented is the real thing, the essential language itself.

Using the Workbooks

The Workbooks are not essential for short intensive courses.

Refer to the notes on **The beginner level** on page 1. The Workbooks can be used in a number of ways:

1 As homework.
2 In class. If they are used in class, the progression of the course will be slowed. This will make the course more thorough for beginners. Even with false beginners the Workbooks can be useful in class. Many of the activities are suitable for paired oral practice. These are noted in the Teacher's Book.
3 A mixture of 1 and 2.

♦ **Written exercises**

Shorter fill-in exercises can be written in the book. Students should write longer exercises on a separate piece of paper. Shorter exercises can also be copied out in situations where writing in the book is not allowed.

♦ **Oral work**

Exercises suitable for oral work are always indicated in the lesson plans. They can be integrated into earlier parts of the lesson.

♦ **Reading development**

Reading development activities are best done at home. Stress that all they have to do is to complete the set task. They need not understand every word.

♦ **Writing**

There is no 'free composition' work in *Grapevine 1*. We feel it is unfair to expect students to cope with free composition at this level. They often have to write creative *sentences*, but longer creative work is held back for the later books in the series.

♦ **Vocabulary development**

Many of the exercises are designed to reinforce vocabulary that has been covered in the main Student's Book. Other exercises are designed to help students guess unfamiliar words. There is a strong recycling element.

♦ **Sounds and spelling**

The sounds exercises can be done without oral checking, but we would advise oral explanation in class, and oral checking in class. The actual exercise can be done at home. The spelling exercises should be self-explanatory.

♦ **Key to exercises**

There is a key to the Workbook exercises at the back of this book.

The optional videos

See page 1, **The optional video component**. The material in the introductory unit and Units 5, 10, 15, 20, 25, 30, and 35 has been designed for use *either* on video cassette or on audio cassette. The audio version is usually shorter. There is no indication in the Student's Book that a unit is available on video. In most schools access to video equipment means timetabling problems, and even if you have video it may be difficult to use the videos at the correct places in the progression. If this is the case, the progression should be maintained by presenting the material on audio cassette. The video can still be used later, as the pictures give so much more information.

The Video Activity Book

A Video Activity Book is available which contains:

– an introduction to the teacher on video exploitation techniques, and for each unit:
– two pages of classroom exploitation exercises;
– a page of exercises related to the video;
– language summaries;
– a transcript of the video tape.

Reading outside the classroom

We would recommend using graded readers in a library system towards the end of the course. You will probably want to select from a wide range of reading schemes. Check the grading scheme with the syllabus of *Grapevine 1*.

We believe that students should have access to a library of supplementary graded readers wherever possible. We also believe that reading outside the classroom increases as checking back by the teacher decreases. Let students choose a reader, and feel free to ignore the exercises provided with it.

Reference material

Students will not need any further reference books. Many of them will want a dictionary, and it would be a good idea to encourage the use of a monolingual (English–English) dictionary right from the beginning. We recommend the *Oxford Elementary Learner's Dictionary of English*. It will also be useful for their second and third years of English, as it has 10,000 headwords.

We believe that grammar books can cause more harm than good *at this level*, and the Grammar summaries in the Student's Book should be adequate. Students may wish to buy a grammar, which will be useful in the second year of English. In that case we would recommend *A Basic English Grammar*, Eastwood and Mackin (OUP).

Final note

We are always interested in feedback from teachers. If you have any suggestions or comments on any of the materials in *Grapevine 1*, please write to us:

Peter Viney & Karen Viney
c/o ELT Division
Oxford University Press
Walton Street
Oxford OX2 6DP

Contents

Introduction English words	12 The Family
1 Fasten seat belts	13 People
2 Self-service	14 How much is it?
3 Is it a star?	15 The Keys
4 Names and addresses	Story for pleasure: Security
5 Lambert and Stacey	16 Directions
6 The London train	17 Marchmain Castle
7 Space station	18 It's mine!
8 What's it like?	19 Asking for things
9 Where is she?	20 Chips with everything
10 Quiz of the Week	21 Mickey can't dance
11 Is there any . . .?	22 What time . . .?

23	Flight 201
24	Comet!
25	K Division Metro Police
	Story for pleasure: The Secret of the Pyramid
26	The weather
27	She doesn't like interviews
28	Wants and needs
29	Regular hours?
30	A day in the life of Dennis Cook
	Story for pleasure: The Third Planet
31	The outback
32	Tracey's first day
33	Beware of pickpockets!
34	A good dinner
35	One dark night
	Story for pleasure: Crocodile Preston
36	The Morgans
37	Having a conversation
38	Going home
39	Offers and suggestions
40	Treasure Island
	Irregular verbs
	Listening appendix
	Vocabulary index
	Grammar summaries
	Workbook key

Introduction

English words

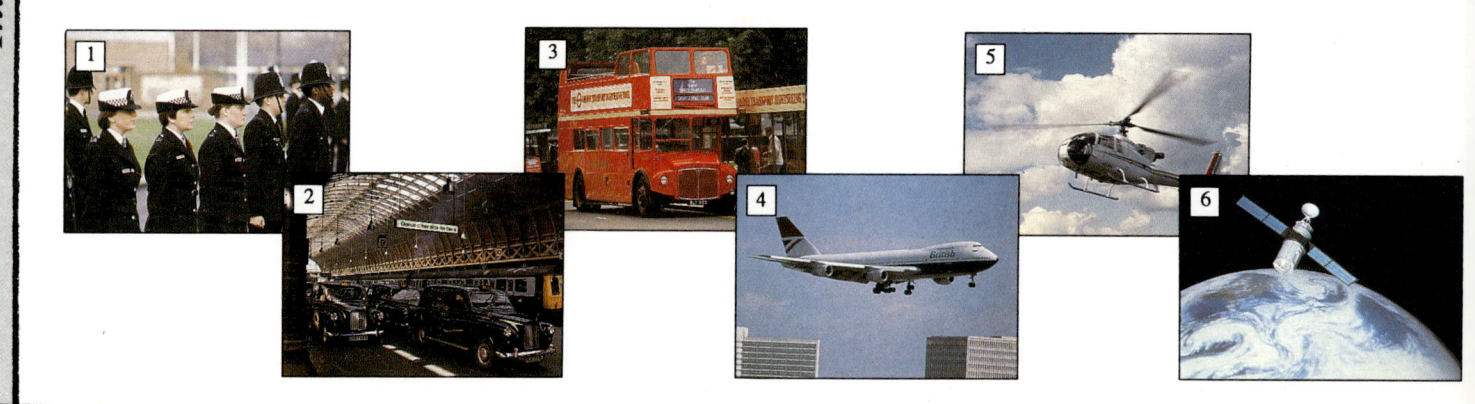

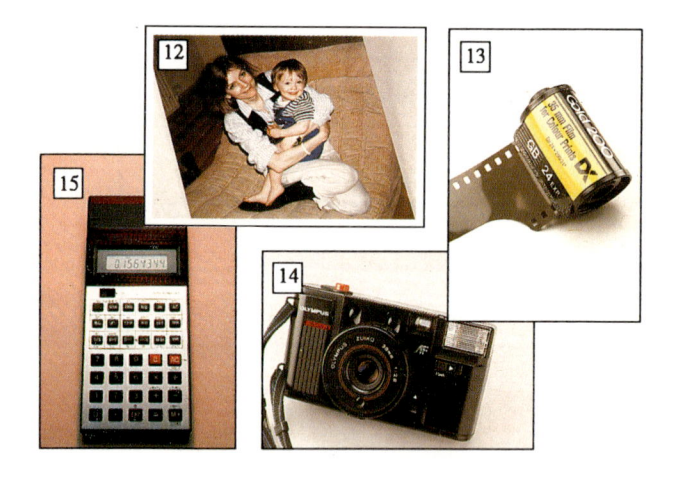

- ☐ taxi
- ☐ jumbo jet
- ☐ police
- ☐ bus
- ☐ satellite
- ☐ helicopter

- ☐ cassette
- ☐ telephone
- ☐ television
- ☐ computer
- ☐ video

- ☐ camera
- ☐ photograph
- ☐ film
- ☐ calculator

- ☐ tennis
- ☐ football

- ☐ hamburger
- ☐ sandwich
- ☐ pizza
- ☐ hot dog

- ☐ restaurant
- ☐ supermarket
- ☐ cinema

◆ General note

This unit is an **optional** introduction to the course. It may be used in the following ways:

◆ If you have a video, it is recommended with the accompanying video tape for all levels of student.

◆ If you are not using video we would recommend using this lesson in class for true beginners.

◆ With false beginners we would suggest setting it as homework **after** completing Unit 1 of the course in a specialized language school. Alternatively, in a normal school situation, it could be set prior to the first classroom contact lesson as pre-reading, and then checked as part of the first contact lesson. The notes which follow only cover the situation of using the material in class.

◆ Oral introduction

Teach *Hello*. Say it to as many students as possible, getting them to respond. Shake hands. Get them to circulate, shaking hands and saying *Hello*. For the rest of the lesson, try to use as much mime and gesture as possible, getting them to follow your instructions and examples in English. You should be speaking while you are demonstrating with gesture. (This is hard work!) eg:
Open your books. (Check they all do so.) *Close your books.* (Check they all do so.)
Open your books – Close your books – Open your books – Close your books – Open your books. Good. Thank you.
Look at this page. (Hold up your book, indicate, check they all follow the instruction.)
Look at this page. Good. Thank you.
Indicate a word (e.g. *taxi*) *Taxi* (scratch your head, search among the pictures, find the taxi, beam with delight and draw an imaginary line with your finger between word and picture.) *Taxi!* Indicate that they should do the same . . . make a Shhh! noise and gesture and demonstrate someone silently matching words and pictures.

◆ Left-hand page: pictures

Students work alone to match the words to the pictures. Check through with the class. Point out that they already 'know' 25 English words. (Either in mother tongue, or by writing *English* . . . 25 on the board.)

Introduction

◆ Right-hand page: photographs

This exercise deliberately uses photographs from different countries, to show that most languages have words in common with English. They should simply study the photographs and mark the 'English' words. Again use demonstration, mime to indicate this.

◆ English / My language

This is a translation exercise, the first and last in the course. The purpose of the translation is to bring out similarities, not differences. Often the difference will be simply spelling changes. (e.g. If the task were performed in English and Welsh, television would translate as *telefision*, taxi as *tacsi*, and so on.)
Students should work alone on this. If you wish them to work in pairs, they will be using the mother tongue in a monolingual situation. This might get them used to paired practice, though you would need to stress that future pair work should be done in English.

◆ English word square

Answers: The answers we would anticipate from beginners are:
1) football 2) jet 3) yes 4) taxi 5) video 6) film 7) disc 8) sandwich 9) no 10) jeans 11) computer(s) 12) television 13) radio 14) police 15) tennis.
When tested on native speakers, these 'non-international' words were added:
16 foot 17 ball 18 tax 19 it 20 ten 21 art 22 by 23 bye 24 sand 25 pat 26 lice 27 put 28 ice 29 vision 30 air 31 and 32 so 33 levis 34 all.
False beginners (and some beginners) may get some of these extra items.

◆ More English words?

Students write any more English words that they know.

◆ Closure

Teach them 'Goodbye'. Say it to as many students as possible, getting them to respond.

Introduction

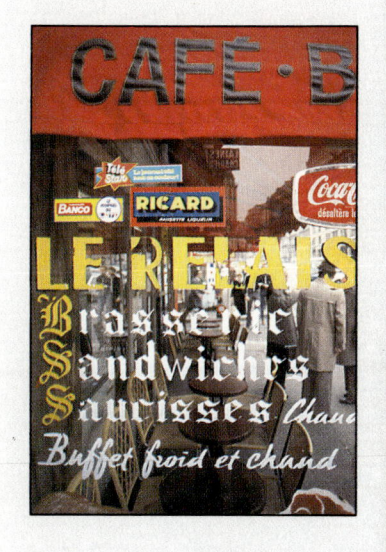

English	My language
video	
telephone	
television	
radio	
computer	
cassette	
camera	
photograph	
film	
sandwich	
buffet	
sport	
pizza	
cafe	
cinema	
taxi	
football	
tennis	
police	
jet	

English word square

Find English words.
8 = good, 10 = very good, 14 = fantastic!

F	O	O	T	B	A	L	L	G	P
H	C	J	E	T	I	Y	E	S	O
J	O	O	L	E	R	M	B	J	L
E	M	V	E	P	A	T	A	X	I
A	P	W	V	I	D	E	O	B	C
N	U	L	I	A	I	N	U	Y	E
S	T	X	S	R	O	N	O	E	K
D	E	J	I	T	F	I	L	M	Z
N	R	Q	O	D	I	S	C	F	C
S	S	A	N	D	W	I	C	H	J

More English words?

Write ten English words.

1 _____ 6 _____
2 _____ 7 _____
3 _____ 8 _____
4 _____ 9 _____
5 _____ 10 _____

Unit one

Fasten seat belts

10 ten 9 nine 8 eight 7 seven 6 six 5 five 4 four 3 three 2 two 1 one

a) I'm Peter Wilson

Listen, and look at the picture.
Write 3, 4, 5, 6, 7, 8, 9, 10.

- [1] Hello.
- [2] *Hello.*
- [1] I'm Peter Wilson.
- [2] *I'm Sarah Kennedy.*

- [ ] Coffee?
- [ ] *Yes, please.*
- [ ] Sandwich?
- [ ] *No, thank you.*

- [ ] *Hello.*
- [ ] Hello.
- [ ] *Are you from Japan?*
- [ ] Yes, I am.

- [ ] Psst!
- [ ] *Yes?*
- [ ] She's Maria Jackson!
- [ ] *Maria Jackson?*
- [ ] Yes, Maria Jackson. She's from Hollywood!

- [ ] *Are you from England?*
- [ ] No, I'm not.
- [ ] *Oh? Where are you from?*
- [ ] I'm from Scotland.

Unit one

Teaching points
Verb *to be* singular forms, personal names, countries.
Numbers: 1–10.
Greetings and offers.
I'm / You're / He's / She's from (England).
I'm not / You aren't / He isn't / She isn't from (England).
Am I / Are you / Is he / Is she from (England)?

Yes, I am. / No, I'm not.
Yes, you are. / No, you aren't.
Yes, he is. / No, he isn't.
Yes, she is. / No, she isn't.
Where am I / are you / is he / is she from?
Listening: matching dialogues to pictures.
Song: (optional) for stress, rhythm, and catenation.

Expressions
Hello. How are you?
Yes, please. / No, thank you.
Yes? Coffee? (offer)

Active vocabulary
coffee   sandwich
Countries: *England / Scotland / The United States / Australia / Spain / Italy / France / Japan / Brazil / Greece /* and countries of your students.
Numbers: 1–10.

Passive vocabulary
The Earth / Mars / stars
Exit / No smoking / Fasten seat-belts / Toilets /
(on illustration).

Classroom vocabulary
Listen / Look / Repeat / Ask / Answer / Write
teacher / student

Audio-visual aids
Cassette. **Optional:** world map / name cards / flash cards of food items or real items.

◆ **Oral introduction**

1 Say: *Hello.* Get class to say *Hello* in chorus, then say *Hello* to individuals to elicit *Hello* in response.

2 Say: *I'm (Susan Brown).* Go to individuals, say *I'm (Susan Brown).* Indicate the students to elicit: *I'm (Carlos Sanchez).* etc.
Write your name on a piece of paper, and put it on your desk. Say: *Write.*
Get students to put name cards on their desks.

3 Say: *He's Carlos Sanchez. She's Marie Lebrun.* Do this with four or five names. (Use flash cards in a single sex class.)
Say: *Repeat!* Go through the names again, getting students to repeat in chorus.

4 Go over to individuals. Say: *You're...?* Get the student indicated to reply: *I'm Yoko Kawasaki.*

5 Point to individuals, say: *He's...*, pause and shake your head to indicate that you do not know. Get the class to finish the sentence, e.g. *He's Peter Schmidt. She's Yoko Kawasaki.* Indicate yourself, say: *I'm...?* to elicit: *You're (Susan Brown).*

◆ **Numbers 1–10**

1 Teach the numbers 1–10. Write them on the board in **numeric** form (1, 2, 3, 4, 5, 6, 7, 8, 9, 10). Point at them and say them aloud. Say *Repeat*, indicating that students should repeat after you.

2 Point to numbers at random and get students to repeat the numbers in chorus. Then point at the numbers, the class in chorus calls out the number.
Repeat, selecting individuals to respond.

3 Pick up a Student's Book. Open it at Unit 1, show the class, and say: *Look at Unit 1.* Indicate the numbers. Indicate that they read them **silently**.

4 Write up the numbers in **written** form (one, two, three, etc.). Repeat the procedure in .2 as often as necessary. Do not overstress pronunciation at this point, nor aim for perfection.

◇ **a I'm Peter Wilson**

1 Say: *Listen and look.* Indicate your ear.
Play the cassette of all five dialogues. Indicate the exercise. [Show them that we can see the speakers (1 & 2) of the first dialogue. They are to write in the numbers of the speakers next to the other dialogues.]

2 Play the cassette of all five dialogues again. Students complete the task. If necessary, play it once more. Check that they all now have the dialogues numbered correctly.

◆ **Dialogue 1 (1, 2)**
Hello / Hello / I'm Peter Wilson...

1 Play the first dialogue. Play it again, pausing for students to repeat after the tape.

2 Paired reading of dialogue. Divide the class into pairs. Indicate a pair and say: *You're one, you're two.* Demonstrate a paired reading of the dialogue (i.e. acting out, not reading).
Get them to read the dialogue in pairs. Say: *Now, you're two, and you're one.*
Get them to read the dialogue again, but now they have reversed roles. This will be the normal pattern for paired reading of a dialogue. Get all the pairs to read through dialogue 1 in this way.

3 Pair work. Students work on the dialogue again, substituting their own names.

4 Class work. Get students to stand up and circulate round the class, introducing themselves to each other and to you. Encourage them to shake hands as they are doing it. Participate yourself.

Unit one

◆ Dialogue 2 (3, 4)
Hello / Hello / Are you from Japan?...

1 Play the dialogue. Play again, pausing for repetition.

2 Paired reading of dialogue (as in dialogue 1.2).

3 Pair work on dialogue, substituting their own country.

◆ Dialogue 3 (5, 6)
Are you from England? / No, I'm not...

1 Play the dialogue. Play again, pausing for repetition.

2 Paired reading of dialogue (as in dialogue 1.2).

3 Pair work, substituting other countries.

4 Class work. Get students to circulate, having conversations (as in dialogues 2 and 3).

◆ Dialogue 4 (7, 8) *Coffee? / Yes, please...*

1 Play the dialogue. Play again, pausing for repetition. Take great care on the question intonation of: *Coffee? / Sandwich? /*

2 Paired reading of dialogue (as in dialogue 1.2).

3 Pair work on dialogue, substituting other items. Suggest things like *7-Up*, *Pepsi-Cola*, *chocolate*, *pizza* – concentrating on items which are the same in the student's country.
Flash cards, **cards with words**, or **real items** can be used here. They can then be passed around the class, to elicit *Yes, please. / No, thank you.*

◆ Dialogue 5 (9, 10) *Psst! / Yes?...*

1 Play the dialogue. Play again, pausing for repetition. Take care over the question intonation of *Yes?* Also of the three ways in which *Maria Jackson* is said.

2 Paired reading of dialogue (as in dialogue 1.2).

3 Pair work on dialogue, substituting the names of students in the class.

b Where's he from? / Where's she from?

Indicate the ten pictures in the book. Get students to draw arrows between the country maps and the country names. Check. Get them to repeat country names. (If necessary, explain *Mars* with a small board diagram – the sun, two dots for planets, the Earth, Mars is the fourth planet.)
Visual aids: optional: take in a world map.

c Conversations

1 Point to one of the pictures of people (any one except Peter Wilson). Read the dialogue. Explain that they have to follow the same pattern for all the pictures, taking it in turns to play A & B. Get them to work on this in pairs. Get some pairs to demonstrate.

2 Students work in the same way as in .1.

3 Students work in pairs, substituting different countries. With less mature students, it may be inadvisable for them to use untrue items with *I'm from...* at this stage. More mature students are doing a role play.

4 Say: *I'm a teacher.* Indicate a student: *She's a student. He's a student.*
Ask questions to individuals: *Is he a teacher? Is she a student?* to elicit: *Yes, he is. / No, he isn't. Yes, she is. / No, she isn't.*
Ask: *Am I a teacher? / Am I a student? / Am I from (England)? / Am I from (France)?* to elicit: *Yes, you are. / No, you aren't.*
Get students to ask similar questions about themselves to elicit: *Yes, you are. / No, you aren't.*
Ask: *Am I from England? Am I from (Italy)? Is he from (Spain)? Is she from the (United States)? Are you from (Australia)? Are you from (Brazil)?* to elicit short answers. Do this with several individuals for each question type.

5 Drill:
(See Introduction note on drills.)
T: *you*
C: *Where are you from?*
Continue: *he / she / Peter Wilson / I / Sarah Kennedy.*

6 Comprehension dictation:
Dictate the numbers 1 to 10 in random order, e.g. *5, 9, 1, 4, 10, 2, 8, 6, 3, 7.* Students write their answers in **numeric** form (1, 2, 3 etc.).

d ♪ Hello

The song is optional. (See Introduction.) It may be chanted instead of sung.

1 Refer students to the picture of the plane. Point to Yoko Suzuki. Say 'She's from Japan.' Get students to do the same in pairs, until someone notices the two Martians near the rear of the plane. Point and say 'He's from Mars. She's from Mars.'

2 Get students to look at the picture under d, and to cover the text. Play the song once.

3 Listen and read. Play the song again. Students follow the text in their books. If you have time, you could get them to repeat the words.

4 Listen and sing. Students sing along.

◆ Workbook

1 The Workbook can be left for homework. If you wish to do it in class, exercises 3 and 4 can be done as pair work. In exercise 3, only one student need have the book open.

2 Exercise 8. After students have completed the exercise, they should list English or International words used in their country. Examples might be: *pizza, compact disc, rewind, turbo* etc.

b Where's he from?/Where's she from?

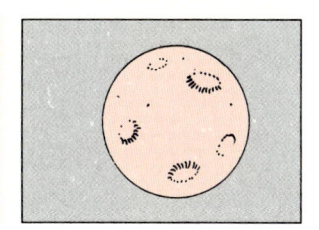

England
Mars
Brazil
Australia
Spain
Japan
The United States
Italy
Greece
France

1 Peter Wilson 2 Sarah Kennedy 3 Monique Lefort 4 Yoko Suzuki 5 Maria Jackson

6 João Medeiros 7 Pedro García 8 Paola Bonetti 9 Zog 10 Eleni Dima

c Conversations

Look at the pictures, and make conversations.

1
A *Is he from France?*
B *No, he isn't.*
A *Is he from England?*
B *Yes, he is.*

2
A *She's Paola Bonetti.*
B *Where's she from?*
A *She's from Italy.*

3
A *Are you from England?*
B *No, I'm not.*
A *Where are you from?*
B *I'm from Australia.*

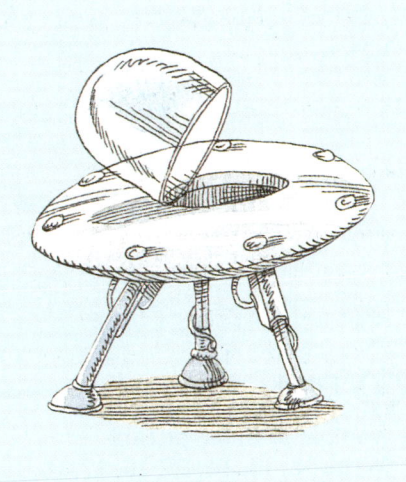

d Hello

Ten, nine, eight, seven, six,
five, four, three, two, one.
Hello, I'm from the stars.
How are you?
Hello, I'm from Mars.
How are you?

Ten, nine, eight, seven, six,
five, four, three, two, one.
Hello, she's from the stars.
How are you?
Hello, she's from Mars.
How are you?

Ten, nine, eight, seven, six,
five, four, three, two, one.
Hello, you're from the Earth.
How are you?
Hello, you're from the Earth.
How are you?

Unit one

Self-service

a Food

Look at 11 in the picture.
Write 12, 13, 14, 15, 16, 17, 18, 19.

11 eleven: a sandwich
12 twelve: a hot dog
13 thirteen: a hamburger
14 fourteen: a salad
15 fifteen: an apple pie
16 sixteen: an orange juice
17 seventeen: an ice cream
18 eighteen: a tea
19 nineteen: a coffee

SANDWICH BAR

cheese sandwich	60p
tuna sandwich	90p
chicken sandwich	80p
tea	40p
coffee	50p
cola	70p

SALAD CENTRE

egg salad	£ 2.20
cheese salad	£ 2.10
chicken salad	£ 2.30
tuna salad	£ 2.40
egg sandwich	90p
apple juice / orange juice	70p
Pepsi-Cola / 7-Up	40p
ice cream	70p
apple pie	80p

11 Good morning.
12 Good morning.
11 A cheese sandwich, please.
12 OK. Anything else?
11 Yes. A tea, please.
12 Here you are.
11 Thanks.

13 Good afternoon.
14 Good afternoon. An egg salad please, and ... er ... a chicken salad.
13 Here you are. Anything else?
14 Yes. An apple pie and an ice cream.
13 OK. That's six pounds, please.
14 Thank you. Goodbye.
13 Goodbye.

Teaching points
Simple restaurant situations. Asking for things. Greetings.
Numbers: 11–20, 30, 40, 50, 60, 70, 80, 90
and
Indefinite article: *a / an*
a coffee / an orange juice.
Listening for specific information.
Reading selectively from lists. Vocabulary set: foods, menus.

Expressions
Good morning / afternoon / evening.
Goodbye / Good night.
A (sandwich) please.   Anything else?   Pardon?   OK.
Here you are.
That's (six pounds), please.   Thanks.
I'm very well, thanks.   And you?   I'm fine.

Active vocabulary
afternoon / apple juice / apple pie / cheese / cheeseburger / chicken / egg / evening / hamburger / ice cream / morning / night / number / orange juice / pence (p) / pizza / pound (£) / salad / tea / tuna
OK.
and
Numbers: 11–20
20, 30, 40, 50, 60, 70, 80, 90

Passive vocabulary
a.m. / desserts / drinks / p.m. / sandwich bar

Classroom vocabulary
box / conversation / in / listening / pizza / put / read / tick / umbrella

Audio-visual aids
Cassette. **Optional:** Flash cards of food items.

Unit two

◆ **Oral introduction**

1 Say *Good morning* (or *Good afternoon / evening* as appropriate). Get class to respond in chorus, then get individuals to respond.

2 Go through numbers 11–20 orally. Write the numbers on the board and point at them at random, getting individuals to respond. Dictate the numbers in random order. Students write them down in **numeric** form (12, 13, 14 etc.).

⟨a⟩ **Food**

1 Focus attention on the picture. Get students to work alone, matching the numbered food items to the picture. They could write the numbers over the appropriate items, as in the example: *a sandwich*.

2 Get students to repeat the food items chorally. Then say (e.g.) T: *eleven*, the class responds *a tea*. Go through the items chorally, then check with individuals.

3 Reverse the process, T: *a tea* C: *eleven* etc.

◆ **Dialogue 1 (11, 12)**

1 Focus attention on the pictures. Demonstrate how to cover the text while looking at the pictures. This is extremely important for future lessons, so explain in the mother tongue if necessary. Play the first dialogue. Play it again, pausing for students to repeat after the tape. Demonstrate *Here you are* by passing an object to a student while saying it. Indicate that students should pass it on around the class, each student saying *Here you are*.

2 Silent reading of the first dialogue.

3 Paired reading of the dialogue. Students reverse roles after the first reading.

4 Focus attention on the Sandwich Bar menu on the left-hand page. Allow students to read it silently for a moment. Check comprehension.
(**Optional:** Use flashcards to do this.)

5 Say *Repeat*. Go through numbers 20, 30, 40, 50, 60, 70, 80, 90 orally. If necessary, write the numbers on the board and point at them, getting individuals to respond.

6 Drill:
(Students look at the menu.)
T: *a cheese sandwich*
C: *sixty p* [piː]
Continue through the menu (chorally, then with individuals).

7 Pair work. Students role play the dialogue, substituting other items from the menu. Encourage them to act it out rather than simply read.

◆ **Dialogue 2 (13, 14)**

1 Exploit as in 1, 2, 3, 4, 7 above (use the Salad Centre menu), but include these activities:

2 Explain *a / an* (before a, e, i, o, and the sound u [ʌ]). Give *egg* and *umbrella* as examples with e and u (use board drawings).

3 Drill:
T: *egg salad*
C: *an egg salad*
Continue: *apple juice / chicken salad / apple pie / cheese sandwich / tea / ice cream / egg sandwich / chicken sandwich / coffee / orange juice / Pepsi-Cola / 7-Up*.

4 Check prices – one pound / two pounds / one pound thirty / one pound twenty / two pounds forty. Point out that it is exactly the same with dollars. If necessary drill the prices on the Salad Centre menu as in dialogue 1.6 and/or write some prices on the board, point and get students to respond chorally and individually.

◆ Dialogue 3 (15, 16)

1 Exploit as above, (use the Hamburger House menu), but include these activities:

2 Check *Good morning / evening / afternoon / night / goodbye*.
Note that *Good morning / afternoon / evening* can mean *Hello* or *Goodbye*. *Good night* can only mean *Goodbye*. If necessary, write up some times. Point to a time, say *Good (evening)*. Get students to respond. Go to the door and wave, say *Good (night)* etc.

3 Check the prices after they have read the menu. Note: fifty p [pi:] **or** fifty pence. Note *one pound fifty* **not** '*one and a half pounds'.

◆ Dialogue 4 (17, 18)

1 Exploit as above, but include the following activities:

2 Get students to circulate, greeting each other as in dialogue 4, and enquiring about other students.

3 Drill:
T: *Lisa*
C: *How's Lisa?*
Continue: *Daniel / you / Sarah / Peter / you*

◆ Numbers 20–90

1 Get students to read the numbers silently. Get them to look back to the numbers 11–20 at the beginning of the lesson.

2 Aural discrimination. Put two columns on the board, labelled A & B.
Write 13, 14, 15, 16, 17, 18, 19 under A,
30, 40, 50, 60, 70, 80, 90 under B.
Call out numbers:
T: *thirteen*   C: *A*
T: *thirty*   C: *B*
Continue:
90 / 17 / 16 / 60 / 15 / 14 / 80 / 40 / 13 / 30 / 50 / 18 / 70 / 19

3 Comprehension dictation. Call out some numbers. Students write them down in **numeric** form. e.g. *13, 40, 15, 60, 70, 18, 90, 14, 19, 80*.

◆ a / an

Focus attention on the summary. Silent reading. If necessary, repeat drill in dialogue 2.3.

b ◆ Four conversations

1 This should be set up with great care. As this is the first blind listening task, it should be made clear that students need not understand everything on the tape, they simply need to understand enough to complete the listening task. Play the cassette right through once to accustom the students to the voices.

2 Focus attention on the listening exercise. Play the first conversation, showing students that the answers have already been marked on the chart.

3 Play the other conversations, one at a time. Students complete the task.

4 Play through the four conversations again, while students check their answers. This can be done in pairs. Make it clear that this is all that they have to do. They can look at the listening appendix later if they wish, but there is no class work with it.

◆ Anagrams

Write a few anagrams of words in the unit on the board. Students unscramble them, e.g. norgae (*orange*), daasl (*salad*), pelap (*apple*), neckich (*chicken*), ate (*tea*).

◆ Workbook

The Workbook can be done as homework.
If you wish to use it in class, exercises 1, 3, and 4 can be done as pair work.

20 twenty   30 thirty   40 forty   50 fifty   60 sixty   70 seventy   80 eighty   90 ninety

Unit two

HAMBURGER HOUSE

hamburger	£ 1.50
cheeseburger	£ 2.00
pizza	£ 1.30
ice cream	£ 1.20
orange juice / apple juice	50p
tea / coffee	50p

a
- a hamburger
- a cheese sandwich
- a tuna salad
- a coffee

an (a e i o u)
- an apple juice
- an egg salad
- an ice cream
- an orange juice

b Four conversations

Listen to the four conversations.
Put ticks [✓] in the boxes.

	1	2	3	4
Salad				
egg	✓			
cheese				
chicken				
tuna				
Sandwich				
egg				
cheese				
chicken				
tuna				
Drink				
orange juice	✓			
apple juice				
tea				
Dessert				
ice cream				
apple pie	✓			

15 Good evening.
16 Good evening. A hamburger, please.
15 Pardon?
16 A hamburger, please. And an orange juice.
15 A hamburger and an orange juice?
16 Yes, please.
15 That's two pounds.
16 Two pounds ... here you are. Thank you.
15 Thank you. Good night.
16 Good night.

17 John!
18 Daniel! Hello, how are you?
17 I'm very well, thanks. And you?
18 I'm fine.
17 And Stephen ... how's Stephen?
18 Oh, he's fine ...

Unit three

Is it a star?

Anne Look!
Laura Where?
Anne Over there. What is it?
Laura I don't know. Is it an aeroplane?
Anne No, it isn't an aeroplane.
Laura Is it a star?
Anne No, it isn't. What is it, Laura?
Laura I don't know, Anne … I don't know …

Mike Is it open?
Ken Yeah. It's open. Look!
Mike What are they?
Ken I don't know. Are they televisions?
Mike No, they aren't televisions.
Ken Are they computers?
Mike No, they aren't. They're videos!
Ken Listen! What's that?
Mike Oh no! It's a police car!

a What is it?/What are they?
radio, cassette player, television, video, speaker, computer
1 *It's a television. / They're televisions.*
Write five more sentences.

Unit three

Teaching points
Singular and plural nouns. Verb to be: *it* and *they* for things.
Identifying objects with:
What is it? / What are they?
It's / isn't a pen / an engine.   They're / aren't pens / engines.
Is it a pen / an engine?
Are they pens / engines?
Yes, it is. / No, it isn't.
Yes, they are. / No, they aren't.
Plurals – formation. Spelling.
Pronunciation of 's' endings: ([s], [z], [ɪz]).
pen / pens   key / keys   watch / watches   dictionary /
dictionaries   knife / knives   man / men   woman / women
Numbers: 1–99 (21, 37 etc.)
Reading: Learning to ignore redundant information.
(Boxes exercise, see ⓐ *What is it? / What are they?*).

Grammar note: indefinite articles (a/an)
The rule that *an* is used before a / e / i / o / u is important (see Unit 2), but it is necessary that students understand clearly that it is the sounds a / e / i / o / u rather than the letters. With false beginners, you could point out *an umbrella* (sound: [ʌ]), but *a university* (sound: [juː]). Equally, we'd say *an 'H'*, but *a 'U'*. Stating this rule would confuse a beginners' class. See **Plural spellings / pronunciation** below.

Expressions
Look! / Listen!   over there.   I don't know.
It's open. / It's OK.
What's that?   Oh, no!

Active vocabulary
aeroplane / book / bus / car / cassette player / computer / cup / dictionary / engine / fork / glass / helicopter / island / it / key / knife / man / orchestra / pen / picture / plate / police / radio / speaker / spoon / star / television / they / umbrella / video / watch / what / woman / listen / look at / open

Passive vocabulary
Bingo / long vehicle / kilometres per hour / Great Britain / that

Classroom vocabulary
between / game / minutes

Audio-visual aids
Cassette. **Optional:** Realia – as many of the objects illustrated as possible.

◆ **Oral introduction**

Optional. Using realia. Take in a collection of real items (two of each), e.g. forks / spoons / knives / cups / plates / glasses / pens / books / dictionaries (plus real items not used in the Student's Book if you wish, e.g. envelopes / pencils / rulers / batteries / cassettes / matches).
Use them to pre-teach and practise:
What is it? It's a (pen). What are they? They're (pens).
Alternatively the realia can be used at the end of the lesson, for a variety of guessing / memory games.

◆ **Dialogue 1 (Anne / Laura)**

1 Focus attention on the picture, check that the text is covered. Play the dialogue. Play it again pausing for students to repeat after the tape, chorally and individually. Point to demonstrate: *over there*. Check *I don't know.* which is taught here as a fixed expression – it is an essential expression in this lesson, and students should be aware that it is a perfectly valid answer to the questions in the lesson (as well as useful throughout the course).

2 Drill:
T: *aeroplane*
C: *Is it an aeroplane?*
Continue: *helicopter / star / Jumbo Jet / UFO*

3 Drill:
T: *It is an aeroplane?*
C: *No, it isn't an aeroplane.*
Continue: *helicopter / star / Jumbo Jet / UFO*

4 Silent reading of the dialogue.

5 Paired reading of the dialogue.

6 Ask questions about objects in the room / on the students' tables (and/or realia), using:
T: *Is it a pen?* S: *No, it isn't. / Yes, it is. / No, it isn't. It's a book. / I don't know.*
T: *What is it?* S2: *It's a book. / I don't know.*
Ask several questions which will elicit *I don't know.* by pointing at more obscure objects, such as an electric socket, a curtain rail, a drawing pin etc. Choose a very obscure item, get them to ask you *What is it?* Say *I don't know.* (Even native teachers should be able to find something. If not, pretend!)

7 Pair work. Students ask and answer as in .6.

◆ **Dialogue 2 (Mike / Ken)**

1 Focus attention on the picture, check that the text is covered. Play the dialogue. Play it again pausing for students to repeat chorally and individually. Use the door, demonstrate: *It's open / It isn't open.*

2 Silent reading of the dialogue.

3 Paired reading of the dialogue.

4 Drill:
T: *televisions*
C: *Are they televisions?*
Continue: *videos / computers / radios / cassette players / speakers.*

5 Drill:
T: *Are they televisions?*
C: *No, they aren't televisions.*
Continue: *videos / computers / radios / cassette players / speakers.*

Unit three

a) What is it / What are they?

1 Focus attention on the pictures of items in cardboard boxes in the lorry. Indicate the row of words (radio, cassette player ... etc.). Write up: *Philips 275 AM/FM Mono.* Scratch your head, say *What is it?* to yourself. Then look at the row of words. Say *Television? No, it isn't. Video? No, it isn't. Ah! It's a radio!* Get them to work silently, matching the words to the boxes. At a very simple level, this is a reading exercise as they are i) beginning to filter out redundant material, ii) guessing from what they know. Do not explain any of the redundant words.

2 Pair work. Having done the matching exercise in .1 above, students work in pairs asking each other about the boxes. Check with individuals.

3 Pair work on the dialogue, substituting other items in the picture.

4 Ask questions about plural objects in the room / on the students' tables (and/or realia), as in dialogue 1.6.

◆ Pictures (21–40)

1 Get students to repeat the numbers 21–40 after you. Write numbers on the board, point at a few, getting the class to call out the numbers chorally. Then select individuals. T: *What is it?* S1: *It's twenty-seven.* etc.

2 Pair work. Students work in pairs, as in .1.

3 Pictures 21–25
Ask questions:
T: *21 – Is it a picture?* S1: *Yes, it is / No, it isn't.*
T: *What is it?* S1: *It's a picture.*

4 Pair work as in .3.

5 Pictures 26–30
Exploit as in .3 and .4 above.

6 Pictures 31–35
Exploit as in .3 and .4 above, (using: *Are they . . .? What are they?*)

7 Pictures 36–40
Exploit as in .3 and .4 above, (using: *Are they . . .? What are they?*)

8 Pair work, using all the pictures, 21–40.
S1: *37*
S2: *What are they?*
S1: *They're watches.*

b) Game

1 Introduce the game, by playing a different version to the one in the Student's Book. A student thinks of one of the singular objects, 21–30. The others ask questions until they guess it.
S1: *Is it a cup?*
S2: *No, it isn't.*
S3: *Is it a fork?*
S2: *Yes it is.*
etc. Repeat the game with pictures 31–40.

2 Students play the memory game in the book in pairs. One in each pair has the book closed.
Alternatively: The game can be extended by using a collection of realia, which the class study before the items are covered with a cloth (or are removed).

c) Bingo!

1 Tell all the students to write nine numbers of their choice (between 21 and 99) in Box A. Then call out numbers. Students cross them off. The first student to cross off all the numbers is the winner.

2 Students then work in pairs. First they write nine numbers of their choice in Box B, making sure that their partners do not see the completed Box B. Each student then calls out numbers in turn. The one who crosses off their numbers after the smallest number of calls is the winner. A class winner can also be found if students note the number of calls.
Note: With slower beginners you may wish to end the lesson at this point.

◆ Plural spellings / pronunciation

1 Check through the plurals, do not give extra examples if the class is finding the vocabulary load difficult.
– the '-es' endings (pronounced [ɪz]) for *glasses / watches / buses*.
– the '-ys' ending of *keys*, other examples you could give are *monkeys / days*.
– the '-ies' ending of *dictionaries*, other examples you could give are *lorries / strawberries*.
– the '-f-' to '-v-' rule of *knife / knives*, other examples you could give are *wives*, *loaves*.
– the irregular plurals of *men* and *women*, other examples you could give are *policemen, policewomen, children*.

2 Dictate 10 plurals to the class. Check on the board.

3 Check the three pronunciations: [s] in *cups*, [z] in *keys*, [ɪz] in *watches*.
Optional: Do an aural discrimination. Put three columns on the board, labelled 1, 2, and 3. Point to 1. Say [s], point to 2, say [z], point to 3, say [ɪz]. Say a number of plurals, students respond 1, 2, or 3.
e.g. T: engines. C: *2*
   T: glasses. C: *3*
   T: cups. C: *1*
Warning: Some students find the [s] and [z] distinction academic, and it will not be worth worrying them unduly about it.

◆ Workbook

The Workbook can be done for homework.
If you wish to use it in class, exercises 3, 4, 5, 6, and 7 can be done as pair work.

Unit three

21 picture
22 fork
23 spoon
24 book
25 car
26 aeroplane
27 engine
28 island
29 orchestra
30 umbrella
31 pen
   pens
32 cup
   cups
33 key
   keys
34 plate
   plates
35 glass
   glasses
36 dictionary
   dictionaries
37 watch
   watches
38 bus
   buses
39 knife
   knives
40 man / woman
   men / women

b Game

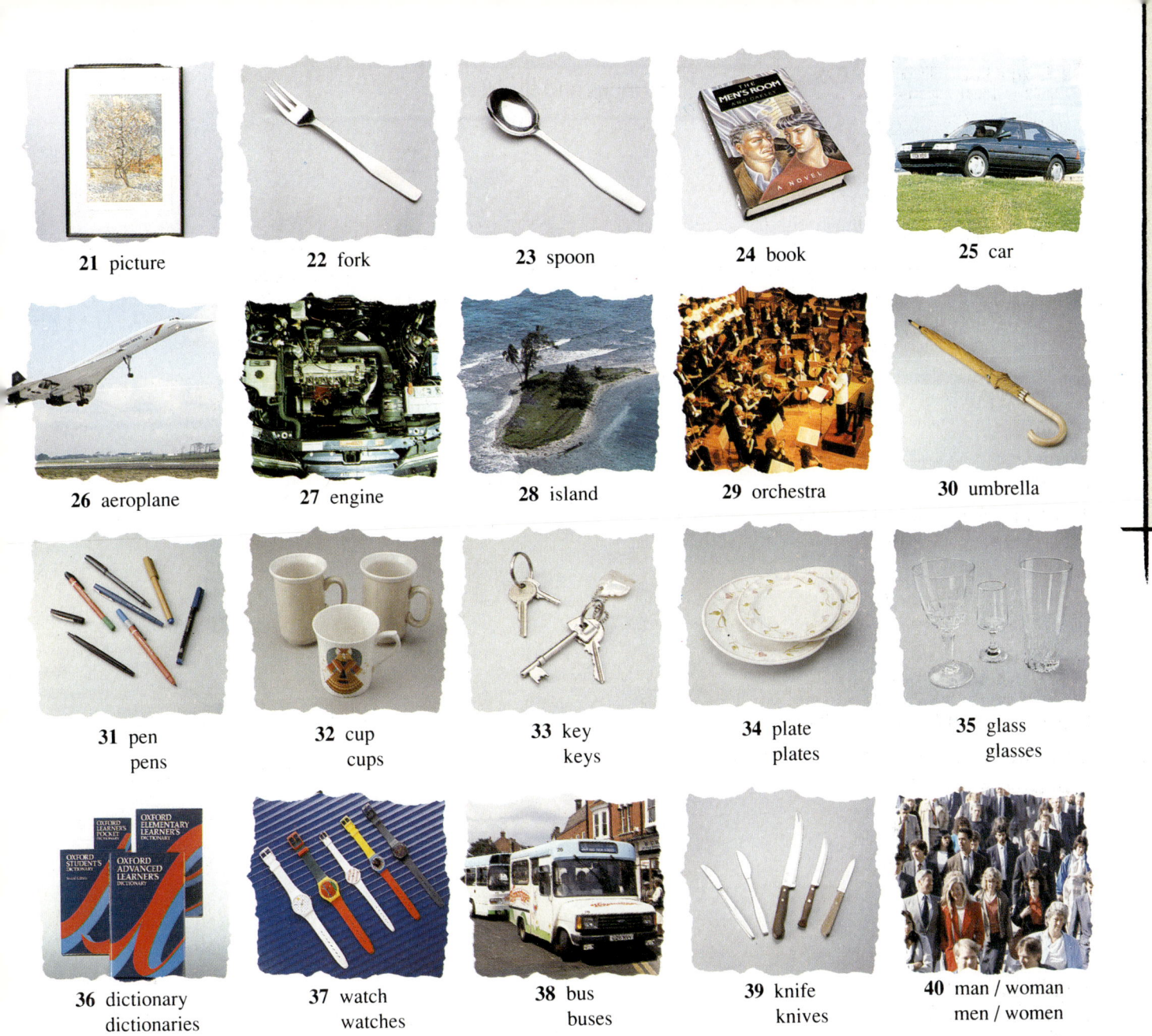

Look at the pictures for two minutes.
Student A: Open the book.
Student B: Close the book.
A *What's number 22?*
B *It's a fork. / I don't know.*
A *What's number 36?*
B *They're dictionaries. /*
  I don't know.

c Bingo!

Write nine numbers (between 21 and 99) in Box 1, and nine numbers in Box 2.

Box 1	Box 2

Unit four

Names and addresses

- What's his name?
- □ I don't know. What's his number?
- Er . . . he's number seven.
- □ Oh! His name's Gary Taylor.
- Gary Taylor? Where's he from?
- □ He's from Liverpool. He's fantastic! Look!

a) What's your name?

Listen to the conversations. Match A E, I O, U Y to the picture.

A Come here, Smith!
E My name isn't Smith . . .
A What *is* your name?
E Taylor. I'm Gary Taylor.
A Oh. What's your number?
E I'm number seven. Smith is number two.
A Oh, sorry.
E That's OK.
A It isn't OK . . . to the dressing room!
E What?
A Go to the dressing room, Taylor! Go now!

I I'm lost!
O Oh dear. What's your name?
I Kevin . . .
O What's your surname, Kevin?
I Stewart.
O And what's your address?
I Um . . . 132 Waterloo Street, Tottenham, London.
O What's your telephone number?
I Um . . . 081–656–4893.

U Name?
Y What?
U What's your name?
Y Paine.
U Paine? Spell it.
Y P-A-I-N-E.
U First name?
Y Darren.
U Address?
Y 207 Redhill Road, Bristol.
U Phone number?
Y Bristol 901332.
U OK, Paine. Come this way . . .

Unit four

Teaching points
Personal information: Names, addresses, telephone numbers.
Possessive adjectives (singular only).
What's my / your / his / her / name? / address? / telephone number?
My / Your / His / Her name's (Taylor). / I'm / You're / He's / She's (Taylor).
(My) address is . . . / (My) phone / telephone number is . . .
What's your surname? / What's your first name? / What are your first names?
Numbers: 100–999.
The Alphabet. Spelling.

Listening for specific information (personal details).
Reading: Extracting relevant information from diagrams:
(Football / tennis programmes, and chart.)

Expressions
Come (here). / Go to (the dressing room.) / Go (now). / Come this way.
Sorry. / That's OK. / It isn't OK. / He's fantastic.
What? (= pardon?) / I'm lost. / Oh dear.
Name? / First name? / Address? / Phone number / Spell it.

Active vocabulary
address / alphabet / double / first name(s) / football / international / name / people / phone / player / surname / telephone / tennis
fantastic / come / go / spell
here / lost / sorry / this way

Passive vocabulary
championship / Czechoslovakia / defender / dressing room / goalkeeper / midfield player / semi-final / striker
Abbreviations: *USA / BBC / ITV / UFO / EEC / VW / MG*

Classroom vocabulary
chart / partner / policeman / policewoman / referee / match (v) / *talk*

Audio-visual aids
Cassette

◆ Oral introduction

Say: *My name's (Susan). What's your name?* Ask several students, getting them to respond with: *My name's (Maria).* etc. Say: *His name's (Pierre). Her name's (Maria).* Ask: *What's his name? What's her name?* about several students.

◆ Dialogue 1 (■, □)

1 Focus attention on the small picture. Check that the text is covered. Set pre-questions: *What's his name? What's his number?* Play the dialogue. Check the answers. Play it again, pausing for students to repeat chorally and individually.

2 Questions:
Ask: *What's his name? Is he number 2? Is he number 11? What's his number? Is he from Manchester? Is he from Barcelona? Is he from Milan? Where's he from? Is he good?*

3 Silent reading of the dialogue.

4 Paired reading of the dialogue.

5 Focus attention on the **football programme** on the right-hand page. Ask students to study it silently for a moment. Say: *Look at number 3. What's his name? Where's he from?*
(Only if students are interested in football, add: *Is he a defender or a striker?*)
Go through the programme like this, asking individuals.

6 Role play. Students role play the first dialogue, substituting other names, numbers, and football teams from the programme.

a) What's your name?

Focus attention on the large picture. Explain that students are going to hear three conversations. They match A E, I O, U Y to the large picture to indicate the speakers. Play the cassette for the three dialogues. Play it again and check.

◆ Dialogue 2 (A, E)

1 Set pre-question: *What number is Smith?* Play the dialogue. Check. Play it again, pausing for students to repeat chorally and individually. Note stress on *What is your name?* Demonstrate *come* and *go.* Say: *Come here. Go to the door. Go to the window.* Students follow your instructions. Demonstrate *sorry* by pretending to confuse students' names – call them by the wrong names and apologize.

2 Drill:
T: *your*
C: *What's your number?*
Continue: *his / my / her / your / her*

3 Silent reading of the dialogue.

4 Questions:
*Is his name Smith? Is his name Brown? What **is** his name? Is he number 4? Is he number 8? What **is** his number? Is he sorry? Is it OK?*

5 Paired reading of the dialogue.

6 Role play. Students role play the second dialogue, substituting other names and numbers from the programme.

7 Pair work. Get students to give instructions with *come* and *go* in pairs, as in .1 above.

◆ Dialogue 3 (I, O)

1 Set pre-question: *What is his telephone number?* Play the dialogue. Check the answer. Play it again, pausing for students to repeat chorally and individually. Check: *one hundred and thirty-two / 01 is pronounced Oh one*

2 Drill:
T: *name*
C: *What's your name?*
Continue: *surname / address / telephone number / name / number*

3 Drill:
T: *name*
C: *What's your name?*
T: *his*
C: *What's his name?*
T: *address*
C: *What's his address?*

Continue:
her
telephone number
number
my
surname
your

4 Silent reading of the dialogue.

5 Paired reading of the dialogue.

6 Role play. Students role play the third dialogue, substituting their own names, addresses, and telephone numbers. They will have problems with the addresses: check the pairs carefully.

◆ Dialogue 4 (U, Y)

1 Set pre-question: *What is his telephone number?* Play the dialogue. Play it again, pausing for students to repeat chorally and individually. Check a, e, and i.

2 Silent reading of the dialogue.

3 Questions:
Ask: *What's his name? What's his surname? What's his first name? What's his address? What's his phone number? Spell Paine.*
Then ask individuals questions about themselves.

4 Paired reading of the dialogue.

5 Role play. Students role play the dialogue, substituting their own names, addresses, and telephone numbers.

b) Numbers

Silent reading. Check: *two hundred* **not** 'two hundreds'.

1 Ask students to say the numbers. Write more 3-figure numbers on the board, point to individuals, and get them to say them.

2 Ask students to say the telephone numbers. Add more 5-figure telephone numbers with double numbers.

3 Comprehension dictation.
Dictate these numbers: *817 / 294 / 500 / 190 / 819 / 340 / 614 / 757 / 727*
Students write the answers in **numeric** form.

c) The alphabet

1 Students repeat the letters of the alphabet, one group of letters at a time. Write some on the board and ask individuals to say them. Point out 'zed' [GB], 'zee' [USA].

2 Students repeat the groups of abbreviations. Check individuals.

3 Ask individual students to spell their names.

4 Call out these letters aloud, asking students to write them down:
a / i / y / e / o / b / e / c / i / a / u / w / v / p / b. Check.

d) Programmes

1 Football programme. Demonstrate that you can ask: *Look at number eight. What's his first name? What's his surname? Spell it. Where's he from?* about any of the players. Students ask and answer in pairs. (The players' names include every letter of the alphabet.)

2 Tennis programme. Exploit as in .1 above.

e) Chart

1 Pair work. Students ask and answer about the people numbered 1 and 2 in the chart.

2 Then they complete the information about themselves.

3 Then they interview their partners, filling in the last space in the chart.

f) Three people

(See also Unit 2, section b) **Four conversations**)

1 Play each conversation twice. Students fill in the information on the second listening.

2 Pair work. Students compare their answers by asking and answering in pairs about the three people. Check the answers with a few questions. Play the cassette again if necessary.

◆ Game: Alphabetical order

Students form a line around the class in strict alphabetical order (Maria before Marie). They do so by circulating and asking other students to spell their first names. If you wish, repeat with family names. This will be a fairly noisy and chaotic activity, but it is fun.

◆ Workbook

The Workbook can be done as homework. Exercise 1 is reading an authentic text for specific information. Explain that you do not need to understand everything in the texts to be able to complete the exercise. NB: No other vocabulary except that needed for the exercise should be explained. Exercises 3 and 4 may be done in class for pair work. Exercise 6 is an oral exercise, and is best done in class. Exercise 7 is matching exercise, designed to focus on letters of the alphabet used in abbreviations. Do not explain meanings.

b) Numbers

100 – one hundred
200 – two hundred
305 – three hundred and five

Number: **188**
Say *one hundred and eighty-eight*.

Telephone number: **21880**
Say *two – one – double eight – oh*.

1 Say these numbers:
   100   104   212   327   439
   561   655   792   848   910

2 Say these telephone numbers:
   33210   55677   48990   311664

c) The alphabet

1 Say:

A	H	J	K			
B	C	D	E	G	P	T	V
F	L	M	N	S	X	
I	Y					
U	W					
O	Q	R	Z			

2 Say:
   USA   ITV   EEC   VW
   BBC   UFO   OK   MG

d) Programmes

Look at number 8 on the football programme.
A *What's his first name?*
B *Gary.*

A *What's his surname? Spell it.*
B *Jones. J-O-N-E-S.*

A *Where's he from?*
B *He's from Liverpool.*

Ask and answer about the other players on the programmes.

Women's Tennis Championship semi-finals

Wimbledon 29 June 2.00pm

Rachel Patworth *(Great Britain)*
v
Martina Kundera *(Czechoslovakia)*

Doris Decker *(United States of America)*
v
Caroline Dundee *(Australia)*

e) Chart

	1	2	You	Your partner
Surname	Brown	Talbot		
First name(s)	Rachel Maria	Gary David		
Address	350 Bridge Street Liverpool	17 North Road Southampton		
Telephone number	051-677-3288	0703-22991		

What's her surname? / What's her first name? / What are her first names?
What's her address? / What's her telephone number?

1 Ask and answer about numbers 1 and 2.
2 Write in your name, address, and telephone number.
3 Talk to your partner. Write in his/her name, address, and telephone number.

f) Three people

Surname	_____	_____	_____
First name(s)	_____	_____	_____
Address	_____	_____	_____
Telephone number	_____	_____	_____

1 Listen to the three people.
  Write in the names, addresses, and telephone numbers.

2 Ask and answer about the people.

Unit four

INTERNATIONAL FOOTBALL ENGLAND v SCOTLAND
WEMBLEY STADIUM 14 MAY 3.00pm

ENGLAND

Goalkeeper
1
Roy Clement
(Southampton)

Defenders
2 Gary Smith (Tottenham)
3 Brian Roberts (Manchester United)
4 Daniel McQueen (Everton)
5 Kevin Fox (Birmingham)

Midfield players
6 Trevor Page (Tottenham)
7 Gary Taylor (Liverpool)
8 Gary Jones (Liverpool)

Strikers
9 Kevin Stevens (Everton)
10 Steve Wade (Manchester United)
11 Darren Fitzroy (Newcastle)

Unit five

Lambert and Stacey

1
Stacey What's the time?
Lambert Eleven thirty.
Stacey They're late.
Lambert Yeah . . . or we're early.
Stacey Listen . . . what's that?
Lambert It's a car. Is it their car?
Stacey Yeah, it is. Come on . . .

2
Stacey Hi!
1st Man Hi. Where's the picture?
Stacey The Picasso.
1st Man Yeah, yeah, the Picasso. Where is it?
Stacey It's in the briefcase. Where are the diamonds?
1st Man They're in the bag.
Stacey Where is the bag?
2nd Man It's in our car.
Stacey
1st Man } Get the bag!

3
1st Man Right . . . here you are.
Stacey Thanks.
Lambert OK, hands on the car! I'm Lambert, she's Stacey. We're detectives . . .
1st Man You're detectives . . .
Stacey Police.
2nd Man They *are* detectives.
1st Man But *we* aren't criminals . . .
Stacey Huh!
1st Man We're customs officers . . . from the airport.
2nd Man We're detectives, too.

4
Stacey OK . . . OK . . .
Lambert Where are your identity cards?
1st Man Our ID cards . . . They're in the car . . .
Lambert Look in their car, Stacey . . .
 Oh no! It's true . . . they are!

H. M. Customs and Excise
Heathrow Airport, London

Surname	Ross
First name(s)	David Charles
Title	Inspector of Customs
Number	W342-6771

Unit five

Optional video component

Teaching points

Verb *to be*; plurals – 1st, 2nd, 3rd person.
We / you / they   are (**detectives**). + Q + Neg.
Possessive adjectives – plural *our / your / their*
Time. *What's the time?*
It's six thirty / seven forty-five / eight o'clock.
Where is it? / are they?
It's in . . . / They're in . . .
early / late   first / second   1st / 2nd
Simple postcard format:
Dear . . . / Best wishes,
Reading: From a handwritten postcard. Extracting information from semi-authentic guest registration card.

Expressions

Yeah. (= yes)   Hi.
Get (the bag).   Right.
Hands on the car!
Go and look.   It's true.
Dear . . .   Best wishes
Do you know . . . ?

Active vocabulary

bag / briefcase / criminal / customs / detective / diamond / hand / identity card / o'clock / plane / room / suitcase / time
early / happy / late / true / second
in / on / get / too

Passive vocabulary

guest / inspector / occupation / passport / photograph / receptionist / registration / title

Classroom vocabulary

classroom / complete / conversation

Redundant vocabulary

Customs and Excise

Audio-visual aids

Cassette. Video cassette (if optional video is to be used).
Realia: single/plural objects.
Clock with moveable hands for ⟨a⟩ **What's the time?** section (**optional**).

Note: With false beginners you will be able to ask more interesting questions as you play the dialogue. The exploitation has been controlled to avoid items outside the students' knowledge (e.g. *who?*). You may wish to do the intensive exploitation quickly (or even miss it out). Note: the four sections of the dialogue are exploited for listening, before any intensive work.

◆ **Oral introduction**

1 Put a pen in a bag. Say *Where is it? It's in the bag.* Take it out. Put two pens in the bag. Say *Where are they? They're in the bag.* Continue, putting objects into bags/desks/books etc, asking individuals: *Where is it? Where are they?*

2 Pair work. Get students to do the same in pairs.

3 Hold up two pens, say: *They're pens.* Bring out two students, say: *They're students.* Ask: *Are they teachers? Are they astronauts? What are they? Are they in a disco? Where are they?* Point to other pairs/groups of students. Ask the same questions.

4 Stand with the students, Say: *We're in the classroom. We aren't in (England). We're in (Spain).* Ask the class (to elicit answers with 'you'): *Are we in a disco? Where are we? Are we in England? Where are we?*
Ask the students standing with you the same questions (to elicit answers with 'we').

◆ **Dialogue 1**

1 Focus attention on the inset picture. Check that the text is covered. Ask *Where are they?* Get students to guess. They may well use the internationally adapted word and say *'in the parking'*: correct this to *'in the car park'*.

2 Set pre-question (pointing to your watch) *What's the time?* Play the dialogue once. Check the answer. Explain *late* and *early*. Write up: *8.55 / 9.00 / 9.05.* (The middle time should be the start of the lesson.) Say: *9.00 is on time. 8.55 is early. 9.05 is late.* Don't explain other items at this point.

◆ **Dialogue 2**

Focus attention on the pictures, check that the text is covered. Draw a diamond shape on the board. Set pre-question: *Where are the diamonds?* Play the dialogue. Check the answer. Demonstrate *Hi* by greeting several students in a friendly way. Get them to respond *Hi*. Then say *Good (morning)*. They should respond *Good (morning)*. (Note: it is usual to reply to a greeting with one in the same register.) Don't explain other items at this point.

◆ **Dialogues 3 and 4**

Focus attention on the pictures, check that the text is covered. Explain *criminal*. Set pre-questions: *Are the men criminals? Are the women criminals?* Play the dialogues. Check the answers.

◆ **Intensive exploitation: dialogue 1**

1 Play dialogue 1 again, pausing for selective repetition. *What's the time? / They're late / Or we're early / Is it their car?*

2 Silent reading of dialogue 1.

3 Point out *They're late. It's their car.* Write up:
1. *they're* 2. *their*. Get students to repeat, showing that the pronunciation is the same. Say:

T: *They're late.* C: *one.* T: *It's their house.* C: *two*
Continue: *It's their car. They're early. They're from England. What's their address?*

4 Drill:
T: *they*
C: *They're late.*
Continue: *I / he / we / you / she / they / John / Sarah and Jane.*

5 Paired reading of dialogue 1.

◆ Intensive exploitation: dialogue 2

1 Play dialogue 2 again, pausing for students to repeat chorally and individually.

2 Drill:
T: *picture*
C: *Where's the picture?*
T: *diamonds*
C: *Where are the diamonds?*
Continue: *pen / books / dictionary / forks / spoons*

3 Silent reading of dialogue 2.

4 Paired reading of dialogue 2.

5 Questions:
Where is the picture? Is it a Van Gogh? What is it? Are the diamonds in the briefcase? Where are they? Where is the bag?

6 Give students instructions: *Get the pen. Get her book. Get his bag.* etc. Make sure they follow the instructions. They do not need to speak. Get them to do the same in pairs.

7 Drill:
T: *my*
C: *It's my car.*
Continue: *his / their / our / her / your / my*

◆ Intensive exploitation: dialogue 3

1 Play dialogue 3 again, pausing for selective repetition. Focus on: *we're detectives. / You're detectives . . . / They **are** detectives . . . But we aren't criminals / We're detectives, too.* Note the changing stress/intonation. Make sure students imitate it.

2 Silent reading of dialogue 3.

3 Paired reading of dialogue 3.

◆ Intensive exploitation: dialogue 4

1 Play dialogue 4 again. There is no need for repetition.

2 Silent reading of dialogue 4.

3 Pair work. Focus attention on the identity card. Ask them to study it for a moment. Then they ask and answer about the ID card in pairs, asking (e.g.) *What's his surname? What are his first names? What's his job? What's his number?* Check by asking a few individuals. Ask a few questions about other students: *What's her surname? What's his first name? Is her name (Maria)?* Ask *What?* etc.

◆ Role play

1 Play all four sections of the dialogue again. Students listen.

2 Role play. Get them to role play the whole dialogue **without books** in groups of four.

◆ a What's the time?

Note: Time is only taught in the *ten twenty, ten forty* style at this stage. It is easier for students to generate than *twenty past ten, twenty to eleven* which appears in Unit 22.

1 Focus attention on the examples, run through them briefly. Ask individuals the time for each of the clocks (or use a classroom clock with moveable hands).

2 Pair work. Students ask and answer about the clocks.

◆ b Questions

1 Focus attention on the postcard. Silent reading.

2 Pair work. Focus attention on the questions. Students ask and answer in pairs.

3 Read the postcard aloud. Ask the questions to individuals as a check.

◆ c Registration

1 Silent reading of the guest registration card.

2 Questions:
What's their surname? What are their first names? Are they students? What are they? Where are they from? What are their passport numbers? What's their address? What's their room number?

3 Pair work. Get them to ask similar questions about the registration card in pairs.

4 Open conversation. Students complete the conversation orally in pairs. It can also be set as a written homework.

◆ d Role play

Students role play a conversation at the hotel, completing a registration card. They should use their own names, addresses etc. Check that they are making up information where necessary (passport numbers). This is an important point about role play that is worth stressing.

◆ Workbook

The Workbook can be done for homework.
If you wish to use it in class, exercises 1, 4, and 5 can be done in pairs.

Unit five

a) What's the time?

A What's the time?
B It's six o'clock.

A What's the time?
B It's ten forty.

A What's the time?
B It's eleven thirty.

Continue:

Dear Sarah and Ben,
Hi! This is a picture of our plane. It's an Airbus. We're in London! Do you know Gary and Eva Ford? Well, they're in London too. They're in our hotel. Our room is number 321, and their room is number 322! Our suitcases aren't in London. But they aren't lost... they're in Manchester. Gary and Eva aren't happy. Their suitcases are in Tokyo!
Best Wishes
Karen and David

Sarah and Ben Franklin
475 Truman Street
Chicago
Illinois
60615 U.S.A.

b) Questions

Ask and answer.
1 Is their plane a Boeing 767?
2 What is it?
3 Are Karen and David in Chicago?
4 Where are they?
5 Are their suitcases in London?
6 Are their suitcases lost?
7 Where are their suitcases?
8 Where are Gary and Eva?
9 What is their room number?
10 Where are their suitcases?
11 Where are Sarah and Ben?
12 What is their address?

c) Registration

Look at the registration card.
Complete the conversation.

Karen Good afternoon.
Receptionist _____ , _____ names?
Karen Our _____ Karen and David Kennedy.
Receptionist _____ students?
Karen No, _____ . We _____ .
Receptionist Where _____ from?
Karen _____ .
Receptionist _____ passport numbers?
Karen _____ and _____ .
Receptionist _____ address?
Karen _____ .
Receptionist OK, you're in room _____ . Where are your suitcases?
Karen Ah! _____ !

HOLIDAY HOTEL
4-8 Stone Street
London SW1 8NT
Tel: (01) 567 1245

Guest Registration Card

Family name: KENNEDY
First name(s): KAREN & DAVID
Occupation: TEACHERS
Nationality: AMERICAN
Passport number(s): 2442890/W318500
Home address: 471 TRUMAN ST. CHICAGO, ILLINOIS, 60615, USA
Room number: 321

d) Role play

Student A is the receptionist at the hotel. Student B is a guest.
Look at the guest registration card.
Have a conversation.

The London train

Driver This is the station.
Philip Thank you. How much is that?
Driver Three pounds fifty.
Philip And where's the ticket office?
Driver It's over there. That's the ticket office. It's next to the entrance.

Diana Good afternoon.
Girl 'Afternoon.
Diana Two tickets to London, please.
Girl Single or return?
Diana Return, please. How much?
Girl Twenty-four pounds.
Diana Here you are.
Girl Thanks.
Diana What time's the next train?
Girl Seventeen forty.

Philip Excuse me!
Guard Yes?
Philip Is this the London train?
Guard No, it isn't. That's the London train over there.
Philip Where?
Guard On platform three.
Philip Thank you.

Unit six

Teaching points

this / that / these / those
here / there
How much is it / this / that?
It's (three pounds fifty.)
Prepositions: *on* (platform three) *next to* (the entrance)
Twenty-four hour clock for timetables: *twenty-one hundred / twenty thirty*
What time? *or*
Listening for specific information (timetables).
Reading for specific information (tickets, timetables).

Grammar note

In this unit *How much?* is used for price, **not** quantity.
Demonstratives (*this*, *that*, *these*, *those*): Although it is useful to introduce the concept with distance, i.e. *this / these* for near things, *that / those* for further away things, you could add the concept of variation – we don't like to give a long list of *this* or *that* references, so alternate between them for variety. *This is a pen, and that's a pencil.* (Though they are at the same distance from the speaker.)

Expressions

'morning   single or return?   How much?   Excuse me!
Well,   Are (these seats) free?   Aren't they?   Come on...

Active vocabulary

door / driver / entrance / girl / hundred / information / office / platform / railway station / taxi / ticket / train
free (= vacant) / return / seat / single / next / next to / What time...?

Passive vocabulary

buffet / car park / departures / destination / guard / left-luggage / news kiosk / waiting room

Classroom vocabulary

chair / make / table / window

Audio-visual aids

Cassette. Some authentic timetables and/or fares lists could be used for reading for specific information with this lesson. Realia for introduction.

◆ Oral introduction

Briefly demonstrate *this*, *that*, *these*, *those* using classroom objects, or optional realia. Point at objects at a distance for *that*, *those*.
Connect the words to **here** (*this*, *these*) and **there** (*that*, *those*).
e.g. *It's here. This is a door.*
They're here. These are chairs.
It's there. That's a table.
They're there. Those are windows.

◆ Dialogue 1 (Driver / Philip)

1 Focus attention on the pictures, check that the text is covered. Play the dialogue. Play it again, pausing for students to repeat chorally and individually.

2 Check *This is the station* (point down at the ground, *We're here.*) *That's the ticket office* (point into the distance, *It's there.*)

3 Silent reading of the dialogue.

4 Paired reading of the dialogue.

⟨a⟩ Where's the ticket office?

1 Focus attention on the large picture of the station. Ask questions to elicit: *It's next to...*
e.g. T: *Where's the information office?* S: *It's next to the waiting room.* Avoid spending undue time on vocabulary teaching.

2 Pair work. Students ask and answer as in .1, using the picture of the railway station.

3 Role play. Students role play a conversation similar to dialogue 1, using the picture of the railway station.

◆ Dialogue 2 (Diana / Girl)

1 Focus attention on the pictures, check that the text is covered. Set pre-questions, *How much? What time?* Play the dialogue. Check the answers. Play it again, pausing for students to repeat chorally and individually. Explain *single*, *return*.

2 Silent reading of the dialogue.

3 Paired reading of the dialogue.

⟨b⟩ How much?

1 Reading for specific information. Go through the **How much?** section orally. Focus attention on the train tickets. Write a chart on the board:

From	To	Price
1		
2		
3		

Ask students to look at the tickets and find the information. Check the answers. Note: the other information on the tickets is redundant language.

2 Students ask and answer in pairs about the tickets.

⟨c⟩ Departures

1 Focus attention on the train departures chart. Note: *sixteen hundred*, and point out that the 24-hour clock is only used for timetables. Ask questions: *What time's the Portsmouth train?* etc. to elicit: *Seventeen thirty*.

2 Pair work. Students ask and answer as in .1.

3 Role play. Students role play a conversation similar to dialogue 2, using the departures board, and substituting different prices. Get one or two pairs to demonstrate in front of the class.

◆ Dialogue 3 (Philip / Guard)

1 Focus attention on the pictures, check that the text is covered. Play the dialogue. Play it again, pausing for choral and individual repetition.

2 Drill:
T: *The London train is here.*
C: *This is the London train.*
T: *The Portsmouth train is over there.*
C: *That's the Portsmouth train.*

Continue:
The Oxford train is over there.
The Manchester train is here.
The Bournemouth train is here.
The Liverpool train is over there.

3 Silent reading of the dialogue.

4 Paired reading of the dialogue.

◆ Role play

Role play. Students role play a conversation similar to dialogue 3, using the departures chart in ⟨c⟩. Get one or two pairs to demonstrate their dialogues in front of the class.

◆ Dialogue 4 (Diana / Man)

1 Focus attention on the pictures, check that the text is covered. Play the dialogue. Play it again, pausing for students to repeat chorally and individually.

2 Drill:
T: *The seats are here.*
C: *Are these seats free?*
T: *The seats are over there.*
C: *Are those seats free?*

Continue:
The tables are here.
The tables are over there.
The chairs are over there.
The chairs are here.

3 Silent reading of the dialogue.

4 Paired reading of the dialogue.

5 Role play, on the dialogue, substituting other vocabulary items. Write up a list:
   1. these seats / this table
   2. the door / the window / the toilet

◆ Dialogue 5 (Diana / Philip)

1 Focus attention on the pictures, check that the text is covered. Play the dialogue. Play it again, pausing for students to repeat chorally and individually.

2 Drill:
T: *My bags aren't here.*
C: *These aren't my bags.*
T: *My pens aren't there.*
C: *Those aren't my pens!*

Continue:
My bags aren't there.
My pens aren't here.
My books aren't there.
My keys aren't here.

3 Silent reading of the dialogue.

4 Paired reading of the dialogue.

5 Play the cassette of all five dialogues again.

⟨d⟩ Announcements

1 Focus attention on the Listening chart. Play the announcements right through twice, getting students to fill in the information on the second listening.

2 Pair work. Students compare their answers in pairs. Check the answers with a few questions. Play the cassette again to confirm if necessary.

◆ Oral practice

1 Check *this/that* again. Put several objects on your desk. Ask a few students *What's this?* Make sure that they reply *That's a (book).* i.e. The object is near you, but far from them.
Follow the same procedure with some plurals, *What are these?* to elicit *Those are (pens)*.
Distribute some realia around the class. Form pairs. Demonstrate that every pair now has some near objects and some far objects to ask about (*What's this? What's that? What are these? What are those?*).

2 Pair work. Get students to ask and answer about the objects freely in pairs.

3 (See Grammar note.) With classes that are confident, put two objects near you. Say *This is a pen, and that's a book.*
Put two groups of objects near you. Say *These are pens and those are books.*
Here *this* and *that*, *these* and *those* are being used simply for variety.

◆ Game (I spy . . .) (Optional)

You could get students to play a guessing game, based on the old game 'I spy . . .' One student thinks of an object, and tells the class the first letter of the object, (a word with 'b'). The class asks questions until they can guess the object, *Is it a book? Is it a ball? Is it a bag?* The game (which can be played at any time in the course) is very limited here due to lack of vocabulary, but it can be used as a way of getting students to use the Vocabulary index at the back of their books. (You could limit the game to words in Units 1 to 6.)

◆ Using authentic materials (Optional)

If you can collect some authentic timetables, they can be used as the basis of the role plays during the lesson, or at this point. They can all be different, and in fact need not be from an English-speaking country (though this would be an advantage). This will involve reading for specific information as part of the role play activity.

◆ Workbook

The Workbook can be done as homework.
If it is done in class, exercises 4 to 8 are suitable for oral pair work. Check that they use the timetable and fare list for the exercises (reading for specific information), but do not explain any vocabulary items.

Unit six

Diana Excuse me ...
Man Yes?
Diana Are these seats free?
Man No, sorry. They aren't.
But *those* seats are free.
Diana Where?
Man Over there. Next to the door.
Diana Thank you.

Diana Philip! Those aren't my bags!
Philip Aren't they?
Diana No. *These* are my bags!
Philip OK. Well, we're here. This is London.

a Where's the ticket office?

Look at the railway station.
A *Where's the ticket office?*
B *It's next to the exit.*
A *Where are the toilets?*
B *They're next to the news kiosk.*
Ask and answer about the station.

b How much?

A *How much is that?* **B** *It's three pounds fifty.*
  How much is it?
  How much?
Ask and answer about the tickets.

c Departures

information	Departures	[17.32]
TIME	**DESTINATION**	**PLATFORM**
17.30	Portsmouth	4
17.35	Oxford, Birmingham, Liverpool	1
17.40	London	3
17.50	Bournemouth, Poole	4
18.10	Winchester	1
18.20	Manchester	3
18.50	Bournemouth, Weymouth	4
19.00	London	3

Note: 16.00 – Say *sixteen hundred* (or *four o'clock*).

A *What time's the Portsmouth train?*
B *Seventeen thirty.*
Ask and answer about the departures board.

d Announcements

Listen. Write the times and platform numbers.

Time	Destination	Platform
1 20.40	London	4
2	Oxford	....
3	Bournemouth	....
4	Manchester, Liverpool	....
5	Portsmouth	....

Unit seven

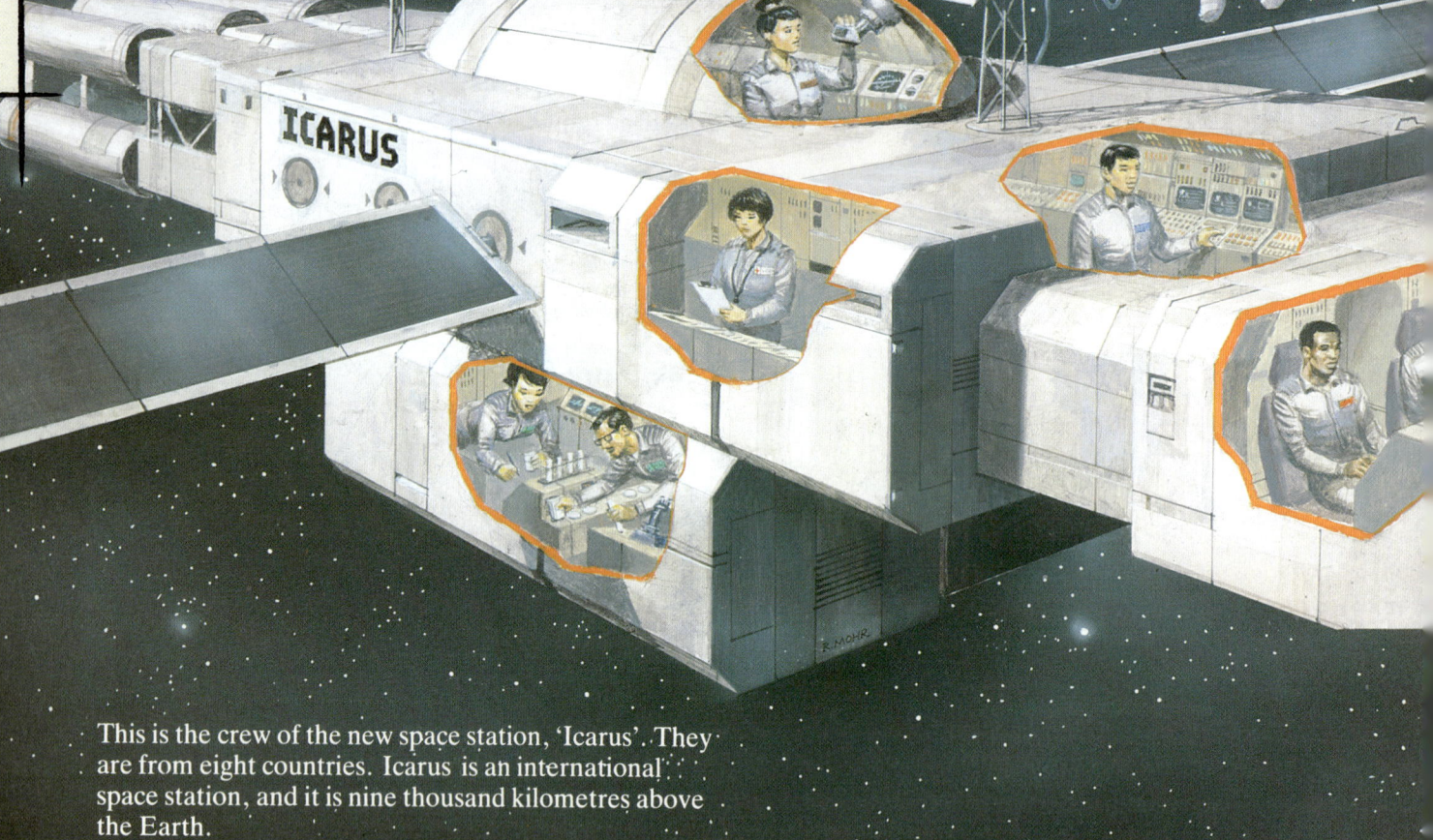

Space station

This is the crew of the new space station, 'Icarus'. They are from eight countries. Icarus is an international space station, and it is nine thousand kilometres above the Earth.

| CLARKE | ASIMOV |

Peter Clarke and Ivan Asimov are the pilots. Peter's American, and Ivan's Russian. Peter's thirty-two, and he's from Los Angeles. Ivan is forty, and he's from Moscow.

| VERNE |

Marie Verne is twenty-nine, and she's the doctor on Icarus. Marie is French. She's from Paris.

| BALLARD |

Mark Ballard is British, and he's the engineer. Mark is thirty-two, and he's from London.

| SUZUKI | MARQUEZ |

Yoko Suzuki and Antonio Marquez are the scientists on the space station. She's thirty-one, and she's from Tokyo. She's Japanese. He's thirty-two, and he's Spanish. He's from Madrid.

| LI |

Li Song is Chinese. He's the computer specialist. He's twenty-eight years old, and he's from Shanghai.

| CABRAL |

Cristina Cabral is Brazilian. She's from Rio de Janeiro, and she's the astronomer on Icarus. She's twenty-nine years old.

1957 Laika, a dog, first traveller in space ... 1961 Yuri Gagarin, first man in space ... 1963 Valentina Tereshkova, first

Unit seven

Teaching points
Who is it? / Who are they? / Who's the doctor? / Who's from Los Angeles?
How old are you? / is she?
I'm twenty-one. / I'm twenty-one years old.
What's your job? / nationality?
What's her job? / nationality?
Nationalities / jobs
Four-figure numbers (1,000).
a / the: *She's a doctor.* / *She's the doctor on the space station.*
Reading for pleasure: the facts about space travel are not exploited. They are there to be read in passing.

Grammar note
The focus of the lesson is facts about people. Exercise ⟨e⟩ shows the use of the definite article (*the*) compared with the use of indefinite articles (*a/an*). We believe that this is a difficult concept for some students, and explanation should be avoided. If it is avoided, most students will find themselves doing the exercise successfully, without even noticing the contrast between *a* and *the*.

Active vocabulary
age / astronomer / country / crew / doctor / Earth / engineer / job / home / kilometre / nationality / pilot / scientist / space / specialist / thousand / town
new / above
American / Brazilian / British / Chinese / French / Japanese / Russian / Spanish

Passive vocabulary
interview / reporter

Classroom vocabulary
badge / chart / close / find / member / think

Redundant vocabulary (for reading, not listed in index)
Years / astronaut / dog / first / meet / moon / skylab / space shuttle / traveller

Audio-visual aids
The texts are **not** recorded.

Optional introduction for false beginners:
Reading material below: **facts about space travel**.

◆ **Oral introduction**

Pretend that you have forgotten students' names.
T: *Who's that?* to elicit, *It's Maria. It's Yoshi*, etc. Get students to test your memory of students' names by pointing, and asking: *Who's that?*

◆ **Pictures and texts on the left-hand page**

Focus attention on the introductory text, and the six texts about the crew of the space station. Pre-reading task (**optional**): Say: 'John' is an English name. Write down: a French name / a Japanese name / a Russian name / a Chinese name / a Spanish name. Ask students to read the texts silently.

⟨a⟩ **Crew chart**

1 Explain the chart at the top of the right-hand page. Draw columns on the board, and complete the chart for Peter Clarke.
Students complete the chart for the other seven crew members, based on their silent reading. They will have to refer back to the six texts in order to complete it.

2 Focus on new vocabulary items by asking questions:
Are the crew from eight countries or six countries?
Is the space station American, or is it international?
Is it on the Earth, or is it above the Earth?
(Demonstrate with your hand *on* the table, and *above* the table.)
Is it nine hundred kilometres above the Earth, or is it nine thousand kilometres above the Earth?
Write '9,000' in numbers.

3 Ask students to study the picture of the space station. Hold up your book, say: *Who is the doctor?*
Ask them to show you on the picture.
Say: *Repeat: pilot, doctor, engineer, scientist, computer specialist, astronomer.*
Students repeat the words chorally and individually. Ask them which words are similar in their own language.

⟨b⟩ **Questions**

1 Focus attention on the questions. Get the students to ask and answer them in pairs, then run through the questions with the class to check.

2 Add more questions:
Who is American? Who is Brazilian? Who is twenty-eight? Who is Chinese? Who is from Tokyo? etc. Remember that students will have to refer to the texts in order to answer, so leave sufficient time for everyone to do this before selecting a student and accepting an answer.

⟨c⟩ **Who is she?**

1 Focus attention on the picture. Get the students to ask and answer in pairs, then run through the questions with the class to check. Be careful with the contraction *who's* and the pronunciation of *who are (who're)*. Note that we do not write this contraction, even though we say it.

2 Ask questions about the class, e.g.
T: *Who's Maria Gonzalez?*
S: *That's Maria Gonzalez over there.*

⟨d⟩ **How old is he?**

1 Focus attention on the example questions and answers. Get the students to ask and answer in pairs; then run through some questions with the class to check.

2 Ask about the class:
How old are you? How old is he? How old is she? (How old am I?)

(**Note:** with school-age students, there will only be two answers from most classes, so keep the activity short. Take care with adult classes, and be careful to avoid embarrassing students.)
You could ask about famous people. You would have to find out their **current ages** before the lesson. If you do this, you could tell students the ages, then make the questions into a memory game. The following dates of birth will help if you cannot find out any current ages before the lesson:
Bruce Springsteen – 23/9/49, Yoko Ono – 18/2/33, Queen Elizabeth II – 21/4/26, Mikhail Gorbachev – 2/3/31, Stephen Spielberg – 18/12/47.

e What's his job?

1 Focus attention on the pictures. Point out the crew's badges next to each of the six texts. Read out the example. Indicate the two possibilities:
*He's **an** engineer. / He's **the** engineer on 'Icarus'.*
*They're pilots. / They're **the** pilots on 'Icarus'.*
Get the students to complete the exercise in pairs. They might like to do it once, answering with the definite article, then again answering with the indefinite article. They have to use the badges to help them. Don't go into complex explanations about definite and indefinite articles at this stage.

2 With school-age classes, ask about famous people, e.g. T: *Madonna. What's her job?* S: *She's a singer / She's a rock star.*
Use a currently famous footballer / President / tennis player / actor / rock singer etc.
(**Avoid: *What's Madonna's job?*** – the possessive is not taught until Unit 12.) Ask: *What's my job?* to elicit *You're a teacher.*
With adult classes, ask: *What's your / his / her / my job?* Then get them to ask each other.

f What's her nationality?

1 Focus attention on the chart. Get students to complete the chart silently. Let them compare their answers in pairs, then check back with the class.

2 Refer them to the examples below the chart. Get the students to ask and answer about the crew in pairs, then run through the questions with the class to check.

3 In a multilingual class, ask: *What's my / your / his / her nationality?*
In a monolingual class, use famous people, as in ⟨d⟩ and ⟨e⟩ above.
e.g. T: *Gorbachev. What's his nationality?* S: *He's Russian.*
Use currently famous living people, politicians, sports personalities, singers, entertainers, etc.
(Again, **avoid: *What's Gorbachev's nationality?*** – the possessive is not taught until Unit 12.)

g Thousands

1 Point out the example (*three thousand **not*** *three thousands*).
Put the numbers on the board, point and get students to say them orally. Add more examples if necessary.

2 Comprehension dictation.
Dictate these numbers. Students write them down in **numeric** form. Dictate 'double four':
4,440   9,800   2,598   5,116   4,330   2,818   1,090
5,717   4,414
Write them on the board for students to self-correct.

h Interviews

Role play. Students work in pairs role playing a reporter and various crew members. Ask one or two pairs to demonstrate in front of the class.

i Game: Who is it?

1 The game is done in pairs, with students taking it in turns to be Student A and Student B.

2 The game can then be done with an individual student at the front of the class, thinking of one of the class members. The others have to guess.
Streets or areas can be substituted for towns where all the students come from one town.

j Who are you?

Pair work. Students interview each other in pairs. Check: ask a few students about their partners: *What's her home town?* etc.

◆ Reading material: facts about space

The reading material at the bottom of the pages (facts about space travel) is designed for reading for pleasure. It is assumed that it will not be exploited in class in any way. It is important for students to read information on occasions with no checking or testing. Of course, if student interest is aroused by the facts, you could spend time on them.
Optional: With false beginners, the facts could be used to introduce the lesson.

◆ Workbook

The Workbook can be done for homework.
If it is done in class, exercises, 1, 2, and 8 can be done as oral pair work.

a Crew chart

Complete the chart.

Name	Age	Nationality	Home town	Job
Peter Clarke				
Ivan Asimov				
Marie Verne				
Mark Ballard				
Yoko Suzuki				
Antonio Marquez				
Li Song				
Cristina Cabral				

b Questions

Ask and answer.
1 Who are the pilots?
2 Who is the astronomer?
3 Who is from Japan?
4 Who is from Paris?
5 Who are the scientists?
6 Who is Spanish?
7 Who is forty years old?
8 Who is the computer specialist?
9 Who is from Rio de Janeiro?
10 Who is thirty-one?

c Who is she?

A Who is she?
B She's Marie Verne. / She's the doctor.
A Who are they?
B They're Yoko and Antonio. / They're the scientists.
Make questions and answers about the crew.

d How old is he?

A How old is Li Song?
B He's twenty-eight. / He's twenty-eight years old.
A How old are Marie and Cristina?
B They're twenty-nine. / They're twenty-nine years old.
Make questions and answers about the crew.

e What's his job?

A What's his job?
B He's an engineer. / He's the engineer on Icarus.
A What are their jobs?
B They're pilots. / They're the pilots on Icarus.
Make questions and answers about the crew.

f What's her nationality?

1 Complete the chart with these words:
Spanish   French   Japanese   Russian
Brazilian   British   Chinese.

The United States _American_	The USSR _____
Britain _____	Spain _____
China _____	Japan _____
Brazil _____	France _____

2 Look at the chart.
A Marie's from France. What's her nationality?
B She's French.
A Where's she from?
B She's from Paris.
Make questions and answers about the crew.

g Thousands

6,000 – six thousand
3,451 – three thousand four hundred and fifty-one
Say these numbers:

| 2,987 | 1,207 | 4,361 | 9,400 | 2,000 |
| 5,100 | 9,001 | 3,820 | 10,000 | 8,510 |

h Interviews

You are a reporter. Interview the crew. Ask about:
name, age, nationality, home town, job.

i Game: Who is it?

Student A: Close your book.
Student B: Look at the space station.
Think of one of the crew.
Student A: Ask questions, and find the crew member.

j Who are you?

Ask another student questions. Write his/her:
name, age, nationality, home town, job.

Unit eight

What's it like?

Is this your new car?

It's the fantastic first prize in our new competition!!!
Win a Jaguar XJ6!
The XJ6 3.6 is £28,000!

Second Prize

Malibu Skier sports
boat - 70 kph
American - £14,750

Third Prize

Four Samsonite *Oyster*
suitcases
British - £320 for the four

Fourth Prize

Sony Walkman personal stereo
Model WM - F66
Japanese - £65

Number the words below from 1 to 6.

☐ fast ☐ British ☐ new
☐ big ☐ beautiful ☐ expensive

Write your name and address on the form, and send it to:

JAGUAR Competition
The Weekend Magazine
P.O. Box 54
London, E2 8RJ

Name: _____
Address: _____
_____
_____

Kate Paul! Look at this letter! I'm the winner of the competition!
Paul What competition?
Kate The competition in *The Weekend Magazine*. I'm the winner ...
Paul What's the prize?
Kate It's a new car.
Paul A new car? What make is it?
Kate It's a Jaguar.
Paul Fantastic! What's it like?
Kate It's beautiful. It's big, and fast ...
Paul ... and it's our car!
Kate Well ... my car ...
Paul What colour is it?
Kate I don't know ...
Paul Look at the letter.
Kate Ergh! It's pink!

a Role play

Make conversations about the 2nd prize, the 3rd prize, and the 4th prize.
Note
What's the prize?
What are they like?
What colour are they?

| white | pink | red | orange | yellow | green | blue | brown | black | gre |

Unit eight

Teaching points
Adjectives.
What is it like? / What are they like?
It's big. / They're big. It's a big car. / They're big cars.
What colour is it? / are they?
It's red. / They're red.
It's a red car. / They're red cars.
What make is it? / are they?
It's a Jaguar. / They're Jaguars.
Nationalities (cont.) *Italian / German / Swedish / Dutch*
Ordinal numbers: *1st to 8th.*
Reading: The competition entry contains redundant material, to encourage students to read selectively.

Grammar note
Adjectives. In English adjectives do not agree with the noun – *big car / big cars, new suitcase / new suitcases.*
The choice of indefinite article depends on whether the word following it starts with a vowel sound, not on whether it is an adjective or a noun (see Unit 2):
an apple / a big apple
a drink / an orange drink

Expressions
Win a (new Jaguar). What (competition)? Look at (the / this) letter. Cut here.

Active vocabulary
beautiful / big / expensive / fast / old / slow / small /
black / blue / brown / green / grey / pink / red / white / yellow /
Germany / German / Holland / Dutch / Italy / Italian /
Sweden / Swedish / Turkey / Turkish
third / fourth / fifth / sixth / seventh / eighth /
boat / calculator / colour / competition / flag / fridge /
hair dryer / jeans / letter / magazine / make / prize / recorder /
shirt / truck / winner / like / win

Passive vocabulary
P.O. Box / below / cut / kitchen / kph / personal / send / sports / boat / stereo

Classroom vocabulary
about / describe / other / role play / shoes / things

Audio-visual aids
Cassette. Realia: A number of coloured objects.

◆ **Oral introduction**

Pre-teach the colours, using a collection of coloured objects.
T: *It's a pen. It's red. It's a red pen.* etc.
Ask: *What is it? What colour is it?* about a number of objects.

◆ **Competition entry form**

1 Focus attention on the competition, 'Is this your new car?'
Get the students to read it silently.

2 Questions:
What's the first prize?
What's the second prize?   Where is it from?
What's the third prize?   Where are they from?
What's the fourth prize?   Where it is from?
What's the name of the magazine?
What's the address of the magazine?

3 Check the meaning of *fast, big, beautiful, new, expensive.* Use classroom objects, mime, and gesture as far as possible.

4 Focus attention on the picture of the car. Point out the words that they must number from 1 to 6. Get students to number from 1 to 6, and to add their names and addresses. Check that the address is in the normal English sequence.
name / street / district / town / post code / country.
If necessary, write up:
Mary Smith
13 Waterloo Avenue
Cowley
Oxford OX5 7ED
England.

5 Questions:
What's first for you? What's second for you? etc. Get students to repeat after you: *first, second, third, fourth, fifth, sixth.* Check chorally and individually.

6 Pair work. Students ask and answer as in .5, comparing their lists.
Write up a list on the board. e.g. / fast – 1 / big – 3 / British – 4 / beautiful – 2 / new – 5 / expensive – 6.
Say that this is 'the winner' of the competition. Find out if a student has these numbers on his/her list. Proclaim them as the winner. (A set of car keys might be an amusing mock 'prize'!)

◆ **Dialogue (Kate / Paul)**

1 Focus attention on the picture, check that the text is covered. Set pre-questions: *What's her prize? What colour is it?* Play the dialogue. Check the answers. Play it again, pausing for students to repeat chorally and individually.

2 Demonstrate *What make is it?* and *What colour is it?* with realia, or classroom objects (the cassette player, a pen, a watch, a calculator etc.). Ask questions: *What colour's your (pen)? What make is it? Ask him / her / me.*

3 Drill: Continue:
T: *his watch*   *her watch*
C: *What make is his watch?*   *those pens*
T: *the suitcases*   *that cassette player*
C: *What make are the suitcases?*   *the personal stereo*

4 Drill: Continue:
T: *the Jaguar*   *the video recorder*
C: *What colour's the*   *the personal stereo*
Jaguar?   *those pens*
T: *the suitcases*   *her bag*
C: *What colour are the suitcases?*

5 Drill: Continue:
T: *it*   *the car*
C: *What's it like?*   *the suitcases*
T: *they*   *the pens*
C: *What are they like?*   *the video recorder*

6 Silent reading of the dialogue.

7 Questions:
Is he the winner, or is she the winner?
What's the prize?
Is the car a BMW? Ask: What make?
Is the car slow? Is it old? Is it small?
What is it like?
Is it blue? Is it yellow? Is it white? Ask: What colour?

8 Paired reading of the dialogue. Make sure that students act out, rather than read.

◇a Role play (2nd, 3rd, 4th prizes)

1 Ask students to study the other prizes silently.

2 Questions:
Where's the sports boat from? What make is it? How much is it? What colour is it?
Get them to ask each other about the suitcases and the personal stereo.
Check through the colours at the foot of the page.

3 Pair work. Students role play conversations about the other prizes. Give them vocabulary they might need while monitoring the pairs.

◇b What make is it?

1 Write 1st, 2nd, 3rd etc. on the board in the contracted forms. Point, and get students to say the full word.

2 Focus attention on the first row of pictures. Check that the questions are covered.
Ask questions:
What is in the first picture? What colour is it?
Is it a Sony? Is it a Panasonic?
What make is it? Is it English? Is it French? What nationality is it? etc.
What is in the second picture? What colour are they? etc.

3 Focus attention on the questions. Silent reading.

4 Pair work. Students ask and answer about pictures 1–4.

5 Pair work. Students go straight into pair work on pictures 5 to 8 (i.e. without preparatory questions from the teacher).

6 Ask questions to individuals about pictures 5 to 8 to check.

7 Say the names of different manufacturers. Students respond with the nationality.
e.g. T: *Boeing* S: *It's American.*
Continue: *Ferrari* (Italian), *Citröen* (French), *Mercedes* (German), *Sony* (Japanese), *Rolls-Royce* (British), *SAAB* (Swedish) etc.

◇c Describe them

1 Go through the examples. Ask about other things to the class as a whole, using:
What's your pen like? What are your shoes like?
Check *old, small, slow* using mime and gesture.

2 Pair work. Students continue in pairs as in ◇b .5.

3 Write:
It's big. It's a big car. They're big. They're big cars.
Get students to copy from the board. Make it clear that the adjective does not agree with the noun. It always remains singular. (See Workbook, exercise 6.) Make it clear that *a* and *an* relate to the next word, not to the noun, e.g. *an* apple but *a* big apple, *a* car but *an* Italian car. (See Workbook, exercise 5.)

4 Write:
It's a car. It's Italian. It's an Italian car.
It's an apple. It's big. It's a big apple.
Get students to copy from the board. If there are problems, do the Workbook exercises as oral drills.

◇d Flags

1 Do the exercise orally with the whole class.

2 Get the students to repeat the exercise in pairs.
(Note: Because we say *red, white, and blue* so often in both Britain and the United States, it sounds odd to native speakers if the word order is changed.)
Ask about other flags: *What colour's your flag?* if it has not been included already.

◆ Word game

Write up the colours in scrambled form. Get students to unscramble them. e.g. dre (red), ergen (green), lube (blue), weylol (yellow), clakb (black), yerg (grey), kinp (pink), theiw (white), worbn (brown).

◆ Game

A student thinks of an object. The others ask Yes/No questions until they can guess what it is. e.g. *Is it red? Is it blue? Is it big? Is it expensive? Is it a car? Is it German? Is it Swedish? Is it British? Is it Italian? Is it fast? Is it beautiful? Is it a Ferrari?* etc. The game can be demonstrated with the whole class, and continued in pairs or small groups.

◆ Workbook

The Workbook can be done for homework.
Exercise 1 can be the basis of extensive paired oral practice.
Exercises 3, 7, and 8 can be done orally in class.
Exercises 5 and 6 can be integrated with the lesson, as oral drills as part of ◇c .3.

Note: This may be a point to explain the difference between: *England, Britain, The United Kingdom, English, British* if the class are puzzled/interested. (Britain is made up of England, Scotland and Wales. The United Kingdom is Britain and Northern Ireland. Everybody from the United Kingdom is British. They can also be called English, Scottish, Welsh or Irish depending on whether they come from England, Scotland, Wales or Ireland. People from Scotland, Wales and Ireland do not like to be called English.)

Unit eight

1st a calculator
grey
Casio
(Japanese)

2nd jeans
blue
Levis
(American)

3rd a shirt
yellow
Lacoste
(French)

4th a fridge
white
Zanussi
(Italian)

5th a car
red
SEAT
(Spanish)

6th a truck
green
Volvo
(Swedish)

7th a hair dryer
black
Philips
(Dutch)

8th a cooker
brown
Neff
(German)

b What make is it?

Look at the first picture.

A *What's the first picture?*
B *It's a calculator.*
A *What colour is it?*
B *It's grey.*
A *What make is it?*
B *It's a Casio.*
A *Is it English?*
B *No. It isn't. It's Japanese.*

Ask and answer about the pictures.

c Describe them

A *My watch is new. It's a Rolex and it's beautiful. It's an expensive watch.*
B *My jeans are old. They're blue, and they're Wranglers. They aren't expensive jeans.*

Talk about other things, with these words:
new / old   big / small   expensive / not expensive
fast / slow   beautiful / not beautiful

d Flags

A *What colour is the Dutch flag?*
B *It's red, white, and blue.*

Ask and answer about the other flags.

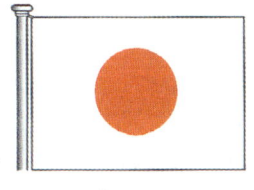

Japan    Sweden    Italy    Germany    Brazil

Holland 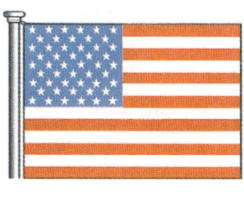   USA    Turkey    Spain    France

Unit nine

Where is she?

- WHERE IS SHE? / SHE'S DOWN THERE! SHE'S ON THAT ROCK.
- SHE'S BELOW US NOW.
- IT'S OK. I'M ABOVE HER.
- OH NO! SHE'S IN THE SEA!
- SHE'S UNDER THE WATER. / PUT ME DOWN!
- IT'S OK. PULL THEM UP.
- RIGHT. THEY'RE IN THE HELICOPTER.
- MY DOG! HE'S DOWN THERE ON THE ROCK. PLEASE, PLEASE RESCUE HIM.
- ERR... IS IT FRIENDLY?

Teaching points

Prepositions of place:
in / on / under / below / above / next to / in front of / behind / down / up
Object pronouns:
me / you / him / her / us / them / it
Where is she?
She's in front of me.
Where are they?
They're next to him.
Who's behind us?
They're behind us.
Pull (them) up. / Put (me) down.
Nationalities: *an / a / the American / Australian / Chinese.*
a / an / the Spanish / British / Dutch / man / woman / person / girl / runner
now
Listening: task listening with a limited aim, finding out the results of a race.
In front (adverbial) appears redundantly in the listening. Do not draw attention to it. It will be understood from *in front of*.

Grammar note

The main focus of this unit is object pronouns and prepositions.

Nationality words ending in *-an*, *-ian*, *-ese* can function as adjectives or nouns, e.g. *an American*, *an American runner*. Nationality words ending in *-ish* and *-ch* only function as adjectives, so we say:
A Spanish man. A man from Spain.
(Note: *Spaniard* is archaic.)

Active vocabulary

class / crewman / dog / metre / race / rock / runner / sea / water / behind / below / down / in front of / under / up
(+ *in / on / above* from previous units; *below* has appeared passively.)
her / him / me / them / us
Australian / friendly
pull

Passive vocabulary

air-sea rescue / co-pilot / window

Classroom vocabulary

draw / plan

Audio-visual aids

Cassette

◆ Cartoon strip

1 Focus attention on the cartoon strip. Note that it will not be possible to separate text and visuals due to the nature of cartoon strips. Play the cassette. Students listen and follow the text and pictures. Play it again, pausing for students to repeat chorally and individually.

2 Demonstrate on/above, under/below, in, up/down. Use a book, a table, and a bag. Ask *Where is it now?* to elicit: *It's on the table. Now it's above the table. It's under the bag. It's in the bag*, etc. Repeat with two objects (e.g. pens), asking *Where are they now?* to elicit: *They're on the table.* etc.

3 Pair work. Students ask and answer in pairs as in .2, using a book, two pens, their table or desk, and a bag or briefcase.

4 Demonstrate object pronouns. Bring out a student of each sex (or use board drawings). Point and say: *Look at me, look at him, look at her, look at them, look at us, look at it.* Point as above and pause, looking quizzical to elicit a choral response. e.g. You indicate yourself and a student, the class says *Look at us*.
Demonstrate *put down* and *pull up*.

5 Focus attention on the cartoon strip again. Play the cassette, one frame at a time, pausing to ask questions. At this point you will be teaching the use of question generators (see Introduction) as well as practising object pronouns.

1 T: *Is she in the sea?* S1: *No, she isn't.* T: *Is she in the helicopter?* S2: *No, she isn't.* T: *Ask him 'Where?'*
S3: *Where is she?* S4: *She's on the rock.*
2 T: *Is she above them or is she below them?*
3 T: *Is he above the helicopter or is he below the helicopter? Is she above him or is she below him?*
4 T: *Is she on the rock? Ask him 'Where?'*
5 T: *Is she on the water? Is she on the rock? Ask him 'Where?'*
6 T: *Are they in the helicopter? Are they in the sea? Ask me 'Where?'*
7 T: *Ask him 'Where?'*
8 T: *Are they in the helicopter? Is the dog in the helicopter? Ask her 'Where?'*
9 T: *Where's the helicopter? Where's the man? What about the dog? Ask her 'Where?'*

6 Pair work. Students ask and answer about the cartoon strip as in .5.

7 Take an object, put it in various places in the room. Ask *Where is it?* Repeat with two objects and *Where are they?*

Unit nine

◆ Preposition diagrams (top of right-hand page)

1 **Either** mask the labels, and ask students what the diagrams represent (*What's this?*), **or** copy the diagrams onto the board, check that the students' books are closed and do the same.

2 Give students time to study the diagrams silently.

3 Drill:
T: *I'm here.*
C: *Look at me.*
T: *He's there.*
C: *Look at him.*
Continue: *She's here. / We're here. / They're over there. / It's here.*

Note: If students have problems with this, extend practice using Workbook, exercises 2 and 5.

a) Where are they?

1 Bring out four chairs, place three of them one behind the other. Place the fourth chair next to the middle one. Sit on the middle chair, put students in the other three chairs. Say (e.g.):
I'm behind her. She's in front of me.
I'm in front of him. He's behind me.
I'm next to her. She's next to me.
Ask questions:
T: *Where is she?*   C: *She's in front of you.*
T: *Where is he?*   C: *He's behind you.*
T: *Where am I?*   C: (e.g.) *You're behind her.*
T: *and?*   C: *You're in front of him.*
T: *and?*   C: *You're next to her.*

2 Focus attention on the plan of the helicopter. Check vocabulary. Read the examples. Ask questions about the location of people on the plan.

3 Pair work. Students ask and answer as in .1.

b) Your class

1 Focus attention on the example class plan. Read through the examples aloud.

2 Ask questions extensively about the location of people in your students' class. e.g. T: *Where's Maria?* S1: *She's next to me. / She's in front of you. / She's behind Roberto.* etc.
Get students to draw a plan, and fill in names on the class plan. (Substitute a different plan to suit your class layout if necessary.)

3 Pair work. Students ask and answer as in .2, using the book.

c) Women's 200-metre race

1 Focus attention on the picture. Briefly check through nationalities of people. (See Grammar note and Workbook, exercise 3 for a summary.)
We can say *an Australian*, *a German*, *the Chinese*, **(-ian, -an, -ese)** but with **-ish** and **-ch** nationalities we have to add another word like *person, man, woman, girl, boy* etc. This point is not worth labouring! If in doubt, add another word to all of them!

2 Explain the listening task. All the students have to do is place the runners in order. The tape has a stop point at the end of the race, then the results are announced. Play the cassette up to the stop point twice. Give the students time to note the order. Demonstrate and encourage the use of notes, like GB for Britain, AUS for Australia etc.
Then play the summary of the result on the tape.
Check the answers.
Ask: *Who is first? Who is second?* etc. If a student doesn't know, say *Ask me / him / her.*
Point out *winner* (Unit 8), *runner* (Unit 9).

◆ Writing / Matching

It is a good idea for students to note new prepositions from now on by using diagrams like the ones in this unit. Draw the diagrams on the board. Get students to copy them and then to write the appropriate preposition next to each diagram.

◆ Game: Where is it?

Send one student from the room. Hide an object, bring the student back in. He / she asks questions, e.g. *Is it on the table? Is it next to the window? Is it in front of Maria, or behind Maria? Is it in front of me or behind me?*
The rest of the class responds. They can add 'hot' (i.e. you're close) or 'cold' (i.e. you're not close).
This could be extended in groups, where one member of each group goes out.

◆ Workbook

The Workbook exercises can be done at home. You may wish to integrate exercises 2 and 5 into the lesson when looking at the preposition diagrams.
Exercises 1 and 4 are suitable for paired oral practice.

Background note for the teacher (register): It is normal in sports commentaries to refer to contestants as 'the English girl', 'The German boy', and so on. However, many women find the use of 'girl' to refer to adult women offensive and patronizing. A good rule is not to use 'girl' where you would not use 'boy' in an equivalent situation. ('Boy' or 'lad' would be equally likely in this situation.)

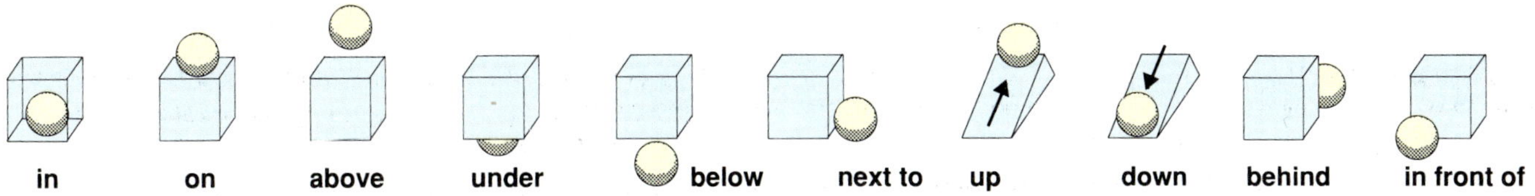

in   on   above   under   below   next to   up   down   behind   in front of

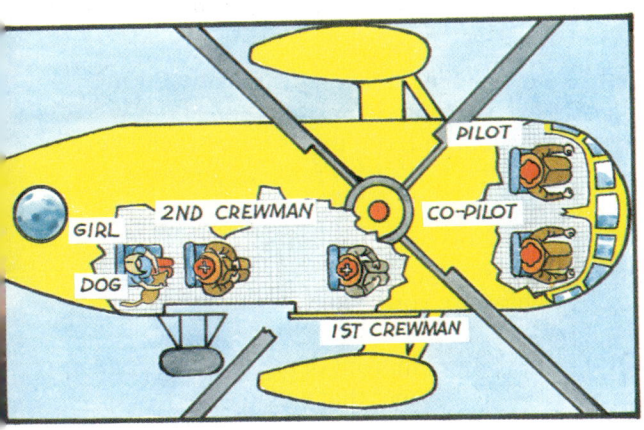

Unit nine

a Where are they?

A *Where's the second crewman?*
B *He's behind the first crewman.*
 He's in front of the girl.
 He's next to the door.

A *Who's behind the co-pilot?*
B *The first crewman is behind the co-pilot.*

Ask and answer about the people in the helicopter, with *Where?* and *Who?*

b Your class

1 Look at this class plan. Look at Maria.
 Who is behind her?
 Who is next to her?
 Who is in front of her?

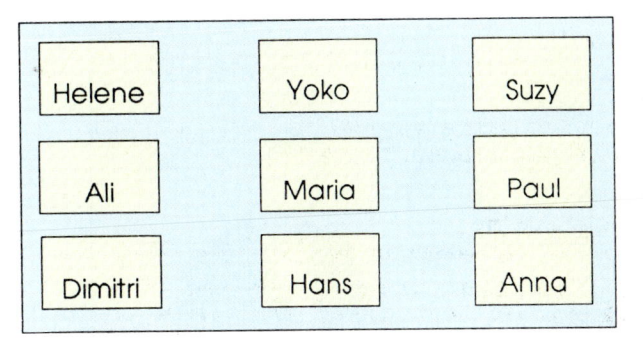

Helene	Yoko	Suzy
Ali	Maria	Paul
Dimitri	Hans	Anna

2 Now look at your class.
 Who is behind you?
 Who is next to you?
 Who is in front of you?
 Draw a plan of your class.

3 Ask and answer about the plan.

c Women's 200-metre race

This is the women's 200-metre race.
Listen to the race, and write the nationalities of the runners on the chart below.

1st _____   4th _____
2nd _____   5th _____
3rd _____   6th _____

Unit ten

Quiz of the Week

Lesley Good evening, ladies and gentlemen! I'm Lesley Crawley, and welcome to 'Quiz of the Week'. There are some wonderful prizes tonight, and here's our first contestant. It's Mr Frank Miller from London!
Lesley Hello, Frank!
Frank Good evening, Lesley.
Lesley And how are you tonight?
Frank Fine.
Lesley Good. You're in front of me, Frank. Stand next to me . . . no, next to me, that's right.
Frank Sorry.
Lesley Right, here is the first question. What is the capital of France?
Frank Er . . . um . . . I don't know . . . er . . .
Lesley I love *Paris* in the springtime, I love *Paris* in the fall . . .
Frank Is it Paris?
Lesley Yes, that's right, Frank! And now the second question! Where is Athens?
Frank Um . . . it's in Greece.
Lesley Yes! That's wonderful! And now the third question! Who is Michael Jackson?
Frank He's a singer!
Lesley That's correct! Open the doors! OK, Frank. Look for ten seconds!

Lesley Well, Frank, in thirty seconds . . . what is there on the table?
Frank Er . . . there's a telephone, um . . . a telephone and a table . . . and there are some glasses . . . and there are some suitcases. Oh! There's a tennis racket . . . Um, is there a typewriter?
Lesley No, there isn't a *typewriter* . . .
Frank Ooh, there's a computer!
Lesley Yes, it's a computer. It isn't a typewriter.
Frank Er . . . there are some books . . . some big books.
Lesley Yes, there are some dictionaries.
Frank Are there any knives and forks?
Lesley No, there aren't any knives and forks, but . . .
Frank Spoons! There are some silver spoons.
Lesley Yes, there are. Look at the time, Frank . . .
Frank Ooh! There's a clock! Um, a gold clock! Er, and golf clubs . . . Um, there's a coffee pot, a silver coffee pot, and a . . .
Lesley That's it! Look at your prizes, Frank!

Unit ten

Optional video component

Teaching points

There's (a book) on the table. / There are some (books) on the table.
There isn't (a pen) on the table. / There aren't any pens on the table.
Is there (an apple) on the table?
Yes, there is. / No, there isn't.
Are there any (apples) on the table?
Yes, there are. / No, there aren't.
What is the capital of (France)? What is the language of (Greece)?
Revision of previously taught nouns and questions.
Stand (next to me).

Expressions

Ladies and Gentlemen! Welcome to ...
Here's the ...   Well, (Frank) ...   That's wonderful!
That's correct.

Active vocabulary

capital / clock / coffee pot / contestant / gentlemen / ladies / language / question / quiz / singer / table / typewriter / correct / gold / Greece / silver / wonderful / stand / welcome / dear / of / any / some

Passive vocabulary

camera / golf club / love / springtime / tennis racket / tonight / week

Classroom vocabulary

another / for / list / student's (possessive)

Audio-visual aids

Cassette, or video cassette (if optional video is to be used).
A number of objects in a carrier bag. Several bags.

◆ Complete dialogue

Focus attention on the picture, check that the text is covered. Play the complete dialogue. Students listen.

◆ Dialogue: section 1

1 Play the first part of the dialogue (to **Frank** Sorry.) again. The text is still covered.

2 Silent reading of the first part of the dialogue.

3 Questions:
T: *What's his name? Are there any prizes? What are they like? Who is the first contestant? What's his first name? What's his surname? Is he from Manchester? Ask him / her 'where?' Is he behind him? Ask him / her 'where?'*

◆ Dialogue: section 2

1 Pre-listening task. Write on the board:
Question 1: ☐ right ☐ wrong
Question 2: ☐ right ☐ wrong
Question 3: ☐ right ☐ wrong.
Explain that students will mark Mr Miller's answers right or wrong as they listen. Play the second part of the dialogue (to **Lesley** ... Look for ten seconds!). Students complete the task. Check briefly.

2 Silent reading of the second part of the dialogue.

3 Questions:
What's the first question? Ask him / her. Answer. Is that right?
What's the second question? Ask him / her. Answer. Is that correct?
What's the third question? Ask him / her. Answer. Is that correct?

4 Paired reading of the second section.

◆ Dialogue: section 3

1 Focus attention on the picture at the bottom of the page. Play the third part of the dialogue (to the end). **Optional:** (with true beginners) play it again, pausing for **selective** repetition, chorally and individually.

2 True / False:
Make statements, students respond 'right' or 'wrong' (as in dialogue: section 2.1), or 'true' or 'false' if you prefer:
There are some glasses.
There are some knives.
There's a typewriter.
There's a computer.
There aren't any forks.
There aren't any spoons.
There isn't a coffee pot.
There isn't a tennis racket.

3 Silent reading of the third section.

4 Questions:
Focus attention on the picture at the top of the right-hand page. Ask Yes / No questions to elicit: Yes, there is. / No, there isn't. / Yes, there are. / No, there aren't.
Is there a typewriter? Is there a computer? Is there a clock? Is there a telephone? Is there a table? Is there a radio? Is there a tennis ball? Is there a tennis racket? Is there a camera: Is there a teapot? Is there a coffee pot? Is there a hair dryer? Is there a pen?
Are there any dictionaries? Are there any glasses? Are there any cups? Are there any briefcases? Are there any suitcases? Are there any golf clubs? Are there any knives and forks? Are there any spoons?

5 Pair work. Students look at the picture and ask and answer as in .4.

6 Questions:
T: *There's a coffee pot. What's it like?* S1: *It's silver. / It's a silver coffee pot.*
T: *There are some dictionaries. What are they like?*
S2: *They're big. / They're blue.* etc.
Continue, asking about the other items on the table.

7 Paired reading of the third section.

8 Pair work. One student in each pair closes their book, and role plays the part of the contestant. The other student role plays Lesley and looks at the book using the picture at the top of the right-hand page. They then role play section 3.

a> Write a quiz

1 Focus attention on the section. Get students to cover the answers. Ask individuals the sample questions. Explain that they are each going to write seven new questions like the ones in the book. Give them time to do this.

2 Pair work. Students use their questions to quiz their partners in pairs.

Optional: If there is time, divide the class into an even number of groups. Each group composes seven questions. Put two groups together. They can conduct a competitive group quiz.

b> Game

Explain that they are going to use the pictures on the right-hand page for a game similar to <a>.2 above. This time there is an information gap, as each student will cover one picture, and study the other. The first student in each pair looks at the picture in the middle of the page, the second student looks at the picture at the bottom of the page.
They should conduct the game as a role play, similar to the third section of the dialogue.

c> Is there a briefcase?

1 Pair work. Students ask and answer about the pictures in pairs.

2 Check through, asking individuals a few questions about each picture.

d> Write a list

1 Go through the instructions. Each student works alone to compose a list, which will consist of selected items from all three pictures, which is then used as the basis for pair work.

2 Language summary.
Write up on the board:

There's a pen on the table.
There are some books on the table.

There isn't a bag on the table.
There aren't any cups on the table.

Is there a pen on the table?
Yes, there is. / No, there isn't.
Are there any books on the table?
Yes, there are. / No, there aren't.

Get students to copy it.

◆ Game: What's in the bag?

1 You will need some carrier bags, and a selection of objects. Prepare a bag with five singular objects (e.g. book, watch, apple, orange, fork) and five pairs of objects (e.g. pens, knives, matches, spoons, cassettes.)
Either: The students have to ask questions until they discover what is in the bag.
Or: Show the contents of the bag once. Students have to make statements until they recall the contents of the bag.

(You may wish to play both variants of the game, noting that the first practises questions, the second practises statements.)

2 Distribute carrier bags, one to each pair or group. The pair (or group) puts a selection of objects in the bag. They then come to the front of the class and play the game with the rest of the class.
The teacher can add questions, e.g.
S1: *Are there any pens in the bag?*
S2: *Yes, there are.*
T: *What are they like? / What colour are they?*
S1: *There's a gold pen, and there are two silver pens.*
T: *Is that correct?*
S2: *No, it isn't. There are two gold pens, and a white pen.*
etc.

◆ Workbook

The Workbook can be done for homework.
If it is done in class, exercises 1 and 3 are suitable for paired oral work. One student should have the Workbook shut for these exercises.
Exercise 7 can be discussed and completed in pairs.

Unit ten

a) Write a quiz

Here are some questions.

1	What is the capital of (Spain)?	It's (Madrid).
2	What is the language of (Turkey)?	It's (Turkish).
3	What nationality is (Stephen Spielberg)?	He's (American).
4	Where is (Milan)?	It's in (Italy).
5	Where is (Princess Diana) from?	She's from (Britain).
6	What colour is the (Japanese) flag?	It's (red and white).
7	Who is (Bruce Springsteen)?	He's (a singer).

Write seven *new* questions. Ask another student.

b) Game

1 Student A: Look at picture two for thirty seconds. Close the book.
What is there in the picture?
2 Student B: Look at picture three for thirty seconds. Close the book.
What is there in the picture?

c) Is there a briefcase?

A *Is there a briefcase in picture one?*
B *Yes, there is. / No, there isn't.*

A *Are there any spoons in picture one?*
B *Yes, there are. / No, there aren't.*

Ask and answer about the pictures.

d) Write a list

Look at the three pictures. Write a list of ten things.

1 _____   6 _____
2 _____   7 _____
3 _____   8 _____
4 _____   9 _____
5 _____   10 _____

Ask about another student's list, with:

Is there a / an _____?
Yes, there's a / an _____ .
No, there isn't a / an _____ .

Are there any _____ ?
Yes, there are some _____ .
No, there aren't any _____ .

Unit eleven

Is there any ...?

In English some things are **countable**, and some things are **uncountable**.

Countable
1 There's an orange in the picture.
2,3,4,5,6 ... There are some tomatoes in the picture. / There are three tomatoes.

tomatoes **3**   orange **1**   apple **0**

Uncountable

There's some milk in the picture.

milk ✓   coffee ✗

a) Chart

Look at the picture, and complete this chart.

potatoes **4**	cheese ✓	eggs ___	lemon ___	biscuits ___
chicken ___	sandwich ___	water ___	meat ___	cola ___
tea ___	bread ___	butter ___	tuna ___	apple juice ___

b) Is there a lemon?

A *Is there a lemon?*
B *Yes, there is. / No, there isn't.*
A *Are there any eggs?*
B *Yes, there are. / No, there aren't.*
A *Is there any milk?*
B *Yes, there is. / No, there isn't.*

Ask and answer about the picture above.

c) True or false?

1 Look at the picture of breakfast.
   Are these sentences true [✓] or false [✗]?
   ☐ There are two eggs on the plate.
   ☐ There's some tea in the jug.
   ☐ There are some cornflakes in the bowl.
   ☐ There isn't any bread on the plate.
   ☐ There isn't any milk in the bowl.
   ☐ There's some butter on the plate.

2 Student A: Write a *true or false?* exercise about lunch. Give it to Student B.
   Student B: Write a *true or false?* exercise about tea. Give it to Student A.

d) What is there?

Look at b) Is there a lemon?
Ask and answer about breakfast, lunch, and tea.

breakfast

lunch

tea

Unit eleven

Teaching points
Countable/uncountable nouns:
There's an orange. / There isn't an orange.
There are some oranges. / There are three oranges. / There aren't any oranges.
There's some milk. / There isn't any milk.
Is there a lemon? / Are there any lemons? / Is there any milk?
in the bowl / the jug / the fridge / San Miguel
on the plate / the helicopters
Revision of food vocabulary.
Reading / completing a form.
Listening: pre-task to focus attention, then for specific items.
Reading: from notes, expanding notes orally into full sentences.

Active vocabulary
airport / biscuit / bowl / bread / breakfast / butter / electricity / food / fruit / gas / hospital / jug / lemon / lunch / meat / medicine / milk / onion / potato / sugar / thing / tea (meal) / tomato / bad / clean / hot

Passive vocabulary
anchovies / antibiotic / chillis / cornflakes / mushrooms / news / nurse / olives / (green) pepper / perfect / pineapple / report / salami / sauce / volcano

Classroom vocabulary
countable / cross (x) / false / form / more / notebook / order / uncountable

Redundant vocabulary (reading text: order form), not listed.
deliver / design / every / midnight

Grammar note
This lesson starts with an overt grammatical explanation, which we feel is particularly useful for the initial teaching of countable and uncountable nouns. Later, in the perfect pizza section, students are invited to explore the concept for themselves.

Audio-visual aids
Cassette. Jug of water and two cups.

◆ Oral introduction

Take in a jug of water and two cups. Say:
There's a jug.
There are two cups.
There's some water in the jug.
There isn't any water in the cups.
Pour all the water into the **two** cups.
Is there any water in the jug? No, there isn't.
Is there any water in the cups? Yes, there is.
Get students to repeat the key sentences.
The jug and water can be used again later.

◆ Introduction: countable and uncountable

Focus attention on the picture. Go through the explanation of countable and uncountable.

a) Chart

Focus attention on the chart. Check that they know what to do. Refer students to the chart. They work individually to complete it.

b) Is there a lemon?

1 Ask students about the picture, to elicit *Yes, there is. / No, there isn't. / Yes, there are. / No, there aren't.*

2 Drill: Continue:
T: *milk*   eggs
C: *There's some milk.*   water
T: *potatoes*   cheese
C: *There are some potatoes.*   biscuits

3 Get students to ask and answer about the picture in pairs.

◆ Breakfast, lunch, and tea

Focus attention on the three pictures. Say 'This is breakfast, this is lunch, and this is tea.' Ask students to study them.

c) True or false?

1 Refer them to the *true / false* exercise. They should work alone to complete it.
Note: This is the first time they have seen the negative sentence in full.

2 Explain the pair work section. They have to write a similar *true / false* routine, then get their partners to complete it.

3 Check the answers to the three *true / false* sections, particularly checking the sentences students have written.

4 Drill (**optional**):   Continue:
T: *coffee*   sugar
C: *There isn't any coffee.*   orange juice
T: *eggs*   potatoes
T: *There aren't any eggs.*   cornflakes

d) What is there?

1 Get students to ask and answer about the pictures in pairs, as in ⟨b⟩.3. This activity can be lengthened or shortened according to how well they seem to have grasped the concept.

2 **Optional.** Students could write lists, entitled *My Breakfast / My Lunch*. They could then ask and answer **about each other's lists** in pairs. i.e. *Is there any milk on your list?* **Note:** They will not have the structures to ask the more logical *Do you have milk for breakfast?* at this stage, which is why we suggest asking about the list rather than the breakfast!

Unit eleven

e) The perfect pizza?

1 This section is designed to let students explore the countable / uncountable concept further. Focus attention on the pizza. Get them to decide which things are countable and which are uncountable. A further concept is: *a green pepper* v *some green peppers* v *some green pepper*.
You could draw on the board: one pepper / three peppers / then some very small bits of diced pepper. We are choosing to use *some pepper* (and *some onion*, *some salami*, *some pineapple*) because it is **part of the whole**, rather than because it's uncountable in the same sense as *water*. If you wish, you could go into the boundaries between countable and uncountable in English:
Countable: peas, beans,
Uncountable: rice, sand, spaghetti.

Get students to make sentences in pairs with: *There's some . . . / There are some . . .*

2 Get them to study The Perfect Pizza order form and write down their own preferences. Do not explain vocabulary, but be sure that they are clear about the meaning of **You choose!**. They can write in anything.

3 Get them to ask each other in pairs about their choice of pizza.

4 Students role play the conversation between the shop and a customer. Refer them back to Units 2 and 4 – they can use minimal sentences. Demonstrate:
A *Yes?* B *A pizza please.* A *What with?* B *Oh, some mushrooms, and some tuna, please.* A *What's your name? What's your address? What's your phone number?* etc.

f) What's in the fridge?

1 Explain the activity carefully. All they do at first is list five countable and five uncountable things that might be in the fridge.
[When they listen to the conversation, they will tick things on their list which are in the fridge. (They do not tick if something is mentioned but is not in the fridge.)
Note: It is irrelevant how many items they can tick (if any). Their list might be entirely different to the contents of the fridge as revealed on the cassette. The purposes of the exercise are i) to get them thinking about the concept and vocabulary and ii) to give them a reason to listen attentively.]

2 Play the cassette once. They tick the items.
Check briefly. Explain:
There are some apples. / There are some oranges. / There is some fruit. / There are some hamburgers. / There are some sausages. / There is some meat.

3 Play the cassette again, pausing to check what *is* in the fridge on the recording.

g) News report

1 i) Focus attention on the picture, check that the text is covered. Pre-listening. Write on the board for students to copy: *gas, electricity, aeroplanes, medicine, helicopters, petrol, doctors, water*
Explain the activity. They are going to listen to a news report. They put a tick [√] next to any words that are in the report. Play the report, students complete the task.
ii) Silent reading. Students read the text, and check their answers to the pre-listening activity. Play the report again.
iii) Questions:
T: *What's the time? What's her name? Where is she? Where's the volcano? What's it like in San Miguel? Is there any water? Is there any clean water? Is there any gas? Is there any electricity? Is there any medicine? Are there any helicopters? Where are they? Where are they from? What's on the helicopters?*

2 i) Focus attention on Gemma's notebook.
Silent reading. Check vocabulary.
ii) Role play. Students role play a conversation between Gemma and the TV station in England, as in the instructions in the Student's Book.

◆ **Dictation**

Dictate:
There are some doctors at the hospital. They're from the USA.
There are some nurses. They're American.
Check back on *they're* and *there are*.

◆ **Practice**

Prepare a plate with spoonfuls of the following **dry** substances (for example):
some sugar, some salt, some pepper, some tea, some coffee, some chocolate.
Pass round the tray getting students to smell the items. Ask *What is it?* to elicit *It's sugar*. Remove the plate from sight. Ask questions:
Is there any sugar on the plate? Is there any milk?
This can be developed into a memory game.

◆ **Game**

This is a variant of *Kim's Game*. Prepare a tray with some countable things, and some uncountable things on it, e.g.
Countable: 2 pens, 2 spoons, 3 books, 1 cassette, 2 forks, 2 plates.
Uncountable: water (in a glass), sugar, salt, pepper, coffee, tea (in dry form!).
Let students study the tray for 30 seconds. Cover the tray with a cloth. Each student makes a list of the contents of the tray from memory. They can then ask questions in pairs, groups, or teams.

◆ **Workbook**

The Workbook can be done at home. The exercises are mainly vocabulary-based.
Exercise 5 is worth checking over in class.
The reading could be done in class, but should not be questioned intensively. You may wish to check the word *lava*.

Unit eleven

e The perfect pizza?

1 Look at the picture.
   What things are countable? What things are uncountable? Make sentences about the picture with:
   There's some ... / There are some ...

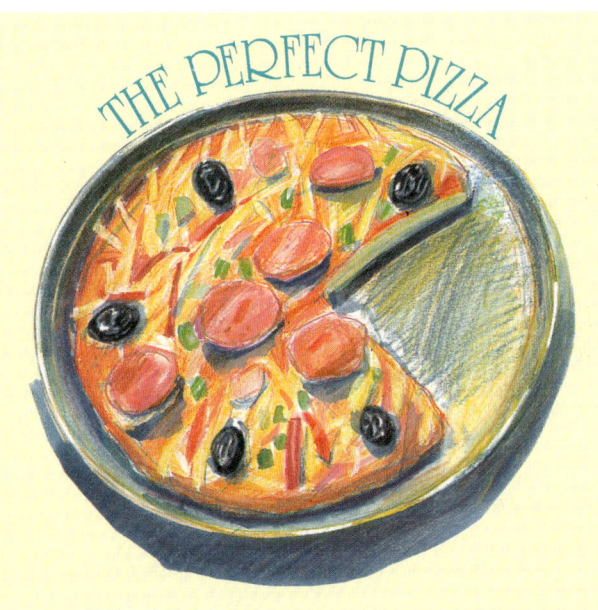

THE PERFECT PIZZA

*We deliver to your door - free!
Telephone us with your order!*

Design your pizza

Large (35cm)   Medium (25cm)   Small (15cm)

A tomato and cheese pizza with:
• mushrooms • green pepper • onion • olives
• hot chillies • tuna • anchovies • salami
• pineapple

You choose!

Telephone: 156462
Open every day: 11.30 a.m. - Midnight

2 Look at the form. What is the perfect pizza for you?

3 Ask a student about his/her perfect pizza.

4 Role play. Telephone the pizza shop with your order.

f What's in the fridge?

1 Guess what's in the fridge. Write a list with five countable things and five uncountable things.

2 Now listen to the conversation about the fridge.
   Put a tick [✓] by the things that are in the fridge and in your list

g News report

1 Listen to this news report.

Good evening, this is Gemma Walker for the six o'clock news. I'm in San Miguel. That's the volcano behind me. It's very bad here. There isn't any gas or electricity, and there isn't any clean water. There are five hundred people in the hospital, and there isn't any medicine there. There are some helicopters from the United States at the airport, and there's some food and there are some antibiotics on the helicopters. Our next report from San Miguel is at nine o'clock.

2 What's it like in San Miguel?
   This is Gemma Walker's notebook:

   TV Report - six o'clock
   • IN SAN MIGUEL - NOT ANY:
   gas/electricity/clean water/medicine
   food/petrol/doctors
   • ON THE HELICOPTERS - SOME:
   food/antibiotics/bread/milk
   bandages/doctors/nurses

You are in England. You are on the telephone to Gemma.
Ask her about San Miguel.
Ask her about the helicopters.

Unit twelve

The Family

TV NEWS　　　　　　　　　　　　　　　　　　　　　　　　　　　　　　　　16th October

ETV's new television series, *The Family,* Wednesdays, 8.00 - 8.50

Meet The Family.

Donald Hewitt
Donald is a very rich man. He's got a computer factory in Cambridge. He's married to Rosemary. They've got three children, two sons and a daughter. He's got a house in Cambridge and a villa in Spain.

Rosemary Hewitt
Rosemary is Donald's wife. She's a writer of romantic novels, and she's very rich, too. She's got a flat in London, and she's got two cars, a Porsche and a Range Rover.

Charles & Amanda Hewitt
Charles is their son. He's 36. His wife's name is Amanda. They've got two children. Amanda's a famous model. Charles is a good businessman, but he isn't a nice person. He hasn't got any friends.

Andrea & Joseph Williams
Andrea is Donald and Rosemary's daughter. She's her father's favourite child. She's a scientist. Joseph is Andrea's husband. He's a doctor. Andrea's 32.

Robin Hewitt
Robin is Charles's and Andrea's brother. He's a rock singer, but he isn't famous. His father isn't happy about Robin's job. He hasn't got any money, and he hasn't got any children. He's 25. He's his mother's favourite child.

Lucy & David
They're Charles's children. Andrea is their aunt. Robin is their uncle. Lucy's Andrea's niece, and David's her nephew. Lucy is seven, and her brother is six. They've got two pets - a dog and a cat.

Peter & Claire
They're Lucy and David's cousins. They're Andrea's children. Peter's four, and his sister is two. Donald is their grandfather and Rosemary is their grandmother. They haven't got any pets.

Teaching points

Have / has got
I / you / we / they 've / have got a sister / some sisters.
He / she 's / hasn't got a sister / any sisters.
I / you / we / they haven't got a sister / any sisters.
He / she hasn't got a sister / any sisters.
Have I / we / you / they got a sister / any sisters?
Has he/she got a sister / any sisters?
+ short answers.
Revision of possessive adjectives, plus genitive ('s).
It's John's car. / They're John's children. / They're John and Mary's children.
It's Charles's house. / They're Charles's children. etc.
What's (your) favourite colour?
Who's (your) favourite singer? / Who are your favourite singers?
Family and Relations: see vocabulary below.
Reading: simple texts.

Grammar note

The main focus is have / has got, which is standard British spoken English. Although it occurs in American English, many speakers consider it sub-standard.
The 'saxon genitive' ending with sibilants (s and z) is in a state of flux. The generally accepted form nowadays is Charles's – which we teach here, but Charles' is often found in text books as well.

Active vocabulary

child/children / parents / father/mother / son/daughter / brother/sister
aunt/uncle / niece/nephew / cousin / husband/wife / family
grandparents (+ grandson / granddaughter / grandfather / grandmother)
businessman / cat / factory / flat / friend / house / money / person / pet / sport / writer
famous / favourite / good / rich
about / has / have / got / is married to

Passive vocabulary

meet / model / novel / programme / questionnaire / rock / romantic / send / series / villa

Classroom vocabulary

sentences / tell

Redundant vocabulary

actor / dinner / fabulous / studio / watch / win

Audio-visual aids

This unit is not recorded. You should have some items of realia.

Unit twelve

◆ **Oral introduction**

Note: This section should be done at speed.
Optional: Points .2 to .7 can be missed with false beginners.

1 Take in a few small items of realia. Put them on the table. Say:
T: *I've got a bag, I've got a book, and I've got some pens. And you?*
Point at students to elicit sentences with *I've got*...
Point at a student, T: *You've got a bag. You've got some books. And me?*
Point at students, elicit sentences with *You've got*...
Go to a student, T: *He's got a pen, he's got some books. And (Juan)?*
Point at students to elicit: *He's got*...
Repeat with a female student: *She's got*...
Indicate two students. T: *They've got some pens. They've got some books. And (Juan) and (Maria)?*
Point at students to elicit: *They've got*...
Stand next to a student. T: *We've got some pens, we've got some books. And you?*
Point at pairs of students to elicit *We've got*...

2 Drill:
T: *I*
C: *I've got some pens.*
Continue: *she / we / they / he / you / I / Mary*

3 T: *I haven't got a cassette player. I haven't got any cassettes.*
Indicate a student. *She hasn't got a cassette player. She hasn't got any cassettes.*
Optional: follow the procedure in .1 with singular and plural negative examples.

4 Drill:
T: *He*
C: *He hasn't got any cassettes.*
Continue: *they / I / she / we / John / you*

5 Say: *Have you got a watch? Repeat. Has she got a watch?*
Ask me. (indicate your watch) to elicit: *Have you got a watch?*
Say: *Yes, I have.* Say: *Ask me... cassette player* to elicit: *Have you got a cassette player?*
Say: *No, I haven't.*
Ask questions: *Have you got a watch / a radio / any pens / any books / a car / a Ferrari / a million (pounds)?*
to elicit: *Yes, I have. / No, I haven't.*

6 Repeat the above procedure with *Has he got a watch? Has she got any pens?* etc.

7 Drill:
T: *they*
C: *Have they got any books?*
Continue: *she / we / I / he / you / Mary*

◆ **Meet The Family**
   Texts: Donald / Rosemary

1 Ask students to open their books. Focus attention on the text. Say: *This is a page from a magazine about television programmes. 'The Family' is a new programme.*

2 Silent reading of the first two texts.

3 Yes / No Questions:
These questions will elicit *is*, *has*, and *have* answers. Ask them at speed.

Is Donald rich? Has he got a factory in Oxford? Has he got a factory in Cambridge? Is it a computer factory? Is he married? What is his wife's name? Have they got ten children? Have they got three children? Have they got two sons? Have they got two daughters? Has he got a house in London? Has he got a house in Cambridge? Has he got a villa in Italy?
Is Rosemary married? Is she a singer? Is she a writer? Is she rich? Has she got a house in London? Has she got a flat? Has she got three cars? Has she got two cars? Has she got a Ferrari? Has she got a Porsche? Has she got a BMW? Has she got a Range Rover?

4 Free reproduction. Check that the text is covered. Say: *Tell me about Donald and Rosemary.*

◆ Texts: Charles / Andrea / Robin

1 Focus attention on the three texts. Silent reading.

2 Correct my statement:
T: *Charles is their grandson.*
C: *No. Charles is their son.*
Continue: *He's 63 / His wife's name is Andrea. / She's a famous writer. / Charles is a bad businessman. / He's a nice person. / He's got some friends. / They've got twenty children.*
Andrea is Charles's daughter. / She's her mother's favourite child. / She's an engineer. / Her husband's a nurse. / She's 23.
Robin is their sister. / He's very famous. / He's a runner. / His father's very happy about his job. / He's got some money. / He's got two children. / He's 52. / He's his father's favourite child.

3 Free reproduction. Check that the text is covered. Say: *Tell me about Charles, Andrea, and Robin.*

◆ Texts: Lucy & David / Peter & Claire

1 Focus attention on the two texts. Silent reading.

2 Questions:
Have Lucy and David got any pets? What have they got?
Have Peter and Claire got any pets?
How old is Lucy? Ask (him) about Claire / Peter / David.

a Competition

1 Focus attention on *The Family* Competition. Explain the *true / false* activity and the ten questions. Do not explain redundant words in the competition. Give students time to complete the task individually.

2 Draw a family tree on the board, with three generations and appropriate spaces for the characters. Write in *Donald*. Ask: *What's his wife's name?* Write it in.
Have they got any children? What are their names? Write them in.
Is (Charles) married? What's his wife's name? Write it in.
Continue:
What's his sister's name? Is she married? What's her husband's name? What's their brother's name? What's Charles's son's name? What's his daughter's name? What are their cousins' names?

3 Draw a diagonal line between Andrea and Lucy. Write *niece / aunt* next to it. Connect other characters to elicit: *aunt / niece; aunt / nephew; uncle / niece; uncle / nephew.* Check all the vocabulary for family relationships.

4 Get students to ask and answer the competition questions in pairs.
Check the possessive of words ending in a sibilant (s or z). Check with a few questions to the class at the end.

b Family

Refer students to the list of words. Get them to ask and answer in pairs.

c How old is she?

Explain the exercise. Students ask and answer in pairs. Check with a few questions to the class at the end.

d What's your favourite colour?
Who's your favourite singer?

Explain the exercise. Students ask and answer in pairs. Check with a few questions to the class at the end.

e Questionnaire

Note: The vocabulary of family relationships is an essential area for students to master, but the teacher will need to be sensitive to the fact that not all students come from 'typical' nuclear families with mother, father, two children. Be careful with questions to students about their family set up.

1 Focus attention on the questionnaire. Get students to ask their partners, and to complete the form with the partner's answers.

2 Get students to change partners, and ask and answer about the previous partner's questionnaire.

f About you and your partner

Get students to write sentences about themselves and their partners, as in the examples. Check through a few of the sentences.

g About your family

1 Ask the questions to the class. Explain the exercise. Students ask and answer in pairs.

2 Pair work. Get students to draw a family tree for their partners by asking / answering in pairs.

◆ Workbook

The Workbook can be done at home.
If the Workbook is done in class, exercises, 1, 3, and 6 can be done orally in pairs.

Unit twelve

The Family Competition
Win our fabulous first prize!
Dinner with the actors in
The Family at the ETV Studio!!!

Are these sentences true [✓] or false [✗]?
- ☐ Donald is Robin's father.
- ☐ Peter is Charles's son.
- ☐ David is Robin's nephew.
- ☐ Charles is Claire's uncle.
- ☐ Andrea is Claire's aunt.
- ☐ Lucy is Andrea's niece.
- ☐ Andrea is Rosemary's daughter.
- ☐ Robin is Rosemary's grandson.
- ☐ Lucy is Donald's granddaughter.
- ☐ Andrea and Joseph are Peter's parents.
- ☐ Rosemary and Donald are Charles's grandparents.
- ☐ Amanda is Charles's wife.

Answer these questions about The Family.

1. Who is Rosemary's daughter?
2. Who are Rosemary's sons?
3. Who is Joseph's wife?
4. Who is Amanda's husband?
5. Who is Lucy's brother?
6. Who is Robin and Charles's sister?
7. Who are Charles's parents?
8. Who is Charles's niece?
9. Who are Robin's nephews?
10. Who are Peter's cousins?

Write your answers on a postcard, and send them to TV News. Watch the first programme for the address.

a) Competition
Look at the competition.
Complete the *true or false* exercise, then ask and answer the questions.

b) Family
Make more questions and answers with:

grandfather	son
grandmother	daughter
grandparents	grandson
parents	granddaughter
children	grandchildren
father	niece
mother	nephew
brother	uncle
sister	aunt
husband	cousin
wife	

c) How old is she?
A *How old is Andrea?*
B *She's thirty-two.*

Ask and answer about the other people in 'The Family'.

d) What's your favourite colour?
Who's your favourite singer?

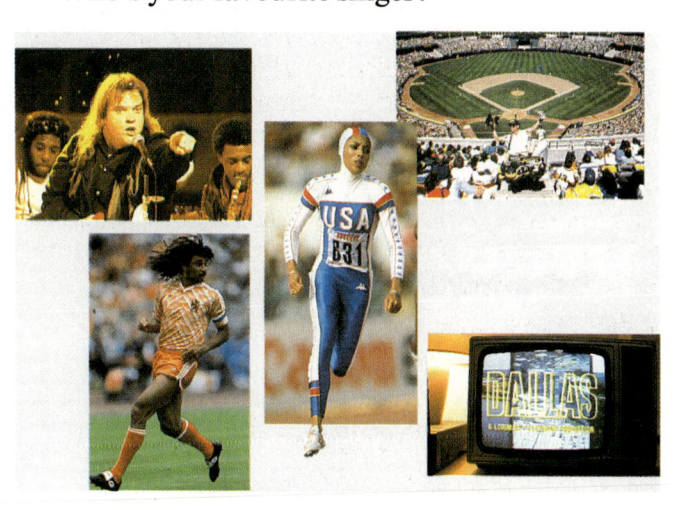

Have you got a favourite colour? What is it?
Have you got a favourite rock singer? Who is it?
Have you got a favourite sport? What is it?
Have you got a favourite sportsperson? Who is it?
Have you got a favourite TV programme? What is it?

Ask another student about his/her favourite people and things.

e) Questionnaire
Ask another student questions with:
Have you got a . . .? / Have you got any . . .?

	Yes	No		Yes	No
brother(s)	☐	☐	pet(s)	☐	☐
sister(s)	☐	☐	house	☐	☐
cousin(s)	☐	☐	flat	☐	☐
aunt(s)	☐	☐	car	☐	☐
uncle(s)	☐	☐			

f) About you and your partner
I've got two brothers.
I haven't got a sister. / I haven't got any sisters.
He's got five uncles.
She hasn't got any cousins.

Make sentences about you and your partner.

g) About your family
A *Has your uncle got any children?*
B *Yes, he has. He's got six children.*
  No. He hasn't got any children.

A *Has your mother got any brothers?*
B *Yes, she has. She's got one brother.*
  No. She hasn't got any brothers.

A *Have your parents got a house?*
B *Yes, they have.*
  No, they haven't. They've got a flat.

Ask and answer with another student.

People

The people at this party are all famous. Mrs Vincent is a cleaner. Mr Brown is a chauffeur. They're on the balcony.

Mrs Vincent Ooh look! That's the American Ambassador ...
Mr Brown Where?
Mrs Vincent Over there. He's the short fat man.
Mr Brown Where?
Mrs Vincent He's wearing a black suit and a black tie.
Mr Brown Oh, yes ...

Mr Brown Who's she?
Mrs Vincent The woman with blond hair?
Mr Brown No. The tall woman over there. She's got dark hair.
Mrs Vincent Is she wearing a long white dress?
Mr Brown Yes, that's her.
Mrs Vincent That's Miss World! She's from Brazil.

Mrs Vincent Ooh! There's Michael George!
Mr Brown Where? What's he like?
Mrs Vincent He's next to Miss World. He's got red hair.
Mr Brown Oh, yes. He isn't wearing a suit!
Mrs Vincent But he's very good-looking.
Mr Brown Tut! He's wearing jeans ... and a T-shirt. That's terrible. Who is he?
Mrs Vincent Don't you know? He's a singer. My daughter's got all his records.

Mrs Vincent There's Jean Collier! Oh, she's got lovely blond hair. Look, over there! She's wearing a pink trouser suit. She's about fifty, you know.
Mr Brown She's fifty-seven.
Mrs Vincent No! Really?
Mr Brown Yes. I'm her chauffeur.
Mrs Vincent Ooh! What's she like?
Mr Brown She's very nice.
Mrs Vincent Is she? Well, she's a wonderful actress.

a ▶ Who are they?

These are the people at the party.
Put the letters (A, B, C, ...) in the spaces.

- [A] The American Ambassador. Short, fat. Black suit.
- [D] Jean Collier, actress. Blond hair. Pink trouser suit. About 50.
- [ ] Gary Trevor, footballer. Brown hair. Pullover. Good-looking.
- [ ] Donna, singer. Young. Orange and green hair. Skirt. Blouse.
- [ ] David Wilson, politician. Blue suit. Moustache. Middle-aged. Glasses.
- [ ] Doris Decker, tennis player. Long curly hair. About 27.
- [ ] Paul Cooper, racing driver. Brown hair. Beard. Green shirt. About 26.
- [ ] Barbara Heartland, writer. Old (87). Long dress. Blue hair. Glasses.
- [ ] Bruno Higgins, boxer. Black. Very tall. Pale blue shirt. Green trousers.
- [ ] Michael George, singer. Red hair. Jeans and T-shirt. Good-looking.
- [ ] Miss World. Tall. Long dark hair. White dress. Brazilian. Good-looking.
- [ ] Suzy Ford, newsreader. Average-height. About 35. Short blond hair.

Teaching points
Describing people.
Revision of: *What's he / she like? How old is (he)?*
What colour is (his) hair? / What colour are (her) eyes?
Has he / she got long hair? / brown eyes?
Yes, he/she has. / No, he/she hasn't.
Present continuous form, restricted to the verb *wearing*.
He's wearing a shirt. / She isn't wearing glasses.
Is he wearing brown shoes?
Yes, he is. / No, he isn't.
Adjective order: *long dark hair / a long white dress.* etc.
Listening: for gist.
Song: for stress, rhythm, and catenation (optional).

Grammar note
The focus of this unit is describing people. As part of this the present continuous tense is used, restricted to the verb *wearing*. This should not be regarded as the formal introduction of the tense, but simply as an exponent of description.
Adjective order: This is restricted to two adjectives in the order 1) quality 2) colour.
Uncountables: Note *hair* is usually uncountable. If you wish to go into this, you could point out that *rice*, *sand*, *spaghetti* are other examples of uncountables. (Though it is theoretically possible to count them, it is totally impractical!)

Expressions
That's right. That's terrible. Really?
Don't you know . . . you know.

Active vocabulary
average / blond / curly / dark / eye / fat / good-looking / long / middle-aged / orange / short / tall / terrible / thin / young / beard / blouse / build / dress / glasses / hair / height / jacket / moustache / party / pullover / record / shoes / skirt / suit / tie / trousers / T-shirt /
about (approximately) / all / with / wear /
Miss / Mr / Mrs

Passive vocabulary
actress / ambassador / boxer / chauffeur / cleaner / letter (ABC) / newsreader / politician / racing driver / alive / clown / crazy / face / just / no (hair)

Classroom vocabulary
chorus / talk about

Audio-visual aids
Cassette. **Optional:** flash cards of people.

Unit thirteen

◆ **Dialogue: section 1 (The Ambassador)**

1 Focus attention on the picture. Allow students time to study it, and to read the introductory sentences. Ask questions:
What's Mrs Vincent's job? Is Mr Brown a cleaner? Ask What? Are they downstairs? Ask 'Where?' Are you famous? Ask me. Are the people at the party famous? Tell me some famous people.

2 Check that the text is covered. Play the dialogue section 1. Then ask students to find the American Ambassador in the picture. Play it again pausing for selective repetition, chorally and individually.

3 Drill:
T: *He*
C: *He's wearing a black suit.*
T: *They*
T: *They're wearing black suits.*
Continue: *I / She / You / The Ambassador / We / He*

4 Silent reading of the dialogue section 1. Point out *Mr* and *Mrs*, and that they are never written out in any other way. (Note that it is now unusual to put a full stop after *Mr*, *Mrs*, *Ms*, *Dr*).

5 Paired reading of the dialogue section 1.

◆ **Dialogue: section 2 (Miss World)**

1 Play the dialogue section 2. Ask students to find Miss World in the picture. Play it again pausing for students to repeat, chorally and individually.

3 Drill:
T: *She's got dark hair.*
C: *Her hair is dark.*
T: *He's got blue eyes.*
C: *His eyes are blue.*
Continue:
She's got blond hair.
They've got brown eyes.
They've got grey hair.
He's got grey eyes.

3 Silent reading of the dialogue section 2.

4 Paired reading of the dialogue section 2.

◆ **Dialogue: section 3 (Michael George)**

1 Set pre-questions:
What's his job? What colour is his hair? What is he wearing?

2 Play the dialogue section 3. Check the answers to the pre-questions. Ask students to find Michael George in the picture. Play it again pausing for selective repetition, chorally and individually.

3 Drill:
T: *He hasn't got a suit.*
C: *No, he isn't wearing a suit.*
Continue: *He hasn't got a tie. / He hasn't got black shoes. / He hasn't got a white shirt.*

4 Silent reading of the dialogue section 3.

5 Paired reading of the dialogue section 3.

◆ **Dialogue: section 4 (Jean Collier)**

1 Set pre-questions:
What colour is her hair? How old is she?

2 Play the dialogue section 4. Check the answers to the pre-questions. Ask students to find Jean Collier in the picture. Play it again pausing for selective repetition, chorally and individually.

3 Drill:
T: *she*
C: *What's she like?*
Continue: *they / he / it / Jean Collier / Ann and Maria*

4 Silent reading of the dialogue section 4.

5 Paired reading of the dialogue section 4.

a Who are they?

Explain the activity. Students read the descriptions silently, then match them with the letters of people in the picture.

b What are they like?

1 What's she like? Look at the examples. Go through them. Ask about the people in the picture:
T: *What's (the Ambassador) like?* S1: *He's short and fat. He isn't good-looking.* The students continue in pairs.

2 How old is he? Ask about someone in the picture as in ⟨b⟩.1. The students continue in pairs.

3 What colour . . . ? Check: His hair *is* brown. / His eyes *are* brown. Go through the examples. The students ask and answer about the people in the picture as in ⟨b⟩.1. Ask about people in the class.

4 Has she got . . . ? Check the vocabulary items for the *Has she got . . . ?* examples. Go through the examples. The students ask and answer about the people in the picture as in ⟨b⟩.1. Ask about people in the class.

5 What is he wearing? Check the vocabulary items for the *What is he wearing?* examples. Go through the examples. The students ask and answer about the people in the picture as in ⟨b⟩.1. Ask about people in the class.

c Who are they talking about?

Explain the activity. Play the cassette once, then play it again while students complete the task. Do not explain any other words in the listening passages. Check the answers.

d Describe them

1 T: *What's Gary Trevor like?* S1: (e.g.) *He's got brown hair. He's wearing a pullover. He's very good-looking. He's young. He isn't fat.*
Ask about the other people in the picture.

2 Explain the activity in the Student's Book. Students have to guess which person in the picture is being described by their partner.

3 Role play. Students work in pairs, role playing Mr Brown and Mrs Vincent talking about people at the party. They may look at the picture, but the text should be covered.

e Game

This involves looking back at pictures from earlier units (or describing other students in the class). One student gives a description, the other guesses who is being described.
Optional: A set of flash cards of famous people can be substituted (or used as an extension). The pictures can be taken from magazines and newspapers.

f ♪ Tall thin Annie

1 Play the song once. Students listen.

2 Allow them to read the lyrics silently.

3 Play it again. Students listen and sing along. If a cassette player is not available, the song can be chanted (or missed out).

◆ Role play: a fashion parade

1 Play some music. Students walk around the room, role playing fashion models. Role play a commentator and describe them. Try to make it humorous, but avoid embarrassment by your selection of students.

2 Then bring out students to replace you as commentator. A few extra clothes items will add interest to this (hats, scarves, belts, jackets). This activity could also be done as group work.

◆ Workbook

The Workbook exercises can be done for homework. Exercises, 7 and 8 are suitable for paired oral work in class.

b What are they like?

Ask and answer about the people at the party.

1 What's she like?
A *What's he / she like?*
B *She's tall / short / average-height.*
  She's thin / fat / average-build.
  He is / isn't good-looking.

2 How old is he?
A *How old is he / she?*
B *He's / she's young / old / middle-aged / about 20.*

3 What colour ...?
A *What colour is her hair?*
B *It's blond / dark / brown / black / red / grey.*
  She's got (white) hair.
A *What colour are his eyes?*
B *They're blue / grey / green / brown.*
  He's got (blue) eyes.

4 Has she got ...?
A *Has she got long / short / curly hair?*
B *Yes, she has. / No, she hasn't.*
A *Has he got glasses / a beard / a moustache?*
B *Yes, he has. / No, he hasn't.*

5 What is he wearing?
A *What is he wearing?*
B *He's wearing jeans / trousers / a suit / a shirt /*
  a pullover / a T-shirt / a jacket.
A *What is she wearing?*
B *She's wearing a dress / a skirt / a blouse /*
  a trouser suit / blue shoes.

c Who are they talking about?

Listen to these three people. They're talking about people at the party. Who are they talking about?

1 _____
2 _____
3 _____

d Describe them

Student A: Describe a person at the party.
Student B: Who is he/she talking about?

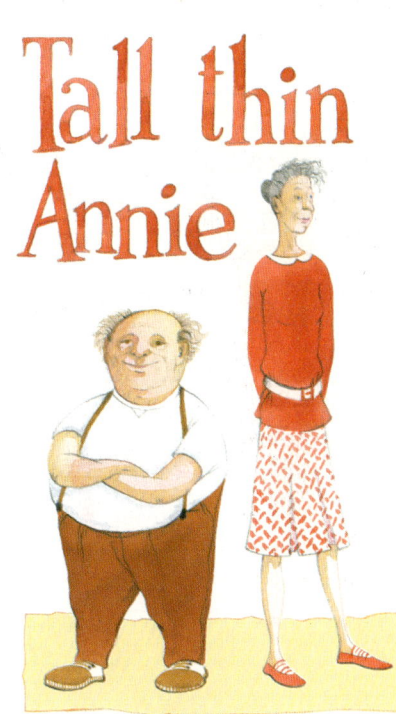

e Game

Student A: Describe a person in Units 1 to 12 or describe a person in the class.
Student B: Who is he/she talking about?

f Tall thin Annie

chorus:
  There's tall thin Annie,
  and short fat Dan.
  She's his woman,
  And he's her man.

She's got grey hair,
and her eyes are blue.
She's not good-looking,
And she's crazy, too.

chorus

He's got no hair,
and his eyes are brown
He's not good-looking,
with the face of a clown.

chorus

She's seventy-four,
He's eighty-five.
They're not good-looking,
but they're alive.

Unit thirteen

Unit fourteen

How much is it?

A Good morning.
B Good morning. Have you got a film for this camera, please?
A What size is it?
B 35 mm.
A 24 or 36-exposure?
B Er ... 36, please.
A What make?
B Kodak, please. How much is it?
A £5.89.
B Thank you.

a) Films

Make conversations.

Student A

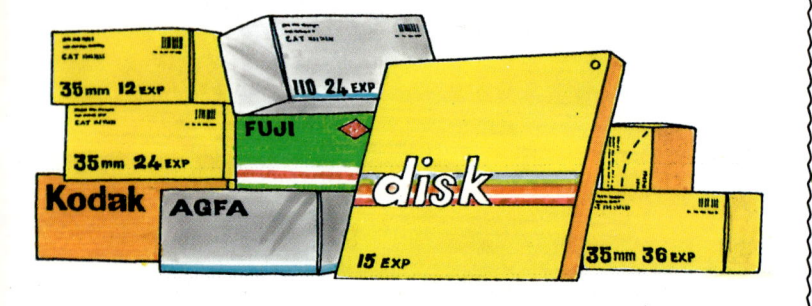

Student B

Prices

	24 exp.	15 exp.	12 exp.	24 exp.	36 exp.
	110	disc	35mm		
Fuji	2.95	1.95	2.20	4.05	5.59
Kodak	2.89	1.99	2.35	4.15	5.89
Agfa	2.75	1.75	2.50	3.99	5.49

C Yes, love?
D How much are the apples?
C 85p a pound.
D And have you got any grapes?
C Yes, love. Black or green?
D Black, please. How much are they?
C £1.60 a pound.
D Right. A pound of apples, and half a pound of grapes, please.
C There you are. That's £1.65 altogether.
D Thanks.

b) Fruit

Make conversations.

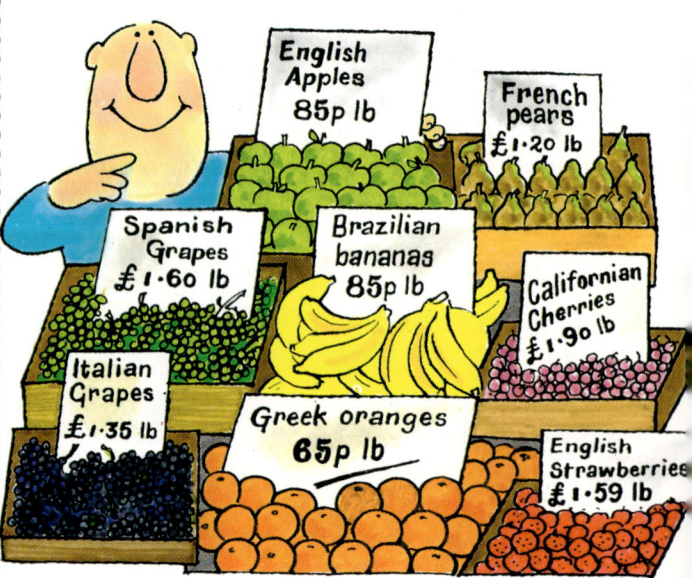

English Apples 85p lb
French pears £1.20 lb
Spanish Grapes £1.60 lb
Brazilian bananas 85p lb
Californian Cherries £1.90 lb
Italian Grapes £1.35 lb
Greek oranges 65p lb
English Strawberries £1.59 lb

One pound (1 lb.) is 0.454 kilos.
Half a pound (½ lb.) is 0.227 kilos.
A quarter of a pound (¼ lb.) is 0.114 kilos.

Unit fourteen

Teaching points
Asking about prices.
How much is this pen? / How much are these pens?
How much is the (tea)?
It's £1.20 / They're 30p a pound. / They're £1.20 each. / That's £3.60 altogether.
What size (is it)? / What flavours (have you got)?
Revision: *this / that / these / those.*
Revision: numbers and prices.
Revision: object Pronouns: *(It's / They're) for him / her / me / us / them / you.*
Reading: Redundant material has been added to the ice cream facsimile (e.g. *Caribbean* pineapple, lemon *dream*).

Grammar note
Don't draw attention to *a 36-exposure film* in Dialogue 1, but if students question it, note that *exposure* is functioning as an adjective in this example. (cf. *a five-pound note, a thirty-centimetre ruler.*)
See Unit 19.

Expressions
Yes, love? Can I help you?
I'm just looking.
Half a pound / quarter of a pound.

Active vocabulary
banana / camera / cherry / film / flavour / grape / half / ice-lolly / millimetre / notebook / pear / pencil / pineapple / postcard / pound (lb.) / quarter / ruler / size / souvenir / strawberry / chocolate / vanilla / large / medium / altogether / each / for

Passive vocabulary
badge / can (v) / disc (film) / doll / exposure / help (v) / jam / marmalade

Classroom vocabulary
nought / point

Redundant vocabulary
authentic / Californian / Caribbean / dream / genuine / made in / surprise / sensation

Audio-visual aids
Cassette. **Optional:** Items of realia (as in the souvenir section) for role play.

◆ Dialogue 1 (A, B)

1 Set pre-question: *How much is the film?* Play the dialogue. Check the answer. Play it again, pausing for students to repeat chorally and individually.

2 Questions:
What size is the film? Is it 24-exposure or 36-exposure? What make is the film? How much is the film?

3 Silent reading of dialogue 1.

4 Paired reading of dialogue 1.

⟨a⟩ Films

1 Focus attention on the **Films** section on the left-hand page. Check through the items (one hundred and ten / thirty-five mill. / disc). Point at the makes of film, ask: *What make is the first film?* etc.

2 Pair work. Refer students to the two boxes, Student A and Student B. Student A is the customer. Student B is the assistant. Student B has to turn the book upside down. They role play two or three dialogues parallel to dialogue 1. They then reverse roles.

◆ Dialogue 2 (C, D)

1 Ask students to list all the *fruit* they know in English. Play the dialogue. Students should tick [√] any items on their list that they hear in the dialogue.

2 Set pre-questions: *How much are the apples? How much are the grapes?* Play the dialogue again, pausing for students to repeat chorally and individually.

3 Drill:
T: *They've got some grapes.*
C: *How much are the grapes?*
Continue:
They've got some lemons / They've got some bananas / They've got some apples / They've got some oranges.

4 Silent reading of dialogue 2.

5 Paired reading of dialogue 2.

⟨b⟩ Fruit

1 Focus attention on the **Fruit** section on the left-hand page. Point out 'lb' for pound weight. Run through the items for pronunciation.
Ask questions. *How much are the pears?* etc. to elicit: *They're one pound twenty a pound.*, etc. Say: *Ask her, 'apples'* to generate: S1: *How much are the apples?* S2: *They're eighty-five p a pound.* etc.
Note: Don't ask where the fruit is from. The nationality labels on the price cards are designed for peripheral reading.

2 Check through the weights. Draw attention to: *half a pound* v. *a quarter of a pound.* Check *0.454 – Nought point four five four kilos.* Say *What's half a pound? What's a quarter of a pound?*

3 Pair work. Students use the prompts and role play dialogue 2, freely substituting items from the **Fruit** section.

4 Get one or two pairs to demonstrate in front of the class.

◆ Dialogue 3 (E, F)

1 Set pre-questions. Write on the board: *How much? – the pen / one postcard / the tea*. Play the dialogue, check the answers. Play it again, pausing for students to repeat chorally and individually. Note the usefulness of *I'm just looking*.

2 Drill:
T: *There's a pen.*
C: *How much is the pen?*
T: *There's some tea.*
C: *How much is the tea?*

Continue:
There's a calculator.
There's some grape juice.
There's some milk.
There's a book.

3 Drill:
T: *There's a pen.*
C: *How much is the pen?*
T: *There are some postcards.*
C: *How much are the postcards?*

Continue:
There's a book.
There are some cassettes.
There are some knives.
There's an umbrella.

[If there are problems, do a third drill, mixing items from .2 (uncountables) and .3 (countables)]

4 Questions:
How much is the pen? How much is one postcard? How much are two postcards? How much are three postcards? How much are the postcards? to elicit: *They're ten p each. How much is the tea? Is it French tea? Ask What.*

5 Silent reading of dialogue 3.

6 Paired reading of dialogue 3.

c Souvenirs

1 Focus attention on the Student A part of the **Souvenirs** section on the right-hand page. Check through the vocabulary. Ask about the priced items only: *How much is the pen? How much is the orange marmalade? How much are the badges?* etc. Be careful to check the answers that require 'each'.

2 Briefly check *this / that / these / those* by asking about classroom objects: *What's this? What's that? What are these? What are those?* Make the distinction between near and far clear with gesture.

3 Pair work. Refer students to the two boxes, Student A and Student B. Student A is the customer. Student B is the shop assistant. Student B has to turn the book upside down. Point out that there are some items with prices, and some without in each list. They role play two or three dialogues parallel to dialogue 3. They then reverse roles. They choose whether to use *this / that / these / those*.

4 Role play. .3 can be extended / enriched by using realia brought into the classroom for the purpose. In which case, ask: *How much is this? / How much are these?* Get the students to choose a price, then write it on a piece of paper and use it as a label. Set up a shop on a table at the front of the class. Souvenirs from the local area could be used. Local prices could be used as well.

5 Get one or two pairs to demonstrate in front of the class.

◆ Dialogue 4 (G, H)

1 Set pre-question: *How much are the ice creams each?* Play the dialogue. Play it again, pausing for students to repeat chorally and individually.

2 Write up on the board:
I . . .	my . . .	me
You . . .	your . . .	you
He . . .	his . . .	him
She . . .	her . . .	her
We . . .	our . . .	us
They . . .	their . . .	them
It . . .	its . . .	it

Get students to repeat chorally. Delete some items from your chart. Get students to complete the gaps. Fill them in, delete other items, and so on.

3 Drill:
T: *That's my ice cream.*
C: *It's for me.*
Continue: *That's her coffee. / That's his milk. / That's their coffee. / That's our Pepsi-Cola. / That's your orange juice.*

4 Check 'altogether'. Write up items with prices, add up the total. Say *That's (xx) altogether.*

5 Questions:
Are the ice creams large or small? Has he got cherry ice cream? Has he got lemon ice cream? Has he got orange ice cream? What flavours has he got? Is the strawberry for a girl or a boy? Is the chocolate for a boy or a girl? Who is the vanilla for? How much are the ice creams each? How much is it altogether?

6 Silent reading of dialogue 4.

7 Paired reading of dialogue 4.

d Ice creams

1 Reading. Focus attention on the **Ice creams** section on the right-hand page. Ask if there's anything wrong / strange about the ice cream advert. Get students to read it silently. (*Genuine, authentic Italian ice cream . . . made in England.*) Check through the vocabulary.

2 Pair work. Students use the prompts and role play dialogue 4, freely substituting items from the Ice creams section. Note that when they ask about the lollies they should ignore the redundant words: e.g. Lemon Dream . . . *What flavour is it? Lemon.*

3 Get one or two pairs to demonstrate in front of the class.

4 Play all four dialogues again.

◆ Workbook

The Workbook can be done for homework.
If it is done in class, exercises 4 and 5 can be done as paired oral practice.

Unit fourteen

E Can I help you?
F Yes. How much is this pen, please?
E It's 40p.
F And how much are these postcards?
E They're 10p each.
F How much is the English tea?
E It's £1.20. Here you are.
F Oh, no. No, thank you. I'm just looking ...

c Souvenirs

Make conversations.

Student A

this / that / the   these / those / the

G Three small ice creams, please.
H What flavour?
G What flavours have you got?
H I've got strawberry, vanilla, chocolate, and coffee.
G OK, one strawberry, one vanilla, and one chocolate, please.
H Right ... who's the strawberry for?
G It's for her.
H And the chocolate?
G It's for him. The vanilla's for me.
H Here you are.
G How much is that?
H They're 60p each ... that's £1.80 altogether.

d Ice creams

Make conversations.

Student B

this / that / the   these / those / the

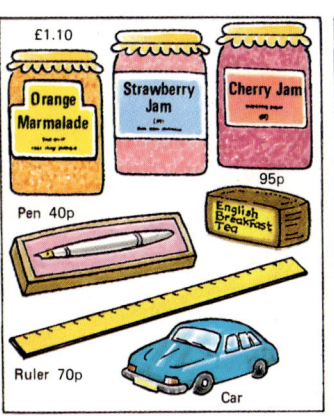

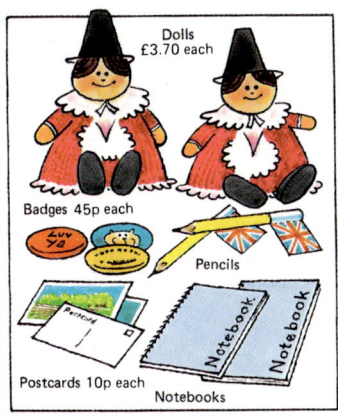

BASILIO'S
Genuine Authentic Italian Ice Cream   Made in England

ICE CREAMS
Small 60p   Medium 85p
Large £1·00
Flavours:
Strawberry · Chocolate ·
Vanilla · Coffee

ICE LOLLIES 70p Each
Orange Surprise · Lemon Dream
Strawberry Sensation
Caribbean Pineapple

Unit fifteen

The Keys

1
Ben There's a programme on television!
Sarah Don't turn on the television, Ben.

4
Sarah Oh no... Ben! Ben, come here. Turn off the television, Ben. Ben, turn off the television and come here... Ben, open this door. Ben. Ben, please!

5
Postman What's wrong?
Sarah It's my little boy. He's inside, and my keys are in there. And the door's locked.
Postman Oh dear. Oh dear. Oh dear.

6
Postman How old is he?
Sarah He's four.
Postman What about the back door?
Sarah That's locked, too.

7
Postman And the windows? Have you got a ladder?
Sarah No, I haven't. Wait here a minute...

8a 8b
Postman Hello? Hello?
Sarah Be quiet! Bad dog! Be quiet! Don't do that! Sit! Sit!... Sorry.

9
Mrs Clark Be careful, dear.
Mr Clark Oh, I'm all right.
Mrs Clark Not you, dear. The garden. Be careful.

10
Sarah Please be careful, Mr Clark.
Mr Clark I'm OK. Help me. Hold the ladder.
Postman OK.

11
Mr Clark It's a very small window.
Postman Put your hand in!
Mr Clark Eh?
Postman Put your hand in! Pull the handle!
Mr Clark What?

12
Postman Pull the handle of the other window.
Mr Clark Oh.
Postman Pull the handle!
Mr Clark It's no good!

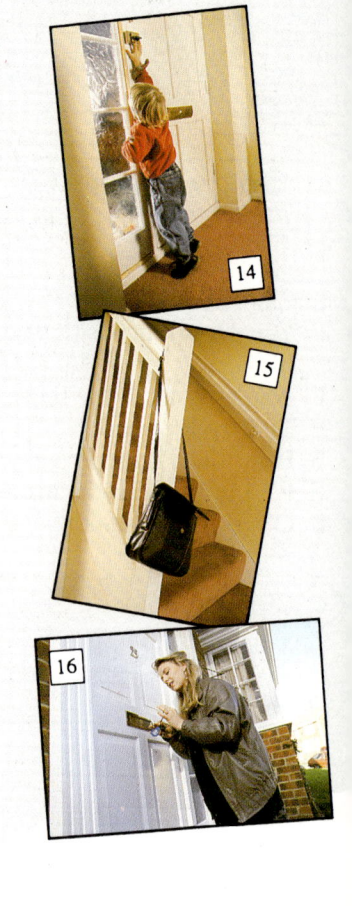

13
Sarah Ben! Turn off the television! *Ben! Come here!*
Ben Hello, Mum.

14
Sarah Ben, the door's locked, and I haven't got my keys. Open the door. It's no good. He's very small, you see.
Mrs Clark Oh dear. Oh dear, oh dear.

15
Sarah Right, Ben. Get my bag. It's in the hall. Have you got it?
Ben Yes.
Sarah Open my bag... and get the purse. Open it. The keys are in the purse. Have you got them?
Ben Yes.

16
Sarah Good boy. Now, come here, and push the keys through the letter-box. Oh no! These are the car keys!

Optional video component

Teaching points
Imperatives: *Open the window. Don't open the window!*
Turn on / off the television. Turn (it) off.
Be quiet. / Be careful.
Help me / him / her / us etc.

Grammar note
Imperatives. The importance of imperatives at this point in a beginner's course is far wider than their straightforward use. Imperatives introduce new verbs in their simplest form (the stem) for the first time, and demonstrate meaning.
Don't: I don't know has been seeded into the course as a fixed formula in earlier lessons, so students will be familiar with *don't*.
Be: If you have avoided grammatical explanations so far, *be* will be unfamiliar. It may be worth pointing out that *am / is / are* are parts of the verb '*be*'.

Expressions
It's no good. Not you. Don't do that!

Examples of the following verbs in the imperative form have appeared in earlier units and/or in class instructions:
ask / come / complete / get / go / help / listen / look / meet / put / read / spell / stand next to / tell / write.

Active vocabulary
box (letter box) / boy / chair / garden / hall / handle / ladder / lock / mum / mummy / paper / postman / prisoner / programme / purse / window
be / close / do / don't / help / hold / move / push / sit / turn on/off / wait / back / careful / little / locked / other / quiet / inside / through

Classroom vocabulary
give / group / instructions / order / outside / polite / request / say(s)

Audio-visual aids
Cassette, or video cassette (if optional video is to be used).

◆ **Oral introduction**

Give a few instructions to the class. e.g. *Listen to me. Stand up. Thank you. Sit down. Maria, please open the window. George, give me your book. Anna, open the door. Carlos, close the door. Come here, go to the door, turn the light on.* etc.
Optional: Get one student out and get them to follow a fairly long sequence of instructions.

◆ **Picture sequence, frames 1–4**

1 Show the students how to cover the text, a row at a time. Ask about the first four pictures.
1 *Where are they? How old is she? How old is he? Who is she?*
2 *Is she in the house? Where is she?*
3 *Is the door open or closed? Where is he? Where is she?*
4 *Is the door locked?*

2 Play the cassette for frames 1–4. Play it again, pausing for selective repetition, chorally and individually. Check the names, Ben and Sarah. *Who is the mother? Who is the son?*

3 Silent reading of the text for frames 1–4.

4 Paired reading of frames 1–4.

◆ **Picture sequence, frames 5–8b**

1 Check that the text is covered. Play the cassette for frames 4–6. Play it again, pausing for selective repetition, chorally and individually.

2 Silent reading of frames 5–8b.

3 Questions:
Is she inside? Ask 'Who?' Is the man a policeman? Ask 'What?' Are her keys outside? Ask 'Where?' Is the door open? How old is the little boy? How old is she? How old is the postman? Is the back door open or is it locked? (Check *front door / back door*.)
Is a window open? Has she got a ladder?

4 Paired reading of frames 5–8b.

◆ **Picture sequence, frames 9–12**

1 Play the cassette for frames 9–12. Play it again, pausing for selective repetition, chorally and individually.

2 Silent reading of frames 9–12.

3 Paired reading of frames 9–12.

◆ **Picture sequence, frames 13–16**

Follow the same procedure as for frames 9–12, but use a bag, purse and keys. Get a student out and give him / her the same instructions. Get a student to give you the same instructions.

Unit fifteen

◆ Picture sequence, frames 17–19

Follow the same procedure as for frames 9–12.

⟨a⟩ Role play

1 Play the whole cassette through, allowing students to follow the text.

2 Explain the activity. It can be done in groups. They role play a parallel situation. Show them the grey shaded box for reference.

◆ Language summary

1 Silent reading of the language summary in ⟨a⟩. Point out the exclamation mark. Note that it is usually optional.

2 Contrast:
Open the window! and *Please open the window.*
Get students to repeat the sentences 1) as orders, 2) as polite requests.
Show that it is **tone of voice**, not the choice of words that usually determines politeness in English.

3 Write the numbers 1–10 on the board. Tell the students to do the same on a piece of paper. Say that you are going to say ten things. They note whether it is an order (1), or a polite request (2).
  1 *Come here, Maria* (say it gently and politely, smile, gesture towards her)
  2 *George! Please come here!* (Stand back, say it as a command)
  3 *Please open the door!* (rudely)
  4 *Give me your pen* (gently, politely, smile, put out your hand)
  5 *Give me your pen!* (a sharp command)
  6 *Listen to me!* (an order)
  7 *Listen* (gently, politely, smiling)
  8 *Stand up!* (an order)
  9 *Sit down, please.* (an order)
  10 *Please look at your books.* (gently, politely, smiling)
Check the answers, stress that the word *please* didn't make sentences polite. It was the tone of voice. There is no need to explain to the class, but body language (smiles and gestures) are equally important in determining politeness.

⟨b⟩ Instructions

1 Check that the texts are covered. Choose a student. Give them the instructions in the book. They have to follow the instructions silently. Do this with both sets. If necessary, add another set or sets.

2 Silent reading of instructions.

3 Pair work. Get students to give, and act upon, instructions in pairs. **Note:** This will be a fairly noisy activity.

4 Check:
Turn on the television. / Turn the television on. – both are correct.
Turn it on. But **'Turn on it'* is wrong in English.

⟨c⟩ What?

Draw attention to the six cartoons. Students can work alone or in pairs to complete the spaces. Check back. Compare the various suggestions.

⟨d⟩ The prisoner

Explain the situation. Get students to read it silently. Invite suggestions. After a few suggestions, refer them to the solution, which is printed upside-down.

◆ Game: Simon Says

Explain the game.
If you say 'Simon says put your hands up', everyone puts their hands up.
If you say 'Put your hands up', no one moves. Anyone who does put their hands up is 'out'. The game continues until only one student is left.
A possible sequence is:
Put your hands up. / Simon says put your hands up. / Simon says stand up. / Sit down. / Simon says sit down. / Simon says open your books. / Simon says close your books. / Open your books. / Stand up. / Simon says open your books. / Close your books. / Put your hands on your head. / Simon says put your hands on your head. / Put your hands down. / Simon says put your hands down. / Put your pen on your book. / Simon says put your pen on your book. / Stand up. / Simon says stand up. / Sit down. / Simon says sit down. / Tell me your name. / Simon says tell me your name. / Simon says be quiet. It can be extended as long as necessary.
Note: There is an authentic American song *Simon Says*, which you could use, but the language in the song is fairly difficult.

◆ Workbook

The Workbook can be done as homework.
If it is done in class, exercises 1 and 6 can be done orally. Exercise 6 can be extended to include other sets of instructions.

17
Sarah Ben, don't go. Come here. Come here, Ben! Don't turn on the television. These aren't the house keys. They're the car keys.

18
Sarah Get the purse. Get mummy's purse. Now push the purse through the letter-box. Push! Push!
Postman Pull!
Sarah Thank you.

19
Ben Push!
Sarah Ben, don't do that! Don't put the purse through the letter-box! Ben!

a Role play

In groups of four, role play the story of the keys.

Come here.
Open the window!
Pull it!
Turn the TV off!
Be quiet!
Don't go there!
Don't open the door!
Don't push it!
Don't turn it on!
Be careful!

b Instructions

Listen. Get up. Get a chair. Put it on the table. Get a book. Put it on the chair. Get a pen. Put it on the book. Go to the door. Push the door. / Pull the door. Open it. Go out. Close the door. Open the door. Come in. Come here. Don't move. Be quiet.

Listen. Get up. Turn on the light. Go to the cassette player. Turn it on. Don't move. Turn it off. Go to the light. Turn it off. Get a chair. Stand on the chair. Be careful. Get on the table. Get off the table. Come here.

Look at the instructions.
Give some instructions to another student.

c What?

Look at the pictures. Complete the spaces.

d The prisoner

This man is a prisoner in this room. The door is locked. The man has got a pen and some paper.
Help him to get out.
Give instructions.

Answer

Get the paper. Push the paper under the door. Get the pen. Push the pen into the lock. Push the key with the pen. Pull the paper under the door. The key is on the paper!

Unit fifteen

Stories for pleasure

Security

"Martha, here's a job for me! Look in the newspaper!"

Bert Ellis is 66. He's retired, but he isn't happy. He's looking for another job.

JOBS

WAITER for small but busy restaurant. 40-hour week. Chelsea. 01-447-9855.

NIGHT SECURITY GUARD for large insurance company. City of London. 5 nights per week. 10 pm to 6 am. Tel: Ms J Cooper, Personnel Manager, 01-243-9088.

VAN DRIVER East London. 42-hour week. Good salary. Clean driving licence essential. Call Tim on 01-554-3361.

"Right, dear... Give me the telephone!"

The next day.

"...and how old are you, Mr Ellis?"

"I'm 66."

"Well, I don't know. It's a job for a young man."

"Please, Ms Cooper. I'm not too old. Really!"

"Hmm... All right, then. Start on Monday."

"Have you got your radio, Bert?"

"Oh, yes. I've got my radio and my torch. See you later."

Monday 11.00 p.m. The offices of Mercia Insurance. Bert is with the other security guard, Dave. Dave is 29.

"Hello, Dave. I'm on the third floor. It's very quiet. Everything's OK."

"That's funny. The lift isn't here now. It's on the fifth floor."

"Ah, here are the stairs..."

"Dave, I'm on the fifth floor. There's a light under a door... and there's a funny smell. It's smoke!"

"Is it a fire? Bert? Don't open the door. Repeat – don't open that door!"

POLICE
FIRE
AMBULANCE
CALL 999

"The money's here... nearly a million pounds..."

"Dave! It isn't a fire. It's cigar smoke. And there are voices. There are people in there!"

Teaching points

This material can be used in a number of different ways:

As extensive reading for pleasure
We would recommend using it for extensive reading for pleasure with most classes. It can be done in class or at home. In this case you will not need any teacher's notes. The material need not be checked or tested in any way.

As extensive listening for pleasure
Where you feel students will benefit from extra listening practice, the story can be used with the recording on cassette.

As reading comprehension material for revision
With classes that need extra revision / consolidation material, the story can be exploited intensively as comprehension material.

Vocabulary & expressions
As the story is intended for reading / listening for pleasure, the vocabulary is not listed in the index. All extra items in the story are for passive comprehension. The extra items are:
cigar / company / fool / guard / hero / idea / insurance / personnel manager / power / smell / smoke / switch / torch / voice
brave / electric / retired / security
calling / repeat / start / touch
really / too
everything / someone
All other items are redundant language.

Audio-visual aids
Optional: Cassette. The material is recorded. It appears between Units 15 & 16.

Stories for pleasure

◆ As extensive reading for pleasure

Reading for pleasure is best done with no pressure or fear of checking or testing. We would suggest that students work alone and read the story with no checking by the teacher. This however would be a good time to point out how to read extensively. Tell students not to stop for difficult words, but to read on to the end of the story. They should mark difficult words with a pencil, and look them up only after completing the whole story.

◆ As extensive listening for pleasure

Note: If you have a listening centre, tell students to listen to the cassette, then read the story, then listen and read. There will be no need for the work below.

1 Play the cassette once with books closed.

2 Write pre-questions on the board:
Bert is ☐ 66 ☐ 26 ☐ 60.
The smoke is on the ☐ 5th ☐ 15th ☐ 3rd floor.
Mr Miles is ☐ the boss ☐ a burglar ☐ another guard.
Bert ☐ is ☐ isn't an old fool.
Play the cassette again, students check the answers.

3 Play the cassette in sections, books closed, pausing to ask questions:
Frame 4: *How old is he? Is he happy? Has he got a job? Is he looking for a job?*
Frame 6: *What's her name?*
Frame 9: *How old is Dave? What's his job? What has Bert got? Where is he? Where is the lift?*
Frame 12: *Where is the light? What is the smell?*
Frame 15: *Is it cigarette smoke? Is it a fire? What is it?*
Frame 18: *Who has got an idea? What is it?*
Frame 21: *Is the door locked?*
Frame 24: *Who is Mr Miles? What about the voices?*
The end: *Is Mr Miles angry? Has Bert got the job?*

4 Students open the books. Play the cassette. They listen and read.

5 Silent reading. Check vocabulary. See reading comprehension exploitation below.

6 Play the cassette again, books closed.

◆ As reading comprehension material for revision

1 Refer students to page one. Silent reading. Don't check vocabulary.

2 Ask them to find words that mean:
A man over 65, or a woman over 60, with no job. (*retired*)
A small, portable light. (*torch*)
Something from a fire or from a cigarette. (*smoke*)

3 Listen and read. Play the cassette. Students listen and read.

4 Play the cassette again, pausing to ask questions as appropriate:
1 Is Bert 56? Ask 'How old?' Has he got a job? Is he happy? Is he retired? Are you retired? Are you happy? How old are you? Ask him / her.
2 Is the job 6 nights a week? Is it 5 nights a week? What's the phone number?
4 What's her name? What's her job?
5 Is the job for an old man or is it for a young man?
7 What's Dave's job? Is he 92? Ask 'How old?' What has Bert got?
8 Where is he? Is it quiet?
9 Is the lift there? Ask 'Where?'
11 Where is he now? Is there a light? Ask 'Where?' Is there a smell? What is it?
13 Is it a fire? Ask 'What?' Are there voices? Ask 'Where?'

5 Page two. Silent reading.

6 Ask them to find words which mean:
idiot, stupid person. (*fool*)
closed with a key. (*locked*)

7 Listen and read. Play the cassette. Students listen and read.

8 Play the cassette again, pausing to ask questions as appropriate:

14 Where's the phone? Is Dave calling his boss? Who is he calling?
15 Who has got an idea? Where's the electric power switch? Is it for all the lights in the town?
18 Is the door open or closed? Is it locked or unlocked?
20 What is the number of the room?
21 Where are the police?
23 Who is Mr Miles?
25 Is Bert sorry?
26/27 Has he got the job or not?

9 Get students to read the story aloud in groups. Get one or two groups to act it out in front of the class.

◆ **Workbook**

There are no Workbook units for the **Story for pleasure** sections.

Stories for pleasure

Cigar smoke? Voices? Don't go in, and be quiet, be very quiet. There's a phone here. I'm calling the police.

No, Dave. Don't call the police. We're the security guards. It's our job.

I've got an idea, Dave. There's an electric power switch here. It's for all the lights on this floor.

Bert! Don't touch that switch!

Now, where's my torch?

Bert! You fool!

It's OK, Dave. The door isn't locked.

Stop! You old fool!

Don't move!!

POW! CRASH! ZONK! KAPOW!

Right, Dave. I've got him! Come up and put the lights on. It's room 503.

Bert, the police are here...

Here he is! He's my prisoner! Not bad for an old fool. Eh?

Oh no, Bert, this is Mr Miles!

Mr Miles? Who's he?

He's the boss of the company!

But...the voices...

Yes. A programme on the television.

Oh dear. I'm sorry, Mr Miles...er, goodbye...

I **AM** an old fool...now I haven't got a job.

SECURITY GUARD HERO gets the wrong man – but he keeps his job!

'He's a very brave man' says company boss Ernest Miles. Mr Miles is in our photograph with 66 year-old security guard, Bert Ellis, from Hackney. Bert, who started work with M...

Unit sixteen

Directions

A Can I help you?
B Yes. I'm looking for a map of the town.
A There are some maps over here. This is a good one.
B How much is it?
A £1.35.
B That's fine. Thank you.

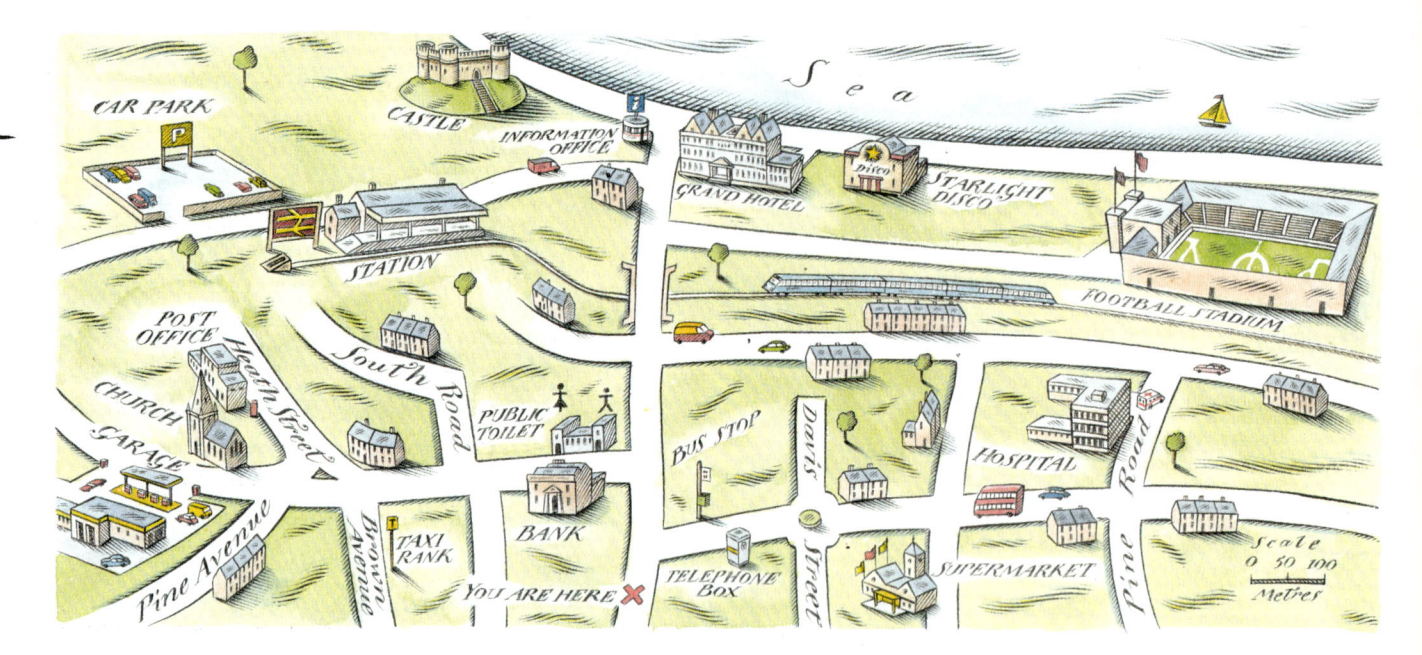

a Asking the way

1 C Excuse me, where's Heath Street?
   D It's first left, then second right.
   C Thank you.

   Make conversations for:
   Brown Avenue / Davis Street / South Road / Pine Road.

2 E Excuse me, is there a bus stop near here?
   F Yes. Go along this street, turn right and it's on the left.

   Make conversations for:
   a public toilet / a telephone box / a bank.

3 G Excuse me, I'm looking for a post office.
   H Go along this street, take the first left, then the second right. It's on the left. You can't miss it.
   G Thank you very much.
   H Not at all.

   Make conversations for:
   a supermarket / a hospital / a taxi rank.

4 I Excuse me, can you tell me the way to the Grand Hotel?
   J Yes, go along this street. Go across the bridge and go straight on to the end. It's on the right at the end of the street.

   Make conversations for:
   the football stadium / the information office / the station.

5 K Excuse me, I'm looking for a garage.
   L A garage? Yes, go along this street, and turn first left. Go straight on for about 400 metres. Go past the church, and it's on the left.
   K Thanks.

   Make conversations for:
   The Starlight Disco / a car park / the Castle.

   M Excuse me, can you tell me the way to the Castle?
   N Sorry, I don't know. I'm a stranger here.

Teaching points
Asking for and giving directions. Consolidation of imperative forms.
Present continuous, in the formula: *I'm looking for . . .*
Turn right / left. Go straight on. / Go past the (church).
First right. / Second left.
Go along this street / across the bridge.
It's on the (left). It's at the end of (this street).
Take the (first right).
Go straight on for about (400 metres).

Expressions
That's fine.
Is there (a bus stop) near here?
Can you tell me the way (to the Grand Hotel)?
You can't miss it.
Not at all. I'm a stranger here.

Active vocabulary
across / along / end / left / past / right / straight on /
avenue / bank / bridge / bus stop / car park / castle / church /
directions / exit / hotel / map / one / post office / stranger /
street / supermarket / telephone box / toilet / way /
take / tell / turn

Passive vocabulary
ask / atlas / cathedral / centre / disco / lighthouse / monster /
plan / public (toilet) / rank (taxis) / stadium / miss

Classroom vocabulary
(give / ask) directions

Audio-visual aids
Cassette. Practice could be extended with a set of local street maps.

Note: The language in this unit has been carefully segmented, and the maps and tasks designed so that the directions students are asked to give will always be possible with the language at their disposal. With some classes it might be possible to extend practice with authentic and / or local maps. However, most authentic maps will require more complex language than students have learned. It is important to realize that we almost never give detailed directions which take someone right across a town. Most directions are localized, and simple. The most useful exponent of the function of 'finding your way around' is probably that in the opening dialogue (A, B) – buying a map.

◆ Dialogue (A, B)

1 Focus attention on the picture of the maps, check that the text is covered. Set pre-question: *How much is the map?* Play the dialogue. Check the answer. Play it again, pausing for choral and individual repetition.

2 Drill:
Note that the purpose of the drill is further familiarization with the present continuous form (see also Unit 13) **not** immediate usefulness.
T: *I*
C: *I'm looking for a map.*
Continue: *they / she / you / he / we / David*

3 Silent reading of dialogue 1.

4 Paired reading of dialogue 1.

5 Pair work on dialogue 1, substituting other titles and prices from the picture.

◇ Asking the way: dialogue 1 (C, D)

1 Focus attention on the map. Check that the text is covered. Check that students have found the starting point on the map, which is marked with a red cross. Play dialogue. Students follow the route on the map. Ask *Where's Heath Street?* Play it again, pausing for choral and individual repetition.

2 Silent reading of dialogue 1.

3 Paired reading of dialogue 1.

4 Students substitute from 'Make conversations for: . . .', using the map to give directions which will follow the pattern in the dialogue.

◇ Asking the way: dialogue 2 (E, F)

1 Follow the same procedure as for dialogue 1 .1–.3, but ask *Where's the bus stop?*

2 Students substitute from 'Make conversations for: . . .', using the map to give directions which will follow the pattern in the dialogue.

◇ Asking the way: dialogue 3 (G, H)

1 Follow the same procedure as for dialogue 1 .1–.3, but ask *Is the post office on the right or the left?* Check *You can't miss it.* and *Not at all.* Note that in English such a response is much less common than in most languages, and is by no means an automatic response to *Thank you.* (You could point out that Americans commonly use *You're welcome*, which is the American English equivalent of *Not at all*. Discourage the translated thought that often leads to *please* as a response to *Thank you.*

2 Students substitute from 'Make conversations for: . . .', using the map to give directions which will follow the pattern in the dialogue.

◇ Asking the way: dialogue 4 (I, J)

1 Follow the same procedure as for dialogue 1 .1–.3, but ask *Where's the Grand Hotel?*

2 Students substitute from 'Make conversations for: . . .', using the map to give directions which will follow the pattern in the dialogue.

◇ Asking the way: dialogue 5 (K, L)

1 Follow the same procedure as for dialogue 1 .1–.3, but ask *Where's the garage?*

Unit sixteen

Unit sixteen

2 Students substitute from 'Make conversations for: . . .', using the map to give directions which will follow the pattern in the dialogue.

⟨a⟩ Asking the way: final dialogue (M, N)

Follow the same procedure as for dialogue 1 .1–.3. There are no substitutions for this dialogue. Point out that it's a very useful response!

⟨b⟩ 🗺 Seaville

1 Focus attention on the street plan of Seaville. Explain the task: They have to listen to four people giving directions. They follow the route on the map, for the first speaker they write '1' on the map at the end of the directions, for the second speaker they write '2', and so on. Play all four sets of directions once for familiarization. Play them again. Students complete the task. Check back.

2 Students work in pairs, and take turns to ask for and give directions to the places listed.

⟨c⟩ Directions game

Students work in pairs. One student chooses a place on one of the maps and gives directions without stating where they lead to. The other student follows their instructions, and finds the place on the map.

⟨d⟩ Computer game

Students work in pairs. Student A directs Student B round the maze to the gold. Then Student B directs Student A from the gold to the exit. Encourage the use of *Don't go that way. / Don't go left, there's a monster. / Don't turn right, turn left.* etc.

◆ Optional extension

1 Authentic maps of the local area can be used for further paired practice – but see the note above.

2 Computer work. If you have access to a computer in the school, a lot of practice can be developed using commercial non-ELT maze-based games, and even the variants of *Donkey Kong / Killer Gorilla*-type games. Students work in groups on the computer (3 or 4 students). The work comes from the language used in directing other students, not from the content of the game.

◆ Workbook

The Workbook can be done for homework.
Exercises 3, 4, 5, 6, and 7 can also be used in class for paired oral practice.
Exercise 8 can be done as a listening exercise, by making it a 'picture dictation' with books closed. Other 'picture dictations' can be evolved along similar lines.

STREET PLAN OF SEAVILLE

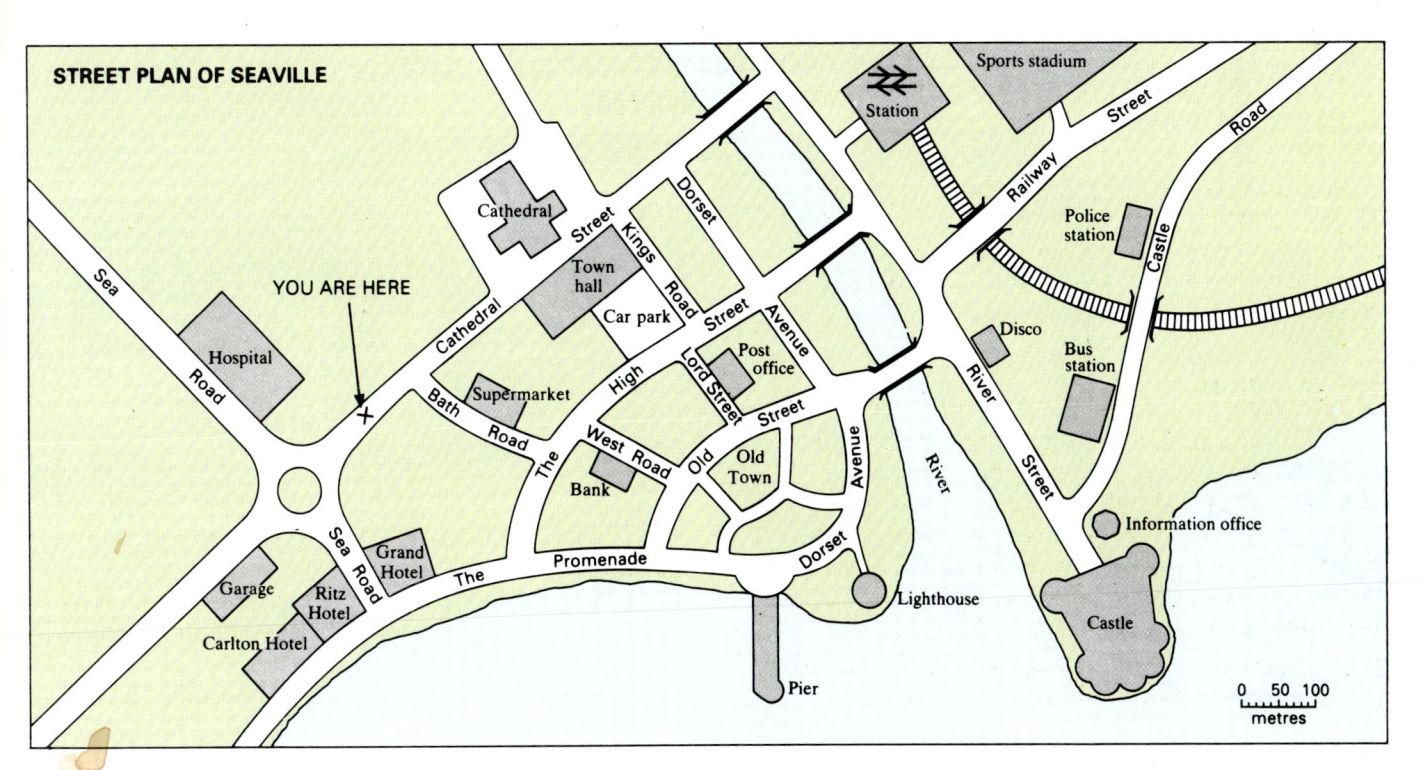

Unit sixteen

b. Seaville

1. You are in Cathedral Street.
   Listen to these four people, and put 1, 2, 3, and 4 on the map.

2. Asking the way in Seaville.

   Student A: Ask the way to the police station / the Ritz Hotel / the lighthouse / the post office.

   Student B: Look at the map.
   Tell your partner the way.

c. Directions game

Student A: Look at the maps.
Give Student B directions to a place on a map.
Student B: What is the place?

d. Computer game

Where is the gold?
Student A: Tell Student B the way to the gold.
Student B: Tell Student A the way to the exit.

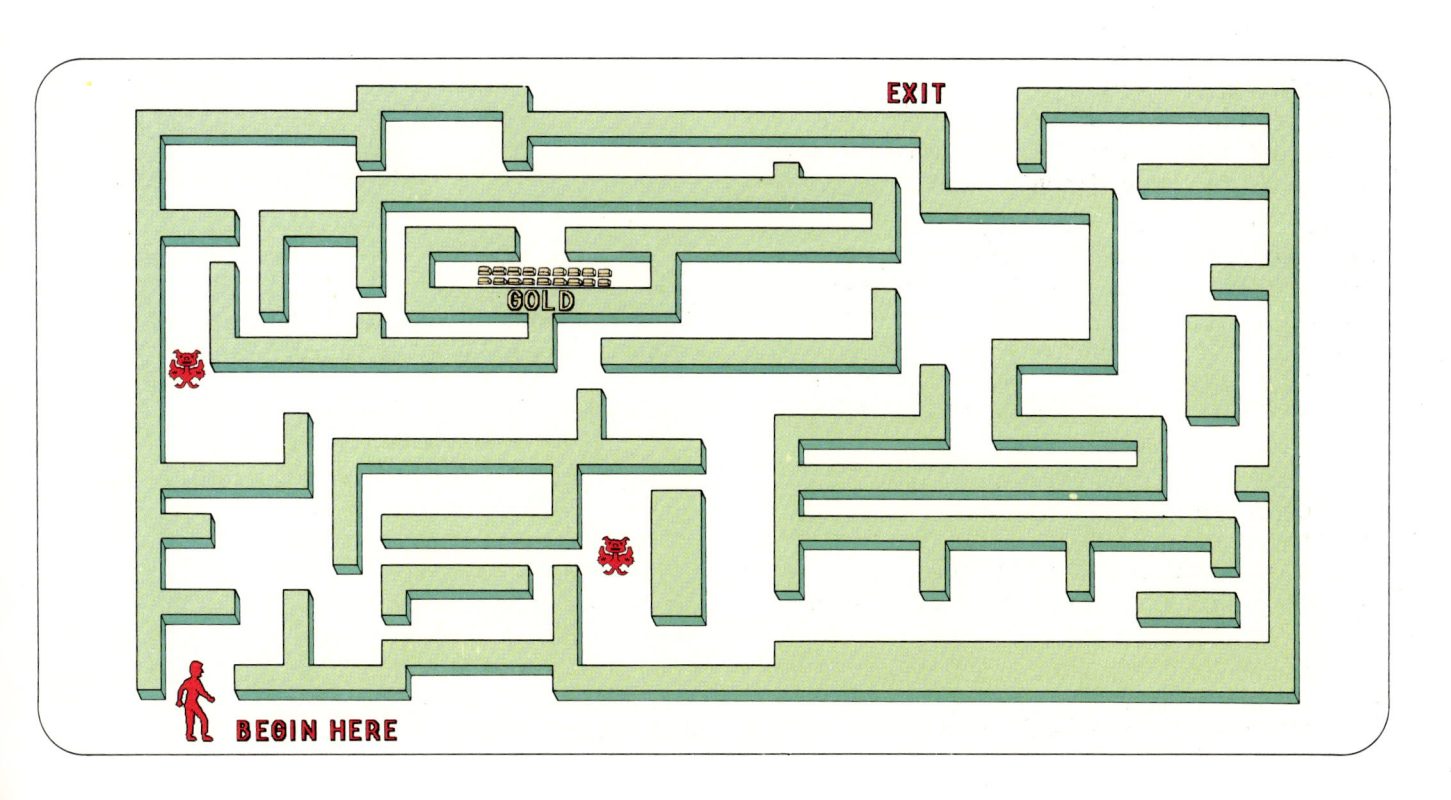

Unit seventeen

Marchmain Castle

Marchmain Castle
OPEN TO THE PUBLIC
Saturdays/Sundays 10.00 - 5.30
ADMISSION: Adults £5.50 Children £2.00

Lady Marchmain Yes?
Mr Wallace Two adults and three children, please.
Lady Marchmain I beg your pardon?
Mr Wallace Two adults and three children, please. How much is that?
Lady Marchmain I'm sorry. It's 5.45 p.m. We're closed.
Mr Wallace Oh, dear. Sorry, kids. They're closed.

Lady Marchmain Oh, well ... er, come in.
Mr Wallace Thanks, love. Are you the guide?
Lady Marchmain The guide? No, I'm not. I'm Lady Marchmain. It's my house.
Mr Wallace Oh! Pleased to meet you. My name's Wallace. Malcolm Wallace ... and this is my wife, Jean.
Lady Marchmain Good afternoon, Mr Wallace ... Mrs Wallace. Er ... follow me.

Mrs Wallace Oh, it's very nice! You've got some lovely pictures!
Lady Marchmain Yes ... there are three paintings by Constable over there, and two Rembrandts on this wall.
Mrs Wallace It's a very big house. How many bedrooms are there?
Lady Marchmain There are eighteen bedrooms.
Mrs Wallace And how many bathrooms?
Lady Marchmain There are two bathrooms.
Mrs Wallace Oh! There aren't very many! We've got two bathrooms in our house, and we've only got three bedrooms!
Lady Marchmain Yes ... well, it's a very old house.

Mrs Wallace That's an enormous table! How many chairs are there?
Lady Marchmain Twenty-four. We've got two dining rooms, this one and our private dining room. There are only six chairs in that one.
Mrs Wallace Oh! What's that?
Lady Marchmain Where?
Mrs Wallace Over there ... in the chair! It's a dead body!
Lady Marchmain No, it isn't. That's my husband, Lord Marchmain. He's asleep.
Mrs Wallace Oh, I *am* sorry. Well, thank you Lady Marchmain. Er ... We're from Manchester. If you're there, come and see our house!
Lady Marchmain Thank you. Oh ... that's £13.
Mrs Wallace Pardon?
Lady Marchmain £13 ... for the tickets.

Teaching points
Revision and consolidation. Extension of greetings. Rooms. Adjectives.
How many? – How many (rooms) are there?
There are only two (rooms). / There aren't (very) many rooms.
How many (aunts) have you / has she got?
I've only got one. / I haven't got (very) many.
Reading for specific information.

Expressions
I beg your pardon? / Come in. / Pleased to meet you. / Follow me. / If you're there, come and see our house.

Active vocabulary
adult / bathroom / bedroom / body / cloakroom / dining room / guide / kids / Lady / Lord / landing / living room / mile / painting / (the) public / stairs / wall /
asleep / closed / dead / lovely / pleased / private / follow / by / downstairs / upstairs / many / only

Passsive vocabulary
beg / belt / cardigan / if

Classroom vocabulary
different / work

Redundant words
The extract from the Guidebook on *Marchmain Castle* is designed for reading development and therefore contains redundant language which will not be exploited.

Audio-visual aids
Cassette

Unit seventeen

◆ Dialogue: section 1

1 Focus attention on the picture, and the notice. Check that the text is covered. Ask questions:
Who is she? Who are they? Where are they?
Play the cassette for the first section of the dialogue. Play it again, pausing for **selective** repetition chorally and individually. Note stress on *How much is that?* Try the sentence with different stress patterns:
*How much **is** that? How much is **that**?*

2 Questions:
How much is an adult's ticket? How much is a child's ticket? Are there two children or three children? Are there two adults or three adults? What's the time? Are they open or closed?

3 Silent reading of section one of the dialogue.

4 Paired reading of section one of the dialogue.

◆ Dialogue: section 2

1 Play the cassette for the second section of the dialogue. Play it again, pausing for **selective** repetition chorally and individually.

2 Silent reading of section two of the dialogue.

3 Paired reading of section two of the dialogue.

◆ Dialogue: section 3

Note: Rembrandt, Constable, Turner, Leonardo (da Vinci), Van Eyke are all famous painters.

1 Set pre-question: *How many bedrooms are there?* Play the cassette for the third section of the dialogue. Play it again, pausing for **selective** repetition chorally and individually.

2 Drill:
T: *There are some bedrooms.*
C: *How many bedrooms are there?*
Continue: *There are some bathrooms / pictures / people / adults / children.*

3 Drill:
T: *We've got two bathrooms.*
C: *Pardon? How many bathrooms have you got?*
Continue: *They've got three bedrooms. / She's got three children. / He's got four paintings. / I've got two cars.*

4 Drill:
T: *bathrooms*
C: *There aren't very many bathrooms.*
Continue: *bedrooms / people / men / women / children.*

5 Silent reading of section three of the dialogue.

6 Questions:
How many paintings by Constable are there? Are there three Rembrandts? Ask How many? Where are they? Is it a big house or a small house? Are there eight bedrooms? Ask How many? Are there eighteen bathrooms? Are there very many bathrooms? Ask How many? Have Mr and Mrs Wallace got one bathroom? Ask How many? Have they got eighteen bedrooms? Ask How many? Is Marchmain Castle an old house or a new house?

7 Paired reading of section three of the dialogue.

◆ Dialogue: section 4

1 Play the cassette for the last section of the dialogue. Play it again, pausing for **selective** repetition chorally and individually.

2 Drill:
T: *How many chairs are there? Three?*
C: *Yes, there are only three.*
T: *How many tickets have you got? One?*
C: *Yes, I've only got one.*
Continue: *How many pictures are there? Two? / How many brothers has she got? One? / How many windows are there? Three? / How many cousins have they got? Two? / How many aunts has he got? One?*

3 Silent reading of part four of the dialogue.

4 Questions:
Are there twenty-six chairs at the table? Ask How many? How many dining rooms have they got? Are there sixteen chairs in the other one? Ask How many? Is that a public dining room or a private dining room? Is there a dead body in the chair? Ask Who? Is he asleep? Where are Mr and Mrs Wallace from? How much are the tickets?

5 Paired reading of part four of the dialogue.

6 Play the whole dialogue.

◇ a Guidebook

1 Focus attention on the reading exercise **below** the guidebook extract. The students are not going to 'read' the guidebook extract in the accepted sense. This exercise is designed to enable students to scan the text for specific pieces of information. **Do not** ask students to read the guidebook silently, and **do not** explain vocabulary in the text. Explain that they answer the questions by referring **quickly** to the text. They will not need to read the text line-by-line in order to do this. (Any items in the text not needed to answer the questions are redundant.) Give them time to do this, checking that they are not trying to read line-by-line or to understand everything in the text.

2 How many? Students ask and answer in pairs as in the examples. Check.

3 Set up pair work using the guidebook extract. Students should ask and answer about the house freely, referring to the guidebook as they wish. Encourage them to use their imaginations as well, and to invent facts about the house. Do not be drawn into vocabulary explanation.

◇ b Houses and flats

1 Focus attention on the house plans. Let students study them silently.

2 Ask the questions in the example, then get students to ask and answer in pairs. They go on to ask about their own flats and houses. Check with a few questions to the class. Ask about their partners' houses / flats.

◇ c How many have you got?

Focus attention on the questionnaire. Explain the task. They can ask more than two students if there is time, circulating around the class.

◇ d How many has she got?

Students change pairs, and ask and answer about their previous partners. Collate the results of the survey on the board.

◆ Project / transfer

Students can be asked to find out a series of facts outside the class. These can be varied in difficulty as you choose. Alternatively, they could work in groups, each group compiling and writing down ten questions for another group to find the answers to.
e.g.
How many teachers are there in this school?
How many students are there in this school?
How many states are there in the USA?
How many rooms are there in the school?
How many people are there in (this city)? / New York? / London? / Mexico City? / Tokyo? etc.
How many discos / hotels / stations etc. are there in this town?
How many cents are there in a dollar? etc.
How many countries are there in Europe / the world / Asia / the United Nations?
How many people are there in the Berlin Philharmonic Orchestra? / a (currently popular) rock group?
How many people are there in a football team? / American football team? / rugby team? / basketball team? / baseball team?
The simpler questions could also be asked in a general teacher–class question session.

◆ Workbook

The Workbook can be done for homework. Some of the exercises are particularly useful for paired oral practice in class – exercises 1, 2, 3, and 4. Exercise 8 (Castle Dracula) is designed for reading for specific information. It should not be exploited intensively.

Famous Houses of Britain: Vol 5: The North

YORKSHIRE

Marchmain Castle
Marchthorpe, Yorkshire. Tel: Marchthorpe 3259
Shipton – 3m. York – 9m. Selby –19m. Leeds – 28m.
Hull – 35m. Manchester – 70m.

Directions
Car: A19 from York, turn right at Shipton.
Bus: Number 14 from York.
Train: To York, then bus or taxi.
There is a large car park (200 cars).
Walk out of the car park, and go across the small bridge.
The ticket office is on the left.

Admission
Open: Saturdays / Sundays 10.00 - 5.30
Closed on weekdays, bank holidays.
Tickets: Adults £3.50, Children £2.00, Students £2.50

Restaurant
Self-service cafeteria next to the house. Lunches, snacks, teas.

Souvenir shop
Behind the cafeteria.

Information
Beautiful house designed by Charles Adams (1635) in lovely gardens. 18 bedrooms. Home of the Marchmain family for 300 years. Many famous paintings - look for two Rembrandts, three Constables, four Turners, two Leonardos, five Van Eykes. Collection of vintage cars (1896 - 1914) in the garages.

a) Guidebook

Look at the information about Marchmain Castle.

1 Put a tick [✓] in the correct box below.

	Yes	No
1 Is the house open at 9.00 in the morning?	☐	☐
2 Is the phone number Marchthorpe 3259?	☐	☐
3 Are students' tickets £2.50 each?	☐	☐
4 Is the ticket office on the right?	☐	☐
5 Is the cafeteria in the house?	☐	☐
6 Is the house open on Sundays?	☐	☐
7 Is the bus from York number 41?	☐	☐
8 Are there two paintings by Leonardo in the house?	☐	☐

2 How many?

A *How many miles is the house from York?*
B *It's nine miles from York.*
A *How many paintings are there by Rembrandt?*
B *There are two paintings by Rembrandt.*

Ask and answer about Marchmain Castle.

3 Student A: Look at the guidebook.
Student B: Close the book and ask about Marchmain Castle.

b) Houses and flats

How many rooms / bedrooms are there?
How many rooms are there upstairs / downstairs?
How many doors / windows / toilets are there?

Ask and answer about the house, the flat, your house or flat, and your bedroom.

c) How many have you got?

A *How many brothers have you got?*
B *I've got two brothers. / I haven't got any brothers.*

Ask two students questions and complete the questionnaire.

	Student 1	Student 2
Family		
brothers		
sisters		
uncles		
aunts		
cousins		
grandparents		
Things		
records / cassettes		
English books		
belts		
pullovers / cardigans		
? (you make the question)		

d) How many has she got?

Work with a different student.
A *How many brothers has he / she got?*
B *He's got two brothers. / She hasn't got any brothers.*

Talk about the other students in your class.

Unit seventeen

It's mine!

It isn't yours! It's mine!
It's mine!
It isn't hers! It's mine.
No, it isn't his. It's ours.
It isn't theirs! It's mine.
It isn't hers! It's my husband's.
There's a five-pound note on the floor. Whose is it?

Sorry!

Man Sorry! Er... whose glasses are these?
Old lady They're mine... thank you.
Man Is this yours?
Old lady The baby food? No, that isn't mine...
Woman It's ours. Thanks.

a Whose is it?/Whose are they?

A *Whose glasses are those? / Whose are the glasses?*
B *They're his / hers / theirs.*

A *Whose baby food is that? / Whose is the baby food?*
B *It's his / hers / theirs.*

Ask and answer about the things on the supermarket floor.

Teaching points
Whose?, *Which one(s)?*, possessive pronouns, vocabulary revision.
Whose is it? / *Whose are they?* *Whose (pen) is it?* / *Whose (glasses) are they?*
Which one is (yours)? / *Which ones are (hers)?*
The (blue) one. / *The (big) ones.*
It's / *They're mine* / *yours* / *his* / *hers* / *ours* / *their* / *Maria's*.
Reference work: using alphabetical order.

Expressions
Come with me.
That's very kind of you.

Active vocabulary
baby / *beer* / *cake* / *floor* / *handbag* / *note* (money) / *sunglasses* / *yoghurt* / *heavy* / *kind*

hers / *his* (possessive pronoun) / *mine* / *ours* / *theirs* / *yours* / *Whose?* / *Which?*

Passive vocabulary
agriculture / *driving* / *encyclopaedia* / *fishing* / *jazz* / *kangaroo* / *physics* / *volume*

Classroom vocabulary
socks / *trainers* / *transparent*

Audio-visual aids
Cassette. Realia. Students' own possessions. Make sure that you have two pens, two books, two pencils of your own. You will need several carrier bags / boxes (one per group) for group work.

Unit eighteen

◆ **Cartoon: the supermarket queue**

1 Focus attention on the cartoon. Play the cassette. Students listen and read. Play the cassette again, pausing for students to repeat chorally and individually. Ask *Whose five-pound note is it?* Check *a five-pound note* **not*** *a five pounds note*.

2 Ask students to come out and form a line as in the cartoon. They re-enact the situation in front of the class.

3 Take pens from two students. Hold one up, say *Whose is it? Is it his or is it hers?* to elicit *It's hers.* Repeat with your pen and a student's, *Whose is this? Is this mine or is it his?* Take two students' pens, hold one up and say, *Whose is this? Is it (Juan)'s or is it (Yoshi)'s?* Continue with other classroom objects.

4 Drill:
T: *It's my pen.*
C: *It's mine.*
Continue: *It's her book.* / *It's our house.* / *It's his calculator.* / *It's their car.* / *It's your pencil.* / *It's Maria's watch.*

◆ **Dialogue: Sorry!**

1 Focus attention on the picture. Check that the text is covered. Play the cassette. Play it again, pausing for students to repeat chorally and individually.

2 Silent reading of the dialogue.

3 Group reading (in groups of three) of the dialogue.

4 Take two books from one student, and two of some other object from another student. Say *Whose books are these? Are they his or are they hers?* Continue: *Whose pencils are these? Are they mine or are they his? Whose pens are these? Are they Maria's, or are they Anna's?* etc. Continue as long as necessary.

◇ **a Whose is it? / Whose are they?**

1 Focus attention on the large picture with the three small pictures of the people from **Sorry!** Explain that all of these things are on the floor of the supermarket. Focus attention on the summary. Silent reading.

2 Pair work. Explain the activity. Point to an object:
T: *What is it?* S1: *It's milk.* T: *Whose is it?* S2: *Is it theirs?*
Make it clear that the answer is a matter of opinion. Students are guessing whose the things are, and there is no definite 'correct' answer. Students ask and answer in pairs.
Note: The only new vocabulary items are *beer*, *sunglasses*, and *yoghurt*.
Students are also revising countable plurals (*glasses*, *biscuits*, etc.) and uncountables (*milk*, *yoghurt*, *baby food*). It is only worth drawing attention to this if they encounter problems. If they do, check through all the pictures asking *What is it?* / *What are they?*

3 Check back with the class, e.g.
T: *Whose are the sunglasses?* / *Whose sunglasses are they?*
S1: *They're hers.* S2: *No, they aren't. They're his!* etc.

4 Put your pen on a student's desk. Say *It's mine! Give it to me.* Get the student to do so. Collect a number of objects. Say: *Whose is it? OK, give it to (her).* Repeat with several objects.

5 Drill:
T: *It's theirs.*
C: *Give it to them.*
Continue: *It's mine.* / *It's ours.* / *It's Maria's.* / *It's his.* / *It's hers.*

6 Role play. Students work in groups of four, role playing the people in the cartoon. They re-enact the dialogue, substituting different objects, and adding *Give it to me.* / *Give them to us.* as appropriate.
Get one or two groups to demonstrate in front of the class.

Unit eighteen

◆ Dialogue: (Susan / Mr Dodds)

1 Focus attention on the picture, check that the text is covered. Play the cassette. Play it again, pausing for choral and individual repetition. Explain *heavy* by lifting things in the classroom, saying *Is it heavy?*

2 Silent reading of the dialogue.

3 Paired reading of the dialogue.

4 Take objects (pens, pencils, rulers, books) from students. Say *Which one is yours? The (red) one or the (blue) one?* to elicit: *The red one's mine, the blue one's hers.*
Which one is mine? The (silver) one or the (gold) one? Do this extensively. **Note:** You may have to teach *the transparent one* (e.g. ballpoint pen) if you are using pens. Only do so if necessary.

b) Which one?

1 Group work. Distribute one carrier bag (or box) to each group. Explain the activity. Each student will put three things in the bag secretly. The other students must not look. Then the contents of the bag are put on the floor or table. Students ask and answer, as in the examples, until all the possessions have been returned.
If there are any problems with *whose* and *which one* the activity can be done twice, once for each form.

2 This can be checked / extended if you go round the class with one carrier bag, collecting one or two things from each student. Put two or three of your own things in the bag as well. Distribute the objects back to their owners by asking questions as in .4 of the Susan / Mr Dodds dialogue.

c) Which ones?

1 Focus attention on the cartoon. Go through the exercise. The word *socks* and *trainers* have not appeared previously. Teach them.

2 Pair work. Students ask and answer in pairs. Check back with the class.

3 Collect items from each student – glasses, two pens, two books, (if culturally acceptable in your teaching situation) shoes. Ask students about the items and return them. *Which ones are yours? Which ones are hers?* etc.

d) Encyclopaedia

1 This is a reference exercise. **Note:** There should be no need to explain any vocabulary items from this exercise. Explain the activity. Get students to work alone on it.

2 Pair work. Get them to check their answers by asking each other about the words in pairs. Check with the class.

3 Get them to ask and answer about other words of their choice.

Note: If your students' mother tongue does not use the roman script it will be worth spending a reasonable amount of time on this exercise. If not, it should be done quickly as reference practice.

◆ Game: alphabetical order

Tell the students you want them to form a line in **strict** alphabetical order (i.e. Maria before Marie). If the students already sit in alphabetical order in your school, they should arrange themselves in a new alphabetical order – by their first names. They should circulate freely, asking each other to spell their names, and deciding on their position. *What's your name? Spell it. What's the second letter? Who's first – Maria or Marie?* etc. This will be a cheerful, but noisy, activity.

◆ Workbook

The Workbook can be done for homework.
If it is done in class, exercise 8 should be done orally in pairs. This would be a good close to the basic lesson plan.

Unit eighteen

Susan Hello, Mr Dodds. Is that bag heavy?
Mr Dodds Hello, Susan. Well, yes, it is.
Susan My car's over there. Come on, come with me...
Mr Dodds That's very kind of you. Thank you.
Susan That's my car... over there.
Mr Dodds Which one? The white one? It's very nice.
Susan No! That's mine next to it. It's the black one!

b Which one?

Work in groups of five or six. The group has got a bag.
Each student puts three or four things in the bag.
The other students don't look.
Put all the things on the floor.

A *Whose is this pen?*
Is this pen yours?
B *It isn't mine.*
It's hers.
It's Maria's.
A *Which pen is yours?*
Which one is hers?
B *The blue one's mine.*
The old one's hers.

Ask and answer about the things.

c Which ones?

Look at the trousers.
A *Which ones are his?*
Which trousers are his?
B *The blue ones are his.*

Ask and answer about the picture.

d Encyclopaedia

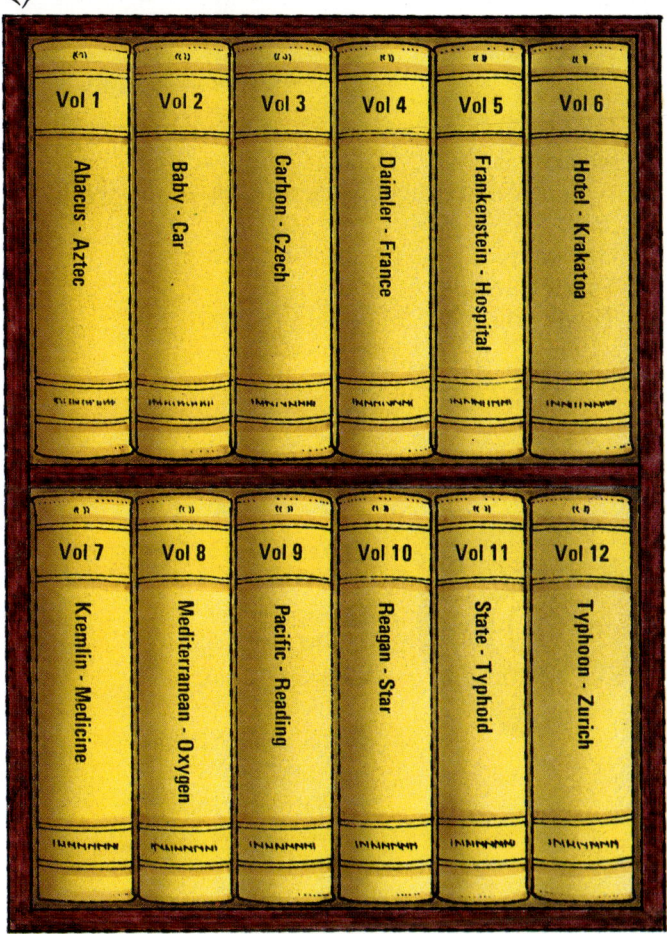

Vol 1	Vol 2	Vol 3	Vol 4	Vol 5	Vol 6
Abacus - Aztec	Baby - Car	Carbon - Czech	Daimler - France	Frankenstein - Hospital	Hotel - Krakatoa

Vol 7	Vol 8	Vol 9	Vol 10	Vol 11	Vol 12
Kremlin - Medicine	Mediterranean - Oxygen	Pacific - Reading	Reagan - Star	State - Typhoid	Typhoon - Zurich

Look at this 12-volume encyclopaedia.
1 You are looking for information in the encyclopaedia.
Which volumes are these words in?

— television   — St. Peter   — Mexico
— computers   — fishing   — London
— driving   — The Beatles   — Queen Anne
— kangaroo   — Mozart   — The Nile
— Hemingway   — agriculture   — The USSR
— physics   — jazz   — Napoleon

2 Work with your partner.
A *Which volume is (Einstein) in?*
B *It's in volume (four).*

Ask about other words.

Unit nineteen

Asking for things

In a record shop

A Yes?
B I'd like *Sixteen Greatest Hits* by Cyndi Lawson, please.
A Would you like the LP, the cassette, or the compact disc?
B Oh, sorry. I'd like the cassette, please.
A That's £6.89.
B Thank you.

THIS WEEK'S TOP 10 ALBUMS

1. **Sixteen Greatest Hits** Cyndi Lawson (Pacific)
2. **How many tears?** 4 U (Shamrock)
3. **Karate King 5** (Film soundtrack) Mario Marietti (Korner Brothers)
4. **Happy or Sad** The plugs (BCS)
5. **Smash, Crash, Bang** Titanium (Polygon)
6. **You wouldn't tell me** Angie Dallas (Pacific)
7. **West Texas Child** Carl Lee Hoover (BCS)
8. **2095** The Duke (IEA)
9. **On stage** The Earrings (Pink Punk)
10. **The Island** Cyndi Lawson (Pacific)

a) The Top Ten

Ask and answer.
1 Which record is number four this week?
2 How many Pacific records are in the Top Ten?
3 How many records has Cyndi Lawson got in the Top Ten?
4 Whose record is number eight this week?
5 Which group is *Smash, Crash, Bang* by?
6 Who is *West Texas Child* by?

Inland Letters and Cards

	60g	100g	150g	200g
1st Class	19p	28p	34p	42p
2nd Class	14p	22p	26p	32p

Overseas Letters (Air)

Zone A (N Africa, Middle East)	30p (10g)
Zone B (Americas, Africa, India, SE Asia)	32p (10g)
Zone C (Australasia, Japan, China)	35p (10g)
Europe (EEC countries)	19p (20g)
Europe (non-EEC) and surface letters	23p (20g)

Please use the postcode and include a return address.

Promoter:
Royal Mail, Room 194A, 33 Grosvenor Place, LONDON SW1X 1PX

In the post office

E I'd like some stamps, please.
F How many?
E I'd like two first class, and one for this airmail letter.
F Where's it going to?
E The United States.
F Put it on the scales, please. Mmm, that's 32p, and two nineteens. That's 70p altogether.
E Thanks.
F Would you like an airmail sticker?
E Yes, I would. Thank you.

b) Book of stamps

1 Find abbreviations for:
   ____gram ____European Economic Community
   ____pence ____South-East ____North.
2 How much is a stamp for a 10-gram letter to:
   ____Japan ____The USA ____Saudi Arabia
   ____France ____Mexico ____Czechoslovakia?

Teaching points

Requests with *would like*.
I'd like (a stamp).
Would you like the (cassette)?
Yes, I would. / No, I wouldn't.
What / Which one / What size / What make would you like?
Who is (it) by? Who is (it) for?
A sixty-minute cassette / A two-hour video tape / A five-pound note.
Reading: extracting information from charts and diagrams.
Reference skills: simple dictionary work.

Expressions

Where's it going to?
I don't know the name in English.
What's its name in English?

Active vocabulary

battery / bottle / cap / compact disc / gram / hour / LP / minute / pair (of trousers) / stamp / video cassette / Walkman / zone /
Africa / America / Asia / Australasia / Europe / India / Middle East
east / north / south / west / airmail / (first) class / dark / light (blue) / like / would

Passive vocabulary

album / card / greatest / hit / inland / lotion / overseas / scales / sticker / sun-tan / surface / EEC (European Economic Community) / N = north / SE = south east

Classroom vocabulary

abbreviation

Redundant vocabulary

(Top ten, stamp book, dictionary extracts) *bang / cell / clothing / container / cover / crash / include / karate / leg / lower / part / promoter / return / sad / soft / sort / soundtrack / stage / tear / tube*

Audio-visual aids

Cassette. A world map would be useful.

◆ In a record shop

1 Focus attention on the picture. Check that the text is covered. Set a pre-question on the board: *How much...?* Play the dialogue. Check the answer. Play it again, pausing for choral and individual repetition. Check *I'd* carefully using front-chaining (forward build-up): *I / I'd / I'd like / I'd like the cassette, please.*

2 Drill:
T: *cassette*
C: *I'd like the cassette, please.*
Continue: *LP / compact disc / record / video cassette*

3 Drill:
T: *cassette / compact disc*
C: *Would you like the cassette, or the compact disc?*
Continue: *this one / that one ... the LP / the cassette ... the new one / the old one ... the small one / the big one*

4 Silent reading of the dialogue.

5 Paired reading of the dialogue.

6 Check that the text is covered. The teacher plays the part of A, and selects a student to respond as B. Run through the dialogue. Then reverse it, so that a student plays the part of A, and the teacher plays the part of B.

⟨a⟩ The Top Ten

1 Focus attention on 'This week's top ten albums'. Let students study it silently for a moment.

2 Ask students to complete the reading exercise silently. Remind them that they do not have to read 'This week's top ten albums' line-by-line in order to do the exercise.

3 Questions. Check the reading exercise, then ask: *Whose record is number one?* to elicit *Cyndi Lawson's record is number one.* Ask four or five questions on this pattern.

Who is 'Happy or Sad' by? to elicit *It's by The plugs.* Ask four or five questions on this pattern. *Which record is number ten?* to elicit *'The Island' by Cyndi Lawson is number ten.* Ask four or five questions on this pattern.

4 Role play. Students use the information in 'This week's top ten albums' in a role play based on the dialogue. They have to make up the prices themselves. To add interest, you could use the current Top Ten (or Top Twenty or Top Thirty) from the local area, or from Britain or the USA. The charts can be found in newspapers, or specialist music magazines. Hi-fi magazines sometimes have classical or jazz charts which could also be used. Alternatively, you could take in a collection of ten authentic LP sleeves, to use as realia. Get one or two pairs to demonstrate in front of the class.

5 Say *Look at the Top Ten. Which record would you like?* Get students to make suggestions. (The current Top Twenty or real albums could be used.)

◆ In the post office

1 Focus attention on the picture of the stamps. Check that the text is covered. Set pre-question: *How many letters has he got?* Play the dialogue. Play it again, pausing for selective choral and individual repetition. Point out *Yes, I would.* and teach *No, I wouldn't.*

2 Silent reading of the dialogue.

3 Paired reading of the dialogue.

4 Check that the text is covered. The teacher plays the part of C. Select a student to respond as D. Then reverse it so that a student plays the part of C, and the teacher plays the part of D. Respond *No, I wouldn't.* at the end.

Unit nineteen

b) Book of stamps

1 Focus attention on the chart 'Inland Letters and Cards' at the top of the left-hand page. Explain 'abbreviation'. Get students to give you examples of abbreviations that they already know – USA, TV, BBC, etc.
Set the first reading exercise.
Check the answers. (Point out that '10g' is 10 grams. Check the abbreviations: N = north, SE = south east.) This can be checked with a small compass on the board, with the principal points on. This means explaining *west* as well. Refer back to 'This week's top ten albums'. Ask *What's number 7?* (West Texas Child). Check EEC = European Economic Community. If students are likely to know, say *Which countries are in the EEC? Which countries are in the Middle East?* etc.
Note: A world map would be useful at this point for checking the continents. Note that 'The Americas' is a little unusual. We usually talk about North America or South America.

2 Set the second reading exercise. Check the answers. Try not to spend too much time on the chart. The students should be able to use it without going into every word. **Do not** explain the small print at the bottom.

3 Role play. Students use the information in the chart as substitutions in a role play based on the dialogue in the post office.

c) One of those

Focus attention on the conversation. Get students to go through the conversation in pairs, taking it in turns to play the customer and the shop assistant. Point out that they should name the things pictured in the fourth box. Refer them to the dictionary extracts in d below.

d) What's its name in English?

1 First note *its* – one of the most common mistakes in written English is to write *it's* (as in *John's*, *Mary's*). Point out that students should use the dictionary to name the items in the fourth box. They **do not** need to understand everything to be able to match the definitions to the pictures. Ask *What abbreviations are there in these examples? What are they?*

2 They should work through the conversation in c again, using the dictionary extracts.

3 Get them to ask each other the names of things in English. Ideally, use monolingual dictionaries, although it can be done using a bilingual dictionary, or by referring back to things pictured in Units 1 to 18 in the book. This will also be useful vocabulary revision.

e) What size?

Explain the exercise. It can be done silently alone, or in pairs.

f) A two-hour cassette

1 Focus attention on the section. Say *An E120 is a two-hour video cassette.*
Ask *What's a C90? / a C30? / a C120? / a C46? / an E180? / an E240?*
Check. *A sixty-minute cassette* **not** **a sixty-minutes cassette.*

2 Check also the use of *an* before the sound of a vowel, therefore *an E180* ('ee' 180).
Write up a few similar abbreviations on the board and ask students to select *a* or *an*:
an A40 car / an F111 plane [an 'eff'] / an H bomb [an 'aiche'] / an IQ test / an L1011 plane [an 'ell'] / an R & B record [an 'arr'] / an SOS [an 'ess'] / a UFO [a 'yoo'] / an X1 plane [an 'ex']

3 Get students to make conversations in pairs as in the example in the Student's Book.

g) Role play

1 Explain the activity. Student A is the customer, Student B is the shop assistant. They role play a conversation.

2 Get one or two pairs to demonstrate in front of the class.

◆ Transfer

Ask questions:
Would you like a cup of tea now? to elicit: *Yes, I would. / No, I wouldn't.*
Make a series of offers on this pattern.
Would you like a lot of money or a lot of friends?
Would you like a big slow car or a small fast car?
Would you like a day at school or a day at the seaside?
Which would you like – a new friend or a new cassette player?
Which (pen) would you like – mine or hers?
Which (bag) would you like – his or yours? etc.

◆ Workbook

The Workbook can be done as homework. Exercise 6 should be explained orally. Exercises 1, 2, and 7 can be done as paired oral practice in class.

c) One of those

Make conversations.

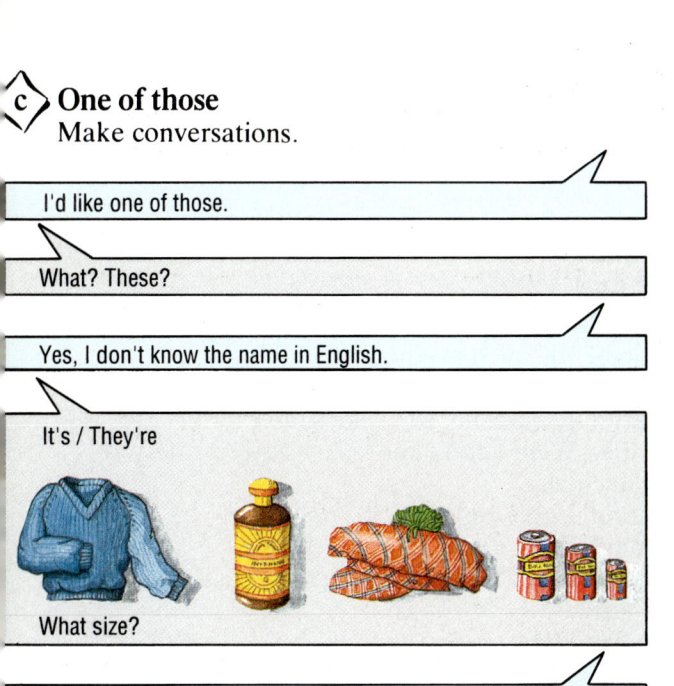

- I'd like one of those.
- What? These?
- Yes, I don't know the name in English.
- It's / They're
- What size?
- Large / Medium / Small — For me
- A / AA / AAA — For my Walkman
- Here you are.
- Thank you.

d) What's its name in English?

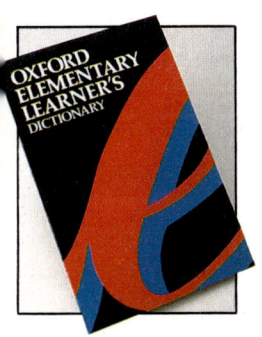

battery /ˈbætərɪ/ n. (pl. batteries) group of cells in a container which give electricity: *I put a new battery into my radio.*
suntan /ˈsʌntæn/ n. brown colour of your skin when you have been in the hot sun. **suntanned** /ˈsʌntænd/ adj.
lotion /ˈləʊʃn/ n. soft liquid that you put on the skin: *suntan lotion.*
pullover /ˈpʊləʊvə(r)/ n. jersey; sweater.
cap /kæp/ n. **1** sort of soft hat. **2** cover for the top of a tube, bottle, etc.

Student A: Read about something in a dictionary. Describe it to Student B.
Student B: What's its name in English? Guess.

e) What size?

Put things from column 1 with things from column 2.

an AA	cap
a three-hour	dress
a large	battery
a sixty-minute	bottle of suntan lotion
a small	video cassette
a size 12	pullover
a size 7	cassette

f) A two-hour cassette

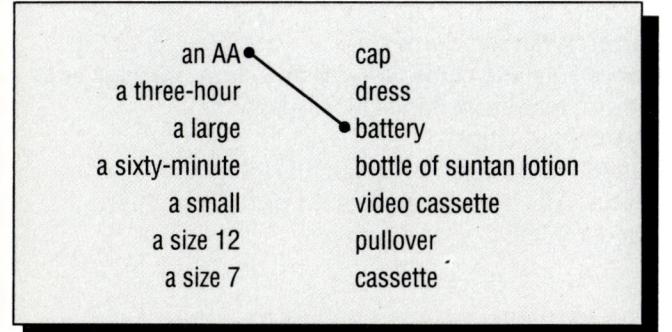

Video cassettes: E120 E180 E240
Cassettes: C30 C60 C90 C120
(An E120 is a <u>two-hour video cassette</u> – **not** two-hour<u>s</u>.)
(A C30 is a thirty-minute cassette, etc.)

A *I'd like a two-hour video cassette, please.*
B *Ah, yes. That's an E120.*
Make more conversations.

g) Role play

Student A is the customer in a clothes shop and is looking for a present. Student B is the shop assistant. Look at the boxes, and have a conversation.

Student A	
Colours	Red, blue, green, yellow, brown, grey dark blue, light blue, etc.
Sizes	Large, medium, small or size 12, size 36, etc.
Make	Benneton, Lacoste, etc.
Who for?	Boyfriend / girlfriend, aunt, grandfather, mother, brother, etc.

Student B

Which colour would you like?
What size would you like?
What make would you like?
Who is it for?

Unit nineteen

Unit twenty

Chips with everything

a 🔲 Lunch

Listen to the conversation in the restaurant.
Number the pictures from 1 to 8.

Martin Excuse me, we'd like a table for two, please.
Waiter Well, I don't know . . . we're very busy at lunchtime.
Martin Is this table free?
Waiter Well . . . yes.
Martin Could we have the menu, please? We're in a hurry.
Waiter Here you are.

Martin Ah, soup. What would you like, darling? They've got tomato or minestrone.
Angela Mmm . . . I'd like the tomato soup. What about the main course?
Martin Oh, I'd like the steak. And you?
Angela Yes, the steak for me, too. And a salad. Not chips.

Martin Excuse me!
Waiter Yes, sir?
Martin We'd like two tomato soups, please.
Waiter Tomato soup's off the menu. We haven't got any.
Angela Could we have two minestrone soups, then?
Waiter Minestrone's off, too.
Angela What *have* you got?
Waiter We've got soup of the day.
Angela What is it?
Waiter Um . . . potato . . .
Angela All right. Two potato soups, then.
Waiter Two . . . potato . . . soups. Anything else?
Martin Yes. We'd like two steaks, please. One rare, and one well-done.
Waiter Steak's off. We haven't got any.
Martin All right. Could we have two chicken, please?
Waiter Chicken's off.
Martin I see. Have you got any fish?
Waiter Uh, uh.

Martin What have you got?
Waiter Egg and chips, hot dog and chips, sausage and chips, hamburger and chips, spaghetti . . .
Martin And chips?
Waiter . . . Bolognese. Spaghetti Bolognese.
Angela All right. Two spaghetti Bolognese, then . . . and a salad.

Optional video component

Teaching points

Requests: *could & would*
Vocabulary for menus and restaurants. Revision.
I / We / He / She / They / You'd like a steak / some chips.
What / How many would you like?
Yes, I / you / he / she / they / we would. No, we / she wouldn't.
Could I / we / have (the menu), please?

Expressions

Sir / Madam. Is this (table) free? (We're) in a hurry.
What about (the main course)? And a (salad), not (chips).
It's off the menu. / It's off. What's wrong with that?

Active vocabulary

chips / dessert / fish / hurry / lunch-time / main course / menu / minestrone / sausage / soup / spaghetti / starter / steak / waiter / could / off (= not on the menu)
busy / rare / well-done / wrong / darling / sir / What about?

Passive vocabulary

bolognese / everything / melon / order / peas / service / soup of the day / VAT (Value Added Tax) / *%* (*per cent*)

Classroom vocabulary

madam / number (v)

Audio-visual aids

Cassette. **Optional:** video cassette.
Optional: some realia – cutlery, plates, tablecloth, menu, etc.

Unit twenty

a) Lunch

1 Pair work. Students work in pairs and list the things they might find on a menu in an English restaurant. Don't offer vocabulary. The exercise is designed to get students to review their own knowledge. Tell them to keep the lists.

2 Focus attention on the photographs on the left-hand page. Check that the text is covered. Explain the task. All they have to do is to number the pictures from 1 to 8.

3 Play the cassette right through. Students complete the task. Do not check or correct the ordering exercise at this stage. **However**, come back to it picture by picture as you go through the sectionalized dialogue exploitation.

4 Play the cassette right through again. Ask them to compare their lists (made in .1) with the dialogue. How many things are both in the dialogue and on their lists? **Note:** this is not a competition – there is no virtue in getting more or less than anyone else. The purpose of the exercise is that thinking about the menu items focuses the mind on the subject area.

◆ Dialogue: section 1 (to ... *Here you are.*)

1 Play the first section of the dialogue. Play it again, pausing for **selective** repetition.

2 Silent reading of the first section.

3 Paired reading of the first section.

◆ Dialogue: section 2
(to ... *And a salad. Not chips.*)

1 Play the second section of the dialogue. Play it again, pausing for **selective** repetition.

2 Silent reading of the second section.

3 Questions:
What soups have they got? Which one would she like? Would he like fish? Ask 'What?' What would she like? Would she like chips? Ask 'What?'

4 Paired reading of the second section.

◆ Dialogue: section 3
(to ... *Two potato soups, then.*)

1 Play the third section of the dialogue. Students listen.

2 Drill:
T: *minestrone soup.*
C: *Could we have two minestrone soups, please?*
Continue: *steak / tomato soup / orange juice / ice cream / potato soup*

3 Silent reading of the third section.

4 Questions:
What would they like? Has the restaurant got any? Have they got any minestrone soup? What have they got? What is it?

5 Paired reading of the third section.

◆ Dialogue: section 4 (to ... *and a salad.*)

1 Play the fourth section of the dialogue. Students listen.

2 Silent reading of the fourth section.

3 Questions:
How many steaks would they like? Would they like two rare steaks? Ask 'What?' Has the restaurant got any steak? Have they got any chicken? What about fish? What have they got?

4 Check pronunciation of *and* in *egg and chips*: *egg 'n' chips*.
Get students to repeat: *egg 'n' chips, chicken 'n' chips, sausage 'n' chips, hamburger 'n' chips, bread 'n' butter, rock 'n' roll.*

5 Paired reading of the fourth section.

◆ Dialogue: section 5 (to the end.)

1 Play the cassette for the fifth section.
Note:
Martin: *What's wrong with that?*
Angela: *You're right! I wouldn't.*
This interaction seems odd if you are not using the cassette. The sound effects make it clear that the salad has arrived and been seen between the two utterances. If you are **not** using a cassette, mime this.
Play it again, pausing for choral and individual repetition.

2 Silent reading of the fifth section.

3 Paired reading of the fifth section.

◆ The menu

Focus attention on the menu. Silent reading. Ask students to tick things mentioned in the dialogue. You should not have to explain too many things, but *peas, melon, side salad* could be demonstrated using flash cards. Suitable pictures can easily be found in magazine adverts. A problem for many students is *salad*, which in England means more than simply *lettuce*, or salad greens. A picture will clear this up.

b Dinner

Explain the listening activity. Play the cassette once. Play it again, students complete the task. Play it again, pausing to check the answers.

c A table for two

1 Get the students to complete the conversation in pairs, referring back to the menu.

2 Get one or two pairs to demonstrate in front of the class.

d Role play

1 Get students to role play a conversation using the menu. Note that the use of realia brought into the class will enhance the role play (e.g. cutlery, plates, a tablecloth, a menu).

2 Set up a group role play. **Optional**: the group could first work to compose the menu they are going to work with instead of using the one in the book. (This will take some time.) The one in Workbook exercise 7 could also be used here, to provide a change.

The role play will work better if the waiter and customers adopt positive characters (e.g. waiter – aggressive, or over-friendly, or dirty, or very superior; the customers – a couple on their first date, a married couple who are angry with each other, a couple where one likes the menu and the other hates it, a couple who can't afford the posh restaurant they're in). Each group could use different characters.

3 Get one or two groups to demonstrate in front of the class.

◆ Workbook

The Workbook can be done at home. Exercise 6 should be explained orally in class. If the Workbook is done in class, exercises 4 and 7 are suitable for paired oral practice. When students write menus in exercise 4, encourage them to fold a piece of paper. The cover should show the name, address and phone number of the restaurant, in the correct order. Students can be encouraged either to illustrate or word-process their menus.

Waiter A salad?
Angela Yes, I'd like a salad.
Waiter You wouldn't.
Angela I would.
Martin She would. What's wrong with that?
Angela You're right. I wouldn't.

Martin Your finger's in my soup.
Waiter It's all right, sir. It isn't hot.
Angela That's it! Come on, Martin.
Waiter Hey! What about your spaghetti? Probably not hungry.

Old England Restaurant

MENU

STARTERS

1	Tomato soup	£1.20
2	Soup of the day	£0.95
3	Minestrone soup	£1.30
4	Melon	£1.95

MAIN COURSES

(All served with chips and peas)

5	Steak	£6.95
6	Chicken	£5.95
7	Fish	£4.95
8	Two hamburgers	£3.95
9	Sausages	£2.95
10	Two eggs	£2.35
11	Hot dog	£2.55
12	Spaghetti Bolognese	£3.50
13	Side salad	£1.50

DESSERTS

14	Ice cream	£1.20
	(strawberry, chocolate, vanilla)	
15	Apple pie	£1.30
16	Fruit salad	£1.40

SERVICE 10% VAT AT 15% INCLUDED

c A table for two

Complete the conversation.

Waiter Good evening, _____ .
You Good evening. _____ a table for two, please.
Waiter Here you are, _____ . This is a nice table.
You Thank you. _____ a menu, please?
Waiter Here you are. Would _____ a starter?
You Yes. _____ for me, and _____ for _____ .
Waiter And _____ main course?
You Please. I _____ , and _____ 'd _____ .
Waiter Right. Anything _____ , _____ ?
You Yes. We'd like desserts. Could _____ and _____ .
Waiter Is that all, _____ ?
You Yes. Thank you.

b Dinner

Listen to these three customers in the Old England Restaurant.
Write their orders on the chart below.
Write the numbers from the menu (e.g. for **chicken** write **6**).

	Starter	Main course	Dessert
1			
2			
3			

d Role play

1 Look at the menu. Make conversations in pairs. Student A is the waiter / waitress. Student B is the customer.

2 Look at the menu. There are two (or three) customers and a waiter in the restaurant. Make conversations in a group of three or four.

Unit twenty

Unit twenty-one

Mickey can't dance

MUSIC MAIL

Meet Independence Day

The number three record this week is *Mickey can't dance*, a song from the album 'This is Independence Day'. But who are Independence Day?
Independence Day are an international group of disabled musicians. They are all in wheelchairs. Paul Thomson is from London. He's 20. He's the guitarist and singer, and he can also play the piano. Jill Raymond, from Canada, is the bass guitarist. She can also sing and play the saxophone. She's 19. Five of the songs on the album, 'This is Independence Day', are by Paul and Jill, including their first hit, *Mickey can't dance*.
Denise Cooper is the keyboard player. She can play the piano, synthesizer, and organ. She's 21, and she's from New Zealand. Julian Wingate is an eighteen year-old American. He's the drummer. Julian can also play the trumpet, and you can hear his trumpet on three of the songs on the album.
Paul says about *Mickey can't dance*: *'It's my favourite song from the album. We're all disabled in this group, but we can all see. There are many wonderful blind musicians, like Stevie Wonder and Ray Charles. The song is about a blind and disabled guitarist.'*

1 Mickey can't dance (Thomson-Raymond)
2 Can't buy me love (Lennon-McCartney)
3 I'd like to tell you...
4 I can help (Billy Sw...
5 One day (Thomson...
6 I can hear music (G...
7 You don't know me...
8 Canadian Forest (Th...
9 Can I call you? (Th...
10 Motown Medley (L...
   I can't get next to y...
   Superstition (S. Wo...
   Can I get a witness...

🎵 Mickey can't dance (*Thomson-Raymond*)

Mickey can't walk,
and Mickey can't run,
and Mickey can't drive a car.
But Mickey can sing,
He can play the guitar,
He's a star . . . he's a star . . . he's a star.

Mickey can't see,
and Mickey can't read,
and Mickey can't do algebra.
But Mickey can sing,
He can play the guitar,
He's a star . . . he's a star . . . he's a star.

Mickey is blind, he can't see anything,
Mickey is blind, he can't read anything.
But Mickey is fine, he can sing anything,
Mickey is fine, he can play anything.

Mickey can't dance,
and Mickey can't swim.
No, Mickey can't go very far.
But Mickey can sing,
He can play the guitar,
He's a star . . . he's a star . . . he's a star.

a Meet Independence Day

Read about Independence Day in the *Music Mail*.

1 Complete this chart.

Name	Age	Nationality	Musical instruments
Paul Thomson			
Jill Raymond			
Denise Cooper			
Julian Wingate			

2 Work with another student. Ask and answer about the group.

A *Who's Paul Thomson?*
B *He's the guitarist and singer.*
A *Where's he from?*
B *He's from London.*
A *How old is he?*
B *He's 20.*
A *Which instruments can he play?*
B *He can play the guitar.*
  He can play the piano. / He can also play the piano.

b Which languages can he speak?

Georges Schmidt is a translator at the United Nations. He's French. He can speak 30 languages. He can also translate from 36 other languages!
(from *The Guinness Book of Records*)
Which languages can he speak? Guess ten of the languages. Write sentences.

Unit twenty-one

Teaching points

Ability: *can* and *can't*.
(I) can read. She (can't) dance. Can (you) sing?
Yes, (I) can. / No, I can't.
Introduction of several new verb stems, including *do*.
What / Which / How many (languages) can you (speak)?

Expressions

The number three record ... (**not** *the third ...*)

Grammar note

He can play the piano. We have followed most grammar books in using *the* with musical instruments.
Note that in conversational English *He can play piano* is both common and acceptable. We would not correct students who followed this usage.
Note that the Southern English pronunciation of *can't* [kɑːnt] is easier to distinguish from *can* [kæn] than is the Northern English / American English *can't* [kænt]. We have chosen to use it in the song.

Active vocabulary

(Many words in this section have appeared in earlier units as classroom or passive vocabulary.)

Can has appeared as a formula: Can I help you?
animal / company / drums / drummer / group / guitar / guitarist / instrument / keyboard / musician / piano / player / saxophone / song / synthesizer / translator / trumpet / whale / wheelchair / word
blind / disabled / far / musical /
anything / also / but /
can / dance / do / drive / hear / play / read / run / see / sing / speak / swim / translate / type / walk / write

Passive vocabulary

abilities / algebra / bass / cheetah / falcon / hi-fi / licence / manager / multinational / New Zealand / PLC (Public Limited Company) / sales representative / swan / type (n) / United Nations
advertising / another
dive / fly / jump / sell

Classroom vocabulary

guess

Audio-visual aids

Cassette

Note: Optional. With false beginners there is no need to use the oral introduction. Begin the lesson with the reading text from the *Music Mail*.

◆ Oral introduction

1 Write a word on the board in very tiny letters. Walk away, look back, say *I can't read it.* Walk closer, repeating *I can't read it.* until you are very close. Then say *Ah! I can read it now.* Say *Can you read it?* Get individuals to say *No, I can't.* Bring one or two close to the board, say *Can you read it now?* to elicit *Yes, I can.*

2 Go to the back of the class, get students to repeat chorally *I can't read it. You can't read it. He can't read it. She can't read it. We can't read it. They can't read it.*

3 Write a word legibly on the board, get students to repeat chorally *I can read it. You can read it. He can read it. She can read it. We can read it. They can read it.*

4 Drill:
T: *I*
C: *I can read it.*
Continue: *he / she / they / we / you / Maria*

5 Drill:
T: *She*
C: *She can't read it.*
Continue: *they / I / he / we / you / John*

◆ Text from the *Music Mail*

Focus attention on the text. Set pre-questions: *How many are there in the group? What is different about this group?* Silent reading. Give them plenty of time. Make sure that they are noting problem words and reading on to the end of the text.

⬥ Meet Independence Day

1 i) Focus attention on the chart. Check that students understand the activity. Get them to complete the chart in pairs by referring back to the text.
ii) Check their answers. Ask questions to elicit Yes / No answers:
e.g. *Is Paul thirty? Is he American? Can he play the guitar? Can he play the drums?*
Go through the whole chart in this way.
iii) Questions:
Who are 'Independence Day'? Are they all English? Ask 'How many?' They're in wheelchairs. Can they walk? Who is Paul Thomson? Who is the bass guitarist? Who is Denise Cooper? Who is the drummer? What is their first record? Who is it by? What is it about?

2 Focus attention on the examples. Get the students to ask and answer in pairs. One student (the questioner) should refer to the text, the other should work from memory as far as possible. If they find this difficult, let them both refer to the text.

◆ ♪ Mickey Can't Dance

Note: See Introduction. The song can be used as a chant if you are not using the cassette.

1 Check that the text is covered. Play the song once through.

2 Play the song, line by line. Pause after each line. Get students to repeat the lines chorally and individually. Explain vocabulary as you are doing it. Demonstrate the actions if necessary.

3 Play the song verse by verse. Ask questions:
Can Mickey walk? Can you walk? Ask him / her / me.
Can Mickey run? Can you run? Ask him / her / me. etc.

4 Listen, read, and sing. Play the whole song. Students follow the text and can sing along.

b) Which languages can he speak?

1 Read the text aloud to the class. Explain the activity. They have to guess what ten of the languages are, and write sentences – *He can speak English* etc.

2 Group work. Students pool their guesses in groups. Ask each group how many languages they have listed between them. Compare the lists. Ask students questions about languages: *Can you speak (Chinese)? Ask him / her / me / each other.* etc. This will work better with adult / multilingual classes. In most situations four or five questions will be quite enough.

c) Game: What can you do?

Explain the activity carefully. The students will circulate round the class, asking each question until they receive a 'yes' answer. They can then go on to the next question. The first student to get a 'yes' answer to every question is the winner.
Important: If you feel nine 'yes' answers are unlikely from your group, you can set a lower target – five or six.
Optional: If you really cannot do this as a whole class activity in your situation, get students to do it in pairs.

d) What can they do?

1 Students use the information they obtained in the game to make third-person sentences about other members of the class as in the example.
Check by asking a few questions.

2 Class survey. Put a chart up on the board. e.g.
  1 speak French   6 do algebra
  2 dance   7 play the guitar
  3 swim 50 metres   8 play the piano
  4 type   9 sing
  5 drive

Ask *How many students can (speak French)?* Put a tick for each student who can. Get the class to make sentences, *Eight students can type. Three students can play the guitar. Seventeen students can sing.*

e) A job interview

1 Focus attention on the job advertisement. Get the students to read it silently.

2 James Hammond / Tricia Miller. Get the students to read James's letter, and Tricia's c.v. (curriculum vitae) silently.

3 Questions:
How old is James? How old is Tricia? Where's he from? Where's she from? Can he drive? Can she drive? Can he speak French? Can she speak French? Can he speak German? Can she speak Italian? How many languages can he speak? Which languages can he speak? How many languages can she speak? Which languages can she speak? Can they type? Who can type 50 words per minute?

4 Set up the role-play interviews. Student A role plays the interviewer and interviews Student B as James, then Student B role plays the interviewer and interviews Student A as Tricia. Check that they ask about the languages of all the countries where the company has got offices. (*Can you speak Japanese? / Dutch? / Greek?*) Get one or two pairs to demonstrate in front of the class.

5 Discussion. Find out who they are going to give the job to, and why.

f) Animal abilities

This section is designed for reading for pleasure. It can just as well be done outside class. If it is done in class, begin with silent reading, then get students to talk about the animals (and other animals if they wish). This section should **not** be exploited intensively.

◆ Closure

If there is time, finish off the lesson by playing the song again, getting students to sing along.

◆ Workbook

The Workbook can be done as homework. Exercise 6 should be explained orally. If it is done in class, exercises 1, 2, and 4 can be done as paired oral practice.

c) Game: What can you do?

Look at these pictures. Ask other students the questions. Put a tick [✓] for *Yes, I can*. Put a cross [✗] for *No, I can't*. The winner is the first student with a tick in all the boxes.

1 Can you sing?
2 Can you speak three languages?
3 Can you type?
4 Can you dance?
5 Can you do algebra?
6 Can you play the guitar or the piano?
7 Can you swim 50 metres?
8 Can you/your father/your mother drive?
9 Can you write a postcard in English?

d) What can they do?

Maria can play the saxophone. Peter can't dance.
Make sentences about other students in your class.

e) A job interview

Read the advertisement and the letters.
Student A: Interview James (Student B) for the job.
Student B: Interview Tricia (Student A) for the job.

Wanted: International Sales Representative
for a multinational computer company.

The company has got offices in England, France, Japan, Spain, Holland, and Greece.

- Can you drive?
- Can you type?
- How many languages can you speak?
- Can you sell computers?

This is a wonderful job - for the right person.

Write to: Lemon Computers PLC
Bovis Street, Bradford, UK.

---

183 Belsize Road,
London,
NW6 2NJ

Dear Sir or Madam,
My name is James Hammond, and I'm 23 years old. I'm a salesman for a hi-fi company at the moment. I can speak French and Spanish. I've got a driving licence, and I can type. I don't know much about computers, but I can learn.

Personal details	
Name	Tricia Miller
Address	17 Dalglish Avenue, Liverpool.
Age	25
Present job	Advertising Manager, 'Computer World' Magazine
Driving Licence	Yes
Typing	50 words per minute
Languages	French, Italian, German, Swedish

f) Animal abilities

- A kangaroo can jump 13.5 metres.
- A blue whale can hear another blue whale 850 kilometres away.
- A cheetah can run at 100 km/h
- One type of swan (the whooper swan) can fly at 8,000 metres.
- A sperm whale can dive to one kilometre under the sea.
- A peregrine falcon can fly at 386 km/h (in a dive from 1,500 metres).

Unit twenty-one

Unit twenty-two

What time...?

ten o'clock

five past eight

ten past three

a quarter past six

twenty past eleven

THIS WEEK IN CASTERBRIDGE
Cinemas

ODEON
Casterbridge 330225

CINEMA 1
Timothy Walton in
THE RETURN OF 007 (PG)
Doors open 2 p.m.
Performances:
2.25 / 4.35 / 6.25 / 8.35

CINEMA 2
Simon Stallion in
RUMBA 5 (18)
Doors open 2.15 p.m.
Performances:
2.40 / 4.20 / 6.40 / 8.20

CANNON CINEMAS
Casterbridge 330033

CANNON 1
Muriel Street / Ben Shawn in
THE FIRST TIME (15)
Performances daily at:
1.50 / 4.10 / 6.50 / 9.10

CANNON 2
New Children's Cartoon
THE MOUNTAIN OF GIANTS (U)
Children half price
Performances daily at:
1.55 / 3.05 / 4.55 / 6.05 / 7.55

Concerts and Ballet

★ **THE ROYAL HALL, CASTERBRIDGE** ★

Monday 8.30
CLASSICAL CONCERT
Charles Dubois & The Quebec Symphony Orchestra
HOLST: *The Planets*
RAVEL: *Bolero*
MAHLER: *5th Symphony*

Tuesday, Wednesday 9.15
ROCK CONCERT
Bruce Sprucetree & The A-Road Band

Thursday, Friday, Saturday 7.45
BALLET
The Yorkshire Ballet in *Swan Lake*

Sunday 7.30
JAZZ CONCERT
The David Miles Group
(David Miles, Rob Carter, Keith Jarrow, Bruce Billford)

Box Office: Casterbridge 220002

five to four

ten to five

a quarter to twelve

twenty to two

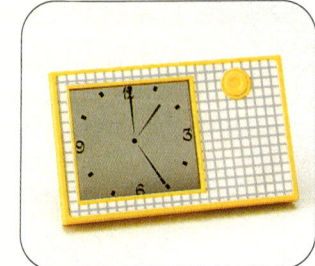

twenty-five past one

half past seven

twenty-five to nine

Teaching points

Time: *half past, a quarter to / past, ten to, twenty past* etc.
What time? (see also Unit 6) / *When?*
Days of the week.
at (*half past ten*) / *on* (*Thursday*)
Position: *at the front / side / back, in the middle, on the left / right.*
Reading for specific information.
Listening for specific information.

Expressions

the first / next / last performance   Can we have (two seats)?
What would you like to see?   Where would you like to sit?

Active vocabulary

ballet / cinema / concert / day / front (place) */ jazz / middle / performance / side / stage / week*

Monday / Tuesday / Wednesday / Thursday / Friday / Saturday / Sunday
classical / last / rock
at (times, place) */ on* days) */ past* (clock) */ to* (clock)
when?

Passive vocabulary

band / box office / cartoon / giant / mountain / price / symphony / daily

Classroom vocabulary

reading

Audio-visual aids

Cassette. A teaching clock with moveable hands would be useful. A set of such clocks would provide paired activity.

Unit twenty-two

Note: Time has been covered in Unit 6, in the form *six thirty / six fifteen / six forty-five* in a timetable situation.

◆ Oral introduction

Optional: Use a clock with moveable hands to teach the time. Go round the clock getting students to repeat chorally and individually. Then set the hands at various times, and ask individuals *What's the time?* This can also be done using your arms to indicate clock positions.

◆ Clock faces

1 Focus attention on the clocks in the Student's Book. Check that the text is covered, go through the clocks as above. If you have no movable clock, write times on the board in the form *6.30* etc.
Ask *What's the time?* to elicit *It's half past six.* etc.

2 Pair work. If you can obtain a number of cardboard clocks with moveable hands (obtainable from educational suppliers specializing in primary materials), issue a clock to each pair. Students ask and answer in pairs. If such clocks are not available, Student A writes *6.45* etc. and asks *What's the time?*; Student B says *It's a quarter to seven*.

3 Check *half past six* v *a quarter to seven*. Note that *It's quarter to seven.* is also possible, though slightly less frequent. (Only if it is relevant in your teaching situation, note that in American English *after* replaces *past*.)

⬧a This Week in Casterbridge

1 Focus attention on 'This Week in Casterbridge' on the left-hand page. Ask the students to look at it silently. As the purpose of the exercise is reading for specific information, you should refuse to explain vocabulary at this stage. They should not read it serially – we never do with this kind of information text.

2 Focus attention on the reading exercise on the right-hand page. This should be done silently by students working alone. They refer back to the text as necessary, scanning for specific information.

3 Check through the answers by asking individuals the questions in the Student's Book. You could explain vocabulary items at this point.

4 Tell students to look back at the 'Cinemas' section. Ask questions about each film:
What time's the first performance? What time's the next performance? What time's the last performance?

5 It is probably not worth explaining the film categories unless students are going to England in the near future, or are in England. If this is the case the categories are:
U – unrestricted, anyone can go; PG – parental guidance – children **can** go, but only with an adult; 12 – you must be over 12; 15 – you must be over 15; 18 – you must be over 18.

6 Focus attention on 'Concerts and Ballet'. Get students to repeat the days of the week, chorally and individually. Ask questions:
What can you see on Monday? etc., to elicit *You can see Charles Dubois on Monday.* etc.

7 Transfer:
Ask questions: *Which film would you like to see? Would you like to see the ballet? What would you like to see?*

Note: The three short conversations (in sections ⬧b, ⬧c, ⬧d) are **not** recorded on the cassette. They are designed for immediate transfer / pair work.

◆ b Cinemas

1 Ask students to look at the conversation. If necessary, they could repeat it chorally after the teacher. Assign pairs. Get the students to act out the conversation in pairs, substituting freely from 'This Week in Casterbridge' on the left-hand page.

2 Choose a student and act out the conversation with him / her.

◆ c Concerts and Ballet

Follow the same procedure as in ◆b Cinemas above. Note Instead of *For which day?*, *Which day for?* is also acceptable.

◆ d The Royal Hall

1 Teach *at the front / back / side, in the middle, on the left / right*. Walk around the room, saying *at the front . . . Repeat, in the middle . . . Repeat*, etc. Then walk to various positions, saying *Where am I?* to elicit *You're at the front.* etc. Point to various students, and say *Where is she? Where is he? Where are they? Where are we?* to elicit *He's at the front. She's at the side. They're on the right. You're in the middle.* **Note:** The left / right confusion can be eased by facing the same way as the class during this exercise.

2 Write up:
AT – the front / the back / the side
IN – the middle
ON – the left / the right
AT the side, ON the left side
Get students to copy it.
Add:
AT – two o'clock.
ON – Wednesday.
Get the students to copy it.

3 Follow the same procedures as in ◆b Cinemas with the conversation, checking that the students refer to the diagram for prices.

◆ e Three conversations

1 Focus attention on the listening exercise. Ask the students to study the multiple-choice answers for a moment.

2 Play the cassette, one dialogue at a time. Students tick the appropriate boxes.

3 Check through the answers by playing the cassette, pausing to confirm / correct the answers. If there are problems with pairs like 14 / 40 and 15 / 50, do a short aural discrimination exercise. They have done this before.
Write:
A – 13, 14, 15, 16, 17, 18, 19
B – 30, 40, 50, 60, 70, 80, 90.
Say: *Thirty*, the students respond *B*. Say *17*, the students respond *A*.

◆ Extension

1 Optional: See notes on Workbook below. Use exercise 4 as a picture dictation to check comprehension of *on the left*, *at the side*, *in the middle*, etc. You could also use pictures, board drawings, or wallcharts to extend practice on this.

2 Authentic extracts from English language newspapers (similar to 'This Week in Casterbridge') could be used for extra paired practice. A different extract could be given to each pair. As the main point is time, the difficulty of the authentic extract should be irrelevant. They are practising seeking specific information, and filtering out redundant material in any case. We have sometimes done this with extracts in five or six different languages in one class, to make the point that you can find the information you need in any language.

3 You could also use things which are happening in the town you are in to give further practice, and to personalize it. Even though the events will not be listed in English, practice on time will still be possible.

◆ Workbook

The Workbook can be done at home. If it is done in class, note that exercise 3 is suitable for paired oral practice, exercise 4 can be done as an oral picture dictation, and that exercise 6 can be expanded into transfer / discussion.

a) This Week in Casterbridge

Look at This Week in Casterbridge, and answer these questions.

1. Which film is at five to two?
2. Which concert is at half past eight, the classical concert or the jazz concert?
3. What time is the rock concert?
4. What can you see on Thursday at The Royal Hall?
5. Which day can you go to a classical concert?
6. When is the first performance of *The Return of 007*?
7. When is the last performance of *The Mountain of Giants*?
8. Which film is Simon Stallion in?
9. What time is the first performance of *Rumba 5*?
10. What time is the next performance of *Rumba 5*?
11. Who is in *The Return of 007*?
12. What's the phone number of The Royal Hall?
13. Who can you see at The Royal Hall on Tuesday and Wednesday?
14. What time is *Swan Lake*?
15. When is the first performance of the Muriel Street film?
16. Where can you see a cartoon film?

b) Cinemas

Look at Cinemas in This Week in Casterbridge.

A *Well, what would you like to see?*
B *What about (Rumba 5)?*
A *OK. When's the (next) performance?*
B *It's at (twenty to seven).*

the first / next / last performance

Make more conversations.

c) Concerts and Ballet

Look at Concerts and Ballet in This Week in Casterbridge.

A *Can I have two tickets for (the Bruce Sprucetree concert), please?*
B *For which day?*
A *(Tuesday), please.*
B *Here you are.*
A *What time is (the concert)?*
B *It's at (a quarter past nine).*

Make more conversations.

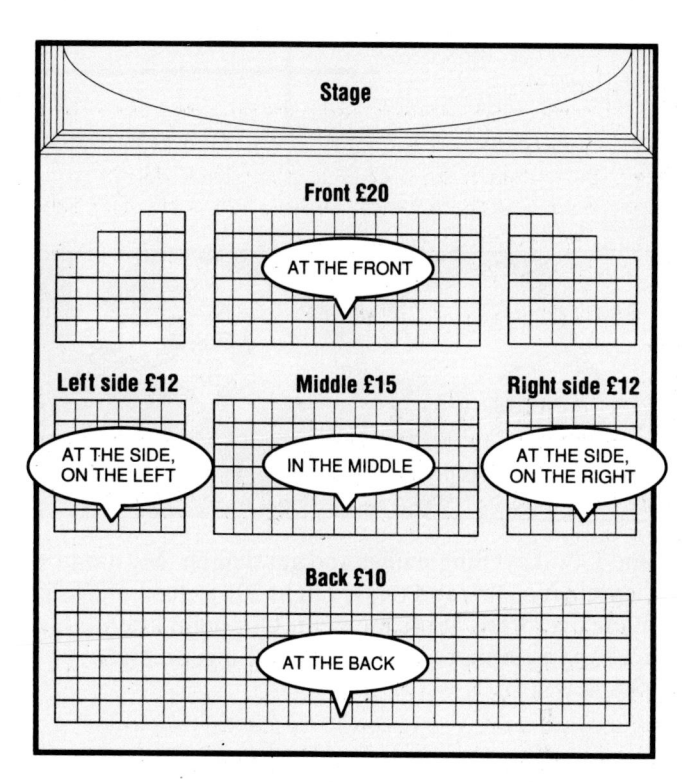

d) The Royal Hall

Look at the plan of The Royal Hall.

A *Have you got any tickets for (Saturday)?*
B *Yes, we have. Where would you like to sit?*
A *Can we have two seats (at the back)?*
B *Yes, that's OK. Here you are . . . (W31 and W32).*
A *Thanks. How much is that?*
B *That's (£20)*
A *And what time is the performance?*
B *(A quarter to eight).*

Make more conversations.

e) Three conversations

Listen to these three conversations.
Put a tick [✓] by the correct answer.

1. a How much are the tickets altogether?
   ☐ £4   ☐ £14   ☐ £40
   b What time's the next performance?
   ☐ 5.20   ☐ 5.40   ☐ 4.40

2. a The tickets are for . . .
   ☐ today   ☐ Thursday   ☐ Tuesday
   b They'd like seats . . .
   ☐ in the middle   ☐ at the side   ☐ at the front
   c The Royal Hall has got seats free . . .
   ☐ at the front   ☐ on the right   ☐ in the middle

3. a The first performance is at . . .
   ☐ 2.05   ☐ 1.55   ☐ 2.55
   b The next performance is at . . .
   ☐ 3.55   ☐ 3.05   ☐ 2.55
   c How much are the tickets each?
   ☐ £3.15   ☐ £350   ☐ £3.50

Unit twenty-two

Unit twenty-three

Flight 201

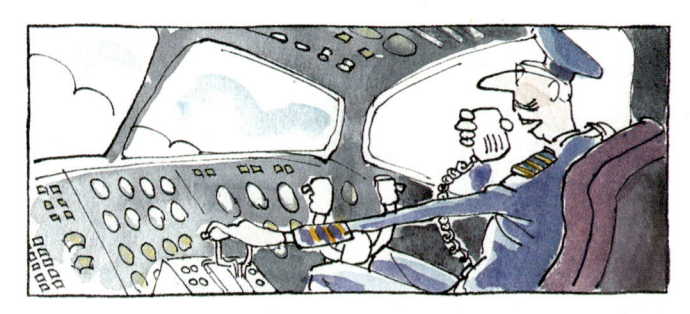

Pilot Good evening, ladies and gentlemen. My name's Captain Yeager, and this is Flight 201 to Rome. We're flying over Paris at the moment. Our flight attendants are serving dinner and drinks. Have a good flight . . . Thank you.

Gina Here's your coffee, Captain.
Pilot Thanks, Gina. Is everything OK?
Gina Oh, yes, sir. The passengers have got their dinners. They're all eating and drinking.
Pilot Good. What's that noise?
Gina I don't know . . .
Pilot Go and look.
Gina Oh! It's an old lady at the front of the plane!
Pilot What's she doing?
Gina Er . . . she's hitting the window, sir . . . with her shoe . . .
Pilot What! Go and stop her!

Gina Excuse me, madam. What are you doing?
Lady It's very hot in here, and I can't open this window. Can you help me, Miss?
Pilot What's wrong, Gina?
Lady Who are you?
Pilot I'm the pilot, madam.
Lady Oh no! Who's flying the plane?
Pilot It's all right, madam. There are two pilots, and it's . . .
Co-pilot Is everything all right?
Lady Who's he?
Co-pilot I'm the co-pilot, madam . . .
Lady But you aren't flying the plane!
Co-pilot No, madam. It's got an automatic pilot!

Teaching points

The present continuous:
I'm / He's / You're reading and *I'm / He's / You're reading (a book).*
I'm not / She isn't / We aren't eating.
Am I / Is he / Are they drinking? What are you doing? / What's she doing?
Spelling: *look / looking*
sit / sitting   serve / serving
Note:
The present continuous form was introduced with *wearing* in Unit 13, and appeared in Unit 16 with *looking for*.

Expressions

at the moment
Have a good flight.
Go and look. Go and stop her.
Is everything OK?
Is everything all right?
What's that noise?

Active vocabulary

attendant / Captain / co-pilot / dinner / flight / moment / noise / passenger
drink / eat / his / serve / sleep / stop
all right / everything / over
(these verbs are in earlier units: *do / fly / listen / look / read / sit / speak / stand / wear*)

Passive vocabulary
automatic

Classroom vocabulary
cold / motor cycle / watch (v)

Audio-visual aids
Cassette. Flash cards illustrating the verbs used may help with practice.

Unit twenty-three

◆ Oral introduction

1 Students were introduced to the present continuous form in Unit 13, with the verb *wearing* and in Unit 16 with *looking for*. Review and check their ability to manipulate the form by asking questions:
What am I wearing? What are you wearing? What's he wearing? What's she wearing? What are they wearing? Is she wearing a dress? Is he wearing a shirt? Who is wearing a red dress?

2 Pair work. Students ask and answer about other members of the class as in .1.

◆ Dialogue: section 1 (Pilot's announcement)

1 Focus attention on the picture, check that the text is covered. Set pre-questions:
What's the flight number?
Where's it going?
Where is the plane now?
Play the cassette. Students write short answers. (*201 / Rome / over Paris.*) Check the answers.

2 Silent reading of the announcement.

3 Questions:
What's the pilot's name? What's the flight number? Is it going to Paris?
Where is it going? Is it over Rome now? Ask 'Where?' Are the flight attendants serving lunch? Ask 'What?'

◆ Dialogue: section 2 (to . . . Go and stop her!)

1 Focus attention on the picture, check that the text is covered. Play the cassette, students listen. Play it again, pausing for selective repetition.

2 Drill:
T: *They*
C: *They're eating.*
Continue: *he / I / she / we / you / the passengers*

3 Drill:
T: *she*
C: *What's she doing?*
Continue: *I / they / he / you / we / the passengers / the old lady*

4 Silent reading of the second section of the dialogue.

5 Questions:
What's Gina's job? Have the passengers got their dinners? What are they doing? Is the old lady at the back of the plane? Is she in the middle of the plane? Ask 'Where?' Is she hitting a flight attendant? Is she hitting the pilot? Ask 'What?' Is she hitting the window with her hand? Ask 'What?'

6 Paired reading of the second section of the dialogue.

◆ Dialogue: section 3 (to the end)

1 Focus attention on the picture, check that the text is covered. Set pre-question: *Who is flying the plane?* Play the cassette, students listen. Check answer. Play it again, pausing for choral and individual repetition.

2 Silent reading of the third section of the dialogue.

3 Questions:
Is it cold on the plane? Is it hot? Is it very hot? Can she open the window? Can Gina help her? Is the pilot flying the plane? How many pilots are there? Is the co-pilot flying the plane? What is flying the plane?

4 Paired reading of sections 3 and 4 of the dialogue. (Student A reads the lady, Student B reads Gina, the pilot, and the co-pilot.)

a What are they doing?

1 Focus attention on the large picture of the plane interior. Explain the activity. Go through the questions, asking individuals, e.g.
T: *There's a man behind her. What's he doing?*
S: *He's reading.*

2 Pair work. Students ask and answer in pairs as in .1.

◆ do – doing

Go through, asking students to repeat after you. Point out the spelling rules:
Doubling final letter: hit – hitting, sit – sitting, put – putting
Deleting final e: serve – serving
Also: dance – dancing, write – writing, drive – driving, type – typing
(All from earlier units in the stem form.) Students may wish to note the extra examples.

b Yes, he is. / No, he isn't.

1 Focus attention on the large picture of the plane interior. Explain the activity. Go through the questions, asking individuals, as in the example. The main point is this sequence:
1 Is he reading?
2 Yes, he is.
3 What is he reading?
4 He's reading a book.

2 Pair work. Students ask and answer in pairs as in .1.

c Traffic jam

Note: This section could be kept fairly close to vocabulary used earlier in the lesson, or it could be used to extend vocabulary with false beginners.

1 There is a variety of activities which can be done with the picture. First go through asking questions to elicit short answers (*Yes, she is. No, she isn't.* etc.) e.g.
T: *Look at the girl on the motor cycle. Is she writing? Is she sleeping? Is she reading?*

2 Go through the pictures, asking:
T: *What are they doing:* S: *They're eating.*
T: *What are they eating?* S: *They're eating hamburgers, I think.*
Students can continue this in pairs.

3 Point at people in the picture, (e.g. the children in the old car).
T: *Are they reading?* S1: *No, they aren't.* T: *Are they sleeping?* S2: *No, they aren't.* T: *Ask 'What?'* S3: *What are they doing?* S4: *They're eating.* T: *And?* S5: *They're drinking.* T: *Ask 'What?'* S6: *What are they drinking?* S7: *They're drinking Pepsi-Cola, I think.*
Students can continue this in pairs.

4 You could ask students to write six sentences about the picture, in class or for homework.

◆ Game

1 This game can be played with the picture, but it would be preferable to use flash cards with pictures of **known** actions (including the verbs from Unit 21 – *dance, type, write, run, read, play the guitar,* etc.)
Show all the flash cards. (With slower classes, they could repeat after you, e.g. *She's running.*) One student comes out and looks at a card. He/she does not show it to the rest of the class. The rest of the class ask **direct** questions until they guess the card, e.g.
Is it a man? Is it a woman? Is she wearing a white skirt? Is she playing tennis?

2 This could also be done as pair work, using earlier pictures in the book.

◆ Mime practice

1 Mime actions. Say, T: *What am I doing?* to elicit:
S1: *You're drinking.* Nod, then gesture, point to imaginary cup / glass. Scratch your head, look puzzled. S2: *You're drinking tea.* Shake your head. S3: *Are you drinking coffee?* Shake your head. S4: *Is it a hot drink?* Shake your head. S5: *It's a cold drink. You're drinking a cold drink.* Nod. S6: *Are you drinking orange juice?* Shake your head. S7: *I know. You're drinking apple juice?* Shake your head. S8: *Is it Pepsi-Cola?* Shake your head. S9: *Are you drinking milk?* Nod, congratulate student.
Obviously, if they guess right too early, change the imaginary drink!
Repeat with *eating / reading / listening to / watching*

2 Get students to come out and do mimes for the class to guess. (This could also be done in groups.)

◆ Workbook

The Workbook can be done at home. The sound exercise, exercise 8, should be explained orally in class.
If it is done in class, exercises 1, 2, 3, and 7 can be done as paired oral practice. However, if the picture sequence in the Student's Book has been done thoroughly it would be a little repetitive to go through exercises 1 and 2 orally.

a) What are they doing?

Look at the picture of the plane.

There's an old lady at the front.
A *What's she doing?*
B *She's hitting the window.*

1 There's a man behind her.
2 There are two women behind him.
3 There's a man behind them.
4 There's a man on the right.
5 There's a woman behind him.
6 There are two people behind her.

Make questions and answers.
Use these words: *stand / drink / listen to / read / sleep / eat.*

do - doing

do - doing	sit - sitting
drink - drinking	eat - eating
speak - speaking	fly - flying
hit - hitting	wear - wearing
stand - standing	serve - serving
sleep - sleeping	read - reading
look - looking	listen - listening

b) Yes, he is./No, he isn't.

Look at a) What are they doing?

There's a man behind the old lady.
A *Is he eating?*
B *No, he isn't.*
A *Is he sleeping?*
B *No, he isn't.*
A *Is he reading?*
B *Yes, he is.*
A *Is he reading a book?*
B *No, he isn't reading a book.*
A *What is he reading?*
B *He's reading a magazine.*

Ask and answer about the other people on the plane.

c) Traffic jam

What are these people doing? Ask and answer.

Unit twenty-three

Unit twenty-four

Comet!

Patrick Good evening. It's midnight, and this is 'World Report' from London. My name's Patrick Shaw. Tonight we're talking about the new comet. People can see it in sixty countries. The huge new comet is travelling through space. It's coming towards the Earth, and it's very near us now. We've got reports from three places.

1 The Sahara Desert

Patrick Our reporter, Jan Lenton, is in the Sahara Desert. Hello Jan. What's happening?
Jan Hello, Patrick. It's one o'clock in the morning here. I'm standing on a hill in the desert. The sky is very clear, and I can see the comet. It's moving across the sky. It's huge and it's very bright. We aren't using television lights, but you can see me. It's amazing!

2 Antarctica

Patrick Mike Worsley is in Antarctica. Hello, Mike. What's happening there? Can you hear me?
Mike Yes, Patrick. We can hear you. Well, we're driving across the ice, and the comet is high in the sky. We can see everything. We're near the sea, but there aren't any penguins on the ice here. They're all swimming in the sea. They're afraid of the comet, I think.

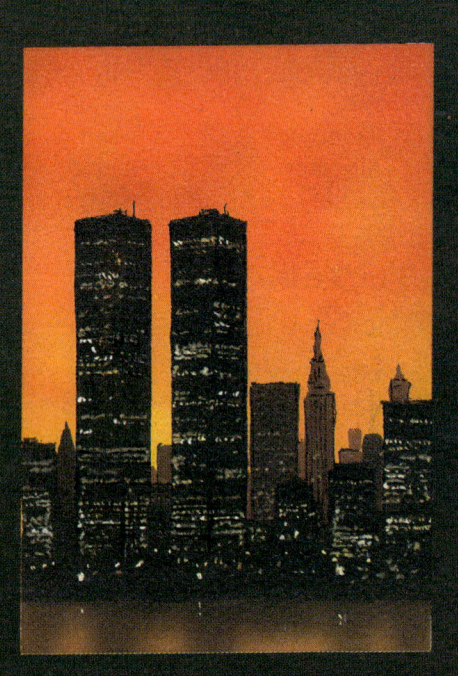

3 New York

Patrick Our last report is from New York City. Hello, New York. What's happening?
Karen Hello, London. This is Karen Buckley from NBC News in New York. It's seven o'clock in the evening here, and there are thousands of people on the streets. They're watching the sky. We can see the comet, and it's fantastic! Some people are taking photographs, some people are singing and dancing in the streets. But many people are afraid. There are thousands of birds in the sky. They're flying away from the city.

Teaching points
Present continuous (continued).
Verbs of movement + prepositions: *moving / travelling / going / coming / driving* + *across / towards / away from / through*
Have: *(I'm) having breakfast / lunch / dinner. What's happening?*
When: *When they're sleeping in England, they're working in Japan.*
When it's 10 a.m. in England, it's 7 p.m. in Japan.
Time: *9 o'clock in the morning / evening. 3 o'clock in the afternoon.*
a.m. / p.m.
Months. Ordinal numbers, 9th–12th. (1st–8th, see Unit 8)
I think (my sister's working). / (My sister's working), I think.

Expressions
It's amazing! / It's fantastic!

Active vocabulary
bird / city / hill / ice / light / month / photograph / place / report / sky / work (n) / world
happen / have / take (photographs) / talk / think / travel / use / work
a.m. / p.m. / midnight / noon / tonight
away / from / near / towards
Time: *ahead of / behind / afraid / amazing / bright / clear / high / huge / January / February / March / April / May / June / July / August / September / October / November / December.*

Passive vocabulary
comet / desert / penguin

Classroom vocabulary
minus / plus

Audio-visual aids
Cassette. **Optional:** A world map would be useful. One with English names for countries would be ideal.

◆ Introduction

1 Check that the text is covered. Play the cassette.
Set pre-questions: *How many countries can people see it in? How many reports have they got?* Play the cassette again. Check the answers.

2 Silent reading of the introduction.

3 Questions:
Is it morning or evening? What's the time? What's his name? Where is he? What is he talking about? Can people see it in 16 countries? Ask *'How many?' What is the comet doing? Is it near the Earth? Is it coming towards the Earth, or is it going away from the Earth? How many reports have they got?*

◆ 1 The Sahara Desert

1 Focus attention on the picture. Check that the text is covered. Play the cassette. Play it again, pausing for choral and individual repetition. Check *What's happening?* carefully. Show that it operates as a formula. e.g. *What's (is) happening? They're (are) watching the comet.*

2 Silent reading.

3 Questions:
What's the reporter's name? Is she in England? Ask *'Where?' Is it one o'clock in the afternoon?* Ask *'What time?' Where is she standing? What's the sky like? What can she see? What's it like? Where is it? Are they using television lights? Can they see her?*

◆ 2 Antarctica

1 Focus attention on the picture. Check that the text is covered. Play the cassette. Play it again, pausing for choral and individual repetition.

2 Silent reading.

3 Questions:
Where is Mike? Can he hear Patrick? What's he doing? Where is the comet? Can they see everything? Are they near the sea? Are there any penguins on the ice? Where are they? What are they doing? Why are they swimming in the sea?

◆ 3 New York

1 Focus attention on the picture. Check that the text is covered. Play the cassette. Play it again, pausing for choral and individual repetition. **Note:** She says *'on the streets'* and *'in the streets'*. Both are possible, correct, and are direct alternatives.

2 Silent reading.

3 Questions:
Is the last report from Washington? Ask *'Where?' Who's speaking from New York? What's her job? Is it seven o'clock in the morning?* Ask *'What time?' Are there any people on the streets?* Ask *'How many people?' Are they watching television?* Ask *'What?' What can they see? What's happening in the streets? Are any people afraid? How many birds are there in the sky? What are they doing?*

4 Play the complete news report through. Students listen.

5 Correct these sentences: e.g.
T: *Patrick's talking about his wife.*
S: *No, he isn't. He's talking about the comet.*
Continue:
People can see it in 160 countries.
It's travelling through London.
It's coming towards Patrick's house.
Jan's standing on Bill in the desert.
The comet's moving across the street.
They are using television lights.
Mike's driving across the desert.
There are some penguins on the ice.
They're all sitting on the sea.
Karen Buckley's a daughter.
There are thousands of animals on the streets.
They're eating apple pie.

Unit twenty-four

Some people are taking money.
Some people are sitting and laughing.
The birds are flying towards the city.

◆ Picture (World Times)

1 A world map is a useful optional visual aid. Focus attention on the picture of the television studio showing time differences (on the right-hand page). Ask students to study it for a moment. Check that they understand the concept. Point out that countries to the west of England have an earlier time, countries to the east have a later time. Point out the examples, and that we say *ahead of* or *behind*. Explain + (plus) and – (minus).

2 Pair work. Students make sentences as in the examples.
How many hours is Athens ahead of London?
It's two hours ahead of London. etc.

a What are they doing?

1 Focus attention on the pictures. Get students to study them for a moment. Check that they are clear on the concept. All these things are happening at exactly the same time. Check *a.m.* (for Latin *ante meridiem*, before noon), *p.m.* (*post meridiem*, after noon).

2 Explain the exercise.
Note: *have breakfast / have lunch / have dinner*. In these examples we cannot use *have got*.
Get students to do it in pairs. Check back with the class. Ask them to describe the pictures in detail.

b When it's 6 a.m. in New York . . .

1 Pair work. Explain the exercise. Students do it in pairs. Check.

2 Get them to try to generate sentences about other towns. A world map could be used to clarify the location of towns, and to remind the students of other towns and countries.

c When they're having breakfast in Rio . . .

1 Pair work. Students ask and answer in pairs.

2 Get them to make sentences about other places. Encourage them to use other verbs where possible.

3 Check back, by getting students to tell you some other sentences. List any new verbs they have used on the board. Check the spelling rule, which they have met in Unit 23:
A *work – working   watch – watching*
B *run – running   swim – swimming*
   hit – hitting   travel – travelling*
C *come – coming   take – taking   use – using*
   have – having   move – moving   drive – driving
   write – writing
(*Where relevant, point out the American spelling, *traveling*. The other examples here still double the consonant in American English.)

d Months

Read through the list of months getting students to repeat chorally after you. Get them to repeat ordinal numbers from *first–twelfth*. (Note: 1st–8th appear in Unit 8.) Note the spellings *fifth*, *twelfth*.

1 Get students to make sentences, e.g.
T: *December?*
S: *December is the twelfth month.*
Continue through the months in random order. (If the class has any difficulty with this, go through in order from 1st–12th.)

2 Pair work. Get students to ask and answer as in the example, *What is the eleventh month? It's November.* etc. Check with a few questions.

e What are they doing now?

1 Go through the examples. Explain that they may replace *mother / friends*, with other examples, such as *Maria, Class 2B, our other teacher, my cousin / uncle / aunt / grandparents, The Queen of England, The President, (a famous person)*, etc. Point out *I think*. Note that it can be placed at either end of the sentence.
I think my sister's playing tennis. My sister's playing tennis, I think.
Point out the comma in the second example.

2 Pair work. Students make sentences in pairs.

◆ Extra practice

Write up this chart on the board:

Midnight	7 a.m.	8 a.m.	9 a.m.	12 noon
sleeping	having breakfast	travelling to work	working	

1 p.m.	5 p.m.	6 p.m.	7 p.m.	7.30 p.m.	11 p.m.
having lunch	working	travelling home	having dinner	watching television	sleeping

Say this is a day in (someone)'s life in England. Point out the time gap between England and the country you are teaching in. (In England, the time gap of the country of one of the students.)
Get students to make sentences, e.g.
When they're having breakfast in England, we're sleeping in Brazil.
When they're working in England, we're watching television in Japan. etc.

◆ Workbook

The Workbook can be done at home. It is worth checking through exercise 1 in class. Exercises 2, 3, and 4 can be done orally in class. Exercise 8 practises simple reference skills. Exercise 9 is designed for reading for gist, and it should be done without vocabulary explanation.

Unit twenty-four

Athens is two hours **ahead of** London. Brazil is four hours **behind** London.

New York, USA. 6 a.m. January 10th

Rio de Janeiro, Brazil. 7 a.m. January 10th

London, England. 11 a.m. January 10th

Nairobi, Kenya. 2 p.m. January 10th

Tokyo, Japan. 8 p.m. January 10th

Sydney, Australia. 10 p.m. January 10th

a What are they doing?

Look at the pictures.
Where is it? What time is it? What are they doing?
Ask and answer.

b When it's 6 a.m. in New York . . .

When it's 6 a.m. in New York, it's 2 p.m. in Nairobi.
1 Make sentences like this about the pictures.
2 Make sentences about other towns.

c When they're having breakfast in Rio . . .

When they're having breakfast in Rio, they're having dinner in Japan.
1 Make sentences like this about the pictures.
2 Make sentences about other towns.

d Months

January	April	July	October
February	May	August	November
March	June	September	December

December is the twelfth month.
1 Make sentences about all the months.

What is the eleventh month?
2 Ask and answer eleven questions like this.

e What are they doing now?

A *What's your mother doing now?*
B *My mother's driving to work. / I think my mother's driving to work.*
A *What are your friends doing now?*
B *My friends are playing tennis. / I think my friends are playing tennis.*
Ask and answer about your family and friends.

Unit twenty-five

K Division Metro Police

Inside

Cobb Well, are you going to take any photographs, or not? Hey, Kennedy! I'm talking to you!
Kennedy Oh, sorry, Sarge. No, it's very quiet. Nothing's happening.
Cobb I'm going to have a sleep. Don't wake me, all right?
Kennedy OK, Sarge.
Voice Hello, Mr Hooper? Are you there? Mr Hooper? It's me, Mrs Harris. Are you all right?

Lady Who are you? What are you doing here? Where's Mr Hooper?
Cobb Er, Mr Hooper isn't here, I'm a friend...
Lady I'm going to phone the police...
Cobb We *are* the police. Look at this, love. Detective Sergeant Cobb, K Division, Metro Police. This is Detective Kennedy. It's all right.
Lady But what are you doing here? What's happening?
Cobb It's police business, love. Don't tell anybody, OK?
Lady Ooh! It's very exciting! I'm Mrs Harris from downstairs. Would you like a cup of tea?
Cobb No, thanks. Goodbye.
Lady Goodbye.
Kennedy She's a nice old lady.
Cobb Yeah. What's happening outside?
Kennedy Nothing. Wait a minute! A car's coming along the street.
Cobb The camera... quick!

a What's happening?

Look at the pictures. Listen to the next part of the story.

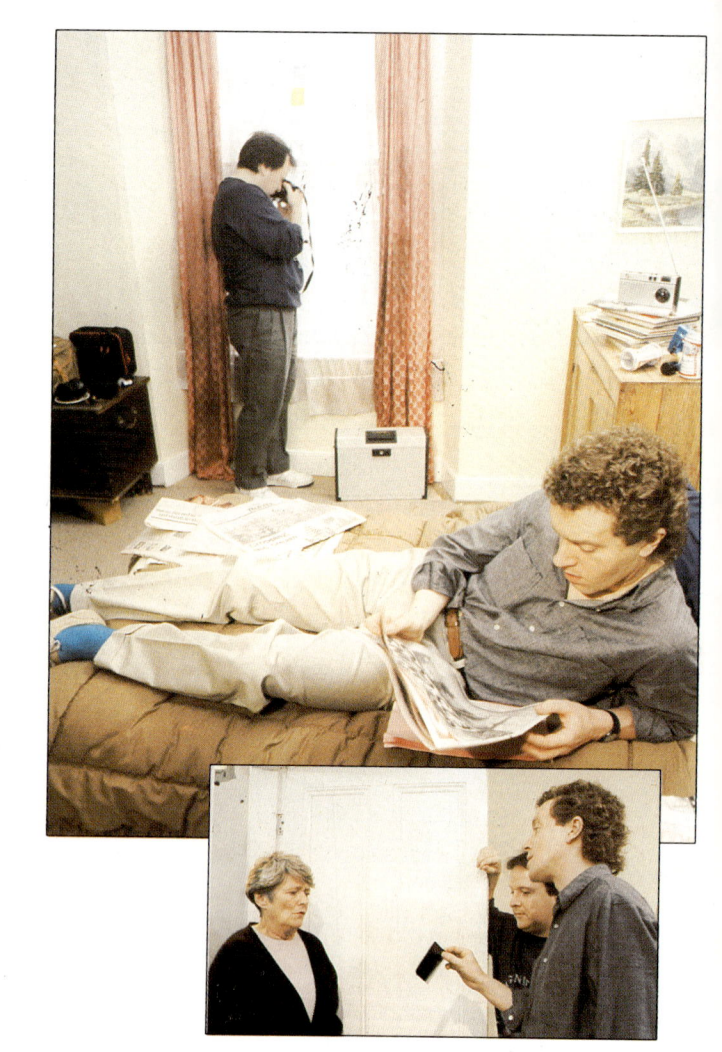

> **Optional video component**
>
> **Teaching points**
> Going to do: future reference. *What are (you) going to do?*
> *(I'm) going to (do it).*
> *(You) aren't going to (do it).*
> *Is (she) going to (do it).*
> Further practice of present continuous.
> *(Are you) going to (do it), or not? Why?*
> *inside / outside / into*
>
> **Expressions**
> *Nothing's happening.*
> *Don't tell anybody.*
> *It's very exciting.*
> *Wait a minute!*
> *Quick! / Hurry! Come on!*
> *How do you do.*
> *I'd like you to meet (my mother). It's nice to see you again.*
>
> **Active vocabulary**
> *gun / robber/robbery / sleep / going / to (do) / phone / rob / start / wake*
> *exciting / nice / quick*
> *anybody / nothing*
> *into / outside*
> *again / Why?*
>
> **Passive vocabulary**
> *business / control / division / sergeant*
>
> **Classroom vocabulary**
> *doorbell / get / into/out of / part / ring (v)*
>
> **Audio-visual aids**
> Cassette. (The listening section for this unit is part of the main dialogue.) **Optional:** video cassette.

Unit twenty-five

Note: The listening section of this lesson, ⟨a⟩ *What's happening?*, forms the middle part of a continuing story, so cannot be missed out.

◆ Oral introduction

1 Say *I'm going to open the door*. Don't move.
T: *Am I opening the door now?* to elicit *No, you aren't.*
Then go and open the door, pausing to ask *Am I opening the door now?* to elicit *Yes, you are.*
Repeat with:
I'm going to close the door. / I'm going to sit down. / I'm going to write on the board.
Get one or two students to come out:
Say *She's going to open the window. / He's going to close the window. / They're going to stand up.* etc.
Go through the sequence above.

2 Drill (**optional**):
T: *I*
C: *I'm going to sit down.*
Continue: *He / We / You / She / They / John*

3 Drill (**optional**):
T: *She*
C: *She isn't going to sit down.*
Continue: *They / We / John / I / He / You*

4 If they've got the point that the manipulation is identical to the present continuous, drills 2 and 3 can be missed. If there are any mechanical difficulties, however, add a short mechanical drill on the question form.
T: *You*
C: *Are you going to sit down?*
Continue: *we / he / they / you / she / John*

◆ Inside

1 Focus attention on the picture, check that the text is covered. Ask students to tell you about the room and the two men.
Say *Who are they?* Get students to make suggestions.

2 Play the cassette down to *The camera . . . quick!*

3 Play the cassette again, pausing for **selective** repetition. Note particularly –
The *going to do* examples. / *It's very quiet, nothing's happening. / Hello, Mr Hooper? / Are you there? Mr Hooper? It's me, Mrs Harris. / We **are** the police. / Don't tell anybody, OK? / What's happening outside?*

4 Silent reading.

5 Questions:
What are their names? What's happening? What's the sergeant going to do? Who's Mr Hooper? Who is the old lady going to phone? Who are Cobb and Kennedy? What's the old lady's name? Is she from upstairs? Ask 'Where?' Would they like a cup of tea? What's happening outside?

⟨a⟩ What's happening?

1 Focus attention on the row of pictures. (The text for this part of the story can be found in the Listening appendix in the Teacher's and Student's Books.) Play the cassette; the students look and listen.

2 Play the cassette again, line by line. Ask questions: *Which picture is it? What's happening? What are they saying? What's going to happen next?*

3 Get students to retell the story using the pictures. This can be done in pairs.

4 Say: *What's going to happen, do you think? What are Craig, Bailey, and Daniels going to do? Why are Cobb and Kennedy watching them? What are Cobb and Kennedy going to do?*
Encourage fairly lengthy speculations.

◆ Outside

1 Focus attention on the picture, check that the text is covered.
Play the cassette, pausing at intervals to ask *What's going to happen next?*

2 Play the cassette again, pausing for **selective** repetition. Note particularly:
I think there's going to be a robbery. / Well, we haven't! / Pleased to meet you. / And I'd like you to meet my mother. / How do you do? / It's nice to see you again.

3 Silent reading.

4 Questions:
What is Craig doing? Is there going to be a robbery today? Have Cobb and Kennedy got guns? Who is Mrs Harris?

5 Paired reading of the Cobb / Kennedy dialogue to *Look! They're over there.*

6 Group role play of the last section of the dialogue.

7 Play the whole unit on the cassette again.

◆ Role play

1 Role play. A formal party. Students work in groups of four – mother, father, daughter, daughter's boyfriend (a drummer in a rock band). They have to make formal introductions. (Workbook, exercise 6 can be used to set this, and / or for written back-up.)

2 This could be extended to a large formal party where everyone has to circulate and make introductions. This is more fun if each student thinks of a persona first (fictional or a famous person). They could be encouraged to mix formal and informal introductions in a humorous way:
Young man: *Hi.*
VIP: *Oh. How do you do?*

⬥b⬥ What are they going to do?

1 Focus attention on the pictures. Show that they are in pairs (1 and 2, 3 and 4, etc.).
Go through the example questions.

2 Pair work. Students ask and answer about the pictures in pairs.

3 Check back by asking the questions to the whole class.

◆ Workbook

The Workbook can be done at home.
If it is used in class, exercises 1, 6, and 7 can be used for paired oral practice.

Outside

Cobb Come on, Kennedy... start the engine... hurry! Tango Delta to Control. Come to the High Street. There's going to be a robbery...

Cobb Where are they? They aren't in the bank...
Kennedy Have they got guns, Sarge?
Cobb I don't know. Why?
Kennedy Well... we haven't!
Cobb Look! They're over there.

Craig Hello! It's Sergeant Cobb. How are you today, Sergeant?
Cobb What are you doing, Craig?
Craig I'm having my lunch, Sergeant. Would you like a chip? Oh, and Sergeant Cobb, these are my friends, Mr Bailey and Mr Daniels.
Daniels Pleased to meet you, Sergeant.
Craig Oh, and I'd like you to meet my mother.
Cobb Your mother?
Craig Yes, she's behind you.
Lady How do you do, Sergeant? It's nice to see you... again.

b What are they going to do?

Look at picture 1.
A *Is he taking a photograph?*
B *No, he isn't.*
A *Is he going to take a photograph?*
B *Yes, he is.*
A *What's he going to do?*
B *He's going to take a photograph.*

Look at picture 2.
A *What's he doing?*
B *He's taking a photograph.*

Make sentences about the pictures.

Unit twenty-five

Stories for pleasure

The secret of the pyramid

Letter:
CENTRAL PRISON, CAIRO, EGYPT
August 4, 1925

Dear Julia,
It's in all of the newspapers. I'm going to be here, in this prison, for thirty years. I'm in prison for the murder of my best friend, Dr Ibrahim. Don't believe the newspapers, Julia. It's not true. I'm not a murderer. Is Dr Ibrahim dead? I don't know.
It's a long story. It begins in April, in my office at the museum...

Professor Dean's office in the Cairo Museum.

— COME IN, DR IBRAHIM. LOOK AT THIS...
— IT'S THE PYRAMID OF KAMUN IV.
— YES. WHAT'S IN THERE?
— NOTHING. IT'S EMPTY. WE KNOW THAT.

— WELL, WE'VE GOT A NEW MACHINE. IT CAN SEE INSIDE THE PYRAMID. DO YOU KNOW THE STORY OF KAMUN IV?
— KAMUN IV? YES. THERE ARE STORIES ABOUT A SECRET. A SECRET IN THE PYRAMID...

The next day. At the pyramid of Kamun IV.

— ALL RIGHT, DR IBRAHIM. TURN ON THE MACHINE. CAN YOU SEE? THERE ARE **TWO** ENTRANCES TO THE PYRAMID! THERE'S THE OLD ONE, THE ONE WE KNOW, AND HERE'S ANOTHER ONE!

May 1925. Twenty men are working on the pyramid.

— PROFESSOR! COME QUICKLY, THERE **IS** ANOTHER ENTRANCE!

— I'M RIGHT! THERE'S A DOOR... AND THERE'S WRITING! CAN YOU TRANSLATE IT, IBRAHIM?
— THAT WRITING IS 4,000 YEARS OLD. DON'T WORRY ABOUT IT.
— IT'S A CURSE. IT SAYS, OPEN THIS DOOR... AND YOU ARE DEAD!

— IT'S LATE. WE CAN'T OPEN TODAY. BUT TOMORROW MORNING... I'M GOING INTO THE PYRAMID!

The next morning.

— WHERE IS EVERYBODY?
— PROFESSOR, WE HAVEN'T GOT ANY WORKERS. THEY'RE AFRAID OF THE OLD CURSE.

— WELL, I'M GOING TO GO IN... ALONE.
— NO, YOU AREN'T. I'M COMING WITH YOU. I'M NOT AFRAID OF AN OLD CURSE.

Teaching points
This material can be used in a number of different ways:

As extensive reading for pleasure
We would recommend using it for extensive reading for pleasure with most classes. It can be done in class or at home. In this case you will not need any Teacher's notes. The material need not be checked or tested in any way.

As extensive listening for pleasure
Where you feel students will benefit from extra listening practice, the story can be used with the recording on cassette.

As reading comprehension material for revision
With classes that need extra revision / consolidation material, the story can be used as comprehension material.

Vocabulary & expressions
As the story is intended for reading / listening for pleasure, the vocabulary is not listed in the index. All extra items in the story are for passive comprehension. The extra items are:
coffin / curse / entrance / ground / machine / matches / mummy (i.e. Egyptian) / murderer / museum / newspaper / prison / pyramid / secret / skeleton / worker
believe / die / murder
empty
best (friend) / (4,000) years old / maybe

Audio-visual aids
Optional: Cassette. The material is recorded and appears between Units 25 and 26.

◆ As extensive reading for pleasure

Reading for pleasure is best done with no pressure or fear of checking or testing. We would suggest that students work alone and read the story with no checking by the teacher. This however would be a good time to point out how to read extensively. Tell students not to stop for difficult words, but to read on to the end of the story. They should mark difficult words with a pencil, and look them up only after completing the whole story. A monolingual (English–English) dictionary would be preferable.

◆ As extensive listening for pleasure

Note: If you have a listening centre, tell students to listen to the cassette, then read the story, then listen and read. There will be no need for the work below.

1 Draw a pyramid on the board. Ask: *What is it? Where are the pyramids?*

2 Play the cassette of Dean's first letter. Ask questions:
Where is he? Is he going to be there for thirteen years or for thirty years? What is he in prison for?
Play the cassette again, students check the answers.

3 Frames 2–5. Set pre-questions: *Where is Professor Dean's office? What can the new machine do?*
Play the cassette with books closed. Check answers.

4 Frames 6–7. Set pre-questions:
How many men are working on the pyramid? How old is the writing?
Play the cassette with books closed. Check answers.

5 Frames 8–10. Explain *curse*. (see .3 below.) Set pre-questions:
Who is afraid of the curse? □ *The workers?*
□ *Professor Dean?* □ *Dr Ibrahim?*
Play the cassette with books closed. Check answers.

6 Frames 11–13 (right-hand page). Set pre-questions:
Where are the two knives? (1 in the skeleton; 2 behind the door)
Play the cassette with books closed. Check answers.

7 Frames 14–22. Set pre-task:
Draw a mummy. Draw a coffin.
Play the cassette with books closed. Check answers.

8 Frame 23, the second letter. Set pre-questions:
Where is the gold now? Where is Dr Ibrahim? (answer: *We don't know.*)
Play the cassette with books closed. Check answers.

9 Students open the books. Play the whole cassette. They listen and read.

10 Silent reading. Check vocabulary.

11 Play the cassette again, books closed.

◆ As reading comprehension material for revision

1 Refer students to page one. Silent reading. Don't check vocabulary.

2 Ask students to tell you the meaning of these words:
pyramid / secret / curse / translate / machine / entrance

3 Vocabulary work:
Is a car a machine? What about a watch? Write down **six** *machines.* Get them to compare their lists in pairs.
Bring a student out. Whisper a 'secret' to them, e.g. *I've got (£50) in my bag / pocket.* Say, *Shhh! Don't tell the class. It's a secret!*
Explain *curse*. Draw a witch on the board. Draw a 'prince'. (Face with a crown.) Point at the prince. Say *The witch is angry with the prince. She's making a curse on him.* Clean off the prince, draw a frog. (or a dog if easier).
Explain *translate*. Ask them to translate these words into their own language:
Hello / Goodbye / Thank you / yes / no / machine / curse / secret.
Ask *Where is the entance to this room? / the school?*

4 Listen and read. Play the cassette for **page one**. Students listen and read. Check roman numerals if necessary: I. II. III. IV. V. VI. VII. VIII. IX. X.

5 Play the cassette again, pausing to ask questions as appropriate:
Frame 1: *What is the year? Where is he? Is he going to be there for thirteen years or for thirty years? What is he in prison for? Who is his best friend?*
Frames 1–4: *Where is his office? Is the pyramid empty? Which pyramid is it? What can the machine do? Is it an old machine or a new machine?*

Stories for pleasure

Frames 5–8: *Are there three entrances? Ask 'How many?' Can the Professor translate the writing? Ask 'Who?' Is it 40,000 years old? Ask 'How old?' When is he going into the pyramid?*

6 Refer students to **page two**. Silent reading. Don't check vocabulary.

7 Ask students to tell you the meaning of these words: *skeleton / coffin / mummy / matches / ground / gold*

8 Vocabulary work:
What's inside an Egyptian coffin? (a mummy). *What's inside an Egyptian mummy?* (a body). *What's inside a body?* (a skeleton).
Ask *Have you got any matches?* (in most schools, of course this would be forbidden, so feign an inquisitorial air!) Mime lighting a match.
Check (with older students) that in English you ask *Have you got a light / any matches?* **Never*** *Have you got 'fire'?*
Ask someone to show you some gold.
Point at the floor. Say *This is the floor.* Point outside the window, indicating the ground, and say *That's the ground.* Ask *Is the ground outside or inside? What about the floor?*

9 Listen and read. Play the cassette for **page two**. Students listen and read.

10 Play the cassette again, pausing to ask questions as appropriate:
Frames 16–22: *Is the secret important? How do they know? Whose is the skeleton? What is the curse on the door? Do they believe it? Do you believe it? Do you believe in curses? Where are the TWO knives?*
Frames 23–29: *What is there in the room? / in the coffin? Where is Dr Ibrahim?*
Frame 30: *Who doesn't believe him? Is Julia going to believe him: What **is** the secret of the pyramid?*

11 Get students to read the story aloud in groups. Get one or two groups to act it out in front of the class.

◆ Workbook

There are no Workbook units for the **Story for pleasure** sections.

Stories for pleasure

The weather

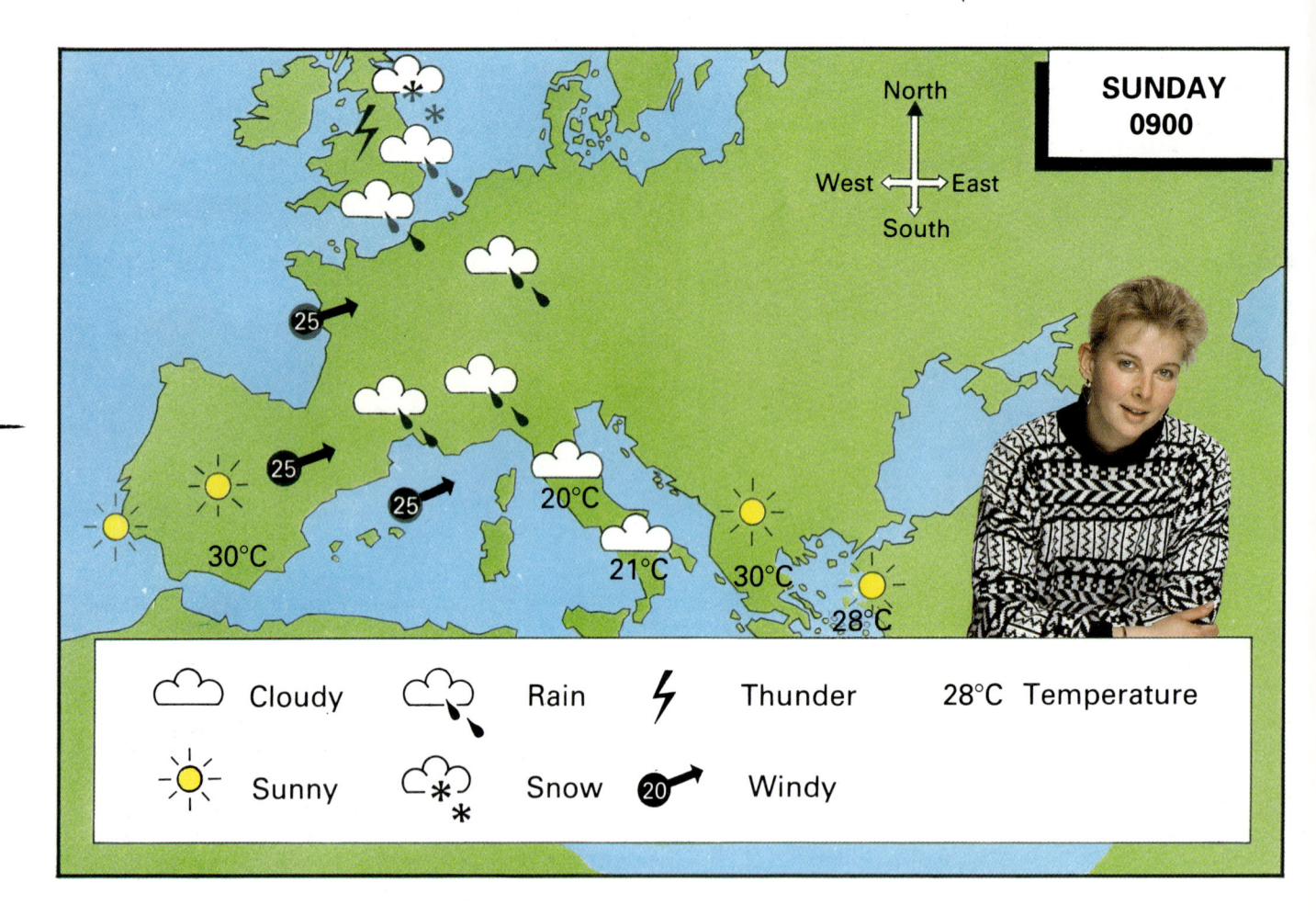

SUNDAY 0900

	Cloudy		Rain	⚡ Thunder	28°C Temperature
	Sunny		Snow	→ Windy	

Good evening. This is Gale Fawcett with the weather forecast for tomorrow. It's Easter Saturday, and a lot of people are going away on holiday. We're going to look at the European weather map for tomorrow morning at 9 o'clock.

First, the bad news. It's raining in Spain at the moment. And the good news? It isn't going to rain tomorrow! It's going to be a hot, sunny day, with temperatures of 30 degrees Celsius.

The rain is going to move into France tonight. Tomorrow is going to be wet and windy in the South of France. In Italy it's going to be a dry day, but cloudy. The temperature there is going to be about 20 or 21 degrees Celsius.

What about Greece? Well, the sun's going to shine there. A very hot day, with temperatures about 30 degrees in Athens, 27 or 28 degrees in the islands.

And Britain? Sorry, but it's going to be a cold, wet day again. It's going to snow in Scotland, and there's going to be thunder in the North of England. Have a nice holiday!

going to future

It	's isn't	going to be	hot / cold. dry / wet. sunny / cloudy. warm / cool.

It	's isn't	going to	rain. snow. thunder.

There's		going to be	rain. snow. thunder.

Unit twenty-six

Teaching points

The weather / 'going to' future (continued).
It's going to be hot / cold / wet / dry / sunny / cloudy / warm / cool.
It's going to rain, snow, thunder.
There's going to be rain / snow / thunder.
Time words:
tomorrow / next week / next month / next year / next summer / next winter
this morning / afternoon / evening
Revision of question words with the 'going to' future.

Expressions

First the bad news . . . / And the good news?
with temperatures of / about . . . Have a nice holiday!
What's the weather like? / going to be like?

Grammar note

1 *A lot of people are going away.* This could be seen as present or future. We don't focus on the present continuous with future reference, and we avoid misleading contrastive work. However, we use the present continuous with future reference from this point.

2 There should be no need to point out that *rain, snow, thunder* in this unit function as both verbs and nouns:
verb: *It's going to snow.*
noun: *There's going to be snow.*
However, it is a possible source of confusion, and can be explained if necessary.

Active vocabulary

Celsius / degree / holiday / Portugal / rain / snow / summer / sun / temperature / thunder / weather / winter / year
go away rain / shine / snow / spend / stay / thunder / watch
cloudy / cold / cool / dry / sunny / warm / wet / windy
tomorrow / next
a lot of / or

Passive vocabulary

Easter / forecast / Yugoslavia

Classroom vocabulary

cloud / weather / forecaster / wind

Audio-visual aids

Cassette. **Optional:** maps of Britain and Europe.

◆ **Weather map**

1 Focus attention on the map of Europe for Sunday at 9 o'clock on the left-hand page. Set pre-question:
She's talking about the weather. Which countries is she talking about?
Encourage students to write the answers in note form, e.g. 'Sp' or 'E' for Spain. (E is the international car identification letter for Spain.)
Check that the text is covered. Play the cassette.

2 Check the answers to the pre-questions.

◆ **Weather forecast – introduction**

1 Focus attention on the map again. Check that the text is covered. Play the cassette for the first paragraph only. Play it again, pausing for selective repetition.

2 Silent reading.

3 Questions:
Is it morning, afternoon, or evening? What's her name? What's her job? (teach: weather forecaster)
Is it Sunday? What day is it? How many people are going on holiday? Ask 'Why?' Which weather map is she going to look at?

◆ **Weather forecast – Spain**

1 Focus attention on the map again. Check that the text is covered. Set pre-question: *What's the weather going to be like in Spain?* Play the cassette for the second paragraph. Ask about the forecast. Play it again, pausing for selective repetition. Check: *There's going to be sun. / It's going to be sunny.*

2 Silent reading.

3 Questions:
What's the bad news? What's the good news? What's the weather like today? What's it going to be like tomorrow? What's the temperature going to be? Is that hot?

◆ **Weather forecast – France & Italy**

1 Focus attention on the map again. Check that the text is covered. Set pre-question: *What's the weather going to be like in France & Italy?* Play the cassette for the third paragraph. Ask them about the weather. Play it again, pausing for selective repetition. Check *cloud / cloudy* and *wind / windy.*

2 Silent reading.

3 Questions:
Is it raining in France now? What's going to happen tonight? Is it going to be dry or wet tomorrow? Is it going to be windy? Is it going to be wet or dry in Italy? Is it going to be cloudy or sunny? Is it going to be warm or cold? What's the temperature going to be?

◆ **Weather forecast – Greece**

1 Focus attention on the map again. Check that the text is covered. Set pre-question: *What's the temperature going to be in Athens?* Play the cassette for the fourth paragraph. Check the answer. Play it again, pausing for choral and individual repetition.

2 Silent reading.

3 Questions:
Tell me about the weather in Greece.

◆ **Weather forecast – Britain**

1 Focus attention on the map again. Check that the text is covered. Say: *What's the weather going to be like in Britain?* Invite suggestions. Write some possibilities on the board in a list: *snow? hot? 30 degrees? windy?* etc.

2 Play the cassette for the last paragraph. Play it again. See how often the things on the cassette match with the list on the board.

3 Silent reading.

4 Correct these sentences: e.g.
T: *It's going to be warm in Britain.*
S: *No, it isn't. It's going to be cold.*
Continue:
It's going to be a dry day in Britain.
It's going to rain in Scotland.
There's going to be thunder in the south of England.
Have a terrible holiday!

◆ **Language summary:** *going to* **future**

1 Ask students to study the language summary silently.

2 Drill:
T: *It isn't going to be hot.*
C: *No, it's going to be cold.*
Continue: *It isn't going to be dry. / It isn't going to be cloudy. / It isn't going to be warm. / It isn't going to be wet. / It isn't going to be cool.*

3 Point out the difference between:
It's going to be wet.
(adjective – there is no need to use the term)
It's going to rain.
(verb – there is no need to use the term)
There's going to be (some) rain.
(noun – there is no need to use the term)
However, if students are aware of grammar, this is a good point to clarify noun, verb, adjective.
After *be* we use an adjective or a noun.
Check adjectives derived from nouns:
sun / sunny   wind / windy   cloud / cloudy

4 Optional: Write three columns on the board labelled **verb**, **noun**, **adjective**. Call out sentences from the weather forecast, get students to tell you what the word describing weather is.

5 Drill:
T: *wet*   C: *It's going to be wet.*
T: *rain*   C: *It's going to rain.*
Continue: *dry / cool / snow / hot / cloudy / thunder / sunny / rain / warm*

a **Monday's weather**

1 Pair work. Refer students to the map. Get them to ask and answer the questions in pairs.
Check back by asking the questions to the class as a whole.

2 Get them to write a weather forecast for one country.

b **Your country**

Pair work. Refer students to the map. Get them to ask and answer the questions in pairs.
Check back by asking the questions to the class as a whole.

c **What are you going to do?**

Ask a few students: *What are you going to do this morning? / this afternoon? / this evening? / tomorrow?* Get them to make sentences.

d **Questionnaire**

1 Explain the activity. Get students to circulate (or work in groups of four). They collect answers from the class.

2 Ask students: *Is he going to watch television? Is she going to listen to music? Is (John) going to stay at home? Is (Maria) going to go out? Is (Juan) going to meet someone?* etc. They answer on the basis of their collected answers.

3 Get students to ask the Wh- questions in pairs. They should note their partners' replies.

4 Ask students about their partners' answers: *Which programme is he / she going to watch?* etc.

5 Pair work. Get students to change partners, and ask about their partner's previous partner as in .1.

◆ **Workbook**

The Workbook can be done at home.
If it is used in class, exercises 2, 5, and 6 can be done in pairs.
Exercise 7 should be explained orally.

MONDAY 1200

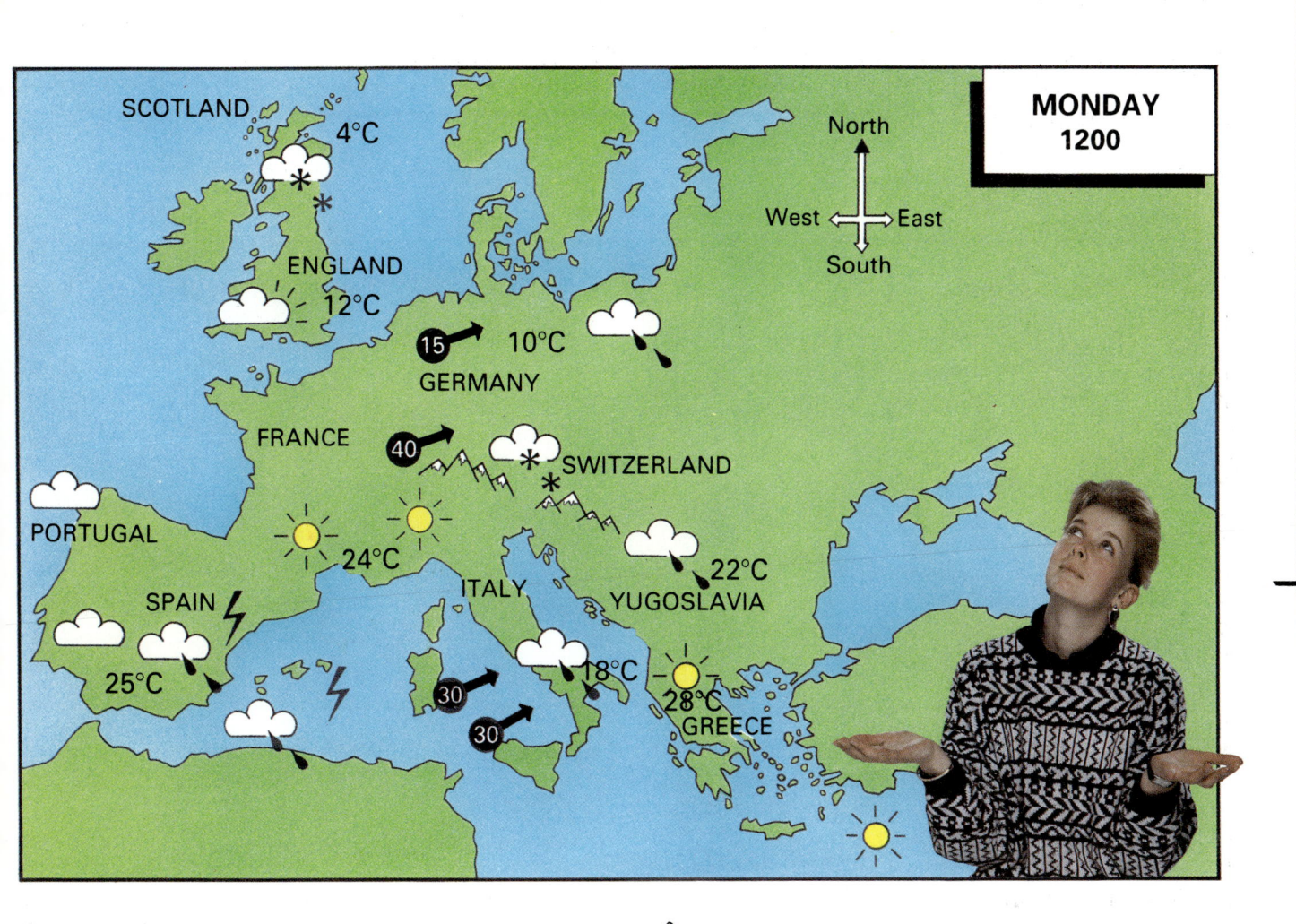

Unit twenty-six

a) Monday's weather

1 Look at the weather map for Monday at 12 o'clock.
What's the weather going to be like in:
France / Spain / Portugal / England / Italy /
Scotland / Greece / Yugoslavia / Germany?
Ask and answer.
2 Write a weather forecast for one country.

b) Your country

What's the weather like today?
What's the weather going to be like | tomorrow?
| next week?
| next month?
| next summer?
| next winter?

Ask and answer.

c) What are you going to do?

What are you going to do | this morning?
| this afternoon?
| this evening?
| tonight?
| tomorrow?

Make sentences.

d) Questionnaire

Are you going to:
☐ stay at home?
☐ watch TV?
☐ listen to music?
☐ go out?
☐ meet someone?

Ask three students.
Put ticks [✓] for yes, and crosses [✗] for no, then ask:

Which programmes are you going to watch?
What are you going to listen to?
Where are you going to go?
When are you going to go there?
What time are you going to come home?
How much money are you going to spend?
How many people are you going to meet / talk to?
Who are you going to meet / talk to?

Unit twenty-seven

She doesn't like interviews

Lisa is a reporter for *Fortnight* magazine. She's interviewing Suzanne Jacklin, the American writer. Suzanne is the author of *Kiss*. The book is a best seller in ten languages, and there is a TV series and a film, too. Her agent, Frank DeVito, is with her.

Lisa Ms Jacklin, is this your first visit to England?
Suzanne Well, er . . . no . . .
Frank No, it isn't. Next question.
Lisa Do you like England?
Suzanne Well, yes, I do . . .
Frank Yes, she does. Next question.
Lisa Do you like English men?
Suzanne Well, er, I . . .
Frank No, she doesn't. No way!
Lisa Ms Jacklin, I like the book *Kiss*, but I don't like the film. Do you like the film?
Suzanne Well, I . . .
Frank She likes it very much. It's a wonderful film, a box office success . . . twenty million dollars in the first week!
Lisa I'm asking her, Mr DeVito.
Frank She doesn't like interviews. I'm answering the questions, OK?
Lisa OK. Does she like the television series of *Kiss*?
Frank Yes, she li . . .
Suzanne DeVito . . .
Frank Yes, Ms Jacklin?
Suzanne Shut up. No, I don't. I don't like the television series, and I don't like the film. That's the end of the interview. Goodbye.

a) Woman of the Week

> **WOMAN OF THE WEEK**
> *Suzanne Jacklin*
> Suzanne is the author of
> **Love in L.A., King, Star, and Kiss**
>
> AGE *37*
> ★
> NATIONALITY *American*
> ★
> FAVOURITE COLOUR *Pink*
> ★
> FAVOURITE SPORT *Swimming*
> ★
> FAVOURITE FOOD *Salad*
> ★
> FAVOURITE DRINK *Champagne*
> ★
> LIKES
> *Old Hollywood films, shopping, reading, cats*
> ★
> DISLIKES
> *New Hollywood films, classical music, dogs, meat*

This is from *Fortnight* magazine.

Make sentences with: *She likes . . . / She doesn't like . . .*

b) Role play

Look at Woman of the Week.
Student A (Lisa): interview Student B (Suzanne Jacklin).

Teaching points
Introduction and manipulation of simple present form (*like*).
Do (you) like swimming?
Yes, (I) do. / No, (I) don't.
Does she like coffee?
Yes, (she) does / No, (she) doesn't.
(I) like coffee. (I) don't like tea.
(He) likes coffee.
(He) doesn't like tea.

Grammar note
1 'I don't know' has been used throughout the course. This unit is confined to the verb 'like', which enables students to concentrate on form. They have met *I'd like* from Unit 19 onwards.
2 Gerunds, e.g. *swimming*, *shopping*, *reading* are introduced, but should not be formally taught.

Expressions
Next question. No way!
A box office success. Shut up!

Active vocabulary
agent / clothes / dollar / film (movie) / hat / million / Ms / music / pop / reading (gerund) / rice / series / shopping (gerund) / story / swimming (gerund) / visit
answer / ask / dislike / does (n't) / interview / like (v) / shut up

Passive vocabulary
author / best seller / bike / champagne / Christmas / fortnight / kiss / no way / soap / opera / soul (music) / success / volleyball

Audio-visual aids
Cassette

Note: Repetition / drill phases (Dialogue .2–.7) are designed for purely mechanical manipulation and should be taken at speed. With false beginners they may be condensed or omitted. In our experience, it is essential for the third person change to be practised mechanically, so that it becomes an automatic response.

◆ **Introductory paragraph**

1 Focus attention on the introductory paragraph. Check that the dialogue below is covered. Get the students to read it silently.

2 Focus attention on the picture. Ask questions: *Which one is Suzanne? What's she like? Which one is Lisa? What's she like? Which one is Frank? What's he like? Where are they?*
What's Lisa's job? Who is she interviewing? What's Suzanne's job? What's Frank's job? Is 'Kiss' a best seller? How many languages can you read it in? Can you see it on television? Can you see it in the cinema? Is Suzanne English? Ask '*What nationality?*'

◆ **Dialogue**

1 Check that the text is covered. Play the cassette. Play it again, pausing for choral and individual repetition. Point out *Ms* – explain that it is useful, as well as being a statement of attitude towards the use of *Miss* and *Mrs*, particularly when replying to letters simply signed *Jane Smith*. (It is said that the origin of *Ms* is a computer efficiency study about mailing lists done by 'Reader's Digest' in the late 1960s.)

2 Say: Repeat!
I like coffee. You like coffee. They like coffee. We like coffee.
*He **likes** coffee. She **likes** coffee. John **likes** coffee. Maria **likes** coffee.*

3 Drill:
T: *I*
C: *I like coffee.*
Continue: *We / She / John / They / You / Maria / He / I*

4 Say: Repeat!
I don't like tea. We don't like tea. They don't like tea. You don't like tea.
*He **doesn't** like tea. She **doesn't** like tea. John **doesn't** like tea.*

5 Drill:
T: *They*
C: *They don't like tea.*
Continue: *He / We / I / Maria / You / She / They / John*

6 Say: Repeat!
Do you like Pepsi-Cola? Do we like Pepsi-Cola? Do I like Pepsi-Cola? Do they like Pepsi-Cola?
***Does** she like Pepsi-Cola? **Does** he like Pepsi-Cola? **Does** Maria like Pepsi-Cola?*

7 Drill:
T: *she*
C: *Does she like Pepsi-Cola?*
Continue: */ I / he / they / Maria / we / John / you*

8 Silent reading of the dialogue.

9 Questions:
*Is this Suzanne's first visit to England? Does she like England? Does she like English men? Does Lisa like the book? Does she like the film? Does Suzanne like interviews? Does she like the television series? Think! Does she like the film? Think! Does she like Frank DeVito? Does she like Lisa? Do **you** like Frank? Do **you** like Suzanne?*

10 Group reading of the dialogue (in threes). Students do this once as a straight reading; then get them to do it again dramatically. Get one or two groups to demonstrate.

⟨a⟩ **Woman of the week**

1 Focus attention on the chart of Suzanne's likes and dislikes from *Fortnight* magazine. Silent reading.

2 Ask questions:
How old is she? Where's she from? What's her favourite colour? / sport? / food? / drink?

Encourage short answers for these questions (Yes, she does. / No, she doesn't.)
Does she like old Hollywood films? new Hollywood films? shopping? reading? classical music? dogs? cats?

3 Pair work. Students ask and answer in pairs as in .2.

4 Students make full affirmative / negative statements about Lisa in pairs: *She likes ... / She doesn't like ...*

b Role play

1 Set up the role play in pairs. Point out that they have the information in the dialogue and the chart to elicit during the interview. Encourage them to act the parts, with Suzanne defensive and aggressive. Point out that they should try and get some new information too. They will have to make this up.

2 Ask the students to pool the new 'information' they have found out about Suzanne.

3 **Optional:** Whole class role play. Act the part of Suzanne yourself, or choose a student to do it. The whole class then becomes a press conference interviewing Suzanne about her likes and dislikes. (An elaborate hat and stole for Suzanne adds to the fun.)

c Likes and dislikes

Focus attention on the large chart 'Likes and dislikes'. Check that the students understand it, particularly the sections on music and TV.

1 Set this as pair work. Make sure that the students check their partner's answers. Make sure that **both** partners have asked questions. If you wish to save time, they could ask about alternate rows on the chart.

2 Put the students with new partners. They are asking and answering about the previous partner's likes and dislikes.

3 Set this as pair work. Make sure that **both** partners have asked questions. If you wish to save time, they could ask about alternate rows on the chart. They need not confine their answers to the examples on the chart.

4 Put the students with new partners. They are asking and answering about the previous partner's likes and dislikes.

5 Get the class to ask you about **your** likes and dislikes in the same way.

6 **Optional:** The results of the questions could be collated on the board as a survey of the class's likes and dislikes. You could then ask: *How many students like swimming? How many like football?* etc.

◆ Written summary

1 Write on the board and get the students to copy:

I	like	swimming.
We	don't like	jazz.
They		football.
You		salad.
He	likes	jeans.
She	doesn't like	pop music.
		tea.
		coffee.

Do you like coffee?   Yes, I do. / No, I don't.
Does he like coffee?   Yes, he does. / No, he doesn't.

This may seem time-consuming, and a similar chart appears in the grammar summaries section, but it is useful with beginners. You could write up the table with the structural words missing and get them to fill them in when they copy.

2 Get students to make true sentences using the written summary.

d The ABC of likes

1 Focus attention on the game. Explain it. Students can make a list on their own, perhaps for homework, or play in groups. If they play in groups they take it in turns to list likes and dislikes, e.g. Student 1 'D', Student 2 'E', Student 3 'F', and so on. Note some playing 'tips' – look at the categories in the example: composers, nationality + noun, makes of (cars etc.), names, colours, colour + noun, animals etc.

2 You may find that students would like to complete the game from A to Z for homework. It's a longer homework than usual, but a motivating one.

◆ Workbook

The Workbook can be done at home. If possible they could send the pen friend letters to a **real** pen friends' organization. If not, they could write to members of a different class in the same school, especially if they are at a similar level.

c Likes and dislikes

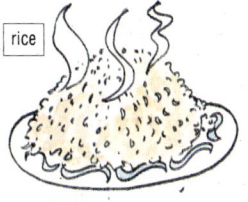

SPORTS: football, tennis, swimming, volleyball

FOOD: steak, salad, chocolate, rice

MUSIC: pop / rock, classical, soul / disco, jazz

CLOTHES: jeans, suits, hats, shirts & ties

T V: soap operas (Dallas etc), animal programmes, police stories, music videos

1 Ask another student questions.
A *Do you like football?*
B *Yes, I do. / No, I don't.*
Put a tick [✓] for yes, and a cross [✗] for no.

2 Work with a different student.
A *Does she like football?*
B *Yes, she does. / No, she doesn't.*
Talk about the answers in **1** above.

3 Work with the same student.
A *Which sports do you like?*
B *I like football and tennis. I don't like swimming.*
Ask and answer.

4 Work with a different student.
A *Which sports does he like?*
B *He likes football and tennis. He doesn't like swimming.*
Talk about the answers in **3** above.

d The ABC of likes

	likes	dislikes
A	apples, Prince Andrew	American food, algebra
B	BMW cars, bikes, blue	brown clothes, Beethoven
C	Christmas, the country	cities, computers, cats
D		

1 Write a list from A to Z.
  (Don't worry about X and Z!)
2 Ask another student about his/her list, and talk about your list.

Unit twenty-seven

Unit twenty-eight

Wants and needs

a) Chris's room

Match things in the picture with the words below.

1. bookcase
2. cupboard
3. waste bin
4. desk
5. light
6. poster
7. shelf
8. plant
9. clock
10. tennis racket
11. mirror
12. carpet
13. curtains
14. wardrobe
15. suitcase
16. bed

Chris is going to college next week. He's tidying his room at home, and his sister, Sally, is helping him. Chris is throwing some things away. He doesn't want them any more, but Sally would like some of his things.

Sally Chris, do you want this poster?
Chris Which one?
Sally This one. The Michael Jackson poster. Do you want it?
Chris No. Put it in the waste bin.
Sally Don't you like Michael Jackson any more?
Chris Oh, yes. I like his music. But I don't want the poster.
Sally Hmm. It's a nice picture.
Chris Would you like it?
Sally OK. Thanks.

Sally What about this plant.
Chris The cactus? No, you can have it.
Sally I don't want it. I don't like it. Anyway, it's dead.
Chris Throw it away, then. Do you want these magazines?
Sally No, thanks.

Sally You've got two bins. Do you need them?
Chris Well...
Sally You only need one. Can I have the blue one?
Chris Yes, all right. I don't need it.

Sally What are these?
Chris Where?
Sally Here. On the bookcase.
Chris Oh, they're my diplomas.
Sally Do you want them? They're very old.
Chris Yes, I do!
Sally Why?
Chris Because... because... Oh, I don't know! I just want them, that's all.

Teaching points
Simple present form with *need*, *want*, *know*.
Negative questions:
Don't you like fish 'n' chips?
(see Unit 13, Expressions – *Don't you know?*)
Would you like (it)? v *Do you like (it)?*
Do you want it? (question) v *Do you want it?* (offer = *Would you like it?*)
because / ..., then. / Anyway ... / any more / just / away / only
Reading for specific information.

Grammar note
One of the most common errors found in non-native speakers is the use of *Do you like...?* in place of *Would you like...?* for offers, and *I like...* in place of *I'd like...* for requests). This unit aims to clarify the difference from the start. Note that *Do you want...?* can function both as a straightforward question and as an offer. This is covered as well. You **may** wish to use the functional terms **offer** and **request** in teaching the difference. We have deliberately not included them on the page for those teachers who prefer to avoid the terminology in the classroom at this point.

Expressions
Throw it away, then. Anyway

Active vocabulary
bed / bookcase / carpet / cupboard / curtains / desk / envelope / floor / ground (floor) / lift / mirror / plant / poster / school / shelf / (tennis) racket / trainers / wardrobe / waste bin
love / need / throw away / want
hungry / thirsty / tidy
any more / anyway / because / just / ..., then. / 'n' (= and)

Passive vocabulary
cactus / CD / college / diploma / earth (= soil) / make-up / store / sunlight

Classroom vocabulary
offer / untidy

Redundant vocabulary
The items in the store guide are redundant.

Audio-visual aids
Cassette

Unit twenty-eight

◆ **Oral introduction: Pair work**

Get students to ask each other about their bedrooms, e.g. *What have you got in your bedroom? Have you got a radio? Have you got any books?* etc. They should find themselves running short of vocabulary. As this happens, bring the activity to a close, and ask them to open their books.

a Chris's room

1 Focus attention on the picture. Ask them to stay in pairs. Ask them to look at the words (1 to 16) below the picture, and to write the numbers on the picture, (**or** find the items in the picture). They can discuss this with their partners.

2 Get them to resume the paired question and answer work (as in the introduction above), this time using the picture to help them.

◆ **Introductory text** (*Chris is going...*)

1 Ask them: *Is your room tidy or untidy?* (Demonstrate with your desk.) *Have you got a lot of old things in your room? Do you want them? Are you going to throw them away?* (Demonstrate.)

2 Silent reading of the introductory text.

3 Questions:
Is Chris going to a new job? Ask 'Where?' What's he doing? Who is helping him? Is Chris throwing things away? Does he want them any more? What would Sally like?

◆ **Dialogue: section 1** (to *OK. Thanks.*)

1 Set pre-questions: *Does Chris want the poster? Does Sally want the poster?* Play the first section of the dialogue. Check the answers. Play it again, pausing for students to repeat chorally and individually. Include these drills in the repetition phrase:

2 Drill:
T: *he*
C: *Does he want it?*
Continue: *you / she / they / Chris / Sally / you*

3 Drill:
Demonstrate the intonation carefully – a friendly offer.
T: *you*
C: *I don't want it. Would you like it?*
Continue: *Sally / they / you / he / your friend*

4 Drill:
T: *Michael Jackson*
C: *Don't you like Michael Jackson any more?*
Continue: *Bruce Springsteen / Madonna / these books / this mirror / that record*
Check *any more / now*

5 Silent reading of the first section of the dialogue.

6 Questions:
Whose poster is it, Chris's or Sally's? What's the picture on the poster? Does Chris like Michael Jackson's music any more? Does Chris want the poster any more? Does Sally like the picture? Does she want the poster? What does Chris say to Sally?

7 Paired reading of the first section of the dialogue.

8 Role play. Refer students to the picture. They role play the first section of the dialogue, substituting other items from the picture. Make sure that 'Sally' is trying to persuade 'Chris' to give her things.

◆ **Dialogue: section 2** (to *No, thanks.*)

1 Check that the text is covered. Set pre-task. *Look at the picture. What are they talking about?*

Point to it. Play the dialogue. Check the answers. Play it again, pausing for students to repeat chorally and individually. Check that *Do you want these magazines?* is an offer, like *Would you like it?* in the first part of the dialogue.

2 Silent reading of the second section of the dialogue.

3 Questions:
Does Chris want the plant? Why not? (Two reasons.) Does Chris want the magazines? What does he say to Sally? Does she want them?

4 Paired reading of the second section of the dialogue.

5 Role play. Refer students to the picture as in section 1.8.

◆ **Dialogue: section 3** (to . . . *I don't need it.*)

1 Check that the text is covered. Set pre-questions: *How many waste bins has he got? Which one does she want?* Play the dialogue. Check the answers.
Play it again, pausing for students to repeat chorally and individually.

2 Silent reading of the third section of the dialogue.

3 Paired reading of the third section of the dialogue.

4 Role play. Refer them to the picture. Ask them to note all the things there are two of. They can then substitute these in a role play of the third part of the dialogue.

◆ **Dialogue: section 4** (to the end.)

1 Check that the text is covered. Set pre-questions: *Why does he want the diplomas?* (Answer: *He doesn't know.*) Play the dialogue. Check the answers. Play it again, pausing for students to repeat chorally and individually.

2 Silent reading of the dialogue.

3 Paired reading of the dialogue.

4 Role play. Refer them to the picture. Ask them to note things that they could substitute for 'diplomas' before starting on the role play.

b **Your room**

1 Check that students understand the activity – and the distinction between *like / need / want* – get them to work alone to compile the lists.

2 Pair work. They ask and answer about each other's lists. Open the activity into a class discussion, where you can check that they understand the distinction.

c **Would you like . . . ? / Do you like . . . ?**

1 At this point, you may wish to explain the teaching point in functional terms. If so, you will have to use the terms **offer** and **request**. You could draw up a chart on the board:

Offer
Would you like some tea?
Do you want some tea?

Request
I'd like that one, please.
I want some tea, please.

Question
Do you like tea?
Do you want that (any more)?

This point is extremely important – see Grammar note above. You could refer to the Workbook exercises at this point in the lesson.

2 Pair work. Refer students to the two conversations. Run through them briefly, then get students to do parallel conversations using the substitutions provided. Check 'n' in *fish 'n' chips*. Get them to repeat: *rock 'n' roll, bread 'n' butter, fish 'n' chips, John 'n' Mary,*

3 Drill (**Optional**):
T: *fish 'n' chips*
C: *Don't you like fish 'n' chips?*
T: *she*
C: *Doesn't she like fish 'n' chips?*
Continue: hamburgers / they / coffee / he / tea / you

◆ **The lift cartoon**

This section is designed for reading for specific information. **Do not explain** vocabulary items. Get students to study the cartoon of the people in the lift. They have to decide which floor the people want by referring to the store guide. They will not be expected to read the store guide from end to end, they should use it as they would a similar guide in the mother tongue – they look for only the information they need.

d **Which floor?**

1 Students work in pairs to decide which floor the people want.

2 Pair work. **Optional:** Students could work co-operatively on the lift cartoon, then go on to ask each other about things in the store, e.g.
S1: *I'm looking for the pens.*
S2: *The pens? They're on the ground floor.*

e **Needs**

This section is designed to promote discussion. Students should try to complete the sentences on their own, then discuss their answers in pairs, groups or as a whole class activity.

◆ **Workbook**

The Workbook can be done at home.
If it is done in class, exercises 2, 3, and 4 are suitable for paired oral practice.

b) Your room

1 Think about your room. Write lists.

(I've got and) I like...	(I've got and) I don't like...	(I've got and) I don't need...	(I haven't got and) I want...
1			
2			
3			

2 Ask another student:
What have you got?
What do you like?
What don't you like?
What don't you need?
What do you want?

c) Would you like...?
Do you like...?

A *Would you like some fish 'n' chips?*
B *No, thanks.*
A *Oh? Don't you like fish 'n' chips?*
B *Yes, I do. But I don't want any now. I'm not hungry.*

A *Do you like Pepsi-Cola?*
B *Yes, I do.*
A *Would you like some now?*
B *No, thanks. I'm not thirsty.*

Make conversations with these words: a hot dog / a hamburger / Pepsi-Cola / chips / coffee / chocolate biscuits / hungry / thirsty.

Speech bubbles in picture:
1. I WANT SOME NEW TRAINERS
2. (person)
3. I LOVE THE NEW MARY QUANT EYE MAKE-UP
4. I'M LOOKING FOR A C.D. OF BEETHOVEN'S 5TH
5. HE NEEDS SOME SCHOOL SHOES
6. WHERE ARE THE CURTAINS?
7. I'D LIKE A NEW SKIRT
8. DESKS...WHICH FLOOR ARE THEY ON?
9. I NEED SOME ENVELOPES
10. WOULD YOU LIKE LUNCH IN THE RESTAURANT? — NO, I'M NOT HUNGRY BUT I'D LIKE A COFFEE

HOUSESTORES PLC STORE GUIDE

Lower Ground Floor	Kitchen equipment ◆ Coffee shop ◆ Hardware ◆ Lighting ◆ Electrical goods ◆ Florist ◆ House plants ◆
Ground Floor	Cosmetics ◆ Stationery ◆ Bookshop ◆ Pharmacy ◆ Confectionery ◆
First Floor	Ladies' fashions ◆ Ladies' shoes ◆ Girls' fashions ◆ Children's clothes ◆ Children's shoes ◆ Babies' clothes ◆ Toys ◆
Second Floor	Sports equipment ◆ Sports clothes ◆ Radio & television ◆ Hi-Fi ◆ Record department ◆ Men's clothes ◆ Men's shoes ◆
Third floor	Furniture ◆ Curtains ◆ Soft furnishings ◆ Fabrics ◆ Bed linen ◆
Fourth floor	Roof-top restaurant ◆ Hairdresser ◆ Toilets ◆ Accounts department ◆

d) Which floor?

Look at the people in the lift. Which floors do they want?

1 __ 2 __ 3 __ 4 __ 5 __ 6 __ 7 __ 8 __ 9 __ 10 __

e) Needs

Plants need sunlight, water, earth.
Complete these sentences:
People need...   Cars need...   Cities need...
Schools need...   Children need...   The world needs...

Unit twenty-eight

Unit twenty-nine

Regular hours?

DO YOU WORK REGULAR HOURS?

There are two kinds of job. Some people work 'regular hours'. In England they work from nine to five, or nine to five thirty every day. In other countries they work in the mornings from eight to one, and in the evenings from five to nine every day. But they always work at the same times every day, for five or six days a week. These are 'regular hours'.

Some people don't work at the same times every day, and they don't work on the same days every week. They work 'irregular hours'. Their lives are very different. They don't see their families every day. They don't get the same money every week.

Here are some examples.

REGULAR HOURS

Tracy lives in London. She works in an office. She begins work at nine every day. She has lunch from twelve thirty to one thirty, and she finishes work at five. She goes out with her friends in the evenings.

Tracy Crabtree

Gurnam lives in Manchester. He works in a factory. He always begins work at eight, and finishes at four thirty. He always works five days a week. He never works on Saturdays and Sundays. He's married, and he's got three children. He sees his family in the evenings every day.

Gurnam Singh

Carmen lives in Spain. She works in a shop. She always begins work at nine o'clock, and works until one thirty. Then she goes home for lunch with her family. She begins work again at five, and works until eight or nine in the evening. She never works on Sundays and Mondays.

Carmen García

IRREGULAR HOURS

Colin works on an oil rig in the North Sea. He works ten hours a day, seven days a week for two weeks. He lives on the oil rig, and sometimes he works twelve or fifteen hours a day. Then he goes home for ten days. Colin lives in Leeds.

Colin Shelton

Shelley is a flight attendant. She lives in Dublin in Ireland, and works for Aer Lingus, the Irish airline. She doesn't come home every night. Sometimes she stays in hotels in European cities. She works for four or five days. Then she has three or four days off.

Shelley O'Connell

George is a famous writer. He lives in New York, and writes detective stories. He writes two books every year. He goes to a hotel, and works eighteen hours a day, seven days a week, for three weeks. He doesn't see anybody. He finishes a book in three weeks. Then he doesn't write for six months.

George Samson

> **Teaching points**
> Present simple for habitual actions.
> with: *live / work / begin / finish / go out / have lunch*
> Frequency adverbs: *always / never / sometimes*
> Time expressions: *every day / every week / month / year / Saturday* etc. *from 9 to 5 / at five in the morning/afternoon/evening / until five / seven hours a day / five days a week / for three weeks/months / on Saturdays / in three weeks*
>
> **Active vocabulary**
> *actor / airline / boxer / director / hours / Ireland / kind (n) / lives (n, pl.) / nurse / officer / president / priest / secretary / teacher / shift*
> *begin / finish / go out / guess / live (v) / European / different / Irish / irregular / regular / same*
>
> *every day / every (week) / until / for (time)*
> *always / never / sometimes*
>
> **Passive vocabulary**
> *oil rig / starting time / workdays*
>
> **Classroom vocabulary**
> *cow / examples / farm / farmer*
> Other words in the listening section are redundant.
>
> **Audio-visual aids**
> Cassette. Note the six texts under Regular hours and Irregular hours are recorded on the cassette. However, you may feel that there is no need to use the cassette to present these texts.

◆ Introductory text

1 Focus attention on the introductory text. Get the students to read it silently. Check that they have understood it, explain the concept of two types of job carefully.

2 Questions:
What are 'regular hours'? What are 'regular hours' in England? What are 'regular hours' in your country? What are 'irregular hours'? Give an example.

◆ Regular hours

Optional: (false beginners only) The class could be divided into three groups. Each group could be assigned a different text. Then students from each group could be put together, and ask about each other's texts.

1 i) Tracy Crabtree. **Either** get the students to read the text silently, **or** play the cassette. (If using the cassette, play it twice. Then get the students to read it silently.)

ii) Questions:
Does Tracy live in Oxford? Ask 'Where?' Does she work in a factory? Ask 'Where?' Does she begin work at ten? Ask 'What time?' When does she have lunch? Ask 'Where?' (Answer: We don't know.) *Does she finish at six? Ask 'What time?' What does she do in the evenings?*

2 i) Gurnam Singh. **Either** get the students to read the text silently, **or** play the cassette. (If using the cassette, play it twice. Then get the students to read it silently.)

ii) Questions:
Where does Gurnam live? Where does he work? What time does he begin work? What time does he finish work? Does he work seven days a week? Does he always work five days a week? Does he always work on Saturdays? When does he work on Sundays? Is he married? Has he got any children? Ask 'How many?' Can he see his family in the evenings?

3 i) Carmen Garcia. **Either** get the students to read the text silently, **or** play the cassette. (If using the cassette, play it twice. Then get the students to read it silently.)

ii) Correct these sentences:
T: *Carmen lives in Italy.*
C: *No, she doesn't. She lives in Spain.*
Continue:
She works in an office.
She begins work at eight o'clock.
She works until ten thirty.
She goes to a restaurant for lunch.
She has lunch with some friends.
She begins work again at two.
She works until five or six in the evening.
She always works on Sundays and Mondays.

◆ Irregular hours

Optional: (false beginners only) The class could be divided into three groups. Each group could be assigned a different text. Then students from each group could be put together, and ask about each other's texts.

1 i) Colin Shelton. **Either** get the students to read the text silently, **or** play the cassette. (If using the cassette play it twice. Then get the students to read it silently.)

ii) Questions:
Where does Colin work? How many hours a day does he work? How many days a week does he work? Does he do this for ten weeks? Does he do this for two weeks? Does he live on the oil rig? Does he sometimes work for twelve hours a day? Does he sometimes work for fifteen hours a day? Does he go home for ten years? Does he go home for ten days? Does he live in London? Ask 'Where?'

2 i) Shelley O'Connell. **Either** get the students to read the text silently, **or** play the cassette. (If using the cassette, play it twice. Then get the students to read it silently.)

ii) Correct these sentences:
Shelley's a pilot.
She lives in England.
She works for British Airways.
She comes home every night.
She stays in night clubs in European cities.
She works for four or five months.
Then she has three or four years off.

3 i) George Samson. **Either** get the students to read the text silently, **or** play the cassette. (If using the cassette, play it twice. Then get the students to read it silently.)
ii) Complete these sentences:
T: *George is a . . .?*
C: *George is a famous writer.*
Continue:
He lives in . . .?
He writes . . .?
He writes two books a . . .?
He goes to . . .?
And works . . .?
for . . .?
He doesn't see . . .?
He finishes a book . . .?
Then . . .?

4 Drill:

T: *She always works on Sunday.*
T: *They*
C: *They always work on Sunday.*
T: *never*
C: *They never work on Sunday.*

Continue:
She
We
sometimes
He
always

a) Whose job?

Get students to discuss which job they would like.

b) Shift work

Go through the text quickly. Check that they understand *shift work*. Discuss whether they would like it or not.

c) Four jobs

1 Explain the activity. Point out that they might get more than one answer. Play the cassette of the first passage. Students do not write at this stage. Show them how to complete the box – ticking the appropriate items in columns 3 and 4.

2 Play the other three passages, this time they complete the chart. If necessary, play all four passages again. Do not exploit the passages intensively.

3 Go through the answers, discussing whether they work regular hours or not. (A pattern of work is the criterion, **not** whether it is a nine-to-five job.)

d) Regular hours?

1 Pair work. Students work in pairs, deciding which of the jobs are regular, and why. (Check *priest, secretary, actor* which have not appeared previously.)

2 Discuss the answers in class.

e) Questions

1 Students ask and answer in pairs. Then ask the questions to the class as a whole.

2 Briefly review the time expressions as listed in the Grammar summaries. Check the position of the three frequency adverbs, *always, never, sometimes*.

3 If necessary, write up for students to copy:
I always have coffee with breakfast.
She never has coffee with breakfast.
He sometimes has coffee with breakfast.

4 Ask questions, to which students reply with one word, *always, never,* or *sometimes*.
Do you have tea / coffee / water with breakfast / lunch / dinner?
Do you watch TV in the evenings? Do you listen to the radio in a car? Do you get up early? Do you get up late on days off? Do you come to this school by car / train / bus etc.?

5 Get them to continue in pairs. Encourage them to make up new questions.

f) Game: Think of a job

This game could take almost a whole lesson, if extra practice is needed. In this case, it should be played in pairs or groups first. Otherwise, get students to play it quickly as a whole class activity.

◆ Workbook

The Workbook can be done as homework.
If it is used in class, exercises 2, 3, and 4 can be done as paired oral practice.

a Whose job?

Look at the jobs on the left.
Whose job would you like? Why?
Which kind of job would you like? A job with regular hours or a job with irregular hours? Why?

b Shift work

Some people work shifts, e.g. police officers, nurses, taxi drivers.
Nurses work in three shifts:
Early shift 6 a.m. – 2 p.m.
Late shift 2 p.m. – 10 p.m.
Night shift 10 p.m. – 6 a.m.
Would you like shift work? Why? / Why not?

c Four jobs

You are going to hear four people. They are talking about their jobs.
Listen and complete the chart.
S M T W T F S = Sunday
Monday
Tuesday
Wednesday
Thursday
Friday
Saturday

Job	Starting time	Workdays tick [✓]	Work on Sundays? tick [✓]			Are they regular hours? [yes/no]
1		S M T W T F S	always	sometimes	never	
2		S M T W T F S	always	sometimes	never	
3		S M T W T F S	always	sometimes	never	
4		S M T W T F S	always	sometimes	never	

d Regular hours?

Do these people work regular hours?
Talk to another student.
 a president
 a rock singer
 a film director
 a pilot
 a waiter
 a nurse
 a teacher
 a writer
 a taxi driver
 an actor
 a secretary
 a boxer
 a doctor
 a reporter
 a priest

e Questions

Ask and answer.
1 What time do you begin work?
2 Do you always finish at the same time?
3 How many hours do you work every day?
4 How many days do you work every week?

Think about someone you know. (Your father, mother, a friend.)
5 What time does he/she begin work?
6 What time does he/she finish?
7 How many hours does he/she work every day?
8 How many days does he/she work every week?

f Game: Think of a job

Every student thinks of a job. One student comes to the front of the class. The class can ask ten questions. The student at the front can answer Yes or No.
1 A *Do you work inside?*
  B *Yes, I do.*
2 A *Do you work in an office?*
  B *No, I don't.*
3 A *Do you always start work at the same time?*
  B *No, I don't.*
4 ...
Can you guess the job in ten questions?

Unit twenty-nine

Unit thirty

A day in the life of Dennis Cook

Dennis Cook lives at 23 Primrose Avenue.

Dennis is 37. He's married. His wife, Tricia, is 34.

Dennis usually wakes up at seven o'clock.

He gets up and goes to the bathroom.

Dennis cleans his teeth, and he shaves.

Then he has a shower.

He goes back to the bedroom, and he puts on his clothes.

Then he goes downstairs, and goes into the kitchen.

He makes a cup of tea.

Then he takes a cup of tea upstairs to Tricia.

They have breakfast. They eat cornflakes, and drink orange juice.

Dennis reads *The Times*, and Tricia listens to the radio.

Dennis leaves the house at 8.15.

He always kisses Tricia.

Then he drives to work.

Unit thirty

> **Optional video component**
>
> **Teaching points**
> Extension of simple present for habitual actions.
> Use of *usually / always* etc.
> *Have breakfast / lunch / dinner / a shower*
>
> **Active vocabulary**
> *case (guitar case) / cornflakes / life / shower / teeth*
> *clean / get out of / kiss / leave / make / put on / shave / wake up*
> *upstairs*
> *usually*
> *then* (time)
>
> **Passive vocabulary**
> *dentist*
>
> **Classroom vocabulary**
> *change* (v)
>
> **Audio-visual aids**
> Cassette. **Optional:** video cassette.

◆ **Pictures 1–6** (to *Then he has a shower.*)

1 Focus attention on the pictures. Show students how to cover the line of text below the pictures, and how to move down to reveal the second set of pictures. Play the cassette. Play the cassette again, pausing for choral and individual repetition. Check *usually* – not **every** day, but 5 or 6 days a week.

2 Drill:
T: *Dennis*
C: *Dennis usually wakes up at 7 o'clock.*
Continue: *They / She / I / We / You / Tricia*

3 Focus attention on the first three pictures. Ask questions:
Whose house is this? Is it number 32 or is it number 23? How old is Dennis? Is he married? Are **you** *married? Is his wife 37?* Ask *'How old?' Does he usually wake up at six?* Ask *'What time?'*

4 Focus attention on pictures 4–6. Ask questions:
Does he get up and go to the kitchen? Ask *'Where?' Does he have a shower first? What does he do first? What does he do then?* (shaves) *What does he do then?* (has a shower)

5 Transfer:
What time do you usually wake up? Ask him / her / me / each other.
Do you usually have a shower? Ask him / her / me / each other.
Do you clean your teeth first? Ask him / her / me / each other.

◆ **Pictures 7–15** (to *Then he drives to work.*)

1 Play the cassette for all nine pictures. Check that the text is covered. Play the cassette again, pausing for choral and individual repetition. Check *always* – every day, seven days a week, 365 days a year.

2 Compare *never, always, usually, sometimes* (see also Unit 29).
He always kisses Tricia – 7 days a week.
He usually kisses Tricia – 5 or 6 days a week.
He sometimes kisses Tricia – 1, 2, 3, or 4 days a week.
He never kisses Tricia – 0 days a week.
Get them to repeat the three examples above.
(With **false beginners**, you may wish to point out that *always* and *never* may be exaggerations in spoken English.)

3 Drill:
T: *usually*
C: *He usually kisses her.*
Continue: *always / sometimes / usually / never / sometimes*

4 Drill:
This is a progressive substitution, and should be set up with care. Give all the examples, then go back and begin again.
T: *He usually kisses her.*
T: *never*
T: *He never kisses her.*
T: *them*
T: *He never kisses them.*
T: *she*
T: *She never kisses them.*
Begin again
He usually kisses her.
Continue: *never / them / she / him / usually / us / sometimes / they / her / we*

5 Silent reading of the text for pictures 9–15.

6 Questions:
Does he put on his clothes in the bathroom? Ask *'Where?' Does he make tea or does he make coffee? Does he make tea in the bedroom?* Ask *'Where?' Does he take the tea downstairs to Tricia? Do they have breakfast in bed?* Ask *'Where?' Do they eat hamburgers?* Ask *'What?' Do they drink whisky?* Ask *'What?' Does Dennis read a book?* Ask *'What?'*
Does Tricia listen to compact discs? Ask *'What?' Does Dennis leave the house at 7.15?* Ask *'When?' Does he kiss Tricia? Does he always kiss Tricia? Does he walk to work or does he drive to work?*

7 Free retelling.
Ask students to close their books. Say: *Tell me about Dennis's morning.* Check that they use *then* to link the actions.

8 Transfer:
Where do you have breakfast? Ask me / him / her. What do you have for breakfast? Ask me / him / her.
Do you have coffee / tea / orange juice with breakfast? Ask me / him / her.
Do you read a newspaper? Do you listen to the radio? Do you watch television? Ask me / him / her.
What time do you leave home? Ask me / him / her.
Do you kiss anybody? Ask me / him / her.

◆ Pictures 16–20 (to ... *at five o'clock*.)

1 Play the cassette for all five pictures. Check that the text is covered. Play the cassette again, pausing for choral and individual repetition.

2 Silent reading of the text for pictures 16–20.

3 Questions:
What is Dennis wearing in picture 16? (teach *suit*). *What is he wearing in picture 18? Why does he change his clothes?* Invite suggestions.
What does Dennis do? (to elicit: *He plays the guitar and sings.*)
Look at picture 18. Is he playing the guitar? What is he doing? When does he usually have lunch?
Look at picture 19.
What does he do in the afternoon? (Check that this elicits *again.*) *How much money does he get?*
Look at picture 20.
What time does he usually stop work? Why is he stopping work today?

4 Transfer:
Get students to tell you about their day at school or work. Check *always* and *usually* by asking *Do you usually do that, or do you always do that?*
If they say *I don't do that*, say *Never?* to elicit, *No, I never do that.*
Also check that they are using *then*.

◆ Pictures 21–25 (to the end.)

1 Play the cassette for all five pictures. Check that the text is covered. Play the cassette again, pausing for choral and individual repetition.

2 Silent reading of the text for pictures 21–25.

3 Correct these sentences:
He comes home at half past twelve.
And kisses the dog.
They usually have dinner at ten o'clock.
In the evening, they play football.
*They **always** go to bed at eleven o'clock ... always, every day.*
Dennis has a very exciting life ...

4 Transfer:
What time do you come home? Ask her / him / me.
When do you usually have dinner? Ask him / me / her.
What do you usually do in the evening? Ask me / her / him.
*Do you **always** do that?*
What time do you usually go to bed? Ask him / her / me.

⟨a⟩ Dennis Cook's day

Pair work. Students ask and answer the questions in pairs.

⟨b⟩ Your day

1 Pair work. Students ask their partners about their typical day, noting the replies.

2 Students then tell their partners about their own typical days.

3 Then they can change pairs, and ask about the other student's previous partner's routine, (**or** you can ask a few students about their partner's responses).

⟨c⟩ Tricia Cook's day

1 Pair work. Students read the notes silently, and then ask and answer about Tricia Cook.

2 Check by asking a few questions to the class.

⟨d⟩ My day

Set this for homework.

◆ Workbook

The Workbook can be done at home.
If it is used in class, exercises 3 and 4 are suitable for paired oral practice.

He gets out of his car, and goes to work.

He opens his case. He plays his guitar.

He usually has lunch at 12.30.

In the afternoon, he plays the guitar again.

He usually stops work at five o'clock.

He comes home at half past five, and kisses Tricia.

They usually have dinner at seven o'clock.

In the evening, they watch television.

And here is the nine o'clock news...

They usually go to bed at eleven o'clock. That's another exciting day in the life of... Dennis Cook.

a Dennis Cook's day

What time does he usually wake up?
What does he do then?
When does he have lunch?
What does he do at work?
What do Dennis and Tricia do in the evening?

Ask another student about Dennis Cook's day.

b Your day

What time do you usually wake up?
What do you do then?
When do you have lunch?
What do you do in the evening?

1 Ask another student about his/her day.
2 Tell him/her about your day.

c Tricia Cook's day

```
 7.00  wake up
 7.45  have breakfast
 8.45  leave home
 9.30  begin work
       (Tricia is a dentist)
 1.00  have lunch
 4.45  finish work
 5.00  drive home
 7.00  have dinner
 7.45  watch television
11.00  go to bed
```

Ask another student about Tricia Cook's day.

d My day

Write about your day.

Unit thirty

Stories for pleasure

The Third Planet

To: Galaxy Central Command, Planet Volkan.
From: Spaceship 40956148
Subject: Solar System, The Third Planet. Report 1.

Spaceship 40956148 is now above the Third Planet in the Solar System. The planet has an area of 510,165,600 square kms. 71% of this is water. There are three types of intelligent life on the planet: 1) *dolphins* 2) *whales* 3) *humans*. Types 1 and 2 are very intelligent, but they live in water. Our people can't live in water. We are going to look at type 3, the humans. My assistant, Space Technician Bizaldo, likes the planet. This is strange. The planet is not beautiful. It is blue and green. I am thinking about my beautiful home on the planet Glom, with its red sky!

Space Commander Zook

To: Galaxy Central Command, Planet Volkan.
From: Spaceship 40956148
Subject: The Third Planet. Report 2. The humans.

The humans are very much like us. They have got two legs, two arms, two eyes etc. But they have only got ten fingers (five on each hand), and they haven't got green hair. They work about eight hours a day. On Glom we work twenty hours a day! (Their day is twenty-four hours, our day is twenty-two hours.) They eat three or four times a day, and sleep for six or eight hours a day. Space Technician Bizaldo thinks they are wonderful. Bizaldo likes eating and sleeping. He sometimes sleeps two or even three hours a day! I am very angry with Bizaldo. Now he wants food three or four times a day, like the humans! Well, he can't have food three times a day. He's a Glommite like me, and we only need one meal a week.

Space Commander Zook

To: Galaxy Central Command, Planet Volkan.
From: Spaceship 40956148
Subject: The Third Planet. Report 3. The humans.

We are now above an island in the north of the Third Planet. There are many different animals on the planet. On this island there is a very important animal, the *dog*. It has got four legs. It lives in houses with the humans! Every day the dogs take the humans out of the houses for a walk. The dogs have got ropes round them, and they pull the humans behind them. The dogs stop and smell trees, and the humans stop too. I think the humans work for the dogs. Space Technician Bizaldo doesn't think I am correct, but he is crazy. The journey home from the Third Planet is only fifteen years in a Glommite spaceship, but Space Technician Bizaldo cannot wait. He wants to go down and walk on the Third Planet! I say, 'Bizaldo, don't be silly! In fifteen more years you can walk on the beautiful orange ground on Glom.' Bizaldo wants to eat food from the Third Planet, too!

Space Commander Zook

Teaching points
This material can be used in a number of different ways:

As extensive reading for pleasure
We would recommend using it for extensive reading for pleasure with most classes. It can be done in class or at home. In this case you will not need any Teacher's notes. The material need not be checked or tested in any way.

As extensive listening for pleasure
Where you feel students will benefit from extra listening practice, the story can be used with the recording on cassette.

As reading comprehension material for revision
With classes that need extra revision / consolidation material, the story can be used as comprehension material.

Vocabulary & expressions
As the story is intended for reading / listening for pleasure, the vocabulary is not listed in the index. All extra items in the story are for passive comprehension. The extra items are:
area / arm / beach / commander / dolphin / finger / fog / galaxy / headache / human / leg / meal / planet / radio-activity / rope / screen / spaceship / stadium / technician / type / whale
square (km) / immediately
call / send / smell
correct / crazy / different / important / intelligent / strange / worried

Audio-visual aids
Optional: Cassette. The material is recorded and appears between Units 30 and 31.

Stories for pleasure

◆ As extensive reading for pleasure

Reading for pleasure is best done with no pressure or fear of checking or testing. We would suggest that students work alone and read the story with no checking by the teacher. This however would be a good time to point out how to read extensively. Tell students not to stop for difficult words, but to read on to the end of the story. They should mark difficult words wih a pencil, and look them up only after completing the whole story.

◆ As extensive listening for pleasure

Note: If you have a listening centre, tell students to listen to the cassette, then read the story, then listen and read. There will be no need for the work below.

1 Play the cassette once with books closed.

2 Report 1. Set pre-questions (write on the board):
Which planet is he talking about? How many types of intelligent life are there on the planet?
Play the cassette again, students check the answers.

3 Refer students to the first report. They listen and read.

4 Silent reading. Check vocabulary. See reading comprehension exploitation below.

5 Play the cassette again, books closed. Give students a chance to discuss the text. Ask (and ask these questions for each report):
What do we know about Zook?
What do we know about Space Technician Bizaldo?

6 Report 2. Set pre-questions (write on the board):
How are Glommites different to humans?
Follow the same procedure, 4–6.

7 Report 3. Set pre-questions (write on the board):
What is the name of the island, do you think?
Follow the same procedure, 4–6.

8 Report 4. Set pre-questions (write on the board):
What are Bizaldo's favourite TV programmes?
Follow the same procedure, 4–6.

9 Report 5. Set pre-questions (write on the board):
Why doesn't Zook like beaches?
Follow the same procedure, 4–6.

10 Report 6. Set pre-questions (write on the board):
Why is Zook going to work on the engines?
Follow the same procedure, 4–6.

11 Report 7. Set pre-questions (write on the board):
Where is Bizaldo? Why?
Follow the same procedure, 4–6.

12 Discussion. Get students to compare life on Glom with life on the Earth. They could be set a written homework, 'A Day on the planet Glom'.

◆ As reading comprehension material for revision

1 **Report one.** Silent reading. Don't check vocabulary.

2 Questions:
What is the name of the third planet? What colour is it? Where is Zook from? What colour is the sky there? What do we know about 1) The Earth, 2) People from Glom.

3 **Report two.** Silent reading.

4 Draw this diagram on the board.

	Earth people	Glommites
Leg		
Arms		
Eyes		
Fingers		
Hair		
Work		
Day		
Eat		

Get students to copy it, and then to complete it by reading the text again.

5 Questions:
What does Space Technician Bizaldo want? Can he have it? Why not?

6 Report three. Silent reading.

7 Questions:
Describe the dogs? What do they do, does Zook think? What do they really do? How many years is the journey to Glom? What does Bizaldo want to do? What colour is the ground on Glom?

8 Report four. Silent reading.

9 Questions:
Why is Zook worried about Bizaldo? Do they laugh on Glom? What are Bizaldo's favourite programmes? Can Mickey Mouse talk? What about Donald Duck? Does Zook understand it? Why not? Who likes Earth music? Why has Zook got a headache?

10 Report five. Silent reading.

11 Correct these sentences:
*The spaceship is over Florida.
They are looking at some dogs.
They're on a seat near the Atlantic Ocean.
They're wearing coats and hats.
They're sitting in the rain.
Zook thinks it's clever.
There is radio and television from suns.
The temperature on the beach is 13°C.
The temperature on Glom is 200°C.
They have wonderful cold baths all the time.
Sometimes there is snow.
Zook wants to go down to the beach.
Bizaldo plays the piano all the time.*

12 Report six. Silent reading.

13 Complete these sentences;
*Bizaldo is very . . .
They are above . . .
There are about . . . down there.
Bizaldo is listening to . . .
He says the big meeting is . . .
The noise . . .
They can see . . .
Some of them have got . . .
Some have pink . . .
Humans do not usually . . .
Zook is going to work . . .
Bizaldo wants to . . .
Zook's headache . . .
He can't . . .*

14 Report seven. Silent reading.

15 Questions:
What is the bad news? Where is Bizaldo? Why? What is Zook going to do? Why?

16 Play the cassette through. Students listen and read. Have a discussion as above.

◆ Workbook

There are no Workbook units for the **Story for pleasure** sections.

To:	Galaxy Central Command, Planet Volkan.
From:	Spaceship 40956148
Subject:	The Third Planet. Report 4. The humans.

I am worried about Space Technician Bizaldo. He watches television programmes from the Third Planet all the time. He thinks they are *funny*. He is watching a television programme now, and he is *laughing*. We never laugh on Glom. His favourite programmes are about two animals, *Mickey Mouse* and *Donald Duck*. In the programmes the mouse and the duck can talk, and they wear clothes. This is silly. There are animals like this on the Third Planet, but they can't talk and they don't wear clothes. I don't understand the programmes. But I don't understand Space Technician Bizaldo. We are recording radio and television programmes from Planet Three. The music is terrible, but Space Technician Bizaldo likes it. He sometimes sings with the music. It is a terrible noise. I have got a headache.

Space Commander Zook

To:	Galaxy Central Command, Planet Volkan.
From:	Spaceship 40956148
Subject:	The Third Planet. Report 5. The humans.

Our spaceship is over another area of the Third Planet. The human name for this area is *California*. Today we are looking at some more humans. They are on a beach near a very big area of water. The humans call it *The Pacific Ocean*. They are sitting on the beach, and they aren't wearing many clothes. They are sitting in the sun. I think this is very silly. We all know about radioactivity from suns. The temperature on the beach is about 30°C. I am thinking about my beautiful Glom, the temperature there is always about 2°C. We have wonderful cold rain all the time, and sometimes on nice days we have fog! Space Technician Bizaldo wants to go down to the beach. He says it is lovely down there! He sings human music all the time now.

Space Commander Zook

To:	Galaxy Central Command, Planet Volkan.
From:	Spaceship 40956148
Subject:	The Third Planet. Report 6. The humans.

Space Technician Bizaldo is very excited today. We are above California again. We are over a big sports stadium. There are about 100,000 humans down there. Bizaldo is listening to a radio programme. He says the big meeting is a *rock concert*. The noise is very bad. We can see the musicians. Some of them have got green hair like us. (Some have pink hair and orange hair too. This is strange. Humans usually do not have green or pink or orange hair.) I am going to work on the spaceship's engines today. Bizaldo wants to listen to the music, and my headache is terrible. I can't stay in the control room with him.

Space Commander Zook

To:	Galaxy Central Command, Planet Volkan.
From:	Spaceship 40956148
Subject:	Space Technician Bizaldo.

I have got very bad news. Space Technician Bizaldo isn't on the spaceship. I am sorry, very sorry. He is on the Third Planet. I can see him on the television screen. He is with the musicians, the ones with green hair. He wants to stay there. I am returning to Glom immediately - alone. The Third Planet is a dangerous place. Don't send any more spaceships here. See you in fifteen years.

Space Commander Zook

Unit thirty-one

The outback

Western Australia is eight times the size of Britain, but it has only one million people. 900,000 of them live in and around the state capital, Perth. The other 100,000 people live in 'the outback', an area of 2,500,000 square kilometres. The area is hot and dry. Temperatures are usually over 30°C in summer, and sometimes over 40°C. It hardly ever rains. Sheep farming is the main occupation, and the farms are called 'sheep stations' in Australia.

Life on a sheep station is very different from life in a town. Houses are sometimes hundreds of kilometres from towns. Some people never go to towns, and never see shops. The sheep stations are very big, and children often ride motor bikes and drive cars.

The children can't go to school, and they hardly ever see a teacher. They have lessons from a two-way radio. It's called 'The School of the Air'. The students can speak to the teacher and other children in the class by radio. They get work by post. The post doesn't come very often, about once a week. Letter-boxes are on the roads, sometimes five or six kilometres from the houses.

There aren't any schools or shops in the outback, but what about doctors? People can talk to doctors by radio, and in an emergency a doctor comes to them by plane. They are called the 'Flying Doctors'.

a) Facts about Western Australia

1 Complete this chart.

Area: _____

Summer temperature: _____

Population of state: _____

Capital: _____

Population of capital area: _____

Population of outback: _____

Main occupation: _____

2 Complete these sentences.
Put *usually, often, sometimes, hardly ever,* or *never* in the spaces.
 1 Children in the outback _____ see a teacher.
 2 They _____ talk to the teacher by radio.
 3 The post _____ comes once a week.
 4 The letter-boxes are _____ five or six kilometres from the houses.
 5 Children _____ drive cars on the sheep stations.
 6 Children _____ drive cars in the towns.
 7 People _____ see a doctor.
 8 Some people _____ go to towns.
 9 The summer temperature is _____ over 30°C.
10 It _____ rains.

Unit thirty-one

Teaching points
Frequency adverbs: (see Units 29 & 30), + *hardly ever / often*.
Word order: *It **usually** rains.* (with 'to be') *It is **usually** wet.*
Questions: *How often do you do it? Do you usually do it?*
It's called (the outback). They're called (Flying Doctors).
by radio / post / telephone
by train / bus / car / on foot
once a week
two or three times a week
Reading: for specific information; talking about new vocabulary items.
Listening: for specific information.

Grammar note
We have been careful to differentiate *often* and *sometimes* from the other freuquency adverbs. Both of them indicate *a number of times* rather than *a percentage of the time*. Many text books over-simplify this leading to mistakes like *I usually go to the cinema*. This would be all right if you added *... on Fridays*. Otherwise, only someone who worked at a cinema would say it.

Expressions
eight times the size of...
It's called...
... very different from ...
What about (doctors)?

Note: The Australian words in the unit are there for interest, and to get students to talk about unfamiliar words. They are redundant, and not indexed. British equivalents, where new, are indexed.

Active vocabulary
emergency / farm / farming / meal / motor bike / occupation / plane / population / post / questionnaire / sheep / snack / state / survey / weekends
Eastern / Northern / Southern / Western / free / main
(to be) called / ride
hardly ever / often / (8) times
around / outside / over (30°C)

Passive vocabulary
area / between / crisps / market research(er) / mosquito / nuts / outback / sex / square (km) / two-way / wild / buy (v)

Redundant vocabulary (Australia)
flying doctor / 'School of the Air' / sheep station
Aussie / brekky / dingo / fish 'n' greasies / mossie / Oz / Pom / Pommie / postie. Note that there is also redundant material in the listening section of the cassette.

Audio-visual aids
Cassette, for listening. The main reading text is not recorded. Take in: a piece of paper, folded in half three times. (See .2 in 'Reading text: The outback' below.)

◆ Reading text: The outback

Note: This text should not be exploited intensively. As long as students can do the exercises given, there will be no need to use detailed comprehension questions.
Optional: With false beginners, you could consider getting students to work in groups of four. One student reads each paragraph, then they work in the group, exchanging information.

1 Books closed. Ask questions: *What do you know about Australia? Where is it? How many people are there? What colour is the flag? Is it a big country or a small country? What language do they speak? What is the capital?* (Canberra) *What's the national airline?* (QANTAS) etc. Explain that they're going to read about one state of Australia, Western Australia.

2 Paragraph 1. Silent reading. Ask them to make three questions beginning *How many people...?* and to answer them. Demonstrate 'twice the size', 'four times the size', 'eight times the size' by unfolding a previously folded piece of paper.

3 Paragraph 2. Silent reading. Ask them to tell you about life on a sheep station. (Free reproduction.)

4 Paragraph 3. Silent reading. Ask them to tell you about schools. (Free reproduction.)

5 Paragraph 4. Silent reading. Ask them to tell you about doctors. (Free reproduction.)

6 Ask them to read the whole text, and to underline these words: *usually, sometimes, often, hardly ever, never*. Ask a few students to give you the sentences the words are in.

◆ a Facts about Western Australia

1 i) Students work alone or in pairs to complete the chart by referring back to the text. As you circulate, check that they are **not** reading the text word by word, but are scanning the text for the specific information required.
ii) Check by asking questions: *What's the area: What's the summer temperature?* etc.

2 Students work alone on the exercise. Then they compare their answers in pairs. Ask a few questions to the class to check. There are alternative possibilities, e.g. apart from 'never' *sometimes* can replace any other frequency adverb. Point this out. For question 2, students may divide equally between *often* and *usually*.

b) What's it called?

Students work alone on the exercise. Then they compare their answers in pairs. Ask the questions to the class to check.

c) Australian words

1 Pair work. Check that the books are closed. Write the Australian words on the board (column 1). Get the students to guess at their meanings. Don't confirm or correct. Then get one student in each pair to open his / her book. The other student will ask *What's 'brekky' called in Britain?* to elicit *It's called breakfast.* They work through the list.

2 They then reverse roles, the second student looks at the book, and the first student asks *What's breakfast called in Australia?* The first student will be working from memory of the list. If it becomes difficult, they can both look at the book.

d) What's this in English?

Pair work. Monolingual groups (e.g. French) should ask *What's (e.g. la porte) called in English?* Multilingual groups can ask *What's a door called in (French)?* Of course, the monolingual group can do it the other way round as well.

e) The weather

The drills are designed to focus on word order. Do them at speed.

1 Drill:
T: *often*
C: *It often rains.*
T: *never*
C: *It never rains.*

Continue:
sometimes
alway
hardly ever
usually

2 Drill:
T: *It*
C: *It's often cold.*
T: *We*
C: *We're often cold.*
T: *sometimes*
C: *We're sometimes cold.*

Continue:
She
always
They
hardly ever
You
often

3 Look at the example sentences. **Optional:** Point out the position of the frequency adverb; before the verb, **except** with the verb 'to be', when it comes after the verb. Ask them to describe the weather in Western Australia, then talk about the weather in other countries as a class discussion. Do not prolong this activity if students have a poor knowledge of climate / geography.
Check *east / eastern   south / southern* [sʌðən] *west / western   north / northern.* Be careful of the pronunciation of *southern*.

◆ Frequency adverb chart

1 Get students to study the chart. (See Grammar note above.) Let students ask you questions.

2 Get each student to think of a true sentence for themselves for each of the frequency adverbs. Ask a few students to give you their examples.

f) Questionnaire

1 Focus attention on the questionnaire. Check *by car / bus / train / bike* but *on foot.* Get students to ask each other in pairs, noting their partner's answers.

2 Get students to change partners. They then ask and answer about the previous partner's replies.

3 Ask a few students the questions, adding *Ask me / him / her.* See the optional project below.

g) Snacks survey

1 Focus attention on the market research form. Explain what students have to do. Note that this listening passage should not be exploited intensively. Play the cassette once. Get students to tick the form on a second listening.

2 Check the answers. While doing this, ask a few students the same questions.
Optional: they could use the form for extra pair work.

◆ Project

1 Refer back to the questionnaire. Students could work to provide a statistical analysis of the answers given, e.g. *15 students usually come to school on foot.* etc.

2 They could also prepare a similar frequency questionnaire with new questions. They could use it within the class, or ideally, they could ask students in a parallel or higher class the questions. Suitable topics might be sport and exercise / entertainment and leisure / methods of travel / buying habits.

◆ Workbook

The Workbook can be done at home.
Exercises 3, 4, 5, and 9 are suitable for pair work.
Note that the reading text on Canada, exercises 7 and 8, is designed for task reading, and that the text deliberately contains items above the level. These should not be explained.

b) What's it called?

Some words are different in Australia.
Answer these questions.
1 What is the 'country outside the towns' called?
2 What are large sheep farms called?
3 What is the radio school called?
4 What are the doctors called?

c) Australian words

A *What's a mosquito called in Australia?*
B *It's called a 'mossie'.*

Ask and answer about the words in the lists.

Australian [Oz]	British English [Pom]
Aussie	Australian
brekky	breakfast
dingo	wild dog
fish 'n' greasies	fish 'n' chips
mossie	mosquito
Oz	Australia
Pom / Pommie	British person
postie	postman / postwoman

d) What's this in English?

What's this (called) in English? / your language?
What are these (called) in English? / your language?

Ask and answer about the names of things in your classroom.

e) The weather

It is <u>usually</u> hot and dry.
It <u>hardly ever</u> rains.
1 Describe the weather in Western Australia.
2 Talk about the weather in:
your country / North Africa / Northern Canada / Southern Europe / Eastern Europe / Britain.
Use these words: *always, usually, often, sometimes, hardly ever, never.*

always	
usually	
often	
sometimes	
hardly ever	
never	

f) Questionnaire

1 Ask another student the questions.
Put a tick [✓] for his/her answers.

Questionnaire

1 Do you usually come to school
☐ by bus? ☐ by train? ☐ by car? ☐ by bike? ☐ on foot? ☐ other?

2 Do you see other students at weekends?
☐ always ☐ usually ☐ often ☐ sometimes ☐ hardly ever ☐ never

3 How often do you listen to records in English?
☐ often ☐ sometimes ☐ hardly ever ☐ never

4 How often do you listen to radio programmes?
☐ often ☐ sometimes ☐ hardly ever ☐ never

5 How often do you speak English outside school?
☐ often ☐ sometimes ☐ hardly ever ☐ never

6 Do you watch television in the evenings?
☐ always ☐ usually ☐ often ☐ sometimes ☐ hardly ever ☐ never

2 Talk to another student about your first partner's answers.

g) Snacks survey

Julie is a market researcher. She does surveys by telephone. She's talking to a man.
This is the survey form. Tick [✓] his answers.

Snacks Survey (for Chockie Bars)
Telephone Surveys plc
Market researcher : Julie Satchi
Call number : 15

Sex ☐ M ☐ F

1 How often do you eat between meals?
☐ often ☐ sometimes ☐ hardly ever ☐ never

2 Do you eat any of these things between meals?
☐ fruit ☐ nuts ☐ crisps ☐ biscuits ☐ chocolate

3 When do you usually have snacks?
☐ mornings ☐ afternoons ☐ evenings ☐ in the night

4 Where do you eat snacks?
☐ at home ☐ at school / the office ☐ in the street
☐ at the cinema

5 How often do you *buy* snacks?
☐ every day ☐ two or three times a week ☐ at weekends
☐ hardly ever

6 Do you know these makes of chocolate?
☐ Nestlé ☐ Suchard ☐ Hershey ☐ Cadbury ☐ Mars
☐ Chockie Bar

7 Would you like a free Chockie Bar? (We can send it by post.)
☐ Yes ☐ No

Unit thirty-one

Unit thirty-two

Tracey's first day

9.00 — OH, MANDY ... THIS IS TRACEY. SHE'S THE NEW TYPIST.
— HI, TRACEY. PLEASED TO MEET YOU.

— 'MORNING, MRS STEELE. IS JACK IN HIS OFFICE?
— NO, MR BURKE. MR NEWBURY ISN'T HERE THIS MORNING.

— OH DEAR. I OWE HIM £20. CAN YOU GIVE IT TO HIM?
— OF COURSE.

— WHO WAS THAT? HE WAS VERY NICE.
— THAT WAS MR BURKE. I DON'T LIKE HIM. HE ...

— HAVEN'T YOU GOT ANY WORK, MANDY?
— SORRY, MRS STEELE.

— HAVE YOU GOT ANY QUESTIONS, TRACEY?
— ER, YES. WHEN'S PAY DAY? I HAVEN'T GOT ANY MONEY AND ... ER ...

May 12 — PAY DAY IS THE 30TH OF THE MONTH.

12.30 — I'M GOING TO LUNCH, TRACEY. PLEASE FINISH THAT LETTER BEFORE LUNCH. SEE YOU AT 1.30.

2.00 — GOOD AFTERNOON, MR NEWBURY. MR BURKE WAS HERE ... I'VE GOT £20 FOR YOU ...

— OH NO! IT WAS IN MY BAG. BUT IT ISN'T THERE NOW!

Teaching points

The past tense of *to be*.
I / He / She / It was / wasn't here.
We / You / They weren't here.
Was I / he / she / it here?
Yes, (it) was. / No, (she) wasn't.
Were we / you / they here?
Yes, (we) were.
No, (you) weren't.
Who was there?
Where were they?
Whose was it? etc.
yesterday
the (30)th of the month   here / there

Expressions

Haven't you got any (work)?   pay day
Are you sure?

Can I borrow your (calculator)?
Poor (Tracey).

Active vocabulary

drawer / pay / typist
borrow / call / give / owe / was / were
before / together / yesterday
empty / poor / sure / of course

Classroom vocabulary

past

Audio-visual aids

Cassette. A few objects – some single (a book), some in pairs (two pens, two knives).

Optional: Points 2 to 6 are important for beginners. With **false beginners** you may wish to skip them. Cover point 1, then go to **Initial listening: pictures 1–10** below.

◆ **Oral introduction**

1 Have a number of objects ready. You will need two of some of the objects (e.g. two pens, two knives).
Put one on the table, ask *Where is it?* to elicit *It's on the table.*
Take it away. Say: *It isn't there now. It was there, but it isn't there now.*
Repeat with two objects. *Where are they?*
Remove them. *They aren't there now. They were there, but they aren't there now.*
Continue with several objects, asking individuals the questions.
Move a student to another place.
Ask *Where is he / she now? Where was he / she?*
Ask the moved student, *Where are you? Where were you?*
Do the same with two students.
Ask *Where are they? Where were they?*
Move to another position.
Ask *Where am I? Where was I?*

2 Choral repetition.
Check the weak, unstressed pronunciation of *was* [wəz] and *were* [wə].
I was there. / He was there. / She was there. / It was there.
We were there. / You were there. / They were there.

3 Repeat .2 with question and negative forms. Check the stressed pronunciation of *was* and *were* with the question form.

4 Drill:
Note: Drills 4, 5, 6 should be taken at speed.
T: *I*
C: *I was there.*
T: *We*
C: *We were there.*
Continue: *She / They / It / You / He / I / John*

5 Drill:
T: *I*
C: *I wasn't there.*
Continue: *You / She / They / He / It / We*

6 Drill:
T: *they*
C: *Were they there?*
Continue: *it / you / he / she / they*

◆ **Initial listening: pictures 1–10**

1 Check that books are closed. Play the cassette for the first half of the story, (frames 1–10, on the left-hand page).
Ask: *Where was the money? Is it there now?*

2 Play the cassette again, pausing for **selective** repetition, both choral and individual. Only repeat key sentences.

◆ **Pictures 1–10**

1 Focus attention on the photo story in the book.
Students read the first row only, silently.

2 Questions:
What's Tracey's job? Is she new? What's Mandy's job? Is Jack in? What's Jack's surname? Who is he, do you think? Does Mr Burke owe him money? How much does he owe him?

3 Focus attention on the photo story in the book.
Students read the second row only, silently.

4 Questions:
Who was the man? What was his name? Does Mandy like him? Is Mrs Steele angry? Why? Has Tracey got any questions? What is her question? When is pay day? What's the day today?

5 Focus attention on the photo story in the book.
Students read the third row only, silently.

6 Questions:
Look at the first picture. *What's the time? Where is Mrs Steele going? When is she going to come back?*
Look at the second picture. *What's the time? Where are they? Who's Mr Newbury? Who was there in the morning? How much has she got for him?*
Look at the last picture. *It isn't in her bag, is it? Was it there?*

7 Play the cassette for pictures 1–10. Students listen and read.

8 Discussion.
Ask questions: *Where is the money, do you think? Who has got it, do you think? Why?*

◆ Initial listening: pictures 11–13

1 Check that books are closed. Play the cassette for the first row of the story, (frames 11–14).

2 Play the cassette again, pausing for **selective** repetition, both choral and individual. Only repeat key sentences.

◆ Pictures 11–13

1 Focus attention on the photo story in the book, the right hand page. Students read the first row only, silently.
2 Questions:
Where was the money? Is she sure? Was she in the office at lunchtime? Ask 'Who?' And Tracey's new, isn't she?

◆ Initial listening: pictures 14–17

1 Check that books are closed. Play the cassette for the next four pictures (frames 14–17).

2 Play the cassette again, pausing for **selective** repetition, both choral and individual. Only repeat key sentences.

◆ Pictures 14–17

1 Focus attention on the photo story in the book, the right hand page. Students read frames 14–17 only, silently.

2 Questions:
Were Mandy and Tracey in the office from 12.30 to 1.30? Where were they? Were they together? Was the office empty?

◆ Initial listening: pictures 18–20

1 Check that books are closed. Play the cassette for the last three pictures (frames 18–20).

2 Play the cassette again, pausing for **selective** repetition, both choral and individual. Only repeat key sentences.

◆ Pictures 18–20

1 Focus attention on the photo story in the book, the right-hand page. Students read the last three pictures only, silently.

2 Questions:
What was in Tracey's bag? What's Mr Newbury going to do? Look at 'Later' (Point to frame 19, with the caption *Later*.).
What does Mandy want? Where is the calculator? What is in the drawer? Where is Tracey now, do you think?

3 Play the cassette for pictures 11–20. Students listen and read.
Say: *What do you think about Mrs Steele? Was she right or wrong? Was Mr Newbury right?* Invite student's opinions.

◆ The past of *be*

Focus the student's attention on the language summary. Go through it. You could put the summary from Grammar summaries on the board for them to copy.

ⓐ Questions

Pair work. Students ask and answer in pairs. Check back.

ⓑ Yesterday

1 Check *yesterday*. *We're at school today – (Tuesday). We were(n't) here yesterday – (Monday).*
Go through the example with the class as a whole. Then students ask and answer in pairs.

2 Students change partners, and ask and answer about their previous partners.

◆ Games

1 There are two games which could be played here. 'Hide and seek' – one student leaves the room. An object is hidden. The student comes back and asks questions. *Is it over here? Was I near it before?* The other students shout *hot* (= near), *warm*, *cool*, or *cold* (*far*).

2 The other game is 'Kim's Game'. Take a tray of objects (singular and plural) into the room. Students study it for 30 seconds. Remove or cover the tray. Students try to remember what was on it. *Was there a pen? Were there any books?* etc. (See Unit 10 for similar ideas done in the present.)

◆ Workbook

The Workbook can be done at home.
If it is done in class, exercises 1, 2, 3, and 9 are suitable for paired oral practice.

The past of *be*

was is the past of *is* and *am*.
Where was it? It wasn't here. / It was there.
Was it in the bag? Yes, it was. / No, it wasn't.
were is the past of *are*.
Where were they? They weren't in the office.
  They were at lunch.
Were they in the restaurant? Yes, they were.
  No, they weren't.

a) Questions

Ask and answer.
1 Where was Mrs Steele / Mandy / Tracey / Mr Newbury at 9 o'clock?
2 Where were they at lunch-time?
3 Where were they at 2 o'clock?
4 Whose money was in Tracey's bag?
5 Where was Mr Newbury's money?

b) Yesterday

1 Talk about yesterday.
  Where were you yesterday?
  Where were you in the
    morning / afternoon / evening?
  Where were you at
    8 o'clock / 11.30 / lunch-time / 3 o'clock /
    6 o'clock / 10 o'clock / midnight?
  Who was with you?

Ask another student.

2 Work with a different student.
  Where was he/she yesterday?
  Where was he/she in the
    morning / afternoon / evening?
  Who was with him/her?

Ask about this student's first partner.

Unit thirty-three

Beware of pickpockets!

Inspector Franklin works for the Metropolitan Police at London's Heathrow Airport. He's talking to his police officers now.

Inspector OK. This man's name is Brian Smith. This is an Identikit picture of him. Remember his face. He's a pickpocket. He always works at airports and seaports. He steals money, credit cards, and passports from travellers. People are usually careful at airports, but in the departure lounges they're sometimes careless. They think they're OK. Now, we've got some police reports about Mr Smith.

Listen. Yesterday morning he was in Aberdeen. There were six robberies at the airport. He was at Heathrow at nine o'clock. There were five robberies. At lunch-time he was in Paris ... five robberies again. Then at two o'clock he was at a railway station in Paris. There were seven robberies.

There were four robberies at the Hovercraft port in Boulogne just before five o'clock French time, one at Dover at five o'clock English time – and two robberies at Victoria Station in London at seven. Last night there were more robberies here at Heathrow. He was on the last flight to Manchester last night.

Policeman But sir, it's impossible! In one day he was in seven places!

Inspector It's *not* impossible. Look at the timetables!

Policeman What was he wearing yesterday?

Inspector He was wearing a long coat, and a hat. He was also wearing glasses yesterday. Last week he was in Amsterdam, and he wasn't wearing glasses then. His hair was short and blond yesterday. But last week it was brown, and last month it was long and black. Last year it was grey.

Policeman It's going to be impossible, sir.

Inspector Not impossible ... but it *is* going to be difficult!

Teaching points
There was . . . / There were . . .
He was wearing (a beard). / They were wearing (hats). / What was (she) wearing?
last night / week / month / year
Extracting specific information from timetables.

Grammar note
This unit introduces some past continuous examples, but the use is restricted to *wearing*. From this point the past continuous can be understood, though we would not expect students to generate other examples. See also Unit 13, the introduction of present continuous with *wearing*.

Expressions
Beware of (pickpockets).
Remember (his face).
It's impossible. / It's not impossible.

Active vocabulary
beware / remember / steal
coat / face / Inspector / officer / passport / pickpocket / port /
timetable
traveller
careless / difficult / impossible
last month / night / week / year

Passive vocabulary
credit card / crossing / Departure Lounge / Hovercraft / Identikit / operation / period / seaport
arrive / depart / shown
local

Classroom vocabulary
scar / sideburns
round / square

Audio-visual aids
Cassette. A wallchart or large picture would be useful for the game. Any scene containing a number of things which the students know the vocabulary for would be suitable. Some authentic timetables could be used to extend the reading for specific information activity.

Unit thirty-three

Optional: With **false beginners** you may wish to skip drills 3–5 in dialogue: section 4. In any case they should be done at speed.

◆ **Introductory paragraph and dialogue: section 1**
(From the beginning to . . . *we've got some police reports about Mr Smith.*)

1 Focus attention on the picture. Check that the text is covered. Set pre-questions *What does Brian Smith steal?* Play the cassette. Check the answer. Play it again pausing for selective repetition, chorally and individually.

2 Silent reading of the introduction and dialogue: section 1.

3 Questions:
Where does Inspector Franklin work? Is he talking to his girlfriend? Ask 'Who?' Who is he talking about? What does Brian Smith do? Where does he work? What does he steal? Who does he steal from? Where are people usually careful? Are they careful in departure lounges? Why? Who are the police reports about?

◆ **Dialogue: section 2**
(From *Listen to . . .* to . . . *There were seven robberies.*)

1 Focus attention on the picture. Check that the text is covered. Set pre-questions: *What time was he at Heathrow? What time was he in Paris?* Play the cassette. Check the answers to the pre-questions. Play it again, pausing for selective repetition, chorally and individually.

2 Silent reading of dialogue: section 2.

3 Drill:
T: *a robbery . . . the airport*
C: *There was a robbery at the airport.*
Continue: *seven robberies . . . the station / a robbery . . . the supermarket / four robberies . . . the bus station / a robbery . . . the restaurant*

4 Questions:
Where was he yesterday morning? Were there three robberies? Ask 'How many?' When was he at Heathrow? How many robberies were there? Where was he at lunchtime? Ask 'How many?' When was he at the railway station? Ask 'How many?'

◆ **Dialogue: section 3**
(From *There were four robberies . . .* to . . . *Look at the timetables.*)

1 Focus attention on the picture. Check that the text is covered. Set pre-question. Write up:
Boulogne _____ Dover _____ Victoria Station _____ Heathrow _____
Tell them that they will have to fill in the times. Play the cassette. Check the answers. Play it again pausing for selective repetition, chorally and individually.

2 Ask them if they can explain why he was in Boulogne and Dover at 5 o'clock. They are about 28 miles apart by sea! Then check *English time*. For most of the year, Britain is one hour behind France, i.e. 5 o'clock English time is 6 o'clock French time. Therefore he was at Dover at 5 o'clock English time, which was 6 o'clock French time. Refer to Unit 24 *Comet* for further information on time zones.

3 Silent reading of dialogue: section 3.

4 Questions:
How many robberies were there at the Hovercraft port? When was that? Was there a robbery at Dover? When was that? How many robberies were there at Victoria Station? When was that? Were there any robberies at Heathrow? When was that? Which flight was he on last night? How many places was he in yesterday? Is it impossible?

Unit thirty-three

◆ **Dialogue: section 4**
(From *What was he wearing yesterday?* ... to the end.)

1 Focus attention on the picture. Check that the text is covered. Play the cassette. Play it again, pausing for selective repetition, chorally and individually.

2 Silent reading of dialogue: section 4.

3 Drill:
T: *He*
C: *He was wearing a coat.*
T: *They*
C: *They were wearing coats.*
Continue: *She / We / I / You / Brian / They*

4 Drill:
T: *I*
C: *I wasn't wearing glasses.*
T: *We*
C: *We weren't wearing glasses.*
Continue: *He / You / They / She / Maria / Charles and Diana*

5 Drill:
T: *this week*
C: *last week*
Continue: *this year / today / this month / this Sunday / this Saturday*

6 Correct these sentences:
He was wearing a short coat.
He wasn't wearing a hat.
He wasn't wearing glasses.
Last year he was in Amsterdam.
He was wearing trousers then.
His hair was long and black yesterday.
Last week it wasn't brown.
Last month it was short and green.
Last year it was blue.
It's going to be impossible.

◆ **Dialogue: sections 1–4**

Play the cassette for dialogue: sections 1–4 again. Students listen and read.

a) Timetables

1 Give the students time to look at the timetables on their own. Don't explain any redundant vocabulary items. Then put them into pairs to work out which flights etc. he was on. Check back with the class as a whole. Draw up a timetable of Smith's movements on the board.

2 Practice could be extended with authentic timetables if you have some available. You could get students to work out itineraries, eg how to get from London to Paris in the quickest / cheapest way. Timetable exercises are easy, even with authentic material. The purpose is to motivate students by making them aware that they could cope in a real situation.

3 Pair work. Explain the activity in the Student's Book. Students work in pairs. Check back with the class.

b) Identikit

Pair work. Focus attention on the three pictures, and the information below them. Get students to ask and answer about the pictures in pairs. Check back briefly with the class.

c) What was he wearing?

1 Pair work. Each student makes a list (based on their imagination). They ask and answer in pairs to discover the contents of each other's lists.

2 They repeat the activity for last month and last year, creating different lists.

d) Two other pickpockets

Explain the activity. Students use the timetables to make up more sentences.

◆ **Transfer**

Ask a few students: *What were you wearing yesterday? / on Sunday?*
Ask me / him / her / each other. When a few students have told you what they were wearing, see if the others can remember: *What was Maria wearing? Was Paul wearing that tie? Was she wearing a skirt?* etc.

◆ **Game**

1 You will need a large wallchart, containing a series of things which they know the vocabulary for. You can show the wallchart to the class for one minute, then put it away. Each student then writes a list from memory. They can compare lists in pairs, or you can ask questions to the class as a whole.

2 This could be turned into a paired game. Issue a series of flash cards, one to each student. You can cut suitable pictures from magazines. They can either 1) ask questions to discover what's on their partner's card, or 2) study a flash card for one minute, then see who can remember most.

◆ **Workbook**

The Workbook can be done at home, except for exercise 3. If it is done in class, exercises 2, 3, and 4 can be done orally in pairs.

a Timetables

Look at the timetables. Which flights was he on? Which trains? Which hovercraft?

From MANCHESTER
Depart Manchester Airport (see Minimum Check-in Times for UK)
Reservations tel 061 2286311
✈ ABERDEEN

From	To	Days 1234567	Depart	Arrive	Flight No.	Air-craft	Class	Stops
		12345 --	0820	0920	BA5690	B11	M	0
		1 --- 5 --	1225	1350	BA5694	HPJ	M	0
		-234 ---	1455	1620	BA5696	HPJ	M	0
		1 --- 5 --	1615	1740	BA5698	HPJ	M	0
		12345 --	1835	2000	BA5688	HS7	M	0
		------ 7	1910	2130	BA867	HS7	M	1

Paris to London (rail/hovercraft)

PERIOD OF OPERATION		A	DAILY	DAILY
Paris Nord	d	0920	1125	1420
Boulogne Hoverport	d	1205	1405	1705
SEA CROSSING		⛴	⛴	⛴
Dover Hoverport	a	1145	1345	1645
London Victoria	a	1353	1553	1853

ALL TIMES SHOWN ARE LOCAL

⛴ Hoverspeed hovercraft with in-flight bar service.
Advance reservation essential. Trains for hovercraft services arrive at and depart from Dover Priory.
A free bus service connects Dover Priory with Dover Hoverport in both directions.

From ABERDEEN
✈ PARIS (Via LONDON HEATHROW)

From	To	Days 1234567	Depart	Arrive	Flight No.	Air-craft	Class	Stops	Transfer Arr.	Airport	Dep.	Flight
		12345 --	1005	1400	BA992	811	CM	1				
		1 ------	1015	1430	BA5607	737	M	1	1140	LHR	1230	BA308
		Daily	1105	1630	BA5609	73S	M	1	1230	LHR	1430	BA312
		123456 -	1400	1830	BA5611	737	M	1	1525	LHR	1630	BA314
		12345 - 7	1535	2030	BA5613	73S	M	1	1700	LHR	1830	BA316
		12345 - 7	1730	2200	BA5615	757	M	1	1855	LHR	2000	BA318

From LONDON
✈ MANCHESTER

From	To	Days 1234567	Depart	Arrive	Flight No.	Air-craft	Class	Stops
		12345 --	0730①	0820	BA4402	757	M	0
		Daily	0930①	1020	BA4422	757	M	0
		Daily	1130①	1220	BA4442	757	M	0
		Daily	1330①	1420	BA4462	757	M	0
		Daily	1630①	1720	BA4492	757	M	0
		Daily	1830①	1920	BA4512	757	M	0
		Daily	2030①	2120	BA4532	757	M	0

From LONDON
✈ PARIS

From	To	Days 1234567	Depart	Arrive	Flight No.	Air-craft	Class	Stops
		123456 -	0640 ①	0840	BA302	757	CM	0
		123 - 56 -	0730 ②	0930	AF807	AB3	CY	0
		Daily	0830 ①	1030	BA304	L10	CM	0
20 Dec		Daily	0930 ②	1130	AF809	AB3	CY	0
22 Dec		12345 - 7	0930 ②	1130	AF809	AB3	CY	0
		Daily	1030 ①	1230	BA306	757	CM	0

From ABERDEEN
✈ LONDON

From	To	Days 1234567	Depart	Arrive	Flight No.	Air-craft	Class	Stops
		12345 --	0700	0825	BA5601	757	M	0
		-----67	0800	0925	BA5603	737	M	0
		12345 --	0940	1105	BA5605	737	M	0
		1 ------	1015	1140	BA5607	737	M	0
		Daily	1105	1230	BA5609	73S	M	0
		123456 -	1400	1525	BA5611	737	M	0
		12345 -7	1535	1700	BA5613	73S	M	0
		Daily	1730	1855	BA5615	757	M	0
		12345 --	1945	2110	BA5619	73S	M	0

b Identikit

Yesterday the name in his passport was Brian Smith. Last week it was Clive Jones. Look at these identikit pictures.

Last week.
Clive Jones.
Amsterdam.

Last month.
Clive Smith.
Rome.

Last year.
Brian Jones.
New York.

What was his name last week?
Where was he?
What was he like?
Ask and answer about the identikit pictures.

c What was he wearing?

1 Student A: What was he wearing last week?
   What do *you* think? Write a list.
   Student B: Ask questions about last week.
2 Do the same for last month and last year.

d Two other pickpockets

Inspector Franklin is looking for two other pickpockets. They were in Manchester, Aberdeen, Paris, and London yesterday.
They were in Manchester at 7 o'clock.
There was one robbery. etc.
Use the timetables and make more sentences.

Unit thirty-three

A good dinner

Man Hello, Mrs Cole?
Mrs Cole Yes?
Man I'm from the Public Health Department.
Mrs Cole Oh, yes?
Man Can I ask you a few questions?
Mrs Cole Well, yes...
Man Did you go to the supermarket this morning?
Mrs Cole Yes. Yes, I did.
Man Which supermarket did you go to?
Mrs Cole I went to Safebury's. I always go to Safebury's.
Man Ah, Safebury's! Did you go to the branch in the High Street?
Mrs Cole Yes, I did.
Man Oh dear. When did you go there?
Mrs Cole I went at 9 o'clock this morning.

Man Did you buy any beef?
Mrs Cole No, I didn't buy any beef. I don't like beef.
Man Oh. Did you buy *any* meat?
Mrs Cole Meat? Yes, I did. I bought some chicken.
Man Chicken? Good. Have you got it now?
Mrs Cole Yes, it's in the fridge.
Man Can you get it, please?
Mrs Cole What? I don't understand. Why...?
Man You can't eat it, Mrs Cole. Five people have got food poisoning. They all bought meat at Safebury's.

Mrs Cole Oh dear. It was very expensive. It was seven pounds fifty.
Man Don't worry, Mrs Cole. Safebury's are going to send you a cheque for fifteen pounds.
Mrs Cole Well, that's all right, then.
Man I'm going to take the chicken. It's going to our laboratory.
Mrs Cole Oh! Oh, yes... well, thank you.
Man Thank *you*, Mrs Cole.

Woman Did you get any beef?
Man No, I didn't. But I got some chicken.
Woman Great!
Man What did you get?
Woman I got some fish at number 23, and some chocolate cake from Mrs Roberts at number 14.
Man Right, we've got dinner. Let's go home!
Policeman Excuse me...
Woman Oh no! The police...

Teaching points

Introduction of simple past tense, restricted in the presentation text to *went, bought, got*. *Had* is introduced in the practice material.
Did you go to the supermarket? Yes, I did. / No, I didn't.
I didn't go to the supermarket. I went to the chemist's.
What did (you) do?
Reading: Jigsaw reading, ordering paragraphs.

Grammar note

The unit is restricted to four common irregular verbs, but four more verbs (3 regular + *put*) appear in the jigsaw reading. These will not be practised or pointed out. They should be understood.

Expressions

Can I ask you a few questions?
Can you get it, please?
They all (bought meat at Safebury's).
Well, that's all right, then.
Great! Let's go home.

Active vocabulary

baker / bath / beef / branch / cheque / chemist / laboratory / list / poisoning / shop / wash (n)
buy/bought / did / had / got / send / went
a few / let's / great!

Passive vocabulary

aspirins / Public Health Department / liquid / rolls / tooth paste / washing up

Classroom vocabulary

find out / jigsaw / mean / paragraph / underline

Redundant vocabulary (jigsaw reading)

accident / crash / drive (n) / garage / knock / moment / motorway / noise / roof / speed / limit / stripes
dark / flashing / suddenly
crash(ed) / put / stop(ped) / wait(ed)

Audio-visual aids

Cassette

Optional: With **false beginners** you may wish to miss out the following points of the introduction: 2, 3, 4, 5. The drills should be taken at speed.

◆ **Oral introduction**

1 Say: *I usually go to the bank on (Fridays = yesterday). I didn't go the bank yesterday. I was very busy. Last night I went to a restaurant. I had a big dinner. But there was a problem ... I didn't have any money.*
Explain that *went* is the past of *go*.
Explain that *had* is the past of *have*.
Points .2 to .5 below should be taken at speed.

2 Repetition: ask students to repeat:
I went to a restaurant. / He went to a restaurant. / They went to a restaurant. / She went to a restaurant. / You went to a restaurant. / We went to a restaurant.

3 Repetition: ask students to repeat;
I didn't go to the bank. / He didn't go to the bank. / We didn't go to the bank. / They didn't go to the bank. / You didn't go to the bank. / She didn't go to the bank.

4 Repetition: ask students to repeat:
Did you go to the bank? / Did we go to the bank? / Did I go to the bank? / Did she go to the bank? / Did they go to the bank? / Did he go to the bank?

5 Drills (**optional**):
Points 2, 3, and 4 can be repeated as simple substitution drills if necessary. (e.g. T: *They* C: *They went to a restaurant.*) This should be avoided with all but the slowest classes.

◆ **Dialogue: section 1**
(to ... *9 o'clock this morning.*)

1 Focus attention on the picture at the top of the left-hand page. Check that the text is covered. Play the cassette. Play it again, pausing for choral and individual repetition. Pay attention to the different ways in which Mrs Cole says *Yes*...

2 Drill:
T: *supermarket – this morning*
C: *Did you go to the supermarket this morning?*
Continue:
bank – yesterday / station – last week / chemist's – last night / cinema – last month / airport – last year.

3 Drill:
T: *I went to the supermarket.*
C: *Which supermarket did you go to?*
Continue: *I went to the bank. / I went to the cinema. / I went to the chemist's. / I went to a restaurant.*

4 Drill:
T: *Did you go there at 9 o'clock?*
C: *Yes, I went at 9 o'clock.*
Continue: *Did they go there yesterday? / Did she go there last night? / Did we go there on Monday? / Did he go there at lunchtime? / Did I go there last week?*

5 Silent reading of dialogue: section 1.

6 Questions:
Is he from the Police Department? Ask 'Where?' Did she go to the supermarket this morning? Did she go to Safeway? Did she go to Sainsbury's? Which supermarket did she go to? Does she often go there? Did she go to the branch in Smith Street? Which branch did she go to? Did she go there at eight o'clock? Ask 'When?'

7 Paired reading of dialogue: section 1.

◆ **Dialogue: section 2** (to ... *meat at Safebury's.*)

1 Check that the text is covered. Play the cassette. Play it again, pausing for choral and individual repetition.

2 Drill:
T: *She doesn't like beef.*
C: *She didn't buy any beef.*
T: *She likes chicken.*
C: *She bought some chicken.*

Unit thirty-four

Continue:
She doesn't like fish. / She likes ice cream. / She likes eggs. / She doesn't like apples. / She likes pizza. / She doesn't like hamburgers.

3 Silent reading of dialogue: section 2.

4 Paired reading of dialogue: section 2.

5 Questions:
Does she like beef? Did she buy any beef? Did she buy any meat? Which did she buy? Has she got it now? Where is it? Can she eat it? How many people have got food poisoning? Where did they all buy meat?

◆ **Dialogue: section 3** (to *Thank you, Mrs Cole.*)

1 Check that the text is covered. Play the cassette. Play it again, pausing for choral and individual repetition.

2 Silent reading of dialogue: section 3.

3 Paired reading of dialogue: section 3.

◆ **Dialogue: section 4** (to the end)

1 Focus attention on the second picture. Check that the text is covered. Play the cassette. Play it again, pausing for choral and individual repetition.

2 Drill:
T: *beef – chicken*
C: *They didn't get any beef, but they got some chicken.*
Continue:
eggs – fish / ice cream – chocolate cake / apples – oranges / salad – potatoes / cheese – bread

3 Silent reading of dialogue: section 4.

4 Questions:
Did he get any beef? What did he get? Did she get any fish? Where did he get it? Did she get any ice cream? Ask 'What?' Ask 'Where?' Who did she get it from? Are they from the Public Health Department?

5 Paired reading of dialogue: section 4.

◆ **Dialogue: sections 1–4**

1 Play the cassette for dialogue: sections 1–4. Students listen.

2 Role play. Students work in pairs and role play the conversations with the householders at Number 23 and Number 14.
When they've done this once, ask them to try it again. This time the trick doesn't work.

⟨a⟩ **Mrs Cole's shopping list**

Pair work. Focus attention on the list. Check the instructions. Get students to ask and answer in pairs. Check back with the class.

⟨b⟩ **Your shopping list**

1 Explain the activity. As each student compiles his / her own list there will be an information gap.

2 Get students to work in pairs.

3 Check with the class, asking what was on students' partners' lists. *Where did (she) go? What did (he) buy?* etc.

⟨c⟩ **Questions**

Students ask and answer in pairs. Check with general questions to the class. Extend with further questions. e.g. *What did you do there?*

⟨d⟩ **Questionnaire**

1 Refer students to the examples with *had* in the past. If necessary, copy the chart from the grammar reference section on to the board and get them to copy it.

2 Explain the activities. Get students to work in pairs. Make sure that they understand that they should give true answers, whether the true answers are on the chart or not.

3 Check back with the class as a whole, asking further questions with: *Where? / When? / What time? / What did you do there?* etc.
Get students to do the pair work again, using these questions.

⟨e⟩ **Jigsaw**

1 Note that this text should not be exploited intensively. The purpose is to understand enough to complete the task and no more. (See Grammar note above.) They will grasp the four new verbs in the past passively (*waited*, *stopped*, *crashed*, *put*). **Do not** be led into an explanation of regular past formation. Explain the task carefully. Give students time to complete it.

2 Read the story aloud to the class, in the correct order.

3 Discuss the story. *Is it true? Why? Why not?*

◆ **Workbook**

The Workbook can be done at home.
If it is done in class, exercises 2, 3, 4, and 9 are suitable for paired oral practice.
Note that practice could be extended by using the times on Bruno's notes, and asking questions with *When* and *What time*.

Unit thirty-four

a) Mrs Cole's shopping list

This is Mrs Cole's shopping list for this morning. She didn't get everything. A tick [✓] means she got it. A cross [✗] means she didn't get it.

```
Safebury's              Chemist           Baker
Chicken ✓               Toothpaste ✓      Bread ✓
Potatoes ✓              Toothbrush ✗      Cakes ✗
Washing-up liquid ✓     Aspirins ✓        Rolls ✓
Tuna fish ✗
Apple juice ✗
```

Look at the list.
Did she go to ...?
Did she buy ...? / Did she get ...?
Ask and answer about Mrs Cole's list.

b) Your shopping list

1 Write a shopping list.
   Say *This is my shopping list for yesterday*.
   Put a tick [*I bought it*] or a cross [*I didn't buy it*] next to the things on the list.
2 Work with another student.
   Ask questions, and find out what's on his/her list.
   Which shops did he/she go to? What did he/she buy?

c) Questions

Ask and answer.
1 Where did you go last weekend?
2 Did you go to the shops?
3 Did you buy anything?
4 What did you buy?
5 Did you get any letters yesterday?
6 How many did you get?

d) Questionnaire

A *Did you have a bath yesterday?*
B *No, I didn't have a bath. I had a shower.*

Ask another student about yesterday.
Underline the answers.
Sometimes the true answer isn't on the chart.
Ask questions with: *Where? When? What time? What?*

e) Jigsaw

There are five paragraphs in this story. They are in the wrong order.
Number them in the correct order, from 1 to 5.

☐ The next morning there was a knock on the door. Sid went to the door. A policewoman was outside. 'Mr Cole?' she said. 'Mr Sidney Cole?' 'Er...yes, that's me,' said Sid. 'Were you on the M40 last night at about eleven o'clock?' 'No,' said Sid. 'No, I wasn't. Not me.' 'Could I see your car please?' said the policewoman.

☐ Just then there was a terrible noise behind them. Two cars crashed, then a third car, then a fourth. The policemen ran to the accident. Sid was alone beside the motorway. He waited for a moment, then he got into the Jaguar and went home...very fast. He put the car into his garage, closed the door, went into his house, and went to bed.

☐ Sid Cole bought a new white Jaguar last week. He got the car last Friday, and that evening he went out for a drive. The Jaguar was very fast, and Sid was going along the M40 motorway at 100mph. Suddenly, there was a blue light behind him, a blue flashing light. It was a police car.

☐ They went to the garage. Sid opened the door. There was a white Jaguar in the garage, but it wasn't his Jaguar. There were red and yellow stripes on the side, and a blue light on the roof. And it had the word **POLICE** on the door.

☐ Sid stopped, and the police car stopped next to him. It was a Jaguar too. 'Get out of your car,' said a policeman. Sid did. He was cold. It was a cold, dark December night. There were two policemen. They were very angry. 'Do you know the speed limit?' said one. 'Yes,' said Sid. '70mph. I'm sorry. It's a new car and...'

Breakfast	before 8.00? tea?	at 8.00? coffee?	after 8.00? fruit juice?
Lunch	at home? at 12.00?	in a restaurant? at 1.00?	at school / work? at 2.00?
Dinner	at home? beef?	in a restaurant? chicken?	at a friend's house? fish?
Bath / shower	bath? in the morning?	shower? in the afternoon?	wash? in the evening?

Unit thirty-five

One dark night

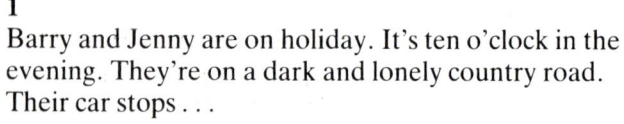

1

Barry and Jenny are on holiday. It's ten o'clock in the evening. They're on a dark and lonely country road. Their car stops...

Jenny What's wrong with it?
Barry I don't know.
Jenny Is there any petrol?
Barry Yes. I put some in this afternoon. I got thirty litres.
Jenny What are we going to do?
Barry I'm going to find a telephone.
Jenny I'm coming with you.
Barry No, it's freezing! You wait here.
Jenny Barry, I'm frightened...

2
Later.
Barry Jenny... it's me. Open the door! Sorry. Did I frighten you?
Jenny No. Did you find a telephone?
Barry No, I didn't find a telephone... But I found a hotel. I went round that corner and I saw it. They've got a room for tonight. We can phone a garage tomorrow. Come on...

3
They're in the hotel room.

Barry Well, what do you think?
Jenny I don't like it.

He goes into the bathroom. There's a noise outside.

Jenny Barry! Did you hear that?
Barry What?
Jenny I heard something. It was a laugh. It was horrible.
Barry I didn't hear anything.
Jenny You were in the bathroom.
Barry Yes, and there aren't any towels. I'm going down to reception.
Jenny OK.
Barry Don't worry, Jenny. I'm not frightened.

Optional video component

Teaching points
Extension of simple past tense, with more common irregular verbs: *saw, heard, found, said, put.*
something / not ... anything / ... anything?
someone / not ... anyone / ... anyone?

Grammar note
A major aim is to enable students to build up a generative framework with the past tense. i.e. If they know the present tense, and the use of the auxiliary, *did,* they will be able to create negatives and questions in the past.

Expressions
I'm frightened. You wait here. What do you think?
What's the matter?
(He was) like (Count Dracula.)
Don't be silly. This isn't funny.

Active vocabulary
corner / corridor / laugh / litre / make-up / matter / reception / toothbrush / tree / towels

find / found / frighten / heard / kill / put / saw / say / said
frightened / funny / horrible / silly / stupid
anyone / someone / something
round

Passive vocabulary
ambulance / chewing-gum / cloak / Count / Halloween / lonely / timer
carefully

Classroom vocabulary
groan / owl / vampire

Audio-visual aids
Cassette. **Optional:** video cassette. **Note:** There are a lot of sound effects on the audio cassette version of the story. When exploiting the cassette, you can stop the tape and say *What was that? / What did they hear?*

◆ Dialogue 1

1 Focus attention on the picture. Check that the text is covered. Play the cassette. (No repetition is suggested here.)

2 Play it again, pausing at appropriate points to ask questions.
What can you hear? / What's wrong with the car? / Is there any petrol? / When did he put petrol in the car? / How much did he put in the car?
What's he going to do? Does she want to come with him? / What's the weather like? / Is he frightened? / Is she frightened?

3 Paired reading of dialogue 1.

◆ Dialogue 2

1 Play the sounds at the beginning of this section of the cassette. Say *What can you hear?* Give vocabulary as necessary.

2 Focus attention on the picture. Check that the text is covered. Play the whole of dialogue 2. Play it again, pausing for choral and individual repetition. Ask *What's the past of 'find'? What's the past of 'see'?*

3 Silent reading of dialogue 2.

4 Questions:
Was she frightened? Did he find a telephone? What did he find? Where did he see it? Have they got a room for tonight? What's he going to do about the car?

◆ Dialogue 3

1 Focus attention on the three photographs above dialogue 3. Ask: *What is it? What are they doing? Describe the man. Describe the room.*

2 Check that the text is covered. Play dialogue 3. Play it again, pausing for selective repetition of the past tense sentences. Ask *What's the past of 'hear'?* Check *some* and *any* (see dialogue 1). Point out *something* and *anything*.

3 Drill:
T: *I heard something.*
C: *I didn't hear anything.*
Continue: *I found something. / I saw something. / I had something. / I got something. / I bought something. / I did something.*

4 Silent reading of dialogue 3.

5 Questions:
Did Jenny hear anything? Did Barry hear anything? What did she hear? What was it like? Why didn't he hear it? Why is he going down to reception?

6 Paired reading of dialogue 3. This should be as dramatic as possible.

◆ Dialogue 4

1 Focus attention on the three photographs above dialogue 4. Ask students to tell you what is happening in them. Get them to guess.

Unit thirty-five

2 Check that the text is covered. Play the cassette for dialogue 4. Play it again, pausing for choral and individual repetition. Check *someone* and *anyone*.

3 Drill:
T: *Who did you see?*
C: *I don't know, but I saw someone.*
T: *What did you see?*
C: *I don't know, but I saw something.*
Continue: *What did you hear? / Who did you find? / Who did you hear? / What did you have? / Who did you see? / What did you buy?*

4 Silent reading of dialogue 4.

5 Questions:
Where did he go? What did he see in the corridor? Describe the man – What was he wearing? Did he have small teeth or did he have big teeth? Is she angry? Why? Did the man go round the corner? Did Barry go round the corner? Did he see the man? Was there anyone there?

6 Paired reading of dialogue 4. This should be as dramatic as possible.

◆ Dialogue 5

1 Check that the text and the final pictures are covered. Play the cassette for dialogue 5. (No repetition is suggested.)

2 Silent reading of dialogue 5.

3 Paired reading of dialogue 5.

4 Focus attention on the final pictures. Ask questions: *What's happening? Why are these people in the hotel? Why are they wearing these clothes? What's Halloween? Do you have Halloween in your country? What are Jenny and Barry going to do now?*

◆ Dialogues 1–5

Play dialogues 1–5 again. Students listen.

◆ Irregular verbs

1 Check that the chart is covered. Give the present tense of a known verb; the class responds chorally with the past:
T: *have* C: *had*
Continue: *say / hear / find / put / go / buy / get / do*

2 Refer them to the chart.

a) On the way here

1 Explain the activity. Students ask and answer in pairs. The *What did you put in your bag?* section works particularly well, but be discrete about asking students to turn out their own bags to check. It can cause embarrassment.

2 Optional: Students could work as a class / in groups to do an analysis of the class's answers. i.e. *How many people saw a police car this morning?* etc.

b) A noise in the night

1 Students should work alone on the exercise. Get them to compare answers in pairs before checking.

2 Check by reading the text allowed to the class, pausing to allow them to call out the missing words.

3 If you wish, this would be a point to explain the use of *something / anything*. You could use the chart in the grammar reference section.

◆ Extension

Note: It is important for students to realize that even if they don't know the past of a particular verb, they can still generate negatives, questions, and short responses (*Yes, I did. / No, I didn't.*) from their knowledge of the present. Exercises 2 and 3 in the Workbook point this out, and gives them practice in doing so. It's worth making a major point about this here.
Start with a drill, which moves from known to unknown (but which is possible because they are generating negatives).

1 Drill:
T: *What did you see?*
C: *I didn't see anything.*
Continue: *What did you hear? / What did you find? / What did you buy? / What did you have for breakfast? / What did you get? / What did you **eat**? / What did you **drink**? / What did you **read**? / What did you **know**?*
Don't go into an individual phase, but stop and point out what the students have been doing. (If it begins as a drill, they probably won't have noticed.)

2 Ask Yes / No questions to follow up the point:
*Did you see anything on TV last night? Did you hear anything on the radio? Did you **drink** anything for breakfast? Did you **drink** coffee? Did you **eat** anything? Did you **eat** eggs? Did you **meet** anyone this morning? Did you **telephone** anyone yesterday? Did you **watch** anything at the cinema last month? Did you **walk** here today? Did you **drive**? Did you **come** on a bus?*
These should elicit: *Yes, I did. / No, I didn't.*

3 Point out that they don't know the past of the verbs in bold above, but that they can find them in a reference book. **Don't teach them here.** Show that they can answer effectively without knowing the past:
Who did you telephone? My friend.
What did you eat? Steak and chips.
Where did you walk to? To school.
Ask a few questions to individuals to elicit answers like this.
What did you eat for breakfast? Who did you meet last night? What did you drink with your breakfast? etc.

◆ Workbook

The Workbook can be done at home. If it is done in class, exercises 2, 3, and 6 can be done orally in pairs. Note that exercises 2 and 3 follow up 'Extension' above.

Irregular verbs

PRESENT	PAST
find	found
see	saw
hear	heard
put	put
say	said

a) On the way here

On the way to this lesson:

Did you see ☐ a police car ☐ a dog ☐ any trees
☐ the teacher ☐ a boat?
What did you see?

Did you hear ☐ an ambulance ☐ a plane
☐ a radio ☐ someone singing?
What did you hear?

Did you find ☐ any money on the street ☐ anything?

Did you put any of these things in your bag / briefcase this morning?
☐ money ☐ food ☐ chewing-gum ☐ make-up
☐ a toothbrush
What did you put in your bag this morning?

Ask and answer with another student.

b) A noise in the night

Complete the spaces with *something*, *someone*, *anything*, or *anyone*.

It was very dark. I found my watch on the table next to my bed. Three o'clock! Then I heard _____ downstairs. What was it? I got out of bed, and went out of the room. I went to the stairs. Then I saw _____ . Was it a light? Carefully, I went downstairs. I didn't say _____ . I was very quiet. Then I heard _____ . It was a woman. 'I'm going to kill him, give me the gun!' she said. I didn't move. Then I heard music. 'Is _____ there?' I said. I heard music again. I went into the living room. There wasn't _____ there, but the television was on! The video recorder has got an automatic timer. Before I went to bed I put the timer on for three o'clock the next afternoon. I went to the video. The timer was on for three o'clock in the morning.

4
Barry Jenny!
Jenny What's the matter?
Barry I went outside . . . and I saw someone in the corridor. He was wearing a long black cloak . . . like Count Dracula.
Jenny Don't be silly, Barry. I *was* frightened, but I'm not stupid.
Barry He was there! I saw him. He had big teeth, and . . .
Jenny This isn't funny, Barry.
Barry Look . . . he went round the corner. And I went after him . . . and there wasn't anyone there.
Jenny What?
Barry I didn't see anyone.

5
Jenny What did you say?
Barry I didn't say anything, there was a noise. Be quiet!
Jenny Barry! That was you!
Barry I said 'Be quiet'! Did you hear that? Come on! I'm not staying here . . . Let's go. .

Unit thirty-five

Stories for pleasure

Crocodile Preston

One of them was wearing high-heeled shoes. She was an old American lady with white hair. I didn't say anything. Her husband had four or five cameras and a big hat. There were two English ladies in their seventies, three boys from New Zealand and a young Canadian couple. They got into the boat.

Ray wasn't there. He was late again. It was hot, very hot - about 32 °C - and it was only ten o'clock.

'When are we leaving?' said the American lady.

'I don't know,' I said. 'We're waiting for the captain.'

They found seats and waited in the sun. The Canadians didn't have any hats. I got two old hats from the back of the boat.

'Here,' I said; 'you're going to need these. It's going to be hot out there.'

They put them on.

'The advertisement said ten o'clock,' said the American man.

'Yes?' I said. 'Well, we usually leave at ten. Today we're late. Sorry.'

Then I saw Ray. He was running towards the boat. He was wearing his white suit, and his face was red. He got onto the boat, and it went down a long way into the water. Ray's a very fat man.

'G'day,' he said. 'It's a nice morning.'

'Good day,' said the tourists. I smiled. In Australian films people always say 'G'day', but the tourists didn't have the right accent.

'G'day Ray,' I said. I was doing my job. Tourists want to see Australia, and hear Australians. That's my job. I'm a professional Australian. What next? Yeah, a joke. Australians always make jokes.

'Did you have a good breakfast, Ray?' I said.

'Yeah,' said Ray. 'Why?'

'I can see it on your jacket. You had eggs, tomatoes, and coffee, right?'

Ray was angry about that one. His jacket *was* dirty. His clothes are always dirty. His boat's dirty, too. Last month I said,

'Ray, why don't you clean the boat?'

'Look,' he said; 'tourists want a journey through the jungle. A dirty boat has got the

Teaching points
This material can be used in a number of different ways:

As extensive reading for pleasure
We would recommend using it for extensive reading for pleasure with most classes. It can be done in class or at home. In this case you will not need any Teacher's notes. The material need not be checked or tested in any way.

As extensive listening for pleasure
Where you feel students will benefit from extra listening practice, the story can be used with the recording on cassette.

As reading comprehension material for revision
With classes that need extra revision / consolidation material, the story can be used as comprehension material.

Vocabulary & expressions
As the story is intended for reading / listening for pleasure, the vocabulary is not listed in the index. All extra items in the story are for passive comprehension. The extra items are:
advertisement / ambience / bottom / camera / captain / control / croc/crocodile / gun / hero / hunter / joke / journey / jungle / nose / shoes / show / teeth / trigger
attack / helped / hit / leave / operate / wait
deep / electric / high-heeled / lucky / professional
Good day / to go quiet / a lot of

Audio-visual aids
Optional: Cassette. The material is recorded and appears between Units 35 and 36.

Stories for pleasure

◆ As extensive reading for pleasure

Reading for pleasure is best done with no pressure or fear of checking or testing. We would suggest that students work alone and read the story with no checking by the teacher. This however would be a good time to point out how to read extensively. Tell students not to stop for difficult words, but to read on to the end of the story. They should mark difficult words with a pencil, and look them up only after completing the whole story.

◆ As extensive listening for pleasure

Note: If you have a listening centre, tell students to listen to the cassette, then read the story, then listen and read. There will be no need for the work below.

1 Paragraph 1 (*One of them was wearing . . .*). Explain 'narrator' – the person telling the story. Set pre-question: *Where was the narrator?* Play the cassette. Get answers.

2 Set pre-questions:
How many were there?
Americans? ____ New Zealanders? ____ Canadians? ____ English? ____
What was the time? ____ What was the temperature? ____
Play the cassette again. Check the answers. Ask them to describe the passengers.

3 Paragraph 2 (*They found seats . . .*). Play the cassette. Ask questions:
Why did he get two hats? When do they usually leave?

4 Paragraph 3 (*Then I saw Ray . . .*). Set pre-question: *Which country are they in?* Play the cassette. Check the answer.

5 Play the cassette again. Ask questions: *Describe Ray. What's the Australian for 'Hello'? What did Ray have for breakfast? How did the narrator know this?*

6 Paragraph 4 (*Ray was angry . . .*). Set pre-question: *What's the narrator's job?*

7 Play the cassette again. Ask questions. *Whose clothes are dirty? What's dirty? What does 'ambience' mean?*

8 Paragraph 5 (*It's a two-hour journey . . .*). Set pre-question: *What's a 'croc'?*

9 Play the cassette again. Ask questions: *What does Ray sell? What did they see? What was the American man doing? Do crocodiles eat people in that part of Australia? Is it true?*

10 Paragraph 6 (*We got to the Tickabaree River . . .*). Set pre-question: *What's the narrator's name?*

11 Play the cassette again. Ask questions: *Who had got a gun? Where was it? Why does he need a gun?*

12 Paragraph 7 (*I saw the big tree . . .*). Play the cassette twice.
Ask the students to tell you what happened. (Free reproduction.)

13 Paragraph 8 (*Tourists always love it . . .*). Set pre-question: *Was it a real crocodile?* Play the cassette.

14 Play the cassette again. Ask: *What was Ray talking about?*

15 Paragraph 9 and 10 (*The old American woman was . . .*). Set pre-question: *Where was the crocodile?* Play the cassette.

16 Play the cassette again. Ask questions: *Describe the crocodile. What do you think is going to happen next?*

17 Paragraph 11 (*Then the crocodile . . .*). Play the cassette. Ask: *What happened?*

18 Paragraph 12 (*The plastic crocodile isn't . . .*). Play the cassette. Ask: *What happened to the plastic crocodile? Do they use it now? Why not?*

19 Play the cassette right through.

20 Get the students to read the story silently.

◆ As reading comprehension material for revision

1 Follow the procedure for extensive listening, **but** get students to read the story silently **after** the initial playing of the cassette. Include the pre-questions and general questions, **but** add the following specific questions for each paragraph:

Stories for pleasure

2 Paragraph 1: *Who was wearing high-heeled shoes? What colour was her hair? Was she old or young? What did her husband have? How old were the English ladies? Were the Canadians two men, two women, or a man and a woman? What was the time? Were the New Zealanders wearing business suits? How do you know?*

3 Paragraph 2: *What was the weather like? What did the advertisement say? Were they late or were they early?*

4 Paragraph 3: *Describe Ray. Why did the boat go down in the water? What accent has the narrator got? What about Ray's accent? Have you got an accent in English? In your own language? What accent is it? What did Ray have for breakfast? How did the narrator know?*

5 Paragraph 4: *Does the narrator like Ray? Does Ray like him? Why was the boat dirty? What do you think 'ambience' means? Who started the engine? Where did they go?*

6 Paragraph 5: *How long is the journey? What did the tourists buy? Who sold it to them? Was it cold? Was it cheap or expensive? Who saw the crocodiles first? Were they awake or were they asleep? Did a small croc come into the river? Which croc came into the river? What do you think of Ray's story?*

7 Paragraph 6: *Did the narrator have his gun? Where was it? Why did the tourists go quiet?*

8 Paragraph 7: Correct these sentences:
He saw a big boat. / He put his hand in the engine. / The Canadian woman shouted. / The crocodile came into the boat. / He fired the gun. / Ray jumped into the water. / He had a fork in his hand. / He kissed the crocodile. / They went for a swim. / The tourists were laughing and joking. / He came out of the water and died. / He had the crocodile's foot in his mouth. / It wasn't a show.

9 Paragraph 8: *How do they operate the crocodile? How many people were in the river?*

10 Paragraph 9 and 10: *Why don't you wear high-heeled shoes on small boats? Is the river very deep? How deep is it? Who was afraid? Who saw the crocodile? Was it a plastic one? Where was it? Where was his knife, do you think? Where did he hit the crocodile? Was he on the menu? What do you think?*

11 Paragraph 11: *What did the crocodile do? Why didn't it eat him? Who was a hero?*

12 Paragraph 12: *What did Ray do with the crocodile? Why? Does Preston go in the river now? Why not?*

◆ **Workbook**

There are no Workbook units for the **Story for pleasure** sections.

Stories for pleasure

right . . . the right . . . ambience.
'What's ambience?' I said. 'You know me, Ray. I'm just a crocodile hunter. I don't understand difficult words.'
Ray doesn't like me, but then I don't like him. But it's a job. I started the old engine and we went up the river.

It's a two-hour journey into the jungle. The tourists bought drinks from Ray. He always sells them warm Pepsi-Cola, at a very high price. Ray talks about the jungle on the journey. And me? I sit at the back of the boat and sleep.
'There they are!' shouted the American woman. I opened one eye. There were some big crocs at the side of the river. They were asleep. They always wake up when the boat goes past. One big old croc came into the river. All the tourists had their cameras. The American man was taking photographs. Ray was in the middle of the talk.
'Yes, crocodiles sometimes eat people,' he said. 'In this part of Australia they eat three or four people every year.'
I smiled. Was it true? I don't know. But the tourists love the stories.
We got to the Tickabaree River, and Ray turned the boat into it.
'But don't worry,' he said. 'Mr Preston is a professional crocodile hunter. He's got his gun.' Ray was looking at me.
'He's got his *gun*,' he said again.
I found the gun at the bottom of the boat. The tourists looked at me.
'Do you need that gun?' said one of the Canadians.
'Oh, yes,' said Ray. 'Sometimes the crocodiles attack small boats.'
The tourists went quiet, very quiet.

I saw the big tree. We were at the right place. I put my hand on a small electric control next to the engine.
The crocodile came out of the water right in front of the boat. Water came into the boat.
'Aargh!' It was the American woman.
'The gun!' said Ray. 'Quick!'
I pulled the trigger. 'Oh no!' I shouted. 'The gun! There's something wrong with the gun!'
Then I was in the water. I had my knife in my hand. I put my arm round the crocodile.

We went under the water. Then I came out of the water with the crocodile and then went under again. The tourists were screaming and shouting.
I came out of the water again, and smiled. I had the crocodile's foot in my hand. It was the end of the show.

Tourists always love it. The electric control operates the plastic crocodile. They're afraid, but then they see it's a joke.
But Ray was shouting. 'Get her! Get her!'
'I've got her!' I said.
'Not the crocodile,' he said; 'the American woman! Look!'

The old American woman was in the river. The high-heeled shoes! You never wear high-heeled shoes on a small boat. I went towards her.

'She can't swim!' shouted her husband.
The water in the Tickabaree River is only about one metre deep, but she was afraid. I got her arms, then I heard Ray again.
'Preston! Be careful! There's a crocodile!'
'Very funny,' I shouted.
'No, behind you! There's a crocodile!'
It wasn't a joke. There it was, a big old croc about two metres away, and it wasn't a plastic one this time. The American woman was in my arms. Then the crocodile was next to us. I didn't have my knife now. I saw its cold eyes and its big teeth. It had a lot of teeth. Then I hit the crocodile. I hit it once on the nose. Was Ray's story true? Do they eat three or four people a year? Was I on the menu for today?

Then the crocodile went. It turned and went away. I was at the boat. They helped us into the boat. Perhaps that old croc just wasn't hungry, or maybe it didn't like me. I don't know, but I was a hero. Me, a hero!

The plastic crocodile isn't in the Tickabaree River any more. The next day Ray put it outside his office. It's an advert for the boat journeys. I don't go in the river now. I was lucky that time, but maybe next time . . . who knows?

Unit thirty-six

The Morgans

Wally Morgan wanted to know about his ancestors. He looked in old books, and visited churches. He discovered a lot of things about his family.

His grandfather, Willy Morgan, played football for England. He was a defender. He played against Scotland in 1923. The game started at 3 o'clock on a Saturday afternoon in May. England scored the first goal at 4.15. Then Willy scored two goals ... both of them for Scotland. He didn't play for England again.

Billy 'Four Eyes' Morgan lived from 1857 to 1886. He moved to the United States in 1879, and in 1886 he was the Sheriff of Rattlesnake County. He died in a gunfight with Jesse James. Billy fired his gun six times, but he didn't kill Jesse. He killed three horses, a dog, the State Governor, and a Deputy Sheriff. Then Jesse killed him. Billy wasn't wearing his glasses.

Wallace Morgan was a pirate. He lived from 1624 to 1657. He worked as a navigator for Captain Elijah Blood. They sailed round the world three times between 1646 and 1657. This was by mistake: Wallace didn't have a map. Finally, in 1657 they arrived in England. Wallace died in his bath. He slipped on the soap and drowned.

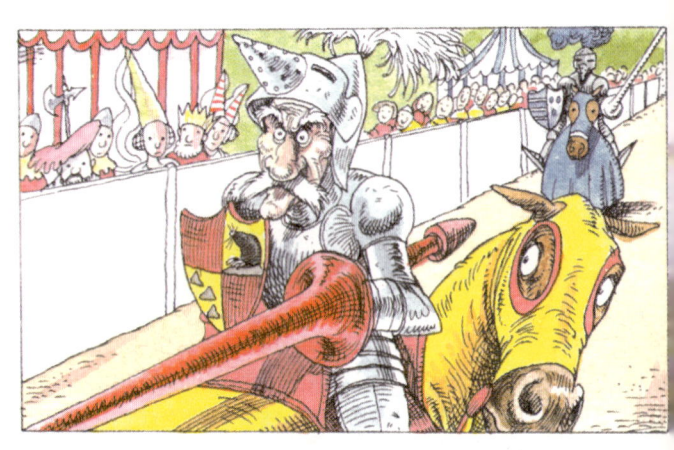

Sir William Morgan lived from 1413 to 1452. He was very romantic. He loved Lady Matilda Potter, the niece of the King. He wanted to marry her. He asked her to marry him in 1432. She said 'No'. He asked her again in 1437, 1441, 1443, and 1450. Finally, she married him in 1452. He died ten minutes after the wedding. His horse stopped on a bridge. He fell off and landed in the river. He was wearing his armour. It weighed 400 kilograms.

a) What happened?

Work with another student.
Make questions and answers about the stories.

Teaching points
The past tense of regular verbs.
Pronunciation of -ed endings. [t], [d], [ɪd].
Spelling rules: *live / lived   kill / killed
marry / married   stop / stopped
What happened?   Finally / then / (three) times / 44 B.C. /
1856 A.D.
He wanted her* **to marry** *him. / He asked her* **to marry** *him.*

Grammar note
There are a large number of regular verbs in this unit. This is deliberate. The purpose is to enable students to generalize the rule, rather than to learn vocabulary.

Active vocabulary
*goal / horse / kilogram / King / mistake / river / wedding
arrive / die / discover / drown / fall / fell / fire / land / marry /
sail / score / slip / weigh
A.D. / B.C. / against / between (time)
both / romantic
finally*

Note: *married* appears in Unit 12.
Previously taught verbs transformed into the past include:
*ask / happen / kill / live / look / love / move / start / stop / visit /
want / work*

Passive vocabulary
*ancestor / armour / deputy / governor / navigator / pirate /
sheriff*
Note: *defender* appears in Unit 4.

Classroom vocabulary
irregular / regular appear in Unit 29.
add / rule / verb

Audio-visual aids
Cassette. Note: The 'Listening' section involves replaying the main text again.

Note: In the pronunciation sections in this lesson, be sure to pronounce [t] and [d] without a semi vowel [tə] and [də]. Note also that students will read most texts silently, and try to generate questions from them **before** listening to the cassette.

◆ Text: Wally Morgan

1 Focus attention on the picture. Check that the text is covered. Play the cassette.

2 Silent reading of the introductory text.

3 Questions:
Note: this section uses want + infinitive (*want to know*). Most students will fail to realize that this is a new structural item. It will reappear later with *want to marry*. Do not draw attention to it unless there are problems.
What's his name? He wanted to know about something. What did he want to know about? He looked in something. What did he look in? He visited something. What did he visit? He discovered something. What did he discover?

4 Explain that the verbs they've learnt in the past tense so far (*went, had, did, bought, saw* etc.) are irregular verbs, and that the most frequent verbs in English are usually irregular. Explain that the verbs in this lesson are regular verbs, and that we form them by adding *-d* or *-ed* to the present. Get them to repeat:
*want / wanted   look / looked   visit / visited
discover / discovered*
Point out the sound of the final *-ed*:
[ɪd] *wanted, visited*
[t] *looked*
[d] *discovered.*

5 Get them to repeat:
*He played for England. He didn't play for Scotland. Who did he play for?
He scored two goals. He didn't score three goals. How many goals did he score?*

◆ Text: Willy Morgan

1 Silent reading of the text. Check vocabulary.

2 Pair work. Get students to ask each other questions about the text. This is a free activity to let them see if they can generate the questions for themselves. If they find it difficult, they can ask Yes / No questions.

3 Play the cassette for 'Willy Morgan'. Get them to repeat *d–d–d–d played* [d], *id–id–id–id started* [ɪd], *d–d–d–d scored* [d].

4 Questions:
What was his grandfather's name? Who did he play football for? Was he a striker? What was he? Who did he play against? When was that? When did the game start? When did England score the first goal? How many goals did Willy score? Who did he score for? Did he play for England again?

◆ Text: Billy 'Four Eyes' Morgan

1 Silent reading of the text. Check vocabulary.

2 Pair work. Get students to ask each other questions about the text.

3 Play the cassette for Billy 'Four Eyes' Morgan. Get them to repeat *d–d–d–d–d lived, moved, died, fired, killed.* [d].

4 Questions:
Did he live from 1856 to 1981? Ask 'When?' Did he move to the United States in 1979? Ask 'When?' Was he the sheriff of El Paso? Where was he the sheriff? Did he die in bed? How did he die? Did he fire his guns four times? Ask 'How many?' Did he kill Jesse? How many horses did he kill? How many people did he kill? What did Jesse do? Was Billy wearing his glasses?

Unit thirty-six

Unit thirty-six

◆ Text: Wallace Morgan

1 Silent reading of the text. Check vocabulary.

2 Pair work. Get students to ask each other questions about the text.

3 Play the cassette for Wallace Morgan. Get them to repeat: d–d–d *lived*, *sailed*, *arrived*, *drowned* [d], t–t–t *worked*, *slipped* [t]. Note: *by mistake*.

4 Questions:
What did Wallace do? When did he live? Who did he work for? What was his job? Did they sail round the world ten times? Ask '*How many?*' *Was that between 1946 and 1957?* Ask '*When?*' *Was it a mistake? Why? When did they finally arrive in England? Did Wallace die in a gunfight?* Ask '*Where?*' Ask '*How?*'

◆ Text: Sir William Morgan

1 Silent reading of the text. Check vocabulary.

2 Pair work. Get students to ask each other questions about the text.

3 Play the cassette for Sir William Morgan. Get them to repeat: d–d–d *loved*, *married*, *weighed* [d], ɪd– ɪd–ɪd *wanted*, *landed* [ɪd], t–t–t *asked*, *stopped*, *slipped* [t].

4 Questions:
(See note above on want + infinitive under 'Introductory text' .3.)
When did he live? Who did he love? Who was her uncle? What did he want to do? When did he ask her to marry him? How many times did he ask her? When did she marry him? When did he die? Did his horse stop under a bridge? Ask '*Where?*' *What happened to him? What was he wearing? How much did it weigh?*

a What happened?

1 Pair work. Get students to go back over the texts asking each other questions again. This time they have heard the teacher's questions.

2 Check back:
What happened to Willy Morgan? What happened to Billy Morgan? What happened to Wallace Morgan? What happened to Sir William Morgan?
Encourage them to use *then* and *finally*.

◆ Regular verbs: spellings

Go through the grammar summary carefully. Check the spelling rules. You could dictate a few examples: *stopped, married, moved, wanted, slipped, hurried, fired, died, sailed*.

b Regular verbs: sounds

1 There is not a separate listening section on the cassette. The listening is done by using the presentation recording again. Go through the instructions. Check the three pronunciations, [t], [d], [ɪd].

2 Play the cassette right through. Students tick the appropriate columns. Check through with the class.

c What's wrong?

1 Explain the activity. Explain A.D. [*Anno Domini* – Latin, in the year of the Lord = after Christ] and B.C. [before Christ]. Students work in pairs, asking and answering about the pictures.
Note that they can usually do this with *didn't have*. Encourage them to use other verbs.

2 Check back on point 1. Ask leading questions.
e.g. 100,000 BC – *When was this? What are they doing in the picture? What are they eating with? Did they eat with knives and forks in 100,000 BC? How did they eat, do you think? So, what's wrong with the picture?*

◆ Transfer

This section is designed to show students that they can generate not only negatives and questions in the past (as practised in Unit 35), but that they can also generate the affirmative form of regular verbs in the past.
Ask questions (+ Ask me / him / her / each other).
Did you live in (this town) in (1989)? Where did you live? When did you move here?
Did you go to this school last year? Which school did you go to? When did you move to this school?
Did you arrive here at 8 o'clock this morning? Ask '*When?*'
Did you look at your book last night? Ask '*When?*'
Did Columbus discover America in 1942? Ask '*When?*'
Did you play (football / tennis / volleyball) last week?
Did you score a goal? Did anyone score a goal?
Did Romeo love Desdemona? Ask '*Who?*'
Did Prince Charles marry Sarah Ferguson? Ask '*Who?*'
Did you have Pepsi for breakfast this morning? Ask '*What?*'
Did your ancestors live (here)? Ask '*Where?*'
Did you watch TV last night? Ask '*Which programme?*'

◆ Workbook

The Workbook can be done at home.
If it is done in class, exercises 2, 7, and 8 can be done orally in pairs.
Students could also question each other in pairs about the text in exercise 2.

Regular verbs: spellings

In English, some verbs are **irregular** in the past:
went, saw, got, bought, fell, etc.
Some verbs are **regular**:
add *-ed*, or *-d* to the present.
Remember these spelling rules:
add -d:
  move, fire, live, die – moved etc.
add -ed:
  want, visit, kill, sail – wanted etc.
change y to ied:
  marry – married, hurry – hurried etc.
double the consonant:
  slip – slipped, stop – stopped etc.

b) Regular verbs: sounds

-d and *-ed* have three different sounds. Sometimes they sound like [t], sometimes they sound like [d], sometimes they sound like [ɪd]. Listen to the cassette. Look at the verbs below, and put a tick [✓] in the correct place.

verb	[t]	[d]	[ɪd]
wanted			
looked			
visited			
discovered			
played			
started			
scored			
lived			
moved			
died			
fired			
killed			
worked			
sailed			
arrived			
slipped			
drowned			
loved			
asked			
married			
stopped			
landed			
weighed			

c) What's wrong?

Picture 1 *They didn't have knives and forks in 100,000 BC.*
  or *They didn't eat with knives and forks in 100,000 BC.*

Unit thirty-six

Unit thirty-seven

Having a conversation

a Which is the friendly conversation?

In English, the **sound** is very important. You can sound friendly, you can sound interested, you can sound happy, you can sound angry, or you can sound afraid.

1 Look at these sentences. Which is the friendly one?
- ■ *Yes, thanks.*
- ■ *Yes, thank you very much. You're very kind.*

Answer:

You don't know. You can't hear the sound.

2 You're going to hear some pairs of conversations. Which is the friendly conversation – conversation A, or conversation B? Put a tick [✓] in the boxes below.

Conversation

1 A ☐	B ☐	4 A ☐	B ☐
2 A ☐	B ☐	5 A ☐	B ☐
3 A ☐	B ☐	6 A ☐	B ☐

b Starting a conversation

How do you start and continue a conversation? There's a right way, and a wrong way! Listen to these two conversations. Which is the right way? Why?

- ☐ Er... It's not very nice today, is it?
- ☐ No, it isn't. Not very nice at all.
- ☐ It's very cold... for Spring.
- ☐ Mmm. The weather forecast was rain for tonight.
- ☐ Was it? Well, it's usually wrong!
- ☐ Yes, but not always. The forecast on Saturday was fog, and it was foggy all day.

- ☐ 'Morning. It's a nice day, isn't it?
- ☐ Yes.
- ☐ Is it going to rain later?
- ☐ I don't know.
- ☐ Oh.

Some ways to start and continue a conversation:

1 In England, talk about the weather.
2 Smile.
3 Sound friendly. Sound interested.
4 Look at the other person. Listen to them.
5 Don't stop the conversation. Answer. Then ask questions.
6 Give more information.

c Conversations about the weather

Make conversations about the weather.
Use some of these words:

| wonderful | lovely | nice |
| not very nice | awful | terrible |

| hot | warm | cool | cold |
| wet | dry | foggy | cloudy | sunny |

| snow | rain | fog | sunshine |

| to rain | to snow | to thunder |
| to be hot / warm / cool / etc |

| spring | summer | autumn | winter |
| January / July / etc |

Teaching points
Strategies for starting and continuing a conversation.
Listening: for tone of voice and expression.
Adjectives, nouns, and verbs (*wet, rain, rain*).
Tag questions:
It's a nice day, isn't it?
It's not very nice, is it?
Revision of weather vocabulary (see also Unit 26).
Gerunds: *I like swimming. I don't like dancing.*
What do you like doing?
do versus *play*
What kind?
sound + adjective (*happy, angry, interested*)
Narration: Telling stories and jokes.
Anyway in narrative.

Expressions
You're very kind.
Anyway / at all / on holiday

Active vocabulary
autumn / comedy / conversation / fog / forecast / horror / joke / neighbour / science fiction / spring / war / western
angry / awful / foggy / important / interested / surprised / valuable
collect / continue / enjoy / smile / sound / take/took
at all

Passive vocabulary
adventure / aerobics / athletics / burglars / drama / hobbies / interests
judo / yoga
folk (music) / Persian (carpet)

Audio-visual aids
Cassette

Unit thirty-seven

ⓐ 😐 Which is the friendly conversation?

Note: This unit begins with a listening exercise which is designed to show the importance of tone and expression in the voice in English. Politeness, or friendliness depend less on the choice of formulas, than on the **way** in which things are said. Get students **to read** the introductory text. Note that if you read it to them, you will have to say the two example sentences in a flat, monotonous voice.

1 Ask students which is the friendly sentence. Then point out the answer – you don't know because you can't hear it. If you wish, demonstrate further by saying:
Give me your pen, Maria in a soft, friendly tone. Lean forward and smile as you say it. Then lean back, and bark out rudely, *Would you be kind enough to give me your pen, please? Thank you very much!* You could give several examples like this.

2 i) Explain the listening exercise. Remind them that it is **how** it is said, not **what** is said that is important.
ii) Play the cassette. Students should put a tick or cross on the initial listening.
iii) Play the cassette again, pausing to check the answers. Don't go into the content of the cassette. Concentrate only on tone and vocal expression.

ⓑ Starting a conversation

1 Explain the activity. As in ⓐ 2 ii), they only have to decide which is the right way, the first conversation or the second one. Play both conversations. Discuss which is the 'right way', and invite suggestions as to why it is the right way.

2 Get students to read the text silently.

3 Go back and play the cassette again. Pause and get them to repeat, chorally and individually. Focus on tone and expression rather than structure. Get students to smile, and use 'inviting' body language as well. Be careful with the intonation of the tag questions. **Note:** If tone is not used in the same way in the mother tongue, students may find this strange, and perhaps embarrassing. If so, be sensitive about individual repetition. You may wish to ask how many of the points are true about their own language. Check *at all*.

4 Point out the tag questions. These are more important for comprehension than student generation, but they are extremely common.

5 Silent reading of the two conversations.

6 Paired reading of the two conversations.

7 Completion drill:
T: *It's a nice day . . .*
C: *It's a nice day, isn't it?*
T: *It isn't very nice . . .*
C: *It isn't very nice, is it?*
Continue: *It's very warm . . . / It isn't wet today . . . / It's cold . . . / It's lovely . . . / It isn't cold for Spring . . . / It isn't right . . . / It's wrong . . .*

8 Focus attention on **Some ways to start and continue a conversation**. Get students to read the text silently.

ⓒ Conversations about the weather

1 Get students to generate conversations about the weather in pairs, using the chart. **Note:** The colour coding will help them to avoid mistakes over the choice of noun, verb, or adjective form.

2 Optional: You could use this section to point out / check grammar. (But we would avoid doing so.)

3 Get a few students out at the front of the class. Say *This is a bus stop. You don't know me. Start a conversation.* The teacher should try and make unpredictable responses in this activity. The students should try to continue. e.g.
S1: *It's a nice day, isn't it:?* T: (fiercely) *Do I know you?*
S2: *It isn't very warm, is it?* T: *No, it isn't. It's very cold indeed. I got up this morning and there was ice on my car. I was freezing! But last year . . . that was really cold! Do you know that . . .* (All taken at very high speed.)

S3: *This rain's terrible, isn't it?* **T:** *Why?*
S4: *It's a lovely day, isn't it?* **T:** *Is it? Not for me . . . I've got a terrible headache and . . .*
S5: *It's awful weather, isn't it?* **T:** *Well, actually I like wet weather. I love thunder! It's very exciting, isn't it?*

d) Talking about interests and hobbies

Say *All right. You can start a conversation. But what are you going to talk about?* Invite suggestions. Someone will bring up interests and hobbies, though they may not know the words in English.
Get students to read through the section silently. Point out that we use the -ing form after *like* and *enjoy*.

1 Pair work. Get students to ask and answer questions. Explain 'collecting things'. Ask what they collect / like collecting. e.g. *stamps, matchboxes, models, records, books* etc. Ask *What do you like collecting? What about your friends / family? What do they collect?*

2 i) Silent reading of the conversation.
ii) Paired reading of the conversation.
iii) Focus attention on the pictures. Check vocabulary. Ask students to give you examples of (e.g.) *a war story, a horror film, a western, a musical.*
iv) Check the use of *play* and *do* with sports.
v) Pair work. Students use the pictures and make more conversations like the example.
vi) Ask students about their partner's interests / hobbies. Ask a few questions generally to the class.
vii) **Optional:** The class could do a statistical analysis to find out the most popular kinds of book, film, record, sport in the class.

e) Telling stories

Point out that in long conversations we often tell stories or jokes.

1 Read *A true story* aloud.

2 Silent reading of *A true story*. Check *anyway*. Retell the story in your own words, as conversationally as possible.

3 Invite students to tell other true stories / anecdotes to the class.

4 Read *A joke* aloud.

5 Silent reading of *A joke*.

6 Invite students to tell other jokes to the class. They will have to translate in their heads.

◆ Homework

Students write out a joke or anecdote for homework. Get some students to tell their jokes / stories at the beginning of a subsequent lesson.

◆ Workbook

The Workbook can be done at home. Months & dates appear in Unit 24, and will appear again in Unit 38. They are revised here.
Exercise 2 can be done in class in pairs, discussing the answers. Exercise 3 is particularly suitable for paired practice. Students can use the questionnaire in pairs, change partners, and ask about the previous partner's answers.

d Talking about interests and hobbies

1 What do you like doing? Ask another student.
Do you like:
____ reading?   ____ swimming?
____ playing sports?   ____ travelling?
____ listening to music? ____ going to the cinema?
____ dancing?   ____ watching videos?
____ collecting things?

Ask more questions like these.

2 What kind? Look at the pictures.
A *Do you like reading?*
B *Yes, I do. Very much.*
A *What kind of books do you like?*
B *I like books about animals, and I enjoy science fiction, too.*
A *What's your favourite book?*
B *I don't know ... Lord of the Rings, I think.*

Make more conversations.

e Telling stories

In long conversations we often tell stories or jokes. Here are some examples.

A true story

I heard a story about a woman in England. One day she saw a large truck outside her neighbours' house. Anyway, she was surprised because her neighbours were on holiday. Then some men came out of her neighbours' door. They had her neighbours' valuable Persian carpets. They put them into the truck. The woman went over to the men and said, 'What are you doing with those carpets?'
'We're taking them to the cleaner's,' said one of the men.
'That's wonderful,' she said. 'Can you take my carpets too?'
'All right,' said the man, and they took her carpets to the truck. Anyway, she never saw them again. The men were burglars.

A joke

A little boy came home after his first day at school. 'What did you do today?' said his mother.
'We did some writing,' said the little boy.
'That's nice. What did you write?' said his mother.
'I don't know,' said the little boy, 'We didn't do reading.'

Tell another student a story or a joke.

Unit thirty-seven

BOOKS: animals | travel | science fiction | novels | romantic novels | detective stories

FILMS / VIDEOS: science fiction | war / adventure | comedy | horror | westerns | musicals | drama

MUSIC: pop | rock | soul / disco | classical | jazz | folk

SPORT

play: football, volleyball, tennis

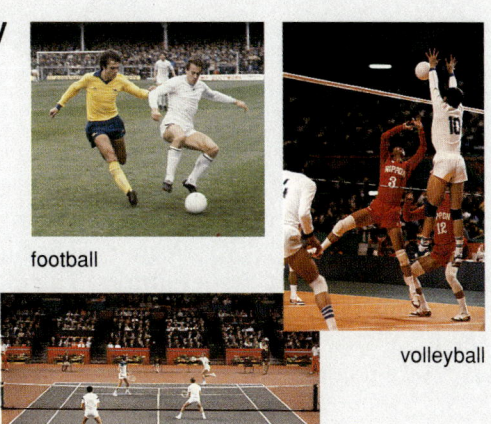

do: athletics,  aerobics,  judo,  yoga

swimming, walking, riding

Unit thirty-eight

Going home

Doris and Harry Flint are English. They're on holiday in San Miguel. It's the last day of their holiday, and they're waiting for their bus to the airport.

Harry Oh dear. When will that bus be here? Look at the time!
Doris Don't worry, love. It'll be here soon.
Harry We'll be late.
Doris No, we won't.
Harry Yes, we will. We'll miss the plane.
Doris No, dear. We won't miss the plane.
Harry Are you sure, Doris?
Doris Yes, I'm sure, Harry. We'll be there on time.
Harry Will we?
Doris Yes. They won't leave without us.
Harry Well, they did last year. We were only ten minutes late. They left without us then.
Doris Well, we won't miss it this year. Here it comes now . . .
Harry Thank goodness for that!

a Questions

Ask and answer.
1 Will you be at school tomorrow?
2 Will you be at school on Saturday?
3 Will you be at school on Sunday?
4 Will you do any homework tonight?
5 What time will you go home tomorrow?
6 What time will you eat this evening?
7 What time will you go to bed?
8 What time will you get up tomorrow?
9 What time will you leave home tomorrow morning?

SAN MIGUEL AIRPORT
FLIGHT DEPARTURES
23 AUGUST   time now 09:15

flight	destination	time	gate
BM 376	GLASGOW	08:30	1
DA 567	MANCHESTER	08:45	4
OR 211	EAST MIDLANDS	09:00	2
BA 889	LONDON - GATWICK	09:15	1
OR 212	NEWCASTLE	09:15	3
DA 569	LUTON	09:45	4
AE 233	BIRMINGHAM	10:05	2
MO 892	BRISTOL	10:25	1

Present: It's 9.15. The flight to London-Gatwick is leaving now.
Past: The flight to East Midlands left at 9 o'clock.
Future: The flight to Luton will leave at 9.45.

b Flight departures

Make sentences about the flights to Glasgow, Manchester, Newcastle, Birmingham, and Bristol.

Teaching points

'll / won't for simple future.
(I) 'll be there. / (We) 'll do it.
(He) won't be there. / (I) won't do it.
Will (I / he / she / we / you / they) be there? / do it?
Yes, (I) will. / No, (we) won't.
Listening: Aural discrimination.

Grammar note

'll should be taught in affirmative sentences, as a contraction of *will* with all persons.
shall is taught in **the question form only** in Unit 39 for offers and suggestions with the first person, but is to be avoided in simple future examples. *shan't* is very rare in modern English and should be avoided.

Expressions

on time
Here it comes now.
Thank goodness for that.

Active vocabulary

birthday / calendar / destination / gate / problem
get married / left (past) / miss / 'll / will / won't / worry
unhappy / on time / soon

Passive vocabulary

independence / national / religious / saint (St.)

Classroom vocabulary

future

Audio-visual aids

Cassette

Unit thirty-eight

◆ **Dialogue**

1 Focus attention on the picture. Check that the text is covered. Ask questions about the picture: *Where are they? What's he like? What's she like? Are they English?*

2 Read the introductory text aloud.
Ask: *What are their names? Where are they? Why are they there? Is it the first day of their holiday? What day is it? Where are they going? What are they waiting for?*

3 Play the cassette of the dialogue. **Note:** *Do not stop the tape too soon. There are sound effects at the end of the dialogue which are important.*
Play it again, pausing for choral and individual repetition. Pay particular attention to *'ll*, which many students find difficult to hear. (**Optional:** See the Listening exercise below, which could be done here if they have serious problems with this.)
Also *It'll be here* **soon**. *We'll be there* **on time**. *Here it comes now.*
It is important that they use the contracted form in future uses, *I will do it* is to be avoided. Include the drills in the repetition phase. Drilling is for pronunciation practice, and to reinforce the use of the contractions, *'ll* and *won't*. It is worth doing even with false beginners.

4 Drill:
T: *We*
C: *We'll be late.*
Continue: *I / He / They / She / You / It / We*

5 Drill:
T: *We*
C: *We won't be late.*
Continue: *He / You / I / It / She / They / We*

6 Drill:
T: *we*
C: *Will we be late?*
Continue: *she / you / it / we / they / I / he*

7 Drill:
T: *We'll be there on time.*
C: *Will we?*

Continue: *She'll miss the plane. / He'll be angry. / You'll be sorry. / They'll be late. / The plane will leave. / I'll be at home.*

8 Silent reading of the dialogue.

9 Paired reading of the dialogue.

10 Play the cassette again. Pause during the sounds at the end.
Ask: *What's happening? Will they be late? Will they miss the plane? Will it leave without them? What will they do?*

11 Role play. Students work in pairs. The bus driver says: 'Another bus will be here in ten minutes.' Role play Doris and Harry's conversation.

12 Group role play. Students work in groups and decide who the other tourists are on the bus. They should also decide what their attitude is to the breakdown. One student takes the part of the bus driver, the other group members role play the angry / anxious tourists. This is an activity for large groups. You may wish to simply split the class into two. If possible, arrange the seats as in a bus.

a **Questions**

1 Go through the questions, asking individuals. Add other days of the week to elicit short answers: *Will we have a lesson next Tuesday?* (etc)? *Will we be at school on Christmas Day? Will you have any lessons on Sunday?* etc.

2 Pair work. Students ask and answer the questions in pairs, noting their partner's answers.

3 Ask students about their partners: *Will he / she be at school tomorrow? What time will he / she leave school today?* etc.

b **Flight Departures**

1 Focus attention on the Flight Departures Board. Go through the examples. Check *past, present, future.*

2 Get students to make sentences in pairs. Check back with the class.

c) You'll finish soon?

1 Explain the activity, which is aural discrimination. Many students fail to hear *'ll* when listening. Play the cassette once. Students tick the sentence they hear.

2 Play the cassette again, pausing to confirm / correct their answers.

d) Dates

1 Get students to say the dates aloud. It may be better to write them on the board, and to point to them for choral and individual responses. You could add more examples.

2 Write *1st December 1989*. Point out that we say *The first of December, 1989* or *December the first 1989*.
Show them that in modern business letters it is now common to write *1 December 1989* rather than *1st December 1989*. It is still said in the same way (*The first of ...*). It is worth mentioning that in Britain, in common with most countries, the abbreviation is 1.12.89. However, in the United States the normal abbreviation for December 1st is 12.1.89.

e) Frank and Betty

1 Read the introductory text aloud. Ask questions:
What's his name? What's her name? What does he do? What does she do? What do they do? Are they married? When did they get married? What's their problem? Why are their jobs a problem?

2 Go through the examples. Students ask and answer in pairs. Check back with the class as a whole.

f) The calendar

1 Explain the activity. Go through the examples. Get students to mark the calendars alone with birthdays of family and friends.

2 Pair work. Students ask and answer about each other's Calendars in pairs. Write up significant birthdays for yourself on the board in abbreviated form (e.g. 1.12). Get students to ask you about the dates as in the examples.

3 Repeat the procedure in pairs with other important days. You may have to help with vocabulary. Check *St. / Saint*. Write up *St. George's St.* Ask students what the abbreviations mean. (*Saint George's Street.*). Point out that St. George is the patron saint of England. (The day is not really celebrated though.)

4 Students change partners and ask and answer about the important dates.

◆ Transfer: Your future

1 Ask students about their future. Write up a date 20 years into the future on the board. Ask questions: *Will you be married? Will you be rich? Will you be poor? Will you be happy? Will you be in this town / country? Will you have children? What do you think you'll look like twenty years into the future? What about the other people in the class? Will you be friends? Will you see them?*

2 Pair work. Get students to ask and answer in pairs in the same way.

3 Discussion questions:
Continue with discussion questions to the class.
*Which of these things do **you** think will be true twenty years into the future?*
Will they be true fifty (or a hundred) years into the future?
Britain will be a republic.
There'll be a space station on the moon.
There'll be no nuclear weapons.
(Your country / Leichtenstein / England) will win the World Cup at football.
There won't be any petrol.
A woman will be the President (of the USA / your country.)
There won't be any wars.
Europe will have one government.
Everybody will drive Korean cars.
Millions of people will die from AIDS.
Things won't be very different.
There won't be any cars.
There won't be any hungry people.
There'll be a world war.
There'll be more robberies.
People will have holidays in space.
(A currently popular singer) will have records in the Top 20.
A lot of cars from today will be on the roads.
(A famous person from today) will be dead.
There'll be cities under the sea.

◆ Workbook

The Workbook can be done at home.
If it is done in class, exercises 1, 2, and 3 can be done orally in pairs.
Exercise 10 can be done in pairs, and might provide a suitable basis for class discussion.

c) You'll finish soon?

'll is sometimes difficult to hear.
Listen to the cassette. Which sentence can you hear?
Put a tick [✓] by the correct one.

1. ☐ I'll leave at 6 o'clock.
   ☐ I leave at 6 o'clock.
2. ☐ We'll arrive at 7.
   ☐ We arrive at 7.
3. ☐ They'll play football.
   ☐ They play football.
4. ☐ I'll have a bath at 8 o'clock.
   ☐ I have a bath at 8 o'clock.
5. ☐ You'll finish soon.
   ☐ You finish soon.
6. ☐ He'll put it there.
   ☐ He put it there.

d) Dates

1 / 12   Say *the first of December*.

Say these dates:

2 / 11	6 / 7	10 / 3
3 / 10	7 / 6	11 / 2
4 / 9	8 / 5	12 / 1
5 / 8	9 / 4	13 / 12

e) Frank and Betty

Frank and Betty are flight attendants. They got married last year. Their jobs are a problem. He hardly ever sees her, and she hardly ever sees him.
Look at their timetables for next week.

Day	Frank	Betty
Monday 11th	London – Paris	New York – London
Tuesday 12th	Paris – Rome	FREE (London)
Wednesday 13th	Rome – Dublin	FREE (London)
Thursday 14th	Dublin – London	London – Miami
Friday 15th	FREE (London)	Miami – New York
Saturday 16th	FREE (London)	New York – London

A *Where will he be on Monday evening?*
B *He'll be in Paris.*
A *Where will she be?*
B *She'll be in London.*
A *Where will he go on Tuesday 12th?*
B *He'll go to Rome.*

Ask and answer about their week.

f) The calendar

1. Look at the calendar. Put a ring around birthdays that are important for you.
   (Your birthday, birthdays of family and friends.)

2. Work with another student. If today is June 9th, and there is a ring around March 3rd and November 22nd, you can make conversations like these:

March 3rd (PAST)

A *Whose birthday is March 3rd?*
B *It's my sister's birthday.*
A *How old was she?*
B *She was fourteen.*

November 22nd (FUTURE)

A *Whose birthday is November 22nd?*
B *It's my mother's birthday.*
A *How old will she be?*
B *She'll be thirty-nine.*

Ask and answer about important dates for you and your partner.

3. Now put a ring around national holidays, religious days, and saints' days, etc.

4. Work with another student.

A *What's important about April 23rd?*
B *It's St. George's Day.*
A *Why is there a ring around July 4th?*
B *It's American Independence Day.*

Ask and answer about the important dates.

Unit thirty-eight

Unit thirty-nine

Offers and suggestions

Offers of help

Man Don't worry, dear. I'll help you.
Lady Pardon?
Man It's a busy road, isn't it? Come on, I'll take you across.
Lady That's very kind of you, but ...
Man Ah! Here's a space in the traffic. Let's go.
Lady Thank you, but ...
Man Shall I carry your shopping bag? It's heavy, isn't it?
Lady Well, yes, but ...
Man There you are!
Lady But I didn't want to cross the road!
Man What? Why didn't you tell me?
Lady You didn't listen!
Man Oh! Er ... Shall I take you back?
Lady No, thank you!

Suggestions

Carol It's no good. It's broken.
Morris But it's Friday night! My favourite programmes are on Friday night.
Carol I know! Shall we go out?
Morris All right, then. Where shall we go?
Carol Shall we go to the cinema?
Morris Oh, no! I don't like the cinema.
Carol Why don't we go to a restaurant?
Morris No. That's too expensive.
Carol All right. Let's go and see some friends.
Morris We haven't got any friends.
Carol I know! The shops are open late on Fridays.
Morris I don't want to go shopping.
Carol Yes, you do. Shall we go and buy a new television?

Offers	Accepting	Refusing
I'll do it.	Yes, please.	No, thank you.
Shall I do it?	Thank you very much.	No, it's all right. I'll do it.
	That's very kind of you.	Thank you, but I can do it.
	That's very nice of you.	That's very kind, but no thanks.

Suggestions	Agreeing	Disagreeing
Shall we do it?	Yes, let's do it.	I don't like (that).
Let's do it.	That's a good idea.	No, I don't want to.
Why don't we do it?	Yes, OK.	No, thanks.
	Yes, all right.	

Teaching points
Offers:
I'll do it. Shall I do it?
Suggestions:
Shall we do it? Let's do it. Why don't we do it?
Where shall we go? What shall we do? Who shall we go and see?
Accepting and refusing offers.
Agreeing and disagreeing with suggestions.
Want + Infinitive (See also Unit 36):
I don't want to do it. / I didn't want to do it.
I want to do it. / I wanted to do it.
Have a headache / a temperature.
Reading: matching dialogues to film titles.

Grammar note
The use of *shall* should be restricted to offers and suggestions (see Unit 38).

Expressions
That's very nice of you.
There you are.
I've got (a headache / a temperature).
That's too expensive.
I don't want to.

Active vocabulary
beach / disco / headache / idea / movie / offer / show / space / suggestion / theatre / traffic
carry / cross / shall
alive / broken / loud / low / tired
anywhere / somewhere / too

Passive vocabulary
Note the structure *Why don't we go to a club **where** the music's playing loud* should be considered passive. It appears in the song.
accepting / agreeing / arm / brakes / disagreeing / elephant / fever / heart / mad / refusing / seaside / soft / volt
forget / where (relative)

Classroom vocabulary
act out

Audio-visual aids
Cassette

Unit thirty-nine

◆ Dialogue 1: Offers of help

1 Focus attention on the picture. Check that the text is covered. Play the cassette.

2 Explain 'offer'. Play the cassette again. Students underline the offers. Check back.

3 Play the cassette again, pausing for selective choral and individual repetition. (Focus on the offers.)

4 Drill:
T: *I can't carry it.*
C: *Shall I carry it?*
Continue: *I can't do it. / I can't phone them. / I can't go there. / I can't do my homework. / I can't help him.*

5 Drill:
T: *I want a drink.*
C: *I'll get you a drink.*
Continue: *I need help. / I'd like a coffee. / I can't carry this bag. / I want a sandwich. / I need some money.*

6 Silent reading of dialogue 1.

7 Paired reading of dialogue 1.

8 Questions:
Was the road busy? Was there a space in the traffic? Did he take her across? Did she want to go across? Did she tell him? Did he listen?

◆ Chart: Offers

1 Focus attention on the chart at the foot of the dialogue. Silent reading.

2 Get them to suggest some alternative responses. Check that *shall* – not *will* – is used for offers.

◆ Dialogue 2: Suggestions

1 Focus attention on the picture. Check that the text is covered. Play the cassette.

2 Explain 'suggestion'. Play the cassette again. Students underline the suggestions. Check back.

3 Play the cassette again, pausing for selective choral and individual repetition. (Focus on suggestions.)

4 Drill:
T: *There's a good film at the cinema.*
C: *OK, shall we go to the cinema?*
Continue: *I want to go to a restaurant. / There's a good football match tonight. / I like swimming. / The shops are open now. / I love dancing.*

5 Drill;
T: *Shall we go out?*
C: *Yes, let's go out.*
Continue: *Shall we watch television? / Shall we go dancing? / Shall we go to a restaurant? / Shall we go for a coffee? / Shall we sit down?*

6 Silent reading of dialogue 2.

7 Paired reading of dialogue 2.

8 Questions:
It isn't Thursday, is it? It's Friday, isn't it? The TV's broken, isn't it? When are Morris's favourite programmes on TV? Does he like the cinema?
Why don't they go to a restaurant? Why don't they go and see some friends? When are the shops open late? Does he want to go shopping? Does she want to go shopping? What does she want to buy?

Unit thirty-nine

◆ Chart: Suggestions

1 Focus attention on the chart. Silent reading.

2 Get them to suggest some alternative responses. Check that *shall* – not *will* – is used for suggestions.

a) Offer to help

1 Explain the activity. Get them to work on it in pairs. They should offer, and their partners should accept or refuse the offer. Check back with the class.

2 Add more situations to which they should respond with an offer:
e.g. *It's very hot in here, and the window's closed. / It's very cold in here, and the window's open. / I can't find my pen. / I need a cup of coffee. / I'm tired. / I haven't got any money. / The board's dirty. / I need some books from the teacher's room. / I'd like a newspaper. / I haven't got a dictionary.* etc.

b) Make suggestions

Get them to make suggestions in pairs. Their partners agree or disagree. Check back.

c) Which film?

1 Focus attention on the four film posters. Ask students about the films. *What kind of film is it?*
(Refer back to Unit 37 for vocabulary if necessary.)

2 Explain the activity. (All they have to do is decide which dialogue comes from which film.)
They should work alone to do this.

3 Ask them for answers. Ask them why they think so.

d) Be a film star!

1 Explain the activity. They are going to act out the conversations in pairs.

2 Explain that they should continue the conversations from their imaginations, again in pairs.

3 Get one or two pairs to demonstrate in front of the class. Ask for class suggestions on the rest of the story.

◆ Extension

1 Situations:
Get students to make suggestions in these situations:
There's a good film on at the (XYZ) cinema. / I'd like a coffee. / The (XYZ) disco is very good. / The new (Italian) restaurant in town is very good. / I love dancing. / There's a good programme on TV. etc.

2 **Optional:** Group work. Take in the entertainments page of a local newspaper. (Either multiple copies, or photocopies of a current one.) Students work in groups, making suggestions about what to do / see. It doesn't matter if the newspaper isn't in English.

e) ♪ Let's Go to a Movie

1 Play the song once. Students listen.

2 Play the song again, checking comprehension. Get them to repeat selected lines chorally.

3 Listen and sing. Students sing along with the cassette.

4 Role play. Students role play the situation of the song. Student A makes a suggestion, student B disagrees with every one, giving a reason. One wants to be the other's boyfriend / girlfriend. The other is not interested.

◆ Role play: The party

The class as a whole improvises a party situation, offering to get each other drinks, food etc, offering to put on records, suggesting a dance, drinks, food, sitting down etc.

◆ Workbook

The Workbook can be done at home.
If it is done in class, exercises 1, 3, and 6 can be done orally in pairs.

a Offer to help

A *I've got a headache.*
B *I'll get you an aspirin. / Shall I get you an aspirin?*
A *Yes. Thank you very much.*
  No, thanks. I'll be all right soon.

Look at the pictures and continue.

I'M THIRSTY
I'M HUNGRY
I HAVEN'T GOT ANY MONEY
I'M TIRED I'D LIKE TO SIT DOWN
THIS BAG'S VERY HEAVY

b Make suggestions

A *Shall we go to the cinema?*
B *Yes, that's a good idea. / No, I don't want to.*

Continue with these words: television / party / dancing / restaurant / disco / theatre / concert.

c Which film?

Look at these four conversations. They are all from films.
One conversation is from *True Hearts in Love*, one is from *Mrs Frankenstein*, one is from *Safari Hospital*, and one is from *Police School 6*.
Which conversation is from which film?

1 □ I'll help you, doctor. I'll help you ...
  ■ Hurry, she can't move her arm.
  □ Shall I turn on the electricity?
  ■ Yes, we'll give her 50,000 volts.
  □ She's moving, doctor. She's alive!

2 ■ But Antonia, I love you. I'll always love you!
  ■ It's no good, Cecil. Let's forget about it.
  ■ I'll do anything for you, Antonia.
  ■ Anything?
  ■ Anything.
  ■ Then go away from here. Go far away!

3 ■ Doctor! Hurry ... or we'll be too late.
  ■ Is that you, Adam? What's wrong?
  ■ It was an elephant, doctor. A mad elephant.
  ■ But I can't drive ... the fever ... I can't see ...
  ■ I'll drive you there, doctor. Shall we take the Land Rover?
  ■ The Land Rover? But Adam ... the brakes ... they don't ...

4 ■ There's someone in there. Let's phone for help.
  ■ There's no time. I'll go in.
  ■ Rod, you can't! You haven't got a gun.
  ■ I'll be all right. Why don't you phone for help?
  ■ No ... no, I'll come with you.
  ■ Thanks, Steve.

d Be a film star!

1 Act out the conversations from the films.
2 What happens next? Can you continue the conversation. Can you tell the story?

e Let's go to a movie

Shall we go to a movie?
Shall we go to a show?
Why don't we go somewhere quiet,
where the lights are soft and low?

I won't go to a movie,
I won't go to a show,
I won't go anywhere with you.
My answer will be 'No'.

Let's go to a party,
Let's go with the crowd.
Why don't we go to a disco,
where the music's playing loud?

I won't go to a disco,
I won't go to a show,
I won't go anywhere with you.
My answer will be 'No'.

I'll take you to the seaside.
Why don't we drive to the sea?
I'll take you to a lovely beach,
where there's only you and me.

I won't go to the seaside,
I won't go to a show,
I won't go anywhere with you.
My answer will be 'No'.

Unit thirty-nine

Unit forty

Treasure Island

Game

You will need something to score with:

You can use a dice.

You can make a spinner.
You will need a piece of card and a pencil.

You can write the numbers on the six sides of a pencil.

You can write the numbers on six pieces of paper.
Then fold the pieces, and mix them up.

You will need a counter:

You can use a coin, or any small object.

Rules

- Any number of players from 2 to 6 can play.

- You are on a desert island. The first person to get to the treasure is the winner.
  You need the *exact* number to get to the end.
  Each player throws the dice, and moves the correct number of spaces.
  Two or more players can be on the same space.

- Follow the arrows (➤➤➤). Each space has a number. Sometimes there will be an instruction. If you land on a red or yellow space, find the instruction in the list, and obey it.

- Red spaces. On the red spaces there are two paths, one to the left and one to the right. When you pass over a red space, read the instruction and continue in the direction it tells you. If you finish on a red space, read the instruction and go in that direction on your next throw.

You can take two things with you:

Choose two things from this list:
a map, a compass, a rope, an axe.
Write them down on a piece of paper.
On some spaces you get more things. You can have two of the same thing. Add a second one to your list.

Instructions

2 You find an axe on the beach. Add it to your list.
3 Have you got a map? YES – Go right; NO – Go left.
4 You remember there's a map on your boat.
  Go back to 1, and add a map to your list.
6 You find a gold coin. Go forward to 14.
8 Did you walk here for this lesson?
  YES – Go to 14; NO – Go to 7.
10 A crocodile attacks you. Go back to 5.
13 Is your birthday between the 1st and 15th of the month?
  YES – Go forward one; NO – Go back to 2.
15 Is the first letter of your surname between A and M?
  YES – Go back to 14; NO – Go on to 16.
17 Have you got an axe?
  YES – Turn right, through the jungle; NO – Go left.
18 You kill a snake. Go forward to 21.
20 Have you got a compass or a rope?
  You lose them in the jungle. Cross them off your list.
22 You find a rope. Add it to your list.
25 A snake bites you. Miss a turn.
27 Have you got a rope?
  YES – Go left across the river; NO – Go right.
28 There is lava from the volcano on the path.
  Wait until it's cold. Miss a turn.
30 You find a compass. Add it to your list.
32 You slip on the path and break your arm. Go back to 26.
34 You sit on your compass. It breaks. Cross it off your list.
36 You're frightened of the volcano. Go back to 26.
  Your rope falls in the river. Cross it from your list.
38 You haven't got any food.
  Go back to 21, and get some coconuts.
40 Did you have a hot drink with your breakfast?
  YES – Go to 41; NO – Go to 39.
42 You are lost. Turn round and go to 33.
  You find a compass on 33. Add it to your list.
43 Have you got a compass?
  YES – Go west (to 48); NO – Go south (to 44).
44 You fall into the lake. The piranhas don't eat you, but go back to 41.
46 Can you swim 400 metres?
  YES – Swim across to 56; NO – Stay on 46.
49 Will you stop studying English when you finish this book?
  NO – Go forward to 53; YES – Go back to 41.
51 What are the past tenses of *go, buy, get*?
  Three correct? – Go left (to 53);
  Any wrong? Go right (fall down the cliff to 52).
54 Is your birthday between January 1st and June 30th?
  YES – Go left (to 56); NO – Go right (to 55).
57 You're thirsty. Go back to 53 for water.
59 You think this is the wrong way. Go back to 50.

Unit forty

Teaching points
Revision. Instructions. *each*.
Note: There are some sentences in the rules and instructions which have not been covered, but these should be understood passively by the students. e.g. *If . . . / When . . . / The first person to get to . . . / something to score with . . . / Continue in the direction it tells you . . .*

Note
The rules and words on the board are covered under vocabulary. Other items in the game instructions are not listed in the main vocabulary index. See **Game vocabulary** below.

Active vocabulary
coin / dice / object / rope / rule / throw (n) / turn (n)
choose / throw
exact

Passive vocabulary
arrow / axe / cliff / compass / counter / jungle / lake / piranha / spinner / swamp / treasure
fold / mix up / obey

Classroom vocabulary
threw

Game vocabulary
Not listed in index.
crocodile (SFP4) / lava (WB11) / path / snake / tenses
break / fall / study

Audio-visual aids
The game can be played without any extra scoring devices or counters. (See: **You will need something to score with.**) However, it would be simple to assemble a box with dice and counters for use with this lesson. You could also make spinners before the lesson, if you have no dice. In the lesson, pencils or pieces of paper are very easy to prepare. Making scorers in class obviously involves comprehension and language practice so is not a waste of time.

Suitable counters: A box of assorted coloured paper clips, map pins, or drawing pins is cheap. Many shops sell counters and dice in packs. Scrabble tiles are also suitable if you have a Scrabble game in the school. Students often enjoy finding their own counters (e.g. decorative pencil tops, hair slides, erasers, coins . . .)

Note: The game takes a group of four or five between 20 and 35 minutes to play.

◆ You will need something to score with

1 Go through the suggestions. Either issue scorers or get students to make their own.

2 Either issue counters, or get students to select their own.

◆ Rules

1 Get students to read the rules silently.

2 Check the rules carefully. Ask questions:
Who is the winner? What do you need to get to the end? So, if you're on Space 58, how many do you need? What about Space 56? Space 55?
Note that two or more players can occupy the same space.
What do you follow? Which spaces have got instructions? Where can you find the instructions? What happens on red spaces? What do you do when you pass over a red space?
i.e. You continue with your turn, e.g. You're on 41. You throw a six. You pause on 43, read the instruction, then count on to six – 50 if you go right, 46 – if you go left. If your throw finishes on a red space, you read the instruction, then continue in that direction when you get your next turn. In each turn you only follow one red, and one yellow instruction – even if that instruction leads you to another yellow space.

◆ You can take two things with you

Explain the instructions. Get them to choose two items each, which must be written down on a list. Some spaces will add things to the list. It is possible to have two or more of the same item as a result.

◆ Playing the game

1 The game may be played in pairs, groups of from 3 to 6, or both. If there are more than 2 players, it may be easier for each student to play on his / her own book. They will have more room. They still take turns.

2 It is best if one players throws, and another player reads out the instructions.

3 You may wish to let the students play in pairs first, before going on to a group game. Go through some expressions they may need:
What did you throw? I threw a six.
What have you got on your list? Add a rope. Cross the axe from your list.
What happened?
How many do you need? I need a four. I threw a three.
Go back to . . . / Go forward to . . .
Bad luck! That was unlucky!
A paired game will take 10–15 minutes. A group game between 20 and 35 minutes.

◆ After the game

Ask students about other board games they have played. Ask why they think they won / lost. Ask what they would do differently if they played it again.

◆ Workbook

The Workbook can be done at home. If it is done in class, the story could be questioned intensively. The sounds exercise should be checked orally.

Unit forty

Irregular verbs

Infinitive	Past tense	Infinitive	Past tense	Infinitive	Past tense	Infinitive	Past tense
be	was/were	feel	felt	light	lit	sit	sat
beat	beat	fight	fought	lose	lost	sleep	slept
become	became	find	found	make	made	speak	spoke
begin	began	fly	flew	mean	meant	spend	spent
bite	bit	forget	forgot	meet	met	stand	stood
break	broke	get	got	pay	paid	steal	stole
bring	brought	give	gave	put	put	swim	swam
build	built	go	went	read	read	take	took
buy	bought	grow	grew	ride	rode	teach	taught
catch	caught	have	had	ring	rang	tear	tore
choose	chose	hear	heard	run	ran	tell	told
come	came	hide	hid	say	said	think	thought
cost	cost	hit	hit	see	saw	throw	threw
cut	cut	hurt	hurt	sell	sold	wake	woke
do	did	keep	kept	send	sent	wear	wore
drink	drank	know	knew	shine	shone	win	won
drive	drove	learn	learnt	shoot	shot	write	wrote
eat	ate	leave	left	shut	shut		
fall	fell	lend	lent	sing	sang		

Listening appendix

Unit two

b) Four conversations

Conversation 1
A Hi.
B Good morning.
A Yeah ... er ... give me an egg salad, please, and ... um ... an apple pie.
B An egg salad and an apple pie. Anything to drink?
A Yeah ... give me an orange juice, please.
B Right.

Conversation 2
A 'Afternoon.
B Good afternoon. Can I help you?
A Yes, please. A tuna sandwich, please ... and ... er ... a chicken sandwich.
B OK. Anything else?
A Mmmm. A drink ... a tea, please. Oh, and an ice cream.
B Fine. That's three pounds fourteen.
A Here you are.
B Thank you. Goodbye.

Conversation 3
A Good evening. A cheese salad, an apple juice ... and an apple pie, please.
B OK. Is that all?
A Yes, that's all. Thank you very much.
B Fine. You can pay over there.

Conversation 4
A Hi.
B Hi.
A A chicken salad and an egg sandwich, please.
B Anything for dessert?
A Oh, yes. Um ... an apple ... no, an ice cream, please.
B An ice cream. Drink?
A An ... no. No, thank you. That's fine.

Unit four

f) Three people

1 Hi, I'm Gary Taylor. That's T–A–Y–L–O–R. I'm a midfield player for Liverpool and England. I'm from Liverpool, and my address is 95 Kennedy Road, Liverpool. OK? 95 Kennedy Road. And my phone number? Oh, that's 051–447–6322.

2 Good morning. My name's Wilson ... Lisa Wilson ... and my address? Yes, it's 161 Snowdon Road ... Snowdon? That's S–N–O–W–D–O–N, Snowdon road, Southampton. Spell Southampton? Oh, all right ... it's S–O–U–T–H–A–M–P–T–O–N. And my phone number? Yes, it's 0703–88664. OK? Yes. I can wait.

3 Hello, I'm Sarah Jones. I'm a student, and I live in London. Where? Oh, I live at number 108, Cambridge Road – that's C–A–M–B–R–I–D–G–E, London SE13. My phone number? Oh, there isn't a telephone in the house.

Unit six

d) Announcements

1 The twenty forty train to London is now leaving from platform four.

2 The twenty-one hundred train to Oxford, calling at Basingstoke and Reading, is at platform two.

3 The twenty-one fifteen departure to Bournemouth is now standing at platform three. Passengers for Brockenhurst take the first three carriages.

4 Passengers for the twenty-one fifty train to Manchester and Liverpool please go at once to platform four.

5 The twenty-two thirty to Portsmouth is now arriving at platform one.

Unit nine

d) Women's 200-metre race

Announcer Well, here we are at the start of the women's two hundred metres.

Starter Ready? On your marks ... get set ...

Announcer They're off. And the Australian's in front. She's very fast ... very fast. The British girl and the Chinese are behind her, and the Spanish girl and the Dutch runner are behind them. Now the German girl is next to the Dutch girl ... oh, she's in front of her. The British girl's in front of the Chinese, yes ... she's just behind the Australian. Oh, look at that! It's the Spanish runner, she's next to the Chinese, now she's in front of her ... Fifty metres to go ... and it's the Spanish girl in front, then the Australian ... the Chinese is behind the British girl, then the German ... and the Dutch girl's behind her ... and that's it!

And here's the result. The Spanish girl is the winner, the Australian is second, the British is third, the Chinese runner is fourth, the German runner is fifth, and the Dutch girl is sixth.

Unit eleven

f) What's in the fridge?

Man Is there any food in the fridge, Janet? I'm really hungry ...
Woman Well, there's some butter, some fruit. And there are some tomatoes.
Man Is that all? Isn't there any meat, or eggs, or anything?
Woman Well, there *are* some eggs, but they're very old. There isn't any chicken left ... or any salad ... and there aren't any hamburgers.
Man What about in the door?
Woman There's some cheese. Ergh! That's very old, too. And some milk. The milk's OK. Oh, and a bottle of Perrier water, well, half a bottle.
Man Oh, well. Let's go to a restaurant, then ...

Unit thirteen

c Who are they talking about?

1 How old? I don't know ... about twenty-five or twenty-six, I think. He's average-build. He's got dark hair ... dark-brown hair, and he's got a beard. He's wearing a short-sleeved shirt. It's kind of green, with ... well, he's wearing bluish trousers. Light-blue trousers.

2 What's she like? Er ... she's good-looking. She isn't tall. She's average-height, I'd say. She's got nice hair. It's blond, and quite short, really. I suppose she's about 35 or 36. She's wearing a brown suit, it's got a nice jacket.

3 What's he like? Umm ... he's average-height, in his twenties, I think. He's got brown hair, it's not very long. He's quite good-looking. He looks very fit ... well, he *is* a sportsman. He's wearing a pullover and trousers, there are a lot of colours in the pullover. I don't like it very much.

Unit sixteen

b Seaville

1 Now, let me think ... yes, go along this street to the end, then go across the river. Turn right and walk along River Street ... about eight hundred metres. The castle's at the end of the street. You can't miss it.

2 Yes ... well, take the first right, go past the supermarket and turn left at the end of the road. Then take the first road on the right. It's called ... er, West Road, I think. You'll see it on your right. It isn't very far. Don't go past it!

3 Ah ... I'm a stranger here myself, actually. But I think I know. Go along this street, go straight past the cathedral ... you can't miss the cathedral, and go straight on to the river. Go across the bridge, and turn ... turn right. Go past the railway station, it's on the left, and carry straight on to the next road on the left. Turn left, and walk along that street. Go over the railway bridge, and it's on your left. It's a long way!

4 You're going the wrong way. Turn round and go along Cathedral Street to Sea Road. Turn left and go straight on to the sea. Turn right at the Promenade ... and it's the second hotel on right. You can't miss it.

Unit twenty

b Dinner

1 **Waiter** Good evening, madam.
Woman Good evening. Could I have the menu, please?
Waiter Certainly, madam. Here it is.
Woman Thank you. What's the soup of the day?
Waiter Chicken.
Woman Fine. A chicken soup, please. And fish and chips.
Waiter Would you like a dessert?
Woman Yes, please. I'd like a fruit salad.

2 **Waiter** Good evening, sir. What would you like?
Man I'd like melon with ham for a starter.
Waiter And the main course?
Man Could I have a steak, please?
Waiter How would you like it?
Man Well-done, please. And could I have a side salad?
Waiter Anything else, sir?
Man Yes, an ice cream, please.
Waiter What flavour would you like?
Man Vanilla, please.

3 **Woman** Could we see the menu, please?
Waiter Yes. Here you are, madam.
Woman Could we have two tomato soups?
Waiter Yes, madam. Anything else?
Woman Yes, we'd like two chicken, please.
Waiter Anything for dessert?
Woman Have you got a fruit salad?
Waiter Yes, madam.
Woman Fine. One fruit salad, and one strawberry ice cream, please.

Unit twenty-two

e Three conversations

1 A Four, please.
B Which film?
A Oh, sorry ... for Rumba 5.
B That's £14.
A What time's the next performance?
B It's at twenty past five.
A Thank you.

2 C Could I have six tickets for The Yorkshire Ballet, please?
D Which day?
C For Thursday, please.
D Where would you like to sit?
C At the front, please.
D We haven't got six seats at the front ... what about the middle?
C Right ... that's fine.

3 E Hello?
F Cannon Cinemas ... Can I help you?
E Er ... yes, what time's *The Mountain of the Giants*?
F The first performance is at five to two, madam.
E Oh dear. That's too early. What time's the next performance?
F Five past three.
E That's OK. How much are the tickets?
F They're three fifty.
E Thank you.

Unit twenty-five

a What's happening?

Cobb It's going to stop ... Yes, it's stopping outside number 20. A man's getting out. Look at that! It's Willy Craig, the bank robber. Come on, are you taking photographs or not?
Kennedy Great! He's going in. He's ringing the door bell.
Cobb The door's opening. I can see Butcher Bailey. Butcher Bailey and Willy Craig. What's happening?
Kennedy They're walking to the car. I can't see the driver ...
Cobb I can ... it's Kevin Daniels.
Kennedy They're getting into the car ... Come on, hurry!

Unit twenty-nine

c) Four jobs

1 Hi, my name's Gary... Gary Miller, and I live in Manchester. Do I work regular hours? Well, I never work on Mondays. I work from ten to one every day. Sometimes I work on Wednesday evenings... or Tuesday evenings. I always work on Saturdays. Oh, but I don't work in the summer. Now, what do I do? I'm a footballer... I play for Manchester United!

2 In the police we work shifts. This month I'm on the early shift, and I begin at 6 a.m. and work until 2 p.m. Sometimes I'm on the late shift, and then I always work from 2 p.m. until 10 p.m. I don't like the night shift. I'm going to be on that next month. The night shift begins at 10 p.m. and finishes at six in the morning. Does my job have regular hours? Well, I don't know, really. I work the same hours every day for a month. But my days off are different every month: this month they're Thursday and Sunday.

3 I start work at five, or half past five in the morning. I'm a farmer. We've got a small farm in the west of England. We stop and have breakfast at eight. We work all day. We finish at six or seven in the evening... sometimes later. Do we have days off? No, we don't! We work seven days a week. The animals never have Sundays off, and we can't! We always work Sunday mornings from six to eight, and again in the afternoon from four to six. We've got sixty cows, and we need to milk them.

Conversation four

I work at home. I'm a computer programmer. I go into the company's office once or twice a week for meetings, but I do all my work in my office at home. It's easy, really. I've got a computer here, a modem – that's a telephone link between my computer and the company's computer – and a telefax machine. I work about thirty-five hours a week. Sometimes I work twelve hours a day, and some days I only work two or three hours. I never work on Saturdays and Sundays. I always get the children from school at four o'clock, and I never work between four and six. In the future I think there are going to be more jobs like mine.

Unit thirty-one

g) Snacks survey

Man 071–115–9872.
Julie Good afternoon. I'm doing a market research survey. Could I ask you some questions, please?
Man Well, I'm busy, but I suppose so...
Julie Thank you. Right... How often do you eat between meals?
Man Are you serious? Oh, I don't know... quite often, really. I mean, every day.
Julie That's fine. And do you eat any of these things? I'm going to read a list. OK?
Man OK.
Julie Fruit?
Man No.
Julie Nuts?
Man No, never.
Julie Crisps?
Man Yes, sometimes.
Julie Biscuits?
Man Uh huh.
Julie Sorry?
Man Yes.
Julie And chocolate?
Man No, hardly ever.
Julie And when do you usually have snacks? I mean, what time of day?
Man Well, in the mornings, and the afternoons... and when I'm watching TV.
Julie And where do you eat snacks?
Man That's a silly question. At home, in the office...
Julie In the street?
Man No, never. Are there any more questions?
Julie No many. How often do you *buy* snacks?
Man Er... every day. Well, nearly every day.
Julie And which of these makes of chocolate do you know? There's another list, I'm afraid.
Man Go on.
Julie Nestlé?
Man Yes.
Julie Suchard?
Man Yes.
Julie Hershey?
Man No. Never heard of it.
Julie Cadbury?
Man Yes.
Julie Mars?
Man Yes.
Julie Chockie Bar?
Man What?
Julie Chockie Bar.
Man Oh, yes. There's an advert on TV. Yes, I know it.
Julie Last question...
Man Good.
Julie Would you like a free Chockie Bar? We can send you one by post...
Man No. Um, ooh, yes, yes, I would. Thanks.
Julie Good. I know you're going to like it.
Man I'm not going to eat it. I don't want it. But my dog loves chocolate...

Unit thirty-six

b) Regular verbs: sounds
The listening exercise uses the text in Unit thirty-six.

Unit thirty-seven

a) Which is the friendly conversation?

1 Conversation A
■ It's a nice day, isn't it?
☐ Yes, it is.

Conversation B
■ It's a nice day, isn't it?
☐ Yes, it is.

2 Conversation A
■ Did you see that programme about Australia last night?
☐ Oh, no, I didn't. Was it good?

Conversation B
■ Did you see *Quiz of the Week* on TV yesterday?
☐ No, I never watch quiz shows.

3 Conversation A
■ Here you are. That's three pounds.
☐ Thank you.

Conversation B
■ There you are. That's two pounds.
☐ Thank you very much.

4 Conversation A
■ Can I help you?
□ Yes, thank you. I'd like some information...

Conversation B
■ Can I help you?
□ Hello. Yes, I want some information...

5 Conversation A
■ Do you often come here?
□ No, hardly ever. It's very nice, isn't it?

Conversation B
■ Do you often come here?
□ Yes, I do. I work here!

6 Conversation A
■ Do you speak English?
□ Yes. Why?

Conversation B
■ Can you speak English?
□ Well, yes... a little.

Unit thirty-eight

<c> You'll finish soon?

1 I'll leave at 6 o'clock.
2 We'll arrive at 7.
3 They play football.
4 I'll have a bath at 8 o'clock.
5 You finish soon.
6 He'll put it there.

Vocabulary index

Note: P = passive vocabulary   C = classroom vocabulary
eg: look-C1, 3 means the word is classroom vocabulary in Unit 1, and taught actively in Unit 3.

a-2
abbreviation-C19
abilities-P21
about-C4, 13
above-7
accepting-P39
actor-29
act out-C39
across-16
actress-P13
A.D.-36
add-C36
address-4
adult-17
adventure-P37
advertisement-P21
aerobics-P37
aeroplane-3
afraid-24
Africa-19
afternoon-2
again-25
against-36
age-7
agent-27
agreeing-P39
agriculture-P18
ahead of (time)-24
air-P19
airline-29
airmail-19
airport-P5, 11
album-P19
algebra-P21
alive-P13, 39
all-13
all right-23
along-16
alphabet-4
also-21
altogether-14
always-29
am ('m)-1
a.m.-P2, 24
amazing-24
ambassador-P13
ambulance-P35
America-P4, 19
American-7
an-2
ancestor-P36
anchovies-P11
and-C1, 2
angry-37
animal-21
announcement-C6
another-C7, P21

answer (v)-C4, 27
answer (n)-C7
antibiotic-P11
any-10
anybody-25
any more-28
anyone-35
anything-21
anything else-2
anyway-28
anywhere-39
apple-2
April-24
are ('re)-1
area-P31
arm-P39
armour-P36
around-31
arrive-P33, 36
arrow-P40
Asia-19
ask-C4, P16, 27
asleep-17
aspirin-34
astronomer-7
at-C1, 3, 22
at all-37
athletics-P37
atlas-P16
attendant-23
August-24
aunt-12
Australasia-19
Australia-1
Australian-9
author-P24
automatic-P23
autumn-37
avenue-16
average-13
away from-24
awful-37
axe-P40
baby-18
back-15
bad-11
badge-C7, P14
bag-5
baker-34
balcony-P13
ballet-22
banana-14
band-P22
bank-16
bass-P21
bath-34
bathroom-17

battery-19
B.C.-36
be-15
beach-39
beard-13
beautiful-8
because-28
bed-28
bedroom-17
beef-34
beer-18
before-32
beg-P17
begin-29
behind-9
behind (time)
below-P8, 9
belt-P17
best seller-P27
Best wishes-5
between-C3, P31, 36
beware-33
big-8
bike-P27
bingo-P3
bird-24
birthday-38
biscuit-11
black-8
blind-21
blond-13
blouse-13
blue-8
board-C6
boat-8
body-17
Bolognese-P20
book-3
bookcase-28
borrow-32
both-36
bottle-19
bought-34
bowl-11
box-C2, 15
boxer-P13, 29
box office-P22
boy-15
brakes-P39
branch-34
Brazil-1
Brazilian-7
bread-11
breakfast-11
bridge-16
briefcase-5

bright-24
British-7
broken-39
brother-12
brown-8
buffet-P6
build (of body)-13
burglar-P37
bus-3
business-P25
businessman-12
bus stop-16
busy-20
but-21
butter-11
buy-P31, 34
by-17
cactus-P28
cake-18
calculator-8
calendar-38
call-32
called (to be)-31
camera-C10, 14
can (v)-P14, 21
can't-P16, 21
cap-19
capital-10
Captain-23
car-3
card (post)-P19
cardigan-P17
careful-15
carefully-P35
careless-33
car park-P6, 16
carpet-28
carry-39
cartoon-P22
case-30
cassette-3
cassette player-3
castle-16
cat-12
cathedral-P16
CD-P28
Celsius (°C)-26
centre-P16
chauffeur-P13
chair-C6, 15
champagne-P27
championship-P4
change (v)-30
chart-C4
cheese-2
cheeseburger-2
cheetah-P21

chemist-34
cheque-34
cherry-14
chewing-gum-P35
chicken-2
child-12
children-12
chilli-P11
Chinese-7
chips-20
chocolate-14
choose-40
chorus-C13
Christmas-P27
church-16
cinema-22
city-24
class (n)-C9
class (1st class)-19
classical-22
clean-11
cleaner-P13, 37
clear-24
cloak-P35
clock-10
close (v)-C3, 15
closed-17
clothes-27
cloud-C26
cloudy-26
clown-P13
class-9
classroom-C5
clean (v)-30
cliff-P40
cloakroom-17
coat-33
coffee-1
coffee pot-10
coin-40
cola-2
cold-C23, 26
collect-37
college-P28
colour-8
come-4
comedy-37
come on-5
comet-P24
compact disc-19
company-21
compass-P40
competition-8
complete-C5
computer-3
concert-22
contestant-10

continue-C5, 37
control-P25
conversation-C1, 37
cooker-8
cool-26
co-pilot-P9, 23
corner-35
cornflakes-P11, 30
correct-10
corridor-35
could (request)-20
Count-P35
countable-C11
counter-P40
country-7
cousin-12
cow-C29
crazy-P13
credit card-P33
crew-7
crewman-9
criminal-5
crisps-P31
cross (x)-C11
cross (v)-39
crossing-P33
cup-3
cupboard-28
curly-13
curtains-28
customs-5
customs officer-P5
cut-P8
Czechoslovakia-P4
'd (would)-19
daily-P22
dance-21
dark-13
dark (blue)-19
darling-20
daughter-12
day-P20, 22
dead-17
Dear ...-5
dear-10
December-24
defender-P4
degree (°)-26
dentist-P30
depart-P33
departures-P6
departure lounge-P33
deputy-P36
describe-C8
desert-P24

desk-28
dessert-P2, 20
destination-P6, 38
detective-5
diamond-5
dice-40
dictionary-3
did(n't)-34
die-36
different-C17, 29
difficult-33
dining room-17
dinner-23
diploma-P28
directions-16
director-29
disabled-21
disagreeing-P39
disc (film)-P14
disco-C5, P16, 39
discover-36
dislike-27
dive-P21
division-P25
do-15, 21
doctor-7
does(n't)-27
dog-9
doing-23
doll-P14
dollar-27
don't-15
don't know-3
door-6
doorbell-C25
double-4
down-9
downstairs-17
drama-P37
draw-C9
drawer-32
dress-13
dressing room-P4
drink (v, n)-23
drink (n)-2
drive (v)-21
driver-6
driving-P18
drown-36
drummer-21
drums-21
dry-26
Dutch-8
each-14
early-5
Earth-P1, 7
earth (soil)-28
east-19
eastern-31
Easter-26
eat-23
egg-2
eighth-8
electricity-11
elephant-P39
emergency-31
empty-32

encyclopaedia-P18
end-16
engine-3
engineer-7
England-1
English-8
enjoy-37
entrance-6
envelope-28
Europe-19
European-29
evening-2
every-29
every day-29
everything-P20, 23
exact-40
example-C29
exciting-25
Excuse me-6
exercise-C11
exit-P1, 16
expensive-8
exposure-P14
eye-13
face-33
factory-12
falcon-P21
fall (v)-36
fall (n) (US =
   autumn)-P10
false-C11
family-12
famous-12
fantastic-4
far-21
farm-C29, 31
farmer-C29
farming-31
fast-8
fasten-P1
fat-13
father-12
favourite-12
February-24
fell-36
fever-P39
few-34
fifth-8
film (for
   camera)-14
film (movie)-27
finally-36
find-C7, 35
find out-C34
fine-2
finish-29
fire (v)-36
first-4
fish-20
fishing-P18
flag-8
flat (n)-12
flavour-14
flight-23
floor-18, 28
fly (v)-P21, 23
fog-37

foggy-37
fold-P40
folk (music)-P37
follow-17
food-11
foot (on foot)-31
football-4
for (price)-P8
for (time)-C3, 29
for (him/her
   etc.)-14
forecast-P26, 37
forecaster-C26
forget-P39
fork-3
form (order)-C11
form
   (competition)-P8
fortnight-P27
found-35
fourth-8
France-1
free (vacant)-6
free-31
French-7
Friday-22
fridge-8
friend-12
friendly-9
frighten-35
frightened-35
from-1
front-22
fruit-11
funny-35
future-C38
game-C3
garden-15
gas-11
gate (airport)-38
gentlemen-10
German-8
Germany-8
get-5
get into-C25
get married-38
get out of-C25, 30
giant-P22
girl-6
give-C15, 32
glass-3
glasses-13
go-4
goal-36
goalkeeper-P4
go away-26
going to do-25
gold-10
golf club-P10
good-12
goodbye-2
good-looking-13
Good morning-2
goodness (Thank)-
   P38

got-34
governor-P36
gram-19
grandchild-12
granddaughter-12
grandfather-12
grandmother-12
grandparent-12
grandson-12
grape-14
great!-34
Great Britain-P3
greatest-P19
Greece-1
Greek-10
green-8
grey-8
groan-C35
ground (floor)-28
group-C15, 21
guard-P6
guess-C21, 29
guest-P5
guest registration
   card-C5
guide-17
guitar-21
guitarist-21
gun-25
had-34
hair-P8, 13
hair dryer-8
half-14
hall-15
Halloween-P35
hamburger-2
hand-5
handbag-18
handle-15
happen-24
happy-5
hardly ever-31
has-12
hat-27
have (got)-12
have-C5, 24
he-1
headache-39
hear-21
heard-35
heart-P39
heavy-18
height-13
helicopter-9
hello-1
help (v)-P14, 15
her-4, 9
here-4
Here you are-2
hers-18
Hi-5
hi-fi-21
high-24
hill-24
him-9
his-4, 18
hit (record)-P19

hit (v)-23
hobbies-P37
hold-15
holiday-26
Holland-8
home-7
home town-7
horrible-35
horror-37
horse-36
hospital-11
hot-11
hot dog-2
hotel-C5, 16
hour-P3, 19
hours (regular
   hours)-19
house-12
hovercraft-P33
How are you?-1
How many?-17
How much?
   (price)-6
How often?-31
How old?-7
huge-24
hundred-6
hungry-28
hurry-20
husband-12
I-1
ice-24
ice cream-2
ice lolly-14
idea-39
identikit-P33
identity card-5
independence-P21,
   P38
if-P17
important-37
impossible-33
in-C2, 5
India-19
information-6
in front of-9
inland-P19
inside-15
inspector-P5, 33
instructions-C15
instrument-21
interested-37
interests-P37
international-P4, 7
interview (n)-27
interview (v)-C7
into-25
Ireland-29
Irish-29
is ('s)-1
island-3
it-3, 9
Italy-1
Italian-8

jam-P14
Japan-1
Japanese-7
jazz-P18, 22
jeans-8
jigsaw-C34
job-7
joke-37
judo-P37
jug-11
juice-2
July-24
jump-P21
June-24
jungle-P40
just-P13, 28
kangaroo-P18
key-3
keyboard-21
kids-17
kill-35
kilogram-36
kilometre-P3, 7
kind (nice)-18
kind (type)-29
kiosk-P6
king-36
kiss (n, v)-P27, 30
kitchen-P8
knife-3
know-3, 5
laboratory-34
ladder-15
ladies-10
Lady-17
lake-P40
land (v)-36
landing-17
language-10
large-14
last-22, 23
late-5
laugh-35
leave (v)-30
left (opp. right)-16
left (past leave)-38
left luggage-P6
lemon-11
let's-34
letter (post)-8
letter (ABC)-C13
licence-P21
life-30
lift-28
light (n)-24
light (blue)-19
lighthouse-P16
like (description)-8
like ('d like)-19
like (v)-27
liquid-P34
list-C10, 34
listen-C1, 3
litre-35
little-15
live (v)-29
lives (pl. n)-29

living room-17	minus-C24	now-4	past (tense)-C32	pot-10	ring-C25
'll (will)-38	minute-C3, 19	no way!-P27	pay-32	potato-11	river-36
local-P33	mirror-28	number-C2, 3	pear-14	pound (£)-2	rob (v)-25
lock-15	Miss-13	number (v)-P8	peas-P20	pound (lb.)-14	robber (n)-25
locked-15	miss (v) (you can't miss it)-P16, 38	nurse-P11, 29	pen-3	president-29	robbery (n)-25
lonely-P35		nuts-P31	pence (p)-2	price-P22	rock-9
long-P3, 13	mistake-36	obey-P40	pencil-14	priest-29	rock (music)-P12, 22
look-C1, 3	mix up-P40	object (n)-40	penguin-P24	prisoner-15	
Lord-17	model-P8, P12	occupation-P5, 31	people-C4, 13	private-17	role play-C5
lost-4	moment-23	o'clock-5	pepper-P11	prize-8	rolls-P34
lot (a lot of)-26	Monday-22	October-24	perfect-P11	problem-38	romantic-P12, 36
lotion-P19	money-12	of-C7, 10	per cent (%)-P20	programme-C4, P12, 15	room-5
loud-39	monster-P16	of course-32	performance-22		rope-40
love (v)-P10, 28	month-24	off (the menu)-20	per hour-P3	programmer-C29	round (shape)-C33
lovely-13	more-C3	offer-C28, 39	period-P33	public-P16, 17	round (direction)-35
low-39	morning-2	office-6	Persian (carpet)-P37	public health department-34	
L.P.-19	mosquito-P31	officer-29			rule-C36, 40
lunch-11	mother-12	often-31	person-12	pull-9	ruler-14
lunch-time-20	motor cycle-C23	Oh dear!-4	personal-P8	pullover-13	run-21
'm (am)-1	motor bike-31	oil rig-P29	pet-12	purse-15	runner-9
mad-P39	mountain-P22	OK-2	phone (n)-4	push-15	Russian-7
madam-C20	moustache-13	old-8	phone (v)-24	put-C2, 9	's (is)-1
magazine-8	move-15	olives-P11	photograph-P5, 24	put (past)-35	's (has)-12
main-31	movie-39	on-5	physics-P18	put on (clothes)-30	's (possession)-12
main course-20	Mr-13	on (Thursday etc.)-22	piano-21	quarter-14	said-35
make (v)-C6, 30	Mrs-13		pickpocket-33	question-10	sail (v)-36
make (n)-8	Ms-27	one (this one)-16	picture-C1, 3	questionnaire-P12, 31	salad-2
make up-P28, 35	multinational-P21	onion-11	pie-2		salami-P11
man-3	mum(my)-15	only-17	pilot-7	quick-25	sales-P21
manager-P21	mushroom-P11	open (adj.)-3	pineapple-P11, 14	quiet-15	same-29
many-17	music-27	open (v)-C3, 10	pink-8	quiz-10	sandwich-1
map-16	musical-21	operation-P33	pirate-P36	race-9	Saturday-22
March-24	musician-21	or-26	piranha-P40	racing driver-P13	sauce-P11
market research-P31	my-24	orange (n)-2	pizza-2	racket-P10, 28	sausage-20
	'n' (and)-28	orange (adj)-13	place-24	radio-3	saw-35
market researcher-P31	name-4	orchestra-3	plan-C9, P16	railway-6	saxophone-21
	national-P38	order (1, 2, 3)-C11	plane-5	rain (v, n)-26	say-C4, 35
marmalade-P14	nationality-7	order (command)-C15	plant-28	rank (taxis)-P16	scales-P19
married-12	navigator-P36		plate-3	rare (meat)-20	scar-C33
marry (v)-36	near-24	order (a meal)-P20	platform-6	're (are)-1	school-28
Mars-P1	need-28	other-C4, 15	play-21	read-C2, 21	science fiction-37
match (v)-C4	neighbour-37	ours-5	player-4, 21	reading-C22, 27	scientist-7
matter (What's the matter?)-35	nephew-12	ours-18	PLC (= Public Limited Company)-P21	refusing-P39	score (v)-36
	never-29	outback-P31		Really?-13	Scotland-1
May-24	new-7	outside-C15, 25		reception-35	sea-9
me-P6, 9	news-P6, 11	overseas-P19	please-1	receptionist-P5	seaside-P39
meal-31	newsreader-P13	over-23	pleased-17	record (n)-13	seat-6
mean (v)-C34	New Zealand-P21	over (more than)-31	plus-C24	recorder-8	seat belts
meat-11	next-6		p.m.-24	red-8	seaport-P33
medicine-11	next (week etc.)-26	over there-3	P.O. Box-P8	referee-C4	second (2nd)-5
medium-14	next to-6	owe-32	point (.)-C14	registration-P5	second (n) (time)-10
meet-P12	nice-P13, 25	owl-C35	poison(-ing)-34	regular-29	
melon-P20	niece-12	painting (n)-17	police-3	religious-P38	secretary-29
member-C7	night-2	pair-19	policeman-C4	remember-33	see-21
menu-20	no-1	pale (blue etc.)-P13	policewoman-C4	repeat-C1	self-service-P2
metre-9	no (not any)-P13		polite-C15	report-P11, 24	sell-P21
midfield-P4	noise-23	paper-15	politician-P13	reporter-P7, 11	semi-final-P4
middle-22	noon-24	paragraph-C34	poor (Tracey)!-32	representative-P21	send-P8, 34
middle-aged-13	north-19	Pardon?-2	pop (music)-27	request-C15	sentences-C12
Middle East-19	northern-31	parents-12	population-31	rescue-P9	September-24
midnight-24	note (money)-18	part-C25	port-33	return (n)-6	sergeant-P25
mile-17	note-C6	partner-C4	Portugal-26	rice-27	series-P12, 27
milk-11	notebook-C11, 14	party-13	postcard-14	rich-12	serve (v)-23
millimetre-14	nothing-25	passenger-23	poster-28	ride-31	service-P20
million-27	nought-C14	passport-P5, 33	post-31	Right-5	seventh-8
mine-18	novel-P12	past (go past)-16	postman-15	right (correct)-10	sex-P31
minestrone-20	November-24	past (clock)-22	post office-16	right (opp. left)-16	shall-39

shave-30
she-1
sheep-31
shelf-28
sheriff-P36
shift-29
shine-26
shirt-8
shoe-C8, 13
shop-C11, P19, 34
shopping (n)-27
short-13
show (n)-39
shower-30
shown-P33
shut up-27
side-22
sideburns-C33
silly-35
silver-10
sing-21
singer-10
single-6
sir-20
sister-12
sit-15
sixth-8
size-14
skirt-13
sky-24
sleep (v)-23
sleep (n)-25
slip (v)-36
slow-8
small-8
smile (v)-37
snack-31
snow (v, n)-26
soap opera-P27
socks-C18
soft-P39
some-10
someone-35
something-35
sometimes-29
somewhere-39
son-12
song-C1, 21
soon-38
sorry-4
soul (music)-P27
sound (v)-37
soup-20
south-19
southern-31
souvenir-14
space (gap)-C13, 39
space-7
space station-7

spaghetti-20
Spain-1
Spanish-7
speak-21
speaker-3
specialist-7
spell-4
spend (money)-26
spinner-P40
spoon-3
sport-12
sports-P8
sportsperson-12
spring-37
springtime-P10
square (km)-P31
square-C33
St. (saint)-P38
stadium-P16
stage-22
stairs-17
stamp-19
stand (v)-10
star-P1, 3
start (v)-25
starter (meal)-20
starting time-P29
state-31
station-6
stay (v)-26
steak-20
stereo-P8
sticker-P19
stop (v)-23
store (shop)-P28
story-27
straight on-16
stranger-16
strawberry-14
street-16
striker-P4
student-C3, 5
stupid-35
success-P27
sugar-11
suggestion-39
suit-13
suitcase-5
summer-26
sun-26
Sunday-26
sunglasses-18
sunlight-P28
sunny-26
sun tan-P19
supermarket-16
sure-32
surface (mail)-P19
surname-4
surprised-37

survey-31
swamp-P40
swan-P21
Sweden-8
Swedish-8
swim-21
swimming (n)-27
symphony-P22
synthesizer-21
table-C6, 10
take-16
take (photos)-24
talk-C4, 24
talk about-C8
tall-13
taxi-6
tea-2
tea (meal)-11
teacher-C1, 29
teeth-30
telephone-P4, 10
telephone box-16
telephone number-4
television-3
tell-C12, 16
temperature-26
tennis-4
terrible-13
thanks-2
thank you-1
that-P3, 6
That's (£1/£2 etc.)-2
the-1
theatre-39
their-5
theirs-18
them-9
then (in that case)-28
then (time)-30
there (opp. here)-6
there (is / are)-10
these-6
they-3, 5
thin-13
thing-C10, 11
think-C7, 24
third-8
thirsty-28
this-6
this way-4
those-6
thousand-7
threw-C40
through-15
throw (n, v)-40
throw away-28
thunder (n, v)-26

Thursday-22
tick-C2 (√)
ticket-6
tidy (adj, v)-28
tie (n)-13
time-5
timer-P35
times (six times)-31
timetable-33
tired-39
title-P5
to-4
to (clock)-22
together-32
toilets-6
tomato-11
tomorrow-26
tonight-P10, 24
too (also)-5
too (big etc)-39
took-37
toothbrush-35
toothpaste-P34
towards-24
towel-35
town-7
traffic-39
train-6
trainers (shoes)-C18, 28
translate-21
translator-21
transparent-C18
travel-24
traveller-33
treasure-P40
tree-35
trousers-13
Trouser-suit-13
truck-8
true-5
trumpet-21
T-shirt-13
Tuesday-22
tuna-2
Turkish-8
Turkey-8
turn (v)-16
turn (n)-40
turn off-15
turn on-15
two-way-P31
type (v)-21
type (kind)-P21
typewriter-10
typist-32
umbrella-3
uncle-12
uncountable-C11

under-9
underline-C34
unhappy-38
United Nations-P21
United States-1
untidy-C28
until-29
up-9
upstairs-30
us-9
usually-30
use (v)-24
valuable-37
vampire-C35
vanilla-14
V.A.T.-P20
vehicle-P3
verb-C36
very-P2, 13
very well-2
video-3
video cassette-19
villa-P12
visit (n)-27
volcano-P11
volleyball-P27
volt-P39
volume-P18
wait-15
waiter-20
waiting room-P6
wake-25
wake up-30
walk-21
Walkman™-P8, 19
wall-17
want-28
want to do-36
war-37
wardrobe-28
warm-26
wash (n)-34
washing up-P34
was(n't)-32
waste bin-28
watch (n)-3
watch (v)-C23, 26
water-9
way-16
we-5
wear-13
weather-26
wedding-36
Wednesday-22
week-P10, 22
weekend-P8, 31
weigh (v)-36
welcome-10

well (adj)-2
well (hesitation)-6
well done (meat)-20
went-34
were(n't)-32
west-19
western (adj)-31
western (film)-37
wet-26
whale-21
What?-3
What about?-20
What time?-6
wheelchair-21
When?-22
Where?-1, 5
where (relative)-P39
Which?-18
white-8
Who?-7
Whose?-18
Why?-25
wife-12
wild-P31
will-38
win-8
window-C6, P9, 15
wind-C26
windy-26
winner-8
winter-26
with-C8, 13
woman-3
wonderful-10
won't-38
word-C8, 21
work (n, v)-C17, 24
workdays-C29
world-P13, 24
worry-38
would-19
write-C1, 21
writer-12
wrong-20
yeah-3
year-26
yellow-8
yes-1
yesterday-32
yoga-P37
yoghurt-18
you-1, 5, 9
young-13
your-4, 5
yours-18
Yugoslavia-P26
zone-19

Grammar summaries

Unit one

Be present singular
Personal pronouns: **I, you, he, she**

I	'm / am / 'm not	
You	're / are / aren't	Peter Wilson. Sarah Kennedy. from England.
He / She	's / is / isn't	

Questions

Am I		Yes, I am. / No, I'm not.
Are you	Peter Wilson? Sarah Kennedy? from England?	Yes, you are / No, you aren't.
Is he / she		Yes, he is. / No, he isn't. Yes, she is. / No, she isn't.

Where	are you / am I / is he / she	from?

Expressions

Coffee?
Yes, please. / No, thank you.
Hello.
How are you?
Yes?

Unit two

Indefinite articles: **a, an**

a | coffee, tea, sandwich, salad, hamburger, pizza

an | apple pie, egg salad, ice cream, orange juice

an *is used before vowel sounds,* ***a*** *is used before consonant sounds.*

Expressions

Good morning.
Good afternoon.
Good evening.
Goodbye.
Goodbye.
Good night.

I'm very well thanks, and you? / I'm fine.
Anything else?
That's (six) pounds, please.
Here you are.
Thanks.
Pardon?

Unit three

Be singular and plural, with things

a / an

It	's / is / isn't / is not	a pen. an engine.
They	're / are / aren't / are not	pens. engines.

Questions

Is	it	a pen? an engine?	Yes, it is. / No, it isn't.
Are	they	pens? engines?	Yes, they are. / No, they aren't.

What is it? / What are they?

Singular and plurals

pen / pens watch / watches
key / keys dictionary / dictionaries

Irregular plurals

knife / knives
man / men woman / women

Expressions

Look! / Listen!
over there.
I don't know.
It's open. / It's OK.
What's that?
Oh no!

Unit four

Personal information: **name, address, telephone number**

What	's / is	your / my / his / her	name? address? telephone number? phone number? number?

Possessive adjectives, singular

My / Your / His / Her	name	is / 's / isn't / is not	Smith.

Personal pronoun – Possessive adjective

I ... my
You ... your
He ... his
She ... her

Expressions

He's fantastic.
Come here. / Come this way. / Go to (the dressing room). /
Go now.
Sorry. / That's OK.
What? (= pardon?)
I'm lost.
Oh dear.
Spell it.

Unit five

Be present tense, plural
Personal pronouns: we, you, they

Affirmative and negative

We You They	're are aren't are not	detectives. early. late. in London.

Questions

Are	we you they	late? criminals? in London?	Yes, we are. No, we aren't.

Possessive adjectives, plural forms

It's	our your their	car. cars.
They're		

Personal pronoun – Possessive adjective

we ... our
you ... your
they ... their

Where is (it)? / Where are (they)?

What's the time?   It's six o'clock / six thirty.
It's in the car. It's in the bag. Hands on the car.

Expressions

Hi.
Yeah. (Yes.)
Right.
Get the (bag).
Put your hands on (the car).
Go and look.
We're early / late.
Dear _____ , / Best wishes.
Do you know ... ?

Unit six

Demonstratives: this, that, these, those
This and these are used for things that are nearer, that and those are used for things that are further away.

This That	is isn't	the London train.
These Those	are aren't	your bags.

Here – this / these   There – that / those

Asking about prices with How much?

How much	is	it? this / that?	One pound fifty. Two pounds seventy.

on platform three / next to the entrance.

Expressions

'Afternoon.
Single or return?
How much?
Excuse me!
Are these (seats) free?
Aren't they?

Unit seven

Questions with Who?

Who	is	he? the pilot? from Paris?
	are	they? the scientists?

Asking about age with How old?

How old	am	I?
	is	he? she? it?
	are	you? they? we?

Asking about jobs and nationality

What	's is	my his her your	job? nationality?
	are	our their your	jobs? nationalities?

I'm twenty-eight. / I'm twenty-eight years old.

Indefinite articles a, an and definite article the

She's a doctor. / She's the doctor on the space station.
He's an engineer. / He's the engineer on Icarus.

Nationalities

American / Russian / Brazilian
British / Spanish
Japanese / Chinese
French

Unit eight

Adjectives

What	's / is	it	like?
	are	they	

It	's / is	big. expensive. fast. blue. new.
They	are	

It's big. / It's a big car.   They're big. / They're big cars.
Note that adjectives in English do not agree with the following nouns.

What colour	is it?	It	's / is	red / yellow / green. grey / black / white. blue / brown.
	are they?	They	're / are	

What make	is it?	It	's	a Jaguar.
	are they?	They	're	Jaguars.

Ordinal numbers

1st / 2nd / 3rd / 4th / 5th / 6th / 7th / 8th

Nationalities

Italian / Swedish / German / Dutch

Expressions

Win a (Jaguar)!
What (competition)?
Fantastic!
Look at (the / this) letter.

Unit nine

Prepositions of place

It's They're She's I'm We're	in on under above below	the sea.

He's They're You're We're I'm She's	next to in front of behind	me. you. him. her. them. us.

Personal pronouns (object form): **me, him, her** etc.
Personal pronouns (subject form): **I, he, she** etc.

Put	me us them him her	down.
Pull		up.

Subject pronoun – Possessive adjective – Object pronoun

I	my	me
you	your	you
she	her	her
he	his	him
we	our	us
they	their	them
it	its	it

Nationalities

-ian	an Australian / the Brazilian
-an	a German / the American
-ese	a Japanese / the Chinese
-ish	a Spanish girl / man / person / the English woman / runner
-ch	a Dutch woman / man / runner / the French girl / boy / person

Unit ten

There is . . . There are . . .

Affirmative and negative

There	is isn't	a	pen	on the table. in the bag.
	are aren't	some any	pens	

Questions

Is	there	a	pen	on the table?
Are		any	pens	

Yes, there is. / No, there isn't.
Yes there are. / No, there aren't.

What's the capital of (France)?
What's the language of (Greece)?

Expressions

Stand (next to me).
Ladies and Gentlemen!
Welcome to . . .
dear
That's correct.
That's wonderful!
Here's the . . .
Well, . . .

Unit eleven

There is . . . with uncountable nouns
See Unit 10 for uses with countable nouns.

Affirmative and negative

| There | is / 's | some | milk. |
| | isn't / is not | any | water. bread. electricity. food. |

Questions

| Is | there | any | water? food? | Yes, there is. / No, there isn't. |

Countable

1 – There's an orange. / There isn't a lemon.
2, 3, 4, 5 . . . etc. – There are some oranges. /
There are three oranges. / There aren't any oranges.

Uncountable

There's some milk. / There isn't any milk.

Unit twelve

Have – have got present tense

Affirmative

| I You We They | 've / have | got | two sisters. some cousins. an uncle. a brother. a car. |
| He She | 's / has | | |

Negative

| I You We They | haven't / have not | got | a sister. an aunt. any cousins. any uncles. |
| He She | hasn't / has not | | |

Questions

| Have | you I we they | got | a brother? an aunt? a car? any sisters? any bread? a house? | Yes, (I, we) have. / No, (you, they) haven't. Yes, (she) has. / No, (he) hasn't. |
| Has | he she | | | |

Possessive (genitive) of nouns
We add *'s* to a name to show possession.
Andrea's / Charles's

He's his brother. / He's John's brother.
It's her car. / It's Andrea's car.
They are their children. / They're John and Mary's children.
They're his pens. / They're Bill's pens.
She's his wife. / She's Charles's wife.
They're their children. / They're Amanda and Charles's children.

Note:
Words ending with an 's' or 'z' can also simply add an apostrophe (') without an extra 's' (e.g. Charles' car), but ('s) is becoming more common nowadays.

What's (your) favourite (colour)?
Who is (his) favourite (singer)?
Who are (her) favourite (singers)?

Expressions

Meet (the family).

Unit thirteen

Describing people

| What | is / 's | he she | like? |
| | are | they | |

| What | colour | is | his her | hair? |
| | | are | his her | eyes? |

| Has | he she | got | long hair? glasses? blue eyes? a beard? |
| Have | you | | |

Describing people using the present continuous tense
(*be* + *verb -ing form*)

Affirmative and negative

He She	's / is / isn't	wearing	a jacket. blue shoes. jeans. a pullover. glasses. suits. ties. shoes.
I	'm / 'm not		
They We You	're / are / aren't		

Questions

Am	I	wearing	a jacket? brown shoes? glasses? jeans? ties? suits? shoes?
Is	he she		
Are	you		
Are	we you they		

Expressions

Don't you know? ... you know.
That's terrible! Really?

Unit fourteen

Asking about prices of singular, plural (countable), and uncountable things

How much	is	it? this (pen)? that (book)?
	are	they? these (pens)? those (books)?
	is	the (tea)? the (jam)?

It's £1.20.
They're 30p a pound.
They're £1.20 each.
That's £3.60 altogether.

What size (is it)?
What flavours (have you got)?

(It's / They're) **for** him / her / me / them / us / you.

Expressions

Yes, love?
Can I help you?   I'm just looking.

Unit fifteen

Imperatives

Come here!   Don't go there.
Push!   Don't pull!
Open the window!   Don't open the window!
Be quiet!   Don't be quiet!

Be	quiet! careful!

Turn on / off (the television). Turn (the television) on / off.

Turn	it the radio the light the lights them	on. off.

Help Listen to	me. him. her. us. them.

Expressions

It's no good.   (That's locked), too.
Not you   What about (the back door)?
Don't do that.

Unit sixteen

Asking for and giving directions

I'm He's She's We're You're They're	looking for	a map. a garage. the station.

Turn right / left.   It's at the end of
Go straight on.   (this street).
Go past (the church).   Take the (first left /
First right / second left.   third right).
Go along this street.   Go straight on for
Go across the (bridge).   about (400 metres).
It's on the left / right.

Expressions

That's fine.
Is there (a bus stop) near here?
Can you tell me the way (to the Grand Hotel)?
You can't miss it.
Not at all.
I'm a stranger here.

Unit seventeen

Quantity: **How many?**

How many	– rooms aunts	are there? have you got? has she got?	There are I've got She's got	six	– rooms. aunts.

I haven't got any. / I haven't got any aunts. /
I've only got (two) aunts.
There aren't any. / There aren't any rooms. /
There are only (two) rooms.

I haven't got (very) many. / I haven't got (very) many books.
There aren't (very) many. / There aren't (very) many books.

Expressions

I beg your pardon?
Come in.
Pleased to meet you.
Follow me.
If you're (there), come and (see our house).
Pardon?

Unit eighteen

Asking about ownership: **Whose?**
Possessive pronouns: **mine, ours,** *etc.*

Whose	– pen	is	it? this? that?	It's They're	mine. yours. his. hers. ours. theirs. Maria's.
	– pens	are	they? these? those?		

Which { one 's/is | yours? / mine? / his? / hers? } ones are { ours? / Maria's? }

The { blue / big / new / red / small / English } { one 's/is | mine. / yours. / his. / hers. } ones are { theirs. / Maria's. }

Expressions

Come with me.
That's very kind of you.

Unit nineteen

Polite requests and offers: **I'd like . . . and Would you like . . . ?**

I'd like (the cassette), please.

Would you like (a stamp)? | Yes, I would. / No, I wouldn't.

What
Which one
What size   would you like?
Which colour
How many

a sixty-minute cassette
a two-hour video cassette
a five-pound note (Unit 18)

Expressions

Where's it going to?
I don't know the name in English?
What's the name in English?

Unit twenty

Requests continued: **Could we / I . . . ?** *and* **I'd like . . .**

Could { I / we } have { the menu? / a steak? / some chips? }

{ I / We / She / He / They } 'd would like { the menu. / a steak. / some chips. }

What / How many would { I / you / he / she / we / they } like?

Yes, (I) would.
No, (I) wouldn't.

Expressions

Sir / Madam
Is this (table) free?
(We're) in a hurry.
What about (the main course)?

And a (salad), (not chips).
It's off the menu. / It's off.
What's wrong with that?

Unit twenty-one

Can (present ability)
Can is a modal verb, and is the same in all persons.

After **can** we use the infinitive without **to**: *I can drive*, etc.

{ I / You / He / She / We / They } { can / can't / cannot } { dance. / sing. / read. / type. / drive. / run. }

Can { you / I / he / she / we / they } { read? / go? / type? / sing? / walk? / drive? } Yes, (I) can. No, (she) can't.

also – He can play the guitar, and he can also play the piano.
all – We're all disabled in this group, but we can all see.

Questions

Which (languages) can you (speak)?
How many (languages) can you (speak)?
What can you do?
Who can (play the guitar)?

Unit twenty-two

Telling the time

What time / When | is | the film? / the concert?

It's at { five / ten / a quarter / twenty / twenty-five } { to / past } two.
       { half past }

It's on Monday / Tuesday *etc.*

It's { in | the middle. / at | the front. / the back. / the side. / on | the left. / the right. }

Expressions

the first / next / last performance
What would you like to see?
Where would you like to sit?
Can we have (two seats)?

Unit twenty-three

Present continuous tense (see also Unit 13):
be + verb **-ing** form

He She It	's is isn't	sleeping. drinking. eating. standing.
I	'm am 'm not	sitting. reading. wearing shoes. serving dinner.
They We You	're are aren't	listening to the radio. reading a book. flying the plane.

Am	I	reading? eating? sleeping?
Is	she he it	sitting? drinking? standing?
Are	you they we	wearing shoes? serving dinner? eating dinner? drinking water? sleeping here?

Spelling:
1. Add **-ing** to the verb: **eating**, **standing**.
2. Verbs ending in **e**: Take away the **e** and add **-ing**, **serve** – **serving**, **have** – **having**.
3. Short verbs ending in vowel – consonant: Double the consonant and add **-ing**, **sit** – **sitting**, **stop** – **stopping**.

What (are you) doing?
What (am I) doing?
What's (she) doing?

Expressions

at the moment
Have a good (flight).
Go and look. / Go and stop her.
Is everything OK? / Is everything all right?
What's that (noise)?

Unit twenty-four

Present continuous tense with prepositions

It's moving across the sky.
They're travelling through space.
We're going towards the Earth.
She's driving away from the city.

When + present continuous tense

When they're sleeping in England, they're working in Japan.

What's happening?	It's coming towards us. They're going away from the city. I'm driving across the ice. She's sleeping.

I think (my sister's working).
(My sister's working), I think.
9 o'clock in the morning / evening
3 o'clock in the afternoon
(He's) having (breakfast / lunch / dinner).
Months: January, February, etc.

Expressions

It's amazing! / It's fantastic!

Unit twenty-five

Going to future: **be** + **going to** + infinitive

Questions

What	am	I	going to	do?
	is	she he it		
	are	you we they		

Affirmative and negative

I	'm 'm not		have a sleep.
He She	's isn't	going to	open the door. be there. get into the car. telephone the police. take a photograph.
They We You	're aren't		

Are you going to (do it), or not?
Is he going to (take it), or not?
Why?
Inside / outside / into

Expressions

Nothing's happening.
Don't tell anybody.
It's very exciting.
Wait a minute!
Quick! / Hurry!
Come on!
Calling all cars ...
How do you do?
I'd like you to meet (my mother).
It's nice to see you again.

Unit twenty-six

Going to future (continued)

Affirmative and negative

| It | 's / isn't | going to be | hot / cold. / wet / dry. / sunny / cloudy. / warm / cool. |

| It | 's / isn't | going to | rain. / snow. / thunder. |

There's going to be rain / snow / thunder.

Future time words

tomorrow / next week / next month / next year / next summer / next winter

this morning / afternoon / evening

Expressions

First the bad news … / And the good news?
with temperatures of / about …
Have a nice holiday!
What's the weather like / going to be like?

Unit twenty-seven

Like, present simple tense

| I / We / They / You | like / don't like | swimming. / jazz. / football. / salad. |
| He / She | likes / doesn't like | pop music. / jeans. / tea. / coffee. |

Questions

| Do | you / they / we / I | like | swimming? / jazz? / football? / salad? | Yes, (I) do. / No, (we) don't. |
| Does | she / he | | pop music? / jeans? / tea? / coffee? | Yes, (she) does. / No, (he) doesn't. |

Expressions

Next question.   A box office success.
No way!   Shut up!

Unit twenty-eight

Present simple tense: **want, need, know**

Affirmative

| I / You / We / They | want / need / know | that. |
| He / She | wants / needs / knows | |

Negative

| I / You / We / They | don't | want / need / know | that. |
| He / She | doesn't | | |

Questions

| Do / Don't | you / they / we | want / need / know | that? |
| Does / Doesn't | he / she | | |

Offers, requests, and questions

Offers

Would you like some tea?
Do you want some tea?

Requests

I'd like some tea.
I want some tea, please.

Questions

Do you like tea?
Do you want that any more?

Expressions

I don't want this one now. / I don't want this one **any more**.
Throw it away.   Anyway, …
…, then.   That's all.

Unit twenty-nine

Present simple tense for everyday habits

| I / You / We / They | work / don't work | every day. / from nine to five. / seven hours a day. / five days a week. / until six. / in the mornings. / on Sundays. / every (Saturday). |
| He / She | works / doesn't work | |

| When / What times / Which days / How many days | do you / does she | work? |

*Frequency adverbs: **always**, **sometimes**, **never***

I / You / We / They	always sometimes never	have	coffee with breakfast. lunch at home. a shower in the mornings.
He / She		has	

Time expressions

every week / month / year / Saturday
in the morning(s) / afternoon(s) / evening(s)
at 6 o'clock
on Sunday(s)
until 6 o'clock
from 9 to 5
for 5 hours / days / weeks / years
in three weeks
eight hours a day / seven days a week / forty weeks a year

Unit thirty

Present simple tense for everyday habits (continued)

I / You	usually always	wake up get up	at	seven o'clock. seven fifteen. half past twelve. one o'clock. five thirty.
She / He		has lunch comes home		

*Questions with **usually***
(**Usually** is another frequency adverb.)

What time do you usually wake up?
When does he usually have lunch?

Have in the present simple tense
(DO NOT use **have got** in these examples.)

Have breakfast / lunch / dinner / a shower

Unit thirty-one

Present simple tense with frequency adverbs
The adverb comes before the verb.

I / You / We / They	always usually sometimes often	watch	TV in the evenings.
She / He	hardly ever never	watches	

Be with frequency adverbs
The adverb comes after the verb.

It	is	always usually often sometimes hardly ever never	hot in summer cold in winter
They	are		

*Questions with **often**, **usually**, and **How often**?*

Do	you	often usually	do it?
Does	she		

How often	do they does he	do it?

It	's / is	called	the outback.
They	're / are		flying doctors.

I usually	go to school	by on	car / train / bus / bike. foot.

Time expressions for frequency

once a week
two or three times a week
ten times a month

Expressions

... very different from
What about (doctors)?
Western Australia is **eight times the size of** Britain.
Australia is **twenty-four times the size of** Britain.

Unit thirty-two

*Past simple tense of **be**: **was** and **were***

Affirmative and negative

I / He / She / It	was wasn't was not	here there	yesterday. at 3 o'clock. in the morning.
We / You / They	were weren't were not		

Questions

Was	I / he / she / it	there?
Were	we / you / they	

Yes, (I / he / she / it) was. / No, (I / he / she / it) wasn't.
Yes, (we / you / they) were. / No, (we / you / they) weren't.

Expressions

Haven't you got any (work)?
pay day
Are you sure?
Can I borrow your (calculator)?
Poor (Tracey)

Unit thirty-three

Past simple tense of be: with there..., some, and any

There	was / wasn't	a	robbery	last	night / week. / month. / year. / Monday.
	were / weren't	some / any	robberies		

Was / Were	there	a robbery / any robberies	last	night? / week? / month?

Yes, there was. / No, there wasn't.
Yes, there were. / No, there weren't.

Past continuous tense was / were + verb + -ing

Present continuous tense: **I am doing.**
Past continuous tense: **I was doing.**

I / He / She	was / wasn't / was not	wearing	a hat. / glasses. / a long coat.
We / You / They	were / weren't / were not		hats. / long coats. / glasses.

What was (she) wearing?
What were (they) wearing?

Expressions

Beware of (pickpockets).
Remember this (face).
It's impossible! / It's not impossible.

Unit thirty-four

Past simple tense: irregular verbs
Many of the most frequent verbs are 'irregular' in the past.
You will need to learn them.

Affirmative and negative

I / You / He / She / We / They	went / didn't go / did not go	to the supermarket / to the bank / there	yesterday. / last Saturday. / last night.

Questions

Did / Didn't	you / I / he / she / we / they	go	there	yesterday? / last week? / last month? / last night? / last year? / at 9 o'clock?

Yes, (I) did. / No, (she) didn't.

When did you go there? — I went there yesterday.
What did he buy? — He bought some chicken.
What did they get? — They got some beef.
What did we have? — We had a cup of tea.
What did you do? — I went home.

Note
Present simple: **I don't do it.** Past simple: **I didn't do it.**
Present simple question: **Do you do it?** Past simple question: **Did you do it?**
You can always make negative sentences and questions in the past if you know the present form of the verb: you simply change **do / does** to **did**.

Expressions

Can I ask you a few questions?
Can you get it, please?
They all (bought meat at Safebury's).
Well, that's all right, then.
Great!
Let's go home.

Unit thirty-five

Past simple tense: irregular verbs (continued)
Indefinite pronouns: something / anything, someone / anyone

Affirmative

I / He / She / You / We / They	saw / heard	something. / someone.

Negative

I / He / She / You / We / They	didn't / did not	see / hear	anyone. / anything.

Questions

Did / Didn't	I / you / he / she / we / they	see / hear	anyone? / anything?

Yes, (I) did. / No, (she) didn't.

Did you find a telephone?
I didn't find a telephone. I found a hotel.

Did you say anything?
I didn't say anything. / I said 'Be quiet!'

Did she put it on the bed?
She didn't put it on the bed. / She put it on the table.

Affirmative: **some, someone, something.**
Negative and questions: **any, anyone, anything.**

Expressions

It's freezing!
I'm frightened.
You wait here.
What do you think?
What's the matter?
(He was) like (Count Dracula).
Don't be silly.
This isn't funny.

Unit thirty-six

Past simple tense: regular verbs

add *-d*	add *-ed*
live / lived	want / wanted
move / moved	look / looked
fire / fired	visit / visted
score / scored	kill / killed
die / died	ask / asked
arrive / arrived	sail / sailed
love / loved	weigh / weighed

-y to *-ied*	double the letter
marry / married	stop / stopped
worry / worried	slip / slipped
hurry / hurried	travel / travelled

What happened?	He scored two goals for Scotland. He killed three horses. He slipped off and landed in the river.

Sequence adverbs with the past tense: **First ... then ... finally**

Expressions

He fired his gun six times.
He lived from 1413 to 1452.
They sailed round the world three times between 1646 and 1657.

Unit thirty-seven

Tag questions: – isn't it? / – is it?

It	's / is	a very nice day, an awful day, a cold day,	isn't it?

It	isn't / is not	very nice, very warm, cold,	is it?

You They	sound	friendly. unhappy. angry.	

-ing form

I you we they	like enjoy	reading. collecting things. swimming. doing aerobics. playing football.
He she	likes enjoys	

We (do / did) some (writing / reading).

Past tenses
come – came   take – took

Expressions

It's very warm ... for Spring.
But not always.
'Morning.
What kind of (books do you like)?
That's wonderful. / That's nice.

Unit thirty-eight

Will for future simple

Affirmative and negative

I You He She We They	'll will won't will not	be (there) do it	tomorrow. soon. on Sunday. next (week).

Questions

Will	I you he she we they	be there? do it?

Yes, (I) will. / No, (we) won't.

What time will (she) be there?
When will (they) do it?

Will *has many uses in English, and future reference is only one of them.*

Dates

August 3rd (August the third, the third of August)

Expressions

Look at the time!
Don't worry.
on time
Here it comes now.
Thank goodness for that!

Unit thirty-nine

Will and shall for offers and suggestions

Offers

Offer	Accepting	Refusing
I'll do it. Shall I do it?	Yes, please. Thank you very much. That's very kind of you. That's very nice of you.	No, thank you. No, it's all right. I'll do it. Thank you, but I can do it. That's very kind, but no thanks.

Suggestions

Shall we	go out(?)
Let's	go to a party(?)
Why don't we	see some friends(?)

Where shall we go?
What shall we do?
Who shall we go and see?

Want to do (want + to infinitive)

I	want don't want wanted didn't want	to	do it. go out. cross the road. be late.

Expressions

That's very nice of you.
There you are.
I've got (a headache / a temperature).
That's too expensive.
That's a good idea.
I don't want to.

Unit forty

Each	player throws the dice. space has a number.

When you pass over a red space, read the instruction.

If you finish on a red space, read the instruction.

Workbook key

unit one

1
1 France 6 United States
2 Brazil 7 Japan
3 England 8 Australia
4 Italy 9 Greece
5 Spain 10 Scotland

2
1 Am I from France?
2 Are you from Spain?
3 Is she from the United States?
4 Is he from Japan?

3
1 Yes, he is.
2 No, I'm not.
3 Yes, she is.
4 No, he isn't.
5 No, she isn't.

4
A Hello.
B *Hello.*
A I'm Paul Smith.
B *I'm (name).*
A Are you from England?
B *No, I'm not.*
A Oh? Where are you from?
B *I'm from (country).*
A Er . . . coffee?
B *Yes, please. (Or No, thank you.)*
A Sandwich?
B *No, thank you. (Or Yes, please.)*

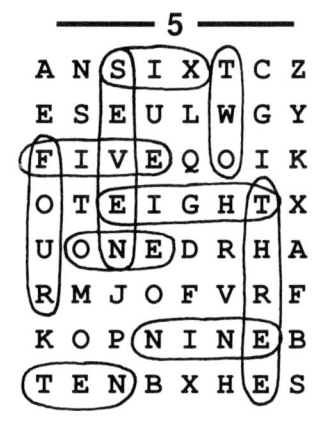

5

A	N	S	I	X	T	C	Z
E	S	E	U	L	W	G	Y
F	I	V	E	Q	O	I	K
O	T	E	I	G	H	T	X
U	O	N	E	D	R	H	A
R	M	J	O	F	V	R	F
K	O	P	N	I	N	E	B
T	E	N	B	X	H	E	S

6

seven	eight	nine
four	five	six
one	two	three
zero		

7
1 one   6 three
2 eight 7 four
3 five   8 nine
4 ten   9 seven
5 two   10 six

8
1 Exit
2 Toilets
3 Fasten seat belts
4 No smoking
5 Self-service

unit two

1
1 How are you?
  Very well thanks. And you?
2 That's four pounds.
  Here you are.
3 Good morning.
  Good morning.
4 Anything else?
  No, thanks.
5 Goodbye.
  Goodbye.
6 An egg sandwich, please.
  An egg sandwich? OK.

2
a coffee, pizza, tea, cheeseburger, salad, sandwich, chicken salad, tuna sandwich, Pepsi-Cola, morning, toilet

an apple juice, ice cream, egg, orange, orange juice, afternoon, evening, exit

3
1 That's seventy pence, please.
2 That's one pound eighty, please.
3 That's forty pence, please.
4 That's one pound ninety, please.
5 That's fifty pence, please.
6 That's one pound thirty, please.
7 That's sixty pence, please.
8 That's one pound fifty, please.
9 That's fifty pence, please.
10 That's sixty pence, please.

4
A Good evening.
B *Good evening. Can I help you?*
A *A hamburger* and *chips* please.
B Anything *else*?
A Yes, *a pizza* and *an apple juice* please.
B Here you *are.*
A Thank you.
B That's *three* pounds *eighty,* please.
A OK, thank you, *good night.*
B Good night.

5
1 seventeen   6 sixteen
2 fifteen   7 twelve
3 thirteen   8 twenty
4 fourteen   9 eighteen
5 nineteen   10 eleven

6
xytsi … *sixty*
eesnyvt … *seventy*
tynnie … *ninety*
yethig … *eighty*
rttyih … *thirty*
wynett … *twenty*
itfyf … *fifty*
roytf … *forty*

7
two - four - six - eight - ten - twelve - *fourteen*
four - eight - *twelve* - sixteen - twenty
five - ten - *fifteen* - twenty
five - eight - *eleven* - fourteen - seventeen

unit three

1
The different words are:
island   key
engine   orchestra
umbrella watch

2
a fork, spoon, knife, cup, plate, glass, television, computer, video, key, car, bus, dictionary, pen, book, speaker, watch, radio, cassette player

an island, engine, umbrella, aeroplane, orchestra

3
43 What is it?
   It's a watch.
44 What are they?
   They're umbrellas.
45 What are they?
   They're forks.
46 What is it?
   It's an aeroplane.
47 What is it?
   It's an ice cream.
48 What are they?
   They're hamburgers.

4

50 What are they?
 They're knives.
51 What are they?
 They're dictionaries.
52 What are they?
 They're keys.

5

Refer to pictures 41–52 in the Workbook exercises 3 & 4.

6

A *What's* that?
B *Where?*
A *Over* there.
B I don't *know* .
A *Is it* a fork?
B *No, it isn't.*
A *Is it* a knife?
B No, *it isn't* a knife.
A Is it a *spoon*?
B Oh yes. It is!

7

Pictures 53–55
Example:
A What's that?
B Where?
A Over there.
B I don't know.
A Is it a (fork)?
B No, it isn't.
A Is it a (knife)?
B No, it isn't a (knife).
A Is it a (cup / car / book)?
B Oh, yes. It is!

8

49 forty-nine
72 seventy-two
51 fifty-one
36 thirty-six
27 twenty-seven
94 ninety-four
63 sixty-three
85 eighty-five
88 eighty-eight
20 twenty
15 fifteen
55 fifty-five

9

56 Great Britain
57 kilometres per hour
58 LONG VEHICLE
59 BUS STOP

unit four

1

1 What's his / her surname? It's ...
2 What are his / her first names? They're ...
3 What's his / her address? It's ...
4 What's his / her telephone number? It's ...

2

1 His name's Roy Clement
2 Your name's Rachel Patworth!
3 Her name's Caroline Dundee.

3

A Hello.
B *Hello.*
A *What's your* name ?
B *(NAME)*
A And *what's your* address ?
B *(ADDRESS)*
A And what*'s your* telephone number ?
B *(TELEPHONE NUMBER)*
A OK. Thank you.
B *Thank you. / Goodbye.*

4

Column A	Column B
Come here.	What?
Owww!	Oh, sorry!
I'm lost.	Oh, dear.
Name?	Peter Smith.
Good evening.	Good evening.

5

200 *two hundred*
455 *four hundred and fifty-five*
734 *seven hundred and thirty-four*
349 *three hundred and forty-nine*
978 *nine hundred and seventy-eight*
896 *eight hundred and ninety-six*
101 *one hundred and one*
611 *six hundred and eleven*
520 *five hundred and twenty*

6

Not to be checked unless done in class.

7

1 BBC	11 UFO
2 JAL	12 ITV
3 USSR	13 CBS
4 WHO	14 UK
5 EEC	15 IQ
6 TWA	16 SOS
7 IBM	17 UNO
8 DIY	18 PLC
9 UHF	19 USA
10 OUP	20 FM

unit five

1

1 They're criminals.
2 They're customs officers.
3 They're police officers.
4 They're suitcases.
5 They're bags.
6 They're briefcases.
7 They're diamonds.
8 They're guns.
9 They're aeroplanes.

2

1 You're students.
2 They're teachers.
3 We're late.
4 They're early.

3

1 Where? 1
2 juice 2
3 island 3
4 tennis 4
5 address 4
6 toilets 6
7 my 4
8 self-service 2
9 plate 3
10 tea 2

4

CROSSWORD

Across	Down
2 my	1 we
4 she's	3 your
8 their	5 his
9 our	6 they
10 you	7 her

5

1 It's eleven twenty-five.
2 It's nine fifteen.
3 It's four o'clock.
4 It's twelve thirty.
5 It's five o'clock.
6 It's seven forty.
7 It's seven twenty.
8 It's ten fifty-five.
9 It's twelve fifty-nine.
10 It's one fifty.
11 It's one thirty-five.
12 It's eight forty-five.

6

1 is	7 is
2 are	8 are
3 are	9 is
4 is	10 are
5 are	11 Are
6 is	12 Are

7

| 1 our | 3 her |
| 2 his | 4 their |

8

A Hi.
B Hi.
A Good afternoon.
B Good afternoon.
A You're late.
B Yes. I'm sorry.
A What's their room number?
B Twenty-five.
A Are we early?
B Yes, we're here first.
A What's the time?
B Eight fifteen.
A Where's the suitcase?
B It's in our room.

9

we / our / is / The / they / Their / our / your / Our or My

unit six

1

1 this	5 these
2 that	6 this
3 these	7 that
4 those	8 those

2

1 is	5 are
2 are	6 Are
3 is	7 Is
4 Are	8 is

3

INFORMATION OFFICE / EXIT / LEFT LUGGAGE / TICKET OFFICE / BUFFET / WAITING ROOM / TOILETS / CAR PARK / TAXIS / BUSES / PLATFORM / NEWS KIOSK / RAILWAY STATION

4

Refer to 'Intercity Savers from London' chart in the Workbook.

5

A What time's the next train to Southampton?
B It's at five forty.
A What time's the next train to Southampton?
B It's at eight forty-five.
A What time's the next train to Southampton?
B It's at ten thirty.
A What time's the next train to Southampton?
B It's at eleven o'clock / twenty-three hundred.
A What time's the next train to Southampton?
B It's at twenty-three forty-five.

6

Man *Good evening.*
You *Good evening.* Two *tickets* to Southampton, *please.*
Man *Single* or *return?*
You Return, *please.*
Man *That's twenty-eight pounds please.*
You Thank *you. What time's the* next train?
Man *It's at twenty forty-five.*
You Thank *you.*

7

Man *Good afternoon.*
You *Good afternoon.* A ticket *to Bournemouth, please.*
Man *Single or return?*
You Return, please.
Man *Seventeen pounds fifty,* please.
You And *what time's the next train?*
Man *It's at thirteen forty-five.*
You OK, *thanks.*

8

A Is this the Manchester / London / Portsmouth train?
B No, it isn't. That's the Manchester / London / Portsmouth train.
A Where?
B It's over there, on platform 4 / 1 / 3.

unit seven

1

Refer to the pictures and information in the Workbook.

2

1 Olga Yeltsov is from Leningrad.
2 Ramon Gutierrez is Spanish.
3 Olga Yeltsov is Russian.
4 Pierre Dubois is French.
5 Mitsuko Tanaka is Japanese.
6 Olga Yeltsov is an astronaut.
7 Mitsuko Tanaka is from Osaka.
8 Ramon Gutierrez is a footballer.
9 Ramon Gutierrez is from Madrid.
10 Pierre Dubois is a film director.

3

1	Who	6	What
2	What	7	Who
3	Who	8	What
4	Who	9	What
5	Who	10	What

4

```
R A J F Q C W E R
U J V R B H G N L
S A M E R I C A N
S P A N I S H A Y
I A B C T K I G M
A N E H I S N S N
N E O P S I E U B
I S F I H O S T
L E U T R D E T H
B R A Z I L I A N
```

5

-ish	-an
British	American
Spanish	

-ian	-ese
Russian	Japanese
Brazilian	Chinese

-ch
French

6

1 It's French.
2 We're British.
3 I'm American.
4 She's Chinese.
5 You're Japanese.
6 He's Russian.

7

2,998 *Two thousand nine hundred and ninety-eight*
4,073 *Four thousand and seventy-three*
3,888 *Three thousand eight hundred and eighty-eight*
7,000 *Seven thousand*
5,001 *Five thousand and one*
1,296 *One thousand two hundred and ninety-six*
9,650 *Nine thousand six hundred and fifty*
8,421 *Eight thousand four hundred and twenty-one*

8

Customs officer Good morning.
You *Good morning.*
Customs officer What's your name?
You *(NAME)*
Customs officer And what nationality are you?
You *(NATIONALITY)*
Customs officer And where are you from? What's your home town?
You *(COUNTRY and HOMETOWN)*
Customs officer How old are you?
You *(AGE)*
Customs officer What's your job?
You *(JOB)*
Customs officer OK, thank you. Goodbye.
You *Goodbye.*

9

1 (They're) detectives.
2 (She's from) Hollywood.
3 (He's) Spanish.
4 (He's) a footballer.
5 (He's) English / British.
6 (She's) from Czechoslovakia.
7 (He's) the England (and / or Southampton) goalkeeper.
8 (They're) American.

10

age	interview
astronomer	kiosk
buffet	platform
driver	return
engineer	scientist
hundred	surname

unit eight

1

Refer to the pictures and information in the Workbook.

2

(Answers to 2, 3, 4, and 6 depend on individual students.)

1 Grey and red.
5 Red, white, and blue.
7 Red or green.
8 White or brown.

3

1	Red	5	Grey
2	Blue	6	Black
3	White	7	Brown
4	Green	8	Pink

— 4 —

The different words are:

big	blue
grey	lost
old	flag
Japanese	personal stereo
white	suitcase

— 5 —

a 2, 3, 4, 9, 10
an 1, 5, 6, 7, 8

— 6 —

1. They're big trucks.
2. They're blue flags.
3. They're American aeroplanes.
4. It's a brown chair.
5. It's a new calculator.
6. They're white shirts.
7. It's a black umbrella.
8. They're expensive suitcases.
9. It's a slow train.
10. They're beautiful pictures.
11. It's an old engine.
12. It's an Italian knife.

— 7 —

Example:
A Look. This is my new *(pen)*.
B Hmmm, *what* make *is it*?
A *It's a (Parker)*.
B *What's it* like?
A Oh, it's *(blue)* and *(beautiful)*.

— 8 —

Open exercise. Students provide own questions and answers.

— 9 —

28,642	50,911
31,900	43,656
40,000	31,808
21,674	75,249

— 10 —

90,876 *ninety thousand eight hundred and seventy-six*
43,006 *forty-three thousand and six*
21,740 *twenty-one thousand seven hundred and forty*
30,000 *thirty thousand*
55,555 *fifty-five thousand five hundred and fifty-five*

— 11 —

Number three is second.
Number eight is third.
Number one is fourth.
Number seven is fifth.
Number two is sixth.
Number five is seventh.
Number four is eighth.

unit nine

— 1 —

1. Where's the pen?
   It's *under* the magazine.
   Where's the magazine?
   It's *on* the table.
2. Who's *in* the sea?
   John's *in* the sea.
3. It's *behind* you!
4. Where's the cup?
   It's *on* the television.
   Where's the television?
   It's *next to* the window.
5. Where are the taxis?
   They're *in front of* the station.
6. The diver is *above* the old ship.
   The old ship is *below* the diver.

— 2 —

1. Look at us!
2. Look at them!
3. Look at her!
4. Look at him / her / it!
5. Look at him!

— 3 —

Refer to the picture in the Workbook.

— 4 —

Picture 2
A Look at him. He's from Paris.
B Where's Paris?
A It's in France.
B Oh, he's French.

Picture 3
A Look at her. She's from Sydney.
B Where's Sydney?
A It's in Australia.
B Oh, she's Australian.

Picture 4
A Look at them. They're from Madrid.
B Where's Madrid?
A It's in Spain.
B Oh, they're Spanish.

— 5 —

I	*my*	me
He	his	*him*
She	her	her
We	our	*us*
They	*their*	them
You	your	*you*
It	its	*it*

— 6 —

behind	rock
below	runner
dog	them
down	under
pull	up
put	us

— 7 —

Examples:
Ambulance is above Mountain Rescue.
Cave Rescue is next to Coastguard.
Fire is next to Police.
Coastguard is next to Mountain Rescue.

— 8 —

1. (Answer depends on students' nationalities.)
2. under
3. from
4. in

unit ten

— 1 —

Examples:
Is there a fridge in the window?
Yes, there is.

Are there any videos in the window?
Yes, there are.

Is there a television in the window?
Yes, there is.

Are there any hair dryers in the window?
Yes, there are.

— 2 —

1	any	4	a
2	a	5	any
3	some	6	an

— 3 —

Refer to the pictures in the Workbook.

— 4 —

1. There are some silver coffee pots.
2. There are some Swedish tennis rackets.
3. There's a Greek cassette.
4. There are some gold pens.
5. There's a new radio.
6. There are some blue and silver curtains.
7. There's an expensive typewriter.
8. There are some fast cars.
9. There's a small calculator.
10. There are some old jeans.

— 5 —

gentlemen, men

ladies, women, ladies' powder room

public conveniences, lavatories, toilets, loos, washroom

— 6 —

1. forty seconds
2. fifteen seconds
3. fifty-five seconds
4. twenty seconds
5. thirty-five seconds
6. fifty-nine seconds

— 7 —

Column A	Column B
singer	record
reporter	magazine
teacher	pen
driver	car
winner	competition
runner	race
photographer	camera
footballer	goal

8

1	9	8
6	4	2
5	3	7

unit eleven

1

countable

apples	cars
oranges	jugs
hamburgers	bowls
eggs	plates
cheeseburgers	cheese
potatoes	sandwiches
sandwiches	olives

uncountable

water	meat
food	bread
electricity	tuna
fruit	salami
sugar	gas
milk	

countable or uncountable

apple juice(s)	orange
mushroom(s)	juice(s)
ice cream(s)	Pepsi-
cheese(s)	Cola(s)
tea(s)	onion(s)
coffee(s)	pineapple(s)
salad(s)	lemon(s)

2

The different words are:
sugar	biscuit
meat	volcano
sauce	milk
hospital	cornflakes

3

1 apple, food, orange, hamburger, egg, cheeseburger, fruit, salad, potato, sandwich mushroom, ice cream, cheese, sugar, meat, bread, cheese sandwich, onion, pineapple, tuna, salami, olive, sauce, biscuit, tomato, cornflakes, green pepper
2 water, tea, coffee, milk, orange juice, Pepsi-Cola
3 volcano, tea, coffee, hamburger, cheeseburger

4

electricity, hospital, gas, nurse, doctor, medicine, antibiotic, water

4

1 There are some clean plates on the table.
2 That is the wrong number.
3 This coffee isn't hot.
4 There isn't any milk in the fridge.
5 There aren't any biscuits on the plate.
6 There is some water in the jug.
7 There aren't any mushrooms on my pizza.
8 There is milk and sugar in your tea.

5

sugar bowl
egg sandwich
orange juice
apple pie
milk jug
coffee pot
tomato sauce
golf club
tennis racket
hair dryer

6

1 Is   4 aren't
2 Are   5 is
3 are / aren't 6 isn't

7

1 She's in a small aeroplane above the volcano of San Miguel.
2 Martin Davis is with her.
3 He's a cameraman.
4 The air is very hot near the volcano.
5 The car's below the helicopter.
6 The car is silver.
7 No, there aren't any people in the car.
8 They're from six countries.
9 The American helicopters are green and brown.
10 They're Sikorskis.
11 The two big white aeroplanes are British.
12 There's food, medicine, doctors and nurses on the planes.

unit twelve

1

1 Zara and Beatrice are Philip's granddaughters.
2 Zara and Peter are Anne and Mark's children.
3 Anne and Sarah are William's aunts.
4 Andrew and Edward are William's uncles.
5 William, Harry, and Peter are Edward's nephews.
6 Zara and Beatrice are Charles's nieces.
7 Anne is Charles's sister.
8 Sarah is Andrew's wife.
9 Zara, Peter, and Beatrice are Harry's cousins.
10 Peter is Zara's brother.
11 Philip is Beatrice's grandfather.
12 Elizabeth is William's grandmother.
13 William, Harry, and Peter are Elizabeth's grandsons.
14 Elizabeth and Philip are Charles's parents.

2

1 have got three
2 has got one
3 has got three
4 has got two
5 have got one
6 has got three
7 have got four
8 have got two
9 have got three
10 has got four

3

1 She's married to Andrew.
2 He's married to Anne.
3 He's married to Diana.

4

1 have   4 have
2 has   5 has
3 have   6 have

5

1 haven't   4 haven't
2 hasn't   5 Haven't
3 haven't   6 Hasn't

6

1 is   6 has
2 has   7 is
3 x   8 has
4 is   9 x
5 x   10 x

7

nephew	M
mother	F
uncle	M
granddaughter	F
grandmother	F
wife	F
son	M
man	M
lady	F

8

The different words are:
car	person
brother	biscuit
green	nephew
have	aunt

9

Answers depend on individual students.

unit thirteen

1

a 1 brown   3 black
   2 blond   4 red

b 1 blue   3 green
   2 grey   4 brown

c 1 tall   4 old
   2 thin   5 good-
   3 short   looking

d 1 trousers 4 tie
   2 shirt   5 shorts
   3 suit

e 1 dress   4 skirt
   2 blouse   5 jacket
   3 trouser suit

2

1 thin   5 old
2 short   6 good
3 short   7 dark
4 late   8 black

3

1 are   4 like
2 His   5 got
3 's   6 wearing

4

a
1 a long white dress
2 dark brown eyes
3 a new silver jacket
4 an old blue shirt
5 a small red car
6 long grey hair

b
1 He's got long brown hair.
2 They've got grey eyes.
3 She is wearing a long white dress.
4 He is wearing a new red pullover.
5 His hair is brown.
6 They are wearing white shirts.

5

A
How old? *42 or 43*
Colour of eyes *pale grey*
Colour of hair *black*
Height *above average*
Clothes *red tie with white stripes, dark blue suit, grey suit, dirty shoes*

B
How old? *18 or 19*
Colour of eyes *dark brown*
Colour of hair *brown*
Height *average*
Clothes *long white shirt, green blouse, white shoes*

C
How old? *70 (in 1989)*
Colour of eyes *bright blue*
Colour of hair *white*
Height *1m 52cm*
Clothes *nice old grey dress, white jacket*

6

Refer to pictures in the Workbook.

7

Answers depend on individual students.

8

Answers depend on individual students.

unit fourteen

1

38p *thirty-eight pence*
£7.76 *seven pounds seventy-six*
55p *fifty-five pence*
£1.49 *one pound forty-nine*
23p *twenty-three pence*
49p *forty-nine pence*
£2.98 *two pounds ninety-eight*
£6.50 *six pounds fifty*
£8.25 *eight pounds twenty-five*
15p *fifteen pence*
£1.99 *one pound ninety-nine*
£4.48 *four pounds forty-eight*

2

1 is   6 are
2 is   7 is
3 are   8 are
4 are   9 are
5 is   10 is

3

rpae   *pear*
wybtrarers   *strawberry*
greaon   *orange*
leapp   *apple*
pegar   *grape*
eeippplan   *pineapple*
yrhecr   *cherry*
mleno   *lemon*

4

1 How much is the coffee?
   It's sixty-five pence a cup.
2 How much are the pencils?
   They're thirty pence each.
3 How much is the pineapple?
   It's one pound fifty.
4 How much are the films?
   They're three pounds forty-nine each.
5 How much is the calculator?
   It's four pounds ninety-nine.
6 How much is the Pepsi-Cola?
   It's fifty pence a glass.
7 How much are the badges?
   They're fifteen pence each.
8 How much is the ice lolly?
   It's forty pence.
9 How much is the sugar?
   It's thirty-seven pence a pound.

5

1 (Large) English potatoes are 90p a kilo.
2 (Best) Italian grapes are £1.20 a pound.
3 (New season) Spanish oranges are 70p for four.
4 White shirts are £16 for two.
5 School notebooks are 50p for two.
6 French (Golden Delicious) apples are 80p a kilo.
7 (24 -exposure) Fuji films are £5 for two.
8 Dutch pears are 79p a pound.

6

1 £6.80   2 £17.20

7

one	two or more
cherry	*cherries*
lady	*ladies*
ice lolly	*ice lollies*
factory	*factories*
dictionary	*dictionaries*
country	*countries*
bus	*buses*
address	*addresses*
glass	*glasses*
potato	*potatoes*
tomato	*tomatoes*

8

lb. *pound*   p *pence*
£ *pound*   km. *kilometre*
$ *dollar*   m. *metre*

9

Examples:
a
1 apple   4 grape
2 orange   5 pineapple
3 pear

b
1 chocolate   3 vanilla
2 strawberry 4 coffee

c
1 orange   3 pineapple
2 lemon

d
1 ruler   4 chair
2 bag   5 cassette
3 pencil   player

unit fifteen

1

1 Be careful! Don't move!
2 Please don't open the window.
3 Open that bag!
4 Hold the ladder!
5 Please help me with my homework.
6 Turn if off!
7 Don't turn it on!
8 Shhh! Be quiet.

2

1 Put it on.
2 Turn them off.
3 Turn it off.
4 Don't turn it on.
5 Put them on.
6 Turn them on.
7 Turn it on.
8 Don't put them on.

3

1 Help her.   4 Help them.
2 Ask them.   5 Ask him.
3 Ask him.   6 Help her.

4

1 Please be careful.
2 Please don't be early.
3 Please don't be stupid.
4 Please be friendly.
5 Please be happy.
6 Please be good.

5

A cup of tea
Instructions

6 Put some tea in the teapot (one spoon for each person, and one 'for the pot')
9 Put milk or lemon in the tea.
2 Turn on the kettle.
1 First, put some water in an electric kettle.
5 Put some hot water in the teapot. Pour it out. The teapot is hot now.
7 Put the water in the teapot.
3 Get a teapot.
8 After 3 or 4 minutes, put the tea in the cups.
4 Turn off the kettle (when the water is 'boiling' - 100° C).

6

Refer to Exercise 5

7

rewind | play
fast forward | stop
record | pause
eject | on-off (POWER)

8

1 Push rewind, wait, push stop, push play.
2 Push rewind, wait until end, push stop, push play.
3 Push fast forward, wait, push stop, push play.

unit sixteen

1

1 on the left
2 at the end
3 along
4 past
5 across
6 on the right

2

Rd. *Road*
St. *Street*
Av. *Avenue*
Cres. *Crescent*
La. *Lane*
Gdns. *Gardens*

3

Examples:
A Excuse me, where's Wood Road?
B Go along Stoney Street, and it's the second on the left.

A Excuse me, where's Jagger Crescent?
B Go along Stoney Street, and it's the third on the right.

A Excuse me, where's Watts' Gardens?
B Go along Stoney Street, and it's the first on the left.

A Excuse me, where's Richards Lane?
B Go along Stoney Street, and it's the second on the right.

4

A Can you tell me the way to the railway station?
B Yes, go *over* the bridge, and go *along* Smith Street. Go *past* the church, and *past* the police station. It's *at* the *end* of the road, *on* the *left*. You can't *miss* it.

5

Refer to the map in the Workbook.

6

Turn *left*, go past the *church*, then *turn* right. Go *over* the bridge, and go *along* the road for *about* 400 metres. *Turn* left at *the* end *of* the road. It's *on* the left.

7

There are some trees behind the house.
There's a house in front of the hill.
There's a bridge across the river.
There's a boat next to the bridge.
There's an aeroplane above the hill.
There's water under the bridge.

8

Refer to drawing instructions in the Workbook.

9

along / church / post / right / left / bridge / along / house / between/ factory / petrol station / in front of / house / miss

10

up *9*   above *7*
under *9*   in front of *9*
down *9*   inside *15*
from *1*   straight on *16*
next to *6*   through *15*
back *15*   along *16*

unit seventeen

1

Refer to the information in the workbook.

2

How many tens are there in sixty? Six.
How many threes are there in nine? Three.
How many sixes are there in forty-eight? Eight.
How many fives are there in twenty-five? Five.
How many nines are there in eighteen? Two.
How many fours are there in sixteen? Four.

3

Refer to the information in the Workbook.

4

1
A How much are the maps each?
B They're £1.25 each.
A How many has she got?
B She's got three.
A How much is that altogether?
B It's £3.75.

2
A How much are the tickets each?
B They're £1.50 each.
A How many have they got?
B They've got two.
A How much is that altogether?
B It's £3.00

3
A How much are the films each?
B They're £5 each.
A How many has she got?
B She's got three.
A How much is that altogether?
B It's £15.

4
A How much are the shirts each?
B They're £15 each.
A How many has he got?
B He's got two.
A How much is that altogether?
B It's £30.

5

Downstairs

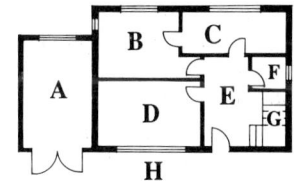

A garage
B dining room
C kitchen
D living room
E hall
F cloakroom
G stairs
H garden

Upstairs

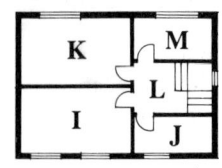

I bedroom 1
J toilet / bathroom
K bedroom 2
L landing
M bedroom 3

---- 6 ----

The different words are:

landing   Lord
bridge   paper
garden   under
go   book
notebook   aeroplane

---- 7 ----

1 He hasn't got very many. He's only got two.
2 They haven't got very many. They've only got four.
3 There aren't very many. There are only three.

---- 8 ----

1 They've got three.
2 a Fifty.
  b Ten.
  c Five.
3 There aren't any.
4 There are three.
5 There are thirty-two.
6 It's open six days a week.
7 There are about one hundred.
8 About five come back.
9 They're 30 Transylvanian glud each.

unit eighteen

---- 1 ----

1 It's theirs.   8 It's hers.
2 They're his.   9 It's theirs.
3 It's ours.   10 It's hers.
4 They're ours.   11 They're theirs.
5 It's hers.   12 It's his.
6 They're his.
7 They're mine.

---- 2 ----

1 Get it for her.
2 Get them for him.
3 Get them for us.
4 Get it for them.
5 Get it for him.

---- 3 ----

1 Who   5 Whose
2 Whose   6 Whose
3 Whose   7 Who
4 Whose

---- 4 ----

1 Who   6 Which
2 Whose   7 What
3 How much   8 Which
4 How many   9 Whose
5 Where   10 What

---- 5 ----

1 The one on the left.
2 The first one.
3 The second one.
4 Bolsover Farm.
5 The one on the left.
6 Blotsford.

---- 6 ----

1 Which ones?
2 Which one?
3 Which ones?
4 Which one?
5 Which ones?
6 Which one?

---- 7 ----

I	me	my	mine
you	*you*	your	*yours*
he	*him*	his	his
she	*her*	her	*hers*
we	*us*	our	*ours*
they	*them*	their	*theirs*
John	*John*	*John's*	*John's*

---- 8 ----

A *Good* morning. Can I *help* you?
B Yes. A (*pound*) of apples, please.
A *Which* ones? The English *ones* or the French *ones*?
B The (*English*) *ones*, please.
A Here you *are*.
B And a pineapple, *please*.
A Which *one*? The big *one* or the *small* one?
B The (*big*) *one*, please.

A Anything else?
B Yes. How *much* are the oranges?
A They're (*20p*) each.
B Four, please.
A Sorry, how *many*?
B Four.
A OK. That's £2.30, *please*.

---- 9 ----

chocolate biscuits
dining room
vanilla ice cream
road map
railway station
car park
football stadium
locked door
taxi rank
blond hair
average height
middle-aged

---- 10 ----

one	two or more
country	countries
body	*bodies*
baby	*babies*
lady	*ladies*
factory	*factories*
glass	glasses
box	*boxes*
sandwich	*sandwiches*

unit nineteen

---- 1 ----

Refer to the information in the Workbook.

---- 2 ----

Refer to the information in the Workbook.

---- 3 ----

1 A three-hour video cassette.
2 A five-pound note.
3 A thirty-centimetre ruler.
4 A seven-inch record.
5 A ten-pound note.
6 A twelve-inch record.
7 A sixty-minute audio cassette.
8 A twelve-volt car battery.
9 A nineteen-inch television.
10 A twenty-pound note.

---- 4 ----

1 don't   11 What's
2 haven't   12 Where's
3 It's   13 He's
4 They're   14 We're
5 I'd   15 It's Maria's
6 Charles's   16 isn't
7 make's   17 Don't
8 hasn't   18 aren't
9 John's   19 Who's
10 They've   20 haven't

---- 5 ----

1 Yes, I have.   5 Yes, they are.
2 Yes, she has.
3 Yes, I would.   6 Yes, it is.
4 Yes, I am.

---- 6 ----

'ee' (meet)	'e' (red)
jeans	egg
free	left
me	tell
be	bed
meat	exit
tea	cherry
Greek	engine
cheese	second
we	dress
clean	get
sea	help
street	pet
green	
she	
he	
medium	
week	
pizza	

---- 7 ----

A Good (*morning*). Can I help *you*?
B Yes, *I'd like* some stamps, please.
A How *many*?
B *I'd like* two first *class*, and one for this airmail *letter*.
A Where *to*?
B To Japan.
A Put *it* on the *scales* please, That's 10 grams … 31 pence.
B How *much* altogether?
A 69p.
B Thanks.
A *Have you got* an *airmail* sticker?
B Yes, I *have*. Thank you.

— 8 —

Europe	Asia	America
France	China	Brazil
Greece	Japan	Mexico
Spain	India	USA
Italy		Canada
Holland		
Germany		
Great Britain		
Sweden		

Africa	Australasia
Egypt	Australia
Nigeria	New Zealand
Kenya	

unit twenty

— 1 —

The correct menu:

Starters
1 Pineapple juice
2 Chicken soup

Main courses
3 Fish and chips
4 Spaghetti Bolognese
5 Side salad
6 Steak and chips

Desserts
7 Ice cream
8 Apple pie

— 2 —

A Could I have the menu, please?
B Here it is, sir.
A Whose is the tomato soup?
B It's mine. Thank you.
A What would she like?
B A rare steak for her, please.
A Would you like a dessert?
B No, thank you. I wouldn't.
A Have you got any fish?
B Sorry, fish is off the menu.
A Could we have two steaks, please?
B Rare, medium, or well-done?
A Is this table free?
B Sorry, it isn't. But that one is.
A We'd like two coffees, please.
B Black or white?
A Could we have two soups, please?
B Tomato or minestrone?
A Which flavour would you like?
B I'd like vanilla, please.

— 3 —

1 Could I have the menu?
2 Is this steak mine?
3 Whose is the strawberry ice cream?
4 I haven't got a fork.
5 She hasn't got a knife.
6 They haven't got any spoons.
7 Are those seats free?
8 He'd like the fish.
9 Could I have some fruit salad?
10 They are in a hurry.

— 4 —

Answers depend on individual students.

— 5 —

well done
tomato soup
dining room
lunch time
compact disc
second class
remote control
long life
airmail
sunglasses

— 6 —

i (big)	i (ice cream)
his	mile
rich	size
which	Chinese
dining room	dining room
him	white
fridge	wife
chicken	write
chips	pie
biscuit	private
milk	like
sticker	mine
winner	pilot
with	knife
single	prize
bridge	my
window	

— 7 —

Example:
Waiter Good evening
You *Good evening. Could I have the menu, please?*
Waiter Here it is. Would you like a starter?
You *Yes, please. I'd like a tomato juice, please.*
Waiter What about the main course?
You *Could I have a pizza, please?*
Waiter Anything for dessert?
You *Yes, a cherry pie, please.*
Waiter Thank you

unit twenty-one

— 1 —

Answers depend on individual students.

— 2 —

Example:
1 No, I haven't.
2 Yes, I would.
3 Yes, it can.
4 Yes, it can.
5 Yes, it can.
6 No, it can't.
7 No, it can't.
8 guitar, trumpet, flute, electric piano.

— 3 —

1 He can swim 20 metres. He can't swim 200 metres.
2 She can drive a car. She can't drive a bus.
3 I can read English. I can't read Chinese.
4 They can write in English. They can't write in Greek.
5 We can run 100 metres. We can't run 10 kilometres.
6 It can make a violin sound. It can't make a saxophone sound.
7 You can do this exercise. You can't do algebra.
8 John can sing. John / He can't dance.
9 My brother can write. My brother / He can't type.
10 My grandmother can walk. My grandmother / She can't run.

— 4 —

Questions:
1 Can you play the guitar?
2 Can you play tennis?
3 Can you drive?
4 Can you type?
5 Can you walk 50 kilometres?
6 Can you read in English?
7 Can you do algebra?
8 Can you dance?
9 Can you sing?
10 Can you do this exercise?

Answers to the questions depend on individual students.

— 5 —

1 Europe	7 Miss
4 Mrs	9 Maria
5 British	10 Lord
6 America	12 Mr

— 6 —

o (dog)	ο (no)
blond	zone
got	road
not	note
orange	hotel
hot	don't
lock	know
long	slow
office	post
doctor	over
wrong	cloakroom
sorry	go
	radio
	hello
	closed

— 7 —

The different words are:

guitar	him
waiter	France
read	apple
theirs	darling

8

Musician: Nationality
Phil Collins: English
Ryuichi Sakamoto: Japanese
Vangelis: Greek
Jean-Michel Jarre: French
Antonio Carlos Jobim: Brazilian
Paco de Lucia: Spanish
Joni Mitchell: Canadian
Ennio Morricone: Italian

unit twenty-two

1

1 It's five past three
2 It's ten past eleven
3 It's a quarter past six.
4 It's twenty past nine
5 It's twenty-five past one
6 It's half past four
7 It's twenty-five to ten
8 It's twenty to twelve.
9 It's a quarter to eight.
10 It's ten to five
11 It's five to seven
12 It's two o'clock.

2

1 It's on the right.
2 It's at the back.
3 It's at the front.
4 It's in the middle.
5 It's at the side, on the left.
6 It's at the side, on the left.
7 3
8 2
9 2
10 8.30

3

Example:
Man Good afternoon. *Can I help you?*
You Yes, *I'd like* two tickets for the Angie Dallas concert, please.
Man *Which* day?
You *(Tuesday)*, please.
Man Where *would you like to* sit?
You Have you got any seats *(at the front)*?
Man Yes, *we have*. Numbers (5 and 6).
You *That's* fine. How much *is* that?
Man *(£15)* each.
You Right, that's £30 altogether. Here you *are*.
Man Thank you.
You What time *does the concert/it start*?
Man It's at *half past* eight.

4

Refer to the drawing instructions in the Workbook.

5

waiter   when
wearing   white
welcome   woman
whale   would
wheelchair wouldn't

6

Answers depend on individual students.

7

1 It's at 11.05.
2 Volcano!
3 The Cosby Show.
4 Terry Wogan.
5 It's on ITV.
6 It's at 7.30.
7 It's at 10.00.
8 The Car Show.
9 It's at 10.20.
10 It's at 11.40.
11 It's at 10.00.
12 It's at 9.25.
13 It's at 8.30.
14 It's at 10.50.
15 It's at 6.00.
16 Quiz of the Week.

8

short	average-height	tall
little	medium	large
small	average	big
thin	average-build	fat
slow	medium	fast
OK	bad	terrible
milli-metre	centi-metre	metre
young	middle-aged	old
short	medium	long
OK	good	wonderful
quarter	half	one

unit twenty-three

1

2 They're reading.
3 He's sleeping.
4 They're eating.
5 She's writing.
6 He's standing.

2

a
1 D   2 C   3 E
4 A   5 B
b
2 He's driving /...a truck.
3 He's writing / ...a letter.
4 They're drinking / ...coffee.
5 They're reading / ...books.

3

2 What's she looking at?
She's looking at a picture.
3 What are they listening to?
They're listening to a/the radio

4

1 eat–eating
drinking   sleeping
reading   playing
looking at listening to
walking   standing
flying   speaking
singing   doing
seeing

2 hit–hitting
stopping   running
sitting   putting

3 serve–serving
dancing   writing
driving   typing

5

1 ...but they're not swimming now.
2 ...but she's not dancing now.
3 ...but we're not speaking English now.
4 ...but you're not reading now.
5 ...but he's not running now.
6 ...but I'm not driving now.

6

1 Is she driving now?
2 Are they speaking English now?
3 Am I playing the piano now?
4 Are we reading now?
5 Are you dancing now?
6 Is he typing now?

7

Picture 1	Picture 2
A man's in a deck chair, eyes open.	The eyes are closed, i.e. he's sleeping
A woman beside him is reading a book.	The book has become a magazine.
She's wearing a white sun hat	The sun hat is black.
A youth with headphones is listening to a Walkman.	The head-phones are connected to a small transistor radio.
A girl on the sand is sipping Pepsi from a can.	The can is now labelled '7-Up'.
A woman is writing a postcard.	She isn't writing anything.
Two youths are hitting a ball with tennis rackets.	The tennis rackets have become baseball bats.
An aeroplane is flying overhead.	A helicopter is flying overhead.

8

a (bad)	a (plane)
battery	plate
bank	station
map	play
taxi	way
have	day
sandwich	train
hand	railway
stamp	take
can	table
gas	radio

platform   paper
stand   name
happy   late
am   lady
at   age

unit twenty-four

1
1 on   7 across
2 above   8 towards
3 over   9 away from
4 through   10 near
5 downstairs 11 under
6 upstairs   12 below

2
2
What time is it?
It's one o'clock in the afternoon.

What's he doing?
He's having lunch.

3
What time is it?
It's nine o'clock in the evening/at night.

What are they doing?
They're having dinner.

3
1 It's moving through space.
2 It's running away from the dog.
3 She's driving across the bridge.
4 He's walking upstairs.
5 The comet's coming towards the Earth.
6 The plane's flying over New York City.

4
Refer to the clock pictures in the Workbook.

5
Refer to the clock pictures in the Workbook.

6
Spelling:
1 go–going
hearing   talking
happening   thinking
working   doing

2 run–ru*n*ning
swimming   travelling

3 wri*te*–writing
coming   using
driving   having
taking   moving

7
He's / She's / They're...
reading a book.
writing a letter / to a friend.
listening to the radio.
talking to John / to a friend.
driving to work / to London.
thinking about lunch / dinner.
having lunch / dinner.

8
February is the second month.
March is the *third* month.
April is the fourth month.
May is the *fifth* month.
June is the sixth month.
July is the *seventh* month.
August is the *eighth* month.
September is the *ninth* month.
October is the *tenth* month.
November is the *eleventh* month.
December is the *twelfth* month.

9
1 Ice and space dust.
2 No.
3 The Sun.
4 Halley's Comet.
5 No.
6 1066.

unit twenty-five

1
2 What are they going to do? *They're going to dance.*
3 What is he going to do? *He's going to type.*
4 What is she going to do? *She's going to sing.*
5 What are they going to do? *They're going to play football.*
6 What is she going to do? *She's going to fly.*
7 What is she going to do? *She's going to swim.*
8 What are they going to do? *They're going to have lunch.*

2
1 When are they going to come home?
2 What time is the film going to start?
3 Where is she going to drive?
4 Who are they going to see?
5 Whose car is he going to use?
6 Why are you going to read that book?

3
1 We aren't going to take any photographs.
2 Are you going to dance?
3 I'm not going to drive to London.
4 Is she going to have lunch?
5 You're going to write a letter.
6 Am I going to see you tonight?

4
Julia Oh, Trevor. I'd like you to meet my mother.
Lady M. How do you do.
Trevor How do you do?
Lady M This is my husband, Lord Mountberg.
Lord M. How do you do, young man?
Trevor Pleased to meet you. It's a nice party.
Lady M. Thank you. Would you like some champagne?
Trevor No, thanks. *I'd like a Pepsi-Cola, please.*

5
1 How do you do?
2 How are you?
3 Hi!

6
1 rob*bing*   4 work*ing*
2 drum*ming*   5 travel*ling*
3 teach*ing*   6 mov*ing*

7
1 run*ner*   7 strik*er*
2 rob*ber*   8 report*er*
3 teach*er*   9 work*er*
4 help*er*   10 travel*ler*
5 drum*mer*   11 walk*er*
6 sing*er*   12 swim*mer*

8
Catherine's saying, 'I'm going to be a pilot.'
Theresa's saying, 'I'm going to be a guitarist.'
Joshua's saying, 'I'm going to be a truck driver.'
Chloe's saying, 'I'm going to be a (ballet) dancer.'
David's saying, 'I'm going to be a policeman.'

9
drive a car
eat an apple
drink some water
take a photograph
sing a song
rob a bank
play tennis
do algebra
type a letter
fly a plane
read a book
speak French
have a sleep

10
-er
teacher   police officer
newsreader   manager
trumpeter   waiter
boxer   factory worker
footballer
composer

-or
doctor   police inspector
translator
conductor

-ist
scientist   saxophonist
guitarist   pianist
bass guitarist   telephonist

unit twenty-six

1

The weather symbols should be positioned as follows:

The North of Scotland
snow / 0° C

The South of Scotland
The North of England
rain / 3° C

The Midlands
rain / WINDY /
(e.g.) 7° C

Wales
The South-West
cloudy

The Midlands
rain / windy /
(e.g.) 7° C

East Anglia
The South-East
sunny / 1 or 2° C

2

1 In the North of Scotland.
2 Cool (10° C) with rain and thunder.
3 5° C.
4 Yes.
5 No.
6 In East Anglia.
7 In the South East.
8 Yes.

3

Individual answers will vary, but should contain the information in Exercise 2.

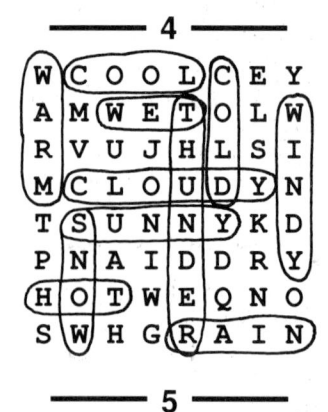

4

(word search grid with circled words: COOL, WET, CLOUDY, SUNNY, HOT, RAIN, WARM, WINDY, DRY)

5

Answers depend on individual students.

6

Answers depend on individual students.

7

u (us)	u (use)
sun	music
butter	menu
bus	United Nations
Dutch	new
number	you
gun	tuna
jug	newspaper
hurry	university
under	avenue
hungry	
umbrella	
uncle	
uncountable	

8

1 It's going to be very windy in Wales.
2 There's going to be thunder in the Midlands.
3 They're going to have a lot of clouds in the South West.
4 It's going to snow in London tomorrow.
5 It isn't going to snow in Liverpool on Sunday.
6 This is the weather forecast for Wednesday.
7 John's going to New York in the USA on Saturday.
8 Maria's going to watch television on Friday evening.
9 I'm going to see Paul and Anna on Thursday.
10 He isn't going to meet Diana on Tuesday.

9

1 windy   3 sunny
2 cloudy 4 sleepy

unit twenty-seven

1

No answers: a reading exercise.

2

Tracey
Nationality: *American*
Likes: *Rock music, swimming, tennis, eating fish*
Dislikes: *Football*

Scott
Nationality: *Australian*
Likes: *Computers, classical music, dancing, jeans, T-shirts*
Dislikes: *Working in a bank, sports*

Donna & Desmond
Nationality: *Irish*
Likes: *Rock music, sport, films, steak*
Dislikes: *Television*

3

Refer to the information in the Workbook about Tracey, Scott, Donna, and Desmond.

4

Answers depend on individual students.

5

1 Does   7 likes
2 Does   8 like
3 doesn't   9 like
4 Do   10 like
5 don't   11 likes
6 don't   12 like

6

Answers depend on individual students.
Yes, I do. / No, I don't.

7

five million
one million four hundred thousand
three million eight hundred thousand
two million six hundred thousand
nine hundred thousand
twenty million
seven million five hundred thousand
one hundred million

8

The different words are:

cool	music
now	penguin
again	at
reading	go
first	water

9

Male
boy, husband, grandson, nephew, uncle

Female
actress, Ms, niece, sister, aunt, girl

Male or female
cousin, baby, driver, guest, police officer, student, author, stranger, person

unit twenty-eight

1

1 desk   9 bed
2 cupboard 10 waste bin
3 curtains 11 poster
4 carpet   12 plant
5 bookcase 13 computer
6 shelf   14 hi-fi
7 mirror   15 light
8 wardrobe

2

Answers depend on individual students.

3

Answers depend on individual students.

4

1 I wouldn't   6 she does
2 I do   7 he would
3 I would   8 he does
4 I do   9 it would
5 she wouldn't 10 it does

5

Example:
1 He likes classical music.
2 She would like a new car.
3 She likes (wearing) jeans.
4 He would like some new trousers.
5 He likes model aeroplanes.

6 She would like a job.
7 They would like to go to the concert.
8 Bill likes the record by Tracey Chapman.

─── 6 ───

1 Q   7 Q
2 R   8 O
3 O   9 O
4 Q   10 R
5 R   11 O or R
6 O or R 12 Q

─── 7 ───

ladies / dictionaries / holidays / strawberries / days / cherries / Sundays / stories / skies / symphonies / companies / keys / batteries / toys / babies / bodies / ways / ice lollies / families / cities

armies / monkeys / valleys / industries / diaries / journeys / plays / laboratories

─── 8 ───

1 Stevens, Barnes, Brown.
2 MacIntosh, MacDonald, MacLeish, MacPherson.
3 Yes.
4 Scotland 3 – England 3.

unit twenty-nine

─── 1 ───

1 No, it doesn't.
2 No, it doesn't.
3 No, you can't.
4 Budmouth 147662.
5 At Children's World.
6 At 10 o'clock.
7 At 6 o'clock.
8 Yes, it does.
9 No, you can't.
10 Yes, they have.
11 No, they don't.
12 No, you can't.

─── 2 ───

Refer to the information in the Workbook.

─── 3 ───

1 12   5 6
2 364   6 6
3 3   7 9
4 5   8 7

─── 4 ───

Tim Well, what are *we* going *to do* today?
Julie I don't *know*. Can I *have* the Holiday Guide?
Tim Yes, here *you are*.
Julie Oh! There's an aquarium! I *like* aquariums.
Tim No, today's Sunday. *It's closed on Sundays.*
Julie Oh, yes. *What about/ How about* the Dinosaur Museum?
Tim Mmmm. What *time does it open*?
Julie *9.30. It closes at 5.30.*
Tim What can you *see* there?
Julie *(Fossils, skeletons, videos)*
Tim I don't *like* museums. *What about/How about* the steam railway?
Julie No, Tim. I *don't like* old trains.
Tim *What about/How about* Children's World?
Julie Tim! We aren't children!
Tim I know, but you can *(see a Wild West town).*
Julie No, Tim. We can go to the beach!

─── 5 ───

1 until   4 a
2 every   5 at
3 on   6 from

─── 6 ───

Answers depend on individual students.

─── 7 ───

want   wants
try   tries
dislike   dislikes
live   lives
do   does
love   loves
finish   finishes
guess   guesses
miss   misses

answer   answers
close   closes
begin   begins

─── 8 ───

1 untidy   9 windy
4 yellow 10 dry
6 our   12 Irish
7 slow

─── 9 ───

a The different words are:

centre   October
United Nations adult
plant   rain
bed   degree

b cupboard

unit thirty

─── 1 ───

Story A
Lord and Lady Mountberg live in Scotland.
They live in an old castle in the Highlands.
They usually get up at 7.00 in the morning,
and ride their horses in the mountains.
They come home and have breakfast at nine.
She always has a bath after breakfast,
then they walk round their farm and speak to
the farm manager, and the farm workers.
They talk about their horses and cows.
Sometimes Lord Mountberg goes and plays
golf for an hour or two.

Story B
Leo Annexe and Mavis Stewart are rock singers.
They play in a famous group, 'Eurobeat'.
They don't get up in the morning. They sleep
until one o'clock or sometimes two o'clock.
In the afternoon, they write songs.
Then they drive into London and practise
guitar and piano in the studio.
They sometimes have a concert in the evening,
and thousands of people come and watch.
After the show they usually speak to
their fans, and to newspaper reporters.
They always ask questions about their lives.

─── 2 ───

Answers depend on individual students.

─── 3 ───

Answers depend on individual students.

─── 4 ───

Answers depend on individual students.

─── 5 ───

1 She always has a shower in the morning.
2 They usually go to bed at half past eleven.
3 It never snows in the Sahara Desert.
4 He always cleans his teeth in the morning.
5 We never have breakfast at school.
6 I sometimes have lunch in a restaurant.

─── 6 ───

1 When do you usually have lunch?
2 Do you always have dinner at home?
3 What does he usually eat for breakfast?
4 What time do they usually leave the house?

─── 7 ───

always / usually
Then/After that
teeth
shower / bath
downstairs
always
of
leaves
to / past
at
English

Maths
from
at
has
a
afternoon
leave
usually
has
Then / After that
watches
listens
reads
usually / always
at
o'clock.

---- 8 ----

o (brown)
town
pound
how
blouse
about
now
south
out
shower
cow

o [do]
do
too

o (for)
floor
orchestra
fourth
sport
your
or
fork
north
cornflakes

to
food

---- 9 ----

1 dry
2 end
3 south
4 irregular
5 different
6 like
7 tell
8 never
9 winter
10 upstairs
11 get up
12 go

---- 10 ----

Answers depend on individual students.

unit thirty-one

---- 1 ----

1 always
2 usually
3 often
4 sometimes
5 hardly ever
6 never

---- 2 ----

1 Tony and Kate often travel 2,000 miles in a day.
2 Duane hardly ever shaves.
3 Yvonne always plays cassettes at work.
4 Yvonne always works in a gymnasium.
5 Yvonne hardly ever eats chips.
6 Tony and Kate sometimes work at night.
7 Yvonne usually teaches in the morning.
8 Duane sometimes goes to California.
9 Tony and Kate never come home for lunch.
10 Yvonne / Duane never wears a uniform.
11 Duane often has hamburgers for lunch.
12 Duane usually wears old jeans.

---- 3 ----

Answers depend on individual students.

---- 4 ----

Answers depend on individual students.

---- 5 ----

Answers depend on individual students.

---- 6 ----

by
bus
train
car
aeroplane
taxi
air
road
sea
rail

on
a bus
a train
an aeroplane
foot

---- 7 ----

A Nova Scotia
B New Brunswick
C Prince Edward Island
D Newfoundland
E Quebec
F Ontario
G Manitoba
H Saskatchewan
I Alberta
J British Columbia
K Yukon
L Northwest Territories

---- 8 ----

1 No.
2 French.
3 Toronto.
4 10,000,000 square kilometres.
5 25 million.
6 10,000.
7 Paris.
8 On the west coast.

---- 9 ----

Refer to the information in the Workbook.

unit thirty-two

---- 1 ----

Where was Marilyn Monroe *from ? She was from the USA / America.*

Mahatma Gandhi *India*
Elvis Presley *the USA / America*
John Lennon *Britain*
Peter Ilyich Tchaikovsky *Russia / the USSR*
Pablo Picasso *Spain*
Leonardo da Vinci *Italy*
Ludwig van Beethoven *Germany*
Napoleon Bonaparte *France*
Florence Nightingale *Britain*

---- 2 ----

1 No, she wasn't.
2 Yes, they were.
3 Yes, she was.
4 Yes, they were.
5 No, they weren't.
6 Yes, she was.
7 Yes, he was.
8 Yes, he was.
9 No, they weren't.
10 Yes, she was.

---- 3 ----

1 Three (or five including Presley and Lennon)
2 Two (or three including Monroe)
3 Two
4 Nightingale
5 Curie
6 Gandhi
7 Mozart, Beethoven, Tchaikovsky, (Presley, Lennon)
8 Presley, Lennon, (Monroe)
9 Monroe
10 Picasso, da Vinci
11 Bonaparte
12 Two

---- 4 ----

Refer to the information in the Workbook.

---- 5 ----

1 Nineteen eighty-nine.
2 Nineteen hundred.
3 Sixteen fifty-nine.
4 Seventeen forty-two.
5 Fifteen hundred.
6 Nineteen ninety-three.
7 Nineteen sixty-eight.
8 Nineteen twenty.
9 Twelve thirty-six.
10 Nineteen seventy-nine.

---- 6 ----

1 We weren't at home yesterday.
2 John Wayne was an American actor.
3 There were three books on the table.
4 He wasn't in his office yesterday.
5 You were at the bank yesterday.

7

1 desk	10 calculator
2 chair	11 cassette
3 waste bin	recorder
4 typewriter	12 dictionary
5 pen	13 ruler
6 plant	14 drawer
7 telephone	15 shelf
8 notebook	
9 pencil	

8

pay day
soul music
flight attendant
fishing boat
oil rig
best seller
soap opera
weather forecast
police sergeant
automatic pilot

9

bright *24*	night *2*
flight *23*	priest *29*
happen *24*	rich *12*
height *13*	straight on *16*
knife *3*	through *15*
light *24*	whale *21*

unit thirty-three

1

Refer to the information in the Workbook.

2

Answers should contain most of this information:

1 He ... round face, bald, long thin mouth, small blue eyes, glasses, about 50.
2 She ... long face, dark curly hair, large brown eyes, small mouth, glasses, about 40.
3 He ... square face, short dark hair, beard, small brown eyes, no glasses, small round mouth, scar, about 35.
4 She ... round face, short blond hair, big blue eyes, wide mouth, no glasses, about 20.

3

Oral pairwork.

4

Answers should contain this information:

She ... long coat, skirt, blouse, cardigan, boots.
He ... long coat, trousers, jacket, shirt, tie, hat.

5

1 She was wearing black boots.
2 He wasn't wearing jeans.
3 They weren't wearing glasses.
4 They were wearing long coats.
5 What were they wearing?
6 She wasn't wearing trousers.

6

1 There were some robberies in Paris.
2 There was a robbery in Dover.
3 There wasn't a robbery in Boulogne.
4 There weren't any robberies in Newcastle.
5 There were five robberies in London.
6 There weren't any robberies in Birmingham.

7

Present	Past
am	was
am not	was not
is	was
isn't	wasn't
are	were
were not	weren't

8

1 We were busy last month.
2 She was happy yesterday.
3 They were in London last night.
4 He was in England last year.
5 He wasn't at school last week.
6 I wasn't wearing a tie yesterday.
7 They weren't wearing coats last night.
8 He wasn't here last month.

9

1 careless		6 arrive
2 thin		7 small
3 spring		8 often
4 impossible		9 bad
5 cold		10 come

10

1 Yes, I <u>can</u>.
2 He <u>was</u> there yesterday.
3 I <u>like</u> rock music.
4 No, she <u>doesn't</u>.
5 <u>Were</u> you at school last week?
6 No, they <u>wouldn't</u>.
7 He usually <u>has</u> breakfast at home.
8 No, they <u>aren't</u>.

unit thirty-four

1

Past
did didn't did didn't went bought got had was weren't

2

Refer to the information in the Workbook.

3

1 *What did she do at the restaurant?* She had lunch.
2 *What did she do at the station?* She bought a first class ticket to London.
3 *What did she do in London?* She bought some clothes.

4

1 No, she didn't.
2 Yes, she did.
3 No, she didn't.
4 No, she didn't.
5 Yes, she did.
6 Yes, she did.
7 No, she didn't.
8 No, she didn't.

5

1 She didn't have a bath at home.
2 She didn't buy (any) chocolate at the garage.
3 She didn't have fish 'n' chips for lunch.
4 She didn't buy a second class ticket at the station.
5 She didn't eat / buy (any) food in London.
6 She didn't drink / buy (any) apple juice at the airport.

6

1 Did she have a bath at home?
2 Did she buy any chocolate at the garage?
3 Did she have fish 'n' chips for lunch?
4 Did she buy a second class ticket at the station?
5 Did she eat / buy any food in London?
6 Did she drink / buy any apple juice at the airport?

7

1 go	6 didn't
2 went	7 Did
3 bought	8 buy
4 didn't	9 get
5 had	10 Did

8

Note that there may be some legitimate variation in answers to this exercise.

Chemist's	**Baker's**
aspirins	bread
toothpaste	rolls
toothbrushes	doughnuts
medicine	cakes
antibiotics	biscuits
hairpins	pizzas
shampoo	chocolate cakes

Garage	**Post office**
petrol	postcards
engine oil	stamps
cars	airmail letters

Clothes shop

skirts	blouses
shirts	trousers
dresses	

9

Example:
A Did you go anywhere last Saturday?
B *Yes, I did.*
A Where did you go?
B *I went to (Safebuy's).*
A Did you buy anything there?
B *Yes, I did.*
A What did you buy?
B *(Some chicken and some milk.)*
A What about last night? Did you go out?
B *Yes, I did.*
A What did you do?
B *(I went to a disco.)*

10

1 I <u>didn't</u> go to the bank.
2 I <u>can't</u> swim.
3 I <u>wouldn't</u> like a new car.
4 I'<u>d</u> like some coffee.
5 He <u>was</u> wearing a long coat.
6 They <u>are</u> sitting in the kitchen.
7 She <u>doesn't</u> like him.
8 They <u>don't</u> usually get up early.
9 I <u>can</u> see you at 6 o'clock.
10 He <u>isn't</u> going to buy any bread.

unit thirty-five

1

Present	Past
go	went
see	*saw*
find	found
hear	*heard*
buy	*bought*
put	put
say	said
have	*had*
do	*did*
got	got

2

1 I didn't do anything.
2 She didn't have anything.
3 I didn't buy anything.
4 They didn't get anything.
5 I didn't hear anything.
6 You didn't find anything.
7 I didn't say anything.
8 We didn't eat anything.
9 I didn't drink anything.
10 They didn't read anything.

3

1 I didn't meet anyone.
2 She didn't watch anything.
3 They didn't know anyone.
4 He didn't like anything.
5 I didn't listen to anyone.
6 She didn't tell anyone.
7 I didn't take anything.
8 He didn't hit anyone.
9 I didn't type anything.
10 They didn't play anything.

4

anyone / something / anything / something / anyone / someone / anyone / someone / something

5

1 He lives in Perth.
2 He was driving across the lonely Nullabar Plain.
3 He heard a strange noise, like electronic music.
4 He saw a light.
5 It was in the sky.
6 It was a Ford Telstar.
7 No, he didn't.
8 Because he was too frightened.
9 He saw it beside the road.
10 He got out of the car, and went to the telephone.
11 It went up into the sky and into the U.F.O.
12 No, he didn't.
13 He telephoned the police.
14 They found a black mark.
15 No, they didn't.
16 He bought it in Eucla.
17 Yes, they did.
18 That was one and a half hours before his telephone call.
19 It's empty country.
20 He bought it last month.

6

Exercise does not require checking.

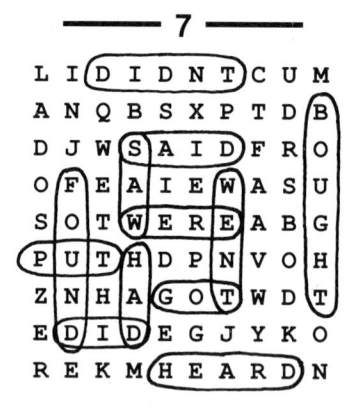

7

```
L I D I D N T C U M
A N Q B S X P T D B
D J W S A I D F R O
O F E A I E W A S U
S O T W E R E A B G
P U T H D P N V O H
Z N H A G O T W D T
E D I D E G J Y K O
R E K M H E A R D N
```

8

The words with the different sounds are:

bought put
need made
gas pool
lord hide
hotel were

9

bought found
said
was
heard
got (but also present)
put cut (but also present)
had
made
saw
hid
did
were

unit thirty-six

1

-d	-ed
arrived	started
moved	rained
scored	visited
fired	snowed
died	asked
	cleaned
	finished
	happened
	played

-y to -ed	double the letter
married	stopped
worried	slipped
hurried	travelled

2

1 1374–1427
2 1396–1427
3 five
4 fifteen
5 1402
6 King Bug XIII
7 1426
8 an elephant
9 1427
10 The elephant slipped and landed on him.

3

lived / to / King / from / to / married / have / was / killed / after / of / in / travelled / between / sister / killed / in

4

Refer to the information in the Workbook.

5

1 to   4 to
2 after   5 to
3 in   6 between

6

1 When did Columbus discover America?
2 When did she arrive at school today?
3 What did they do last night?
4 How many women did he marry?
5 What happened yesterday?
6 What time did she start her homework?

7

sound [t]
worked   asked
looked   stopped
liked   slipped

sound [d]
arrived   killed
discovered   loved
married

sound[ɪd]
started   wanted
visited   needed

8

Note: these answers are printed upside-down in the Workbook.

1. 1492
2. 6
3. 1980
4. 1969
5. radium
6. Lee Harvey Oswald
7. England
8. China
9. Argentina
10. Juliet

9

-er	-or
baker	governor
farmer	author
traveller	doctor
boxer	director
officer	inspector
teacher	actor
footballer	senator
newsreader	
singer	

unit thirty-seven

1

1. The first of January 1974
2. The second of February 1991
3. The third of March 1989
4. The fourth of April 1999
5. The eleventh of May 1996
6. The twelfth of June 1901
7. The twentieth of July 1998
8. The thirtieth of August 1904
9. The twenty-first of September 1902
10. The twenty-second of October 1994
11. The fifteenth of November 1997
12. The thirty-first of December 1993

2

Note: Answers may depend on individual student.

1. No.
2. Yes.
3. Because it was best before 31 January.
4. No.
5. No.
6. No.

3

Answers depend on individual students.

4

1. I did karate for an hour, then I had a shower.
2. I did judo for 45 minutes, then I had a sauna.
3. I did yoga for two hours, then I had a cup of tea.
4. I did weight training for 45 minutes, then I had a bath.

5

1. never   4. always
2. always   5. always
3. never   6. never

6

1. isn't it?   4. is it?
2. is it?   5. is it?
3. isn't it?   6. isn't it?

7

bathroom   18
bed   January
twelve   (Mr)

8

1. had   7. stopped
2. took   8. worked
3. put   9. asked
4. got   10. happened
5. bought   11. killed
6. heard   12. arrived

9

The different words are:

foot	had
Thursday	because
swimming	drama
thought	someone
yesterday	Ms.

10

1. 2
2. 6
3. 9. What? / What about? / What time? / When? / Where? / Which? / Who? / Whose? / Why?
4. 30

unit thirty-eight

1

1. Yes   4. Yes
2. No   5. Yes
3. Yes   6. No

2

1. Oxford.
2. Cambridge.
3. Winchester.
4. They are having a tour of the colleges, the Sheldonian Theatre, and Blenheim Palace.
5. They visited the colleges of Cambridge University.
6. They will see Shakespeare's house. In the evening they will see *Romeo and Juliet* at the Royal Shakespeare Theatre.

3

Refer to the information in the Workbook.

4

1. I'll be on holiday on 30 August.
2. We'll be at home soon.
3. The bus won't leave without us.
4. Will you be at school tomorrow?
5. Will they miss the plane?
6. I won't see you next week.

5

Past	Present	Future
was	is	'll be
wasn't	isn't	won't be
were	are	'll be
weren't	aren't	won't be
did	do	'll do
left	leave	'll leave
met	meet	'll meet
saw	see	'll see

6

1. I'll   7. can't
2. won't   8. doesn't
3. didn't   9. I'd
4. wasn't   10. Let's
5. weren't   11. John's
6. don't   12. When'll

7

1. can't   8. aren't
2. won't   9. wasn't
3. doesn't   10. weren't
4. don't   11. isn't
5. didn't   12. 's
6. 'd   13. let's
7. 'm   14. 're

8

travelling / shopping / slipping / putting / hitting / sitting / running / swimming / travelled / shopped / slipped

9

Answers depend on individual students, but should use many of the words given in the Workbook.

10

Story A

Wicked Wickham will be in town on Sunday. He's the best stunt motorcyclist in the world, and he's going to jump over eight buses. Last year he jumped over seven buses at a football stadium. He'll be on a 1250 c.c. Honda motorcycle and he'll ride his bike at 100 m.p.h. along a wooden platform before he jumps over the buses.

He broke his arm and leg last year when he fell off his motorcycle.
He wasn't wearing a crash helmet.

Story B
Prince Charles will be in Oxford tomorrow.
He's going to open a new bus station.
He'll arrive at the station at half past ten.
Thousands of people will be there.
He'll have lunch with the Mayor of Oxford, and he'll meet local school children in the streets around the bus station.
He was here last year when he met representatives of the university, and shook hands with some of the students.

unit thirty-nine

1
1 C   5 G
2 E   6 H
3 A   7 D
4 F   8 B

2
1 Shall   5 I'll
2 don't   6 Can
3 Let   7 Can
4 we   8 I'll

3
A *Can* I get you a drink?
B Thanks. *I'll* have a Pepsi-Cola.
A All right. Shall *I* get you a sandwich?
B Please.
A What *sort would you* like?
B *I'll* have a cheese and *tomato* sandwich.
A OK. I'll go *and* get them. Shall *we* sit over there?
B Right. *I'll* get two chairs.
A OK, I won't *be* long.

4
Answer depends on individual students. Refer to the Student's Book lesson.

5
play a guitar
carry a bag
cross the road
miss the bus
have a shower
switch on the light
visit friends
wear armour
score a goal
do yoga

6
1 Starship Captain
2 Across America By Bicycle
3 The Lost Pyramid
4 Soldiers of the King
5 The Sheriff of Shane's Crossing
6 Laughing on the Bus, Playing Games with the Faces
7 The Monster of the Castle
8 The Mystery of the Missing Secretary
9 Always in my Heart
10 English-Portuguese, Portuguese-English

7
Answers depend on individual students.

8
Example:
I can see your light,
it's always shining,
in the dark of *night*.
Oh, I love to see the moon,
when it shines in *June*.
Please, please don't *go*
Please don't say *no*.
I feel so sad and blue,
every time I think of *you*.

unit forty

1
1 drink   6 wake up
2 drive   7 throw
3 know   8 make
4 sing   9 ride
5 swim   10 spend

2
1 eat   6 send
2 sleep   7 sit
3 win   8 find
4 meet   9 fly
5 speak   10 run

3
1 didn't eat
2 didn't meet
3 didn't fly
4 didn't sleep
5 didn't run
6 didn't win
7 didn't drink
8 didn't begin
9 didn't swim
10 didn't wake up

4
ir (sir)   **ay** (say)
work   eight
thirty   day
German   pay
nurse   weigh
heard   shave
first   May
Turkey   way

o (no)   **ar** (car)
show   part
know   park
so   scar
low   dark
throw   far
               pardon

oo (too)   **or** (for)
June   thought
do   bought
threw   poor
soon   port
through   forty
moon   north
spoon   saw
               fork

5
3 Annie looked around ...
1 It was a wet and grey Saturday morning ...
5 Annie turned the key again ...
2 Annie turned into a narrow street ...
4 The truck driver pushed his horn twice ...

6
1 saw
2 a place for cases and bags at the back of a car
3 made a noise like a person with a bad cold or influenza.
4 a button on a car that makes a warning noise

7
a
The different words are:
gold   beach
offer   young
order   elephant
did

b
goodbye

Notes

Notes

Notes

Notes

Notes

Acknowledgements

We would like to thank everyone involved in producing, piloting, and designing *Grapevine* 1 for their efforts and inspiration.

We would particularly like to thank our editors David Wilson (Student's Book, Teacher's Book, Workbooks) and Tim Blakey (Video Activity Book), together with Michael Daniell, Simon Murison-Bowie, Cristina Whitecross, and Suzanna Harsanyi for their editorial support and encouragement.

On the art and design side of the Student's Book, Teacher's Book, and Workbooks, we would like to thank the designer, Pearl Bevan, her team (E. Mitchell, L. Darroux, J. Hill), and the art editor, Katy Wheeler. For the design of the Video Activity Book, our thanks go to Phil Hall. We are grateful to Malcolm Price for handling the production of all components. Our thanks are also due to the team of actors and technical crew who brought the video to life, and particularly to our producer, Rob Maidment, and director, Bob Speirs.

For the audio cassettes, we are grateful to James Richardson (Producer) and Vince Cross (music).

We would like to add our thanks to the Oxford University Press ELT representatives around the world, for their help, insights, and friendship during the last ten years.

The authors and publishers are grateful to the following institutions and their staff for piloting *Grapevine* and for providing invaluable comment and feedback:

LinguaSec, Madrid, Spain; Cambridge English Studies, La Coruña, Spain; I.B. Fernando Herrera, Sevilla, Spain; Teach In Language and Training Workshop SRL, Rome, Italy; Oxford School of English SRL, Udine, Italy; Four Seasons Language School, Hamamatsu, Japan; Alec School of Languages, Tokyo, Japan; Shizuoka Seika Gakuen, Shizuoka, Japan; Sociedade Brasileira de Cultura Inglesa, Belo Horizonte, Brazil; Colegio Ward, Ramos Mejia, Pcia. de Buenos Aires, Argentina; Riyadh Language Institute, Riyadh, Saudi Arabia; Lanis Language School, Volos, Greece; Marinou Language School, Athens, Greece; Stamatopoulou Language School, Athens, Greece.

The publishers would like to thank the following for their permission to reproduce photographs:

Ace Photo Agency/Mike Bluestone, Gabe Palmer, Diane Miller 12
Allsport/Simon Brut 9; David Cannon, Tony Duffy,
Bob Martin, Don Smith 12
Austin Rover 3
Barnaby's Picture Library 37
David Cannon 12
John Cleare Mountain Camera 37
Colorsport - Introduction, 37
Compix 31
Greg Evans Photo Library 3, 37
The Image Bank/Derek Berwin, Kay Charnush, Gary Cralle, Brett Froomer, Larry Gatz, Garry Gay, Antonio Rosario, Steve Schatzberg, M Tchereukoff, Trevor Wood, - Introduction, Unit 3; Cliff Feulner, Ted Kawalerski, Elyse Lewin, Christa Peters, 12; Steve Krongard 31
Jaguar Cars 8
Luton & District Transport 3
Adrian Meredith - Introduction, 3, 5
NEFF (UK) Ltd 8
Philips 8
Photographers Library 38
Rex Features Ltd/John Rogers 12
Seat 8
Sony (UK) Ltd 8, 19
Viewfinder - Introduction, 3, 38
Volvo 8
Waterski International, Joe McCarthy 8
Zanussi Ltd 8

and the following for their time and assistance:

Science Studio, Oxford
Levi Strauss UK
Sylvesters, Oxford

The publishers would also like to thank Guinness Publishing Limited for permission to credit adapted information (in Unit 21) to *The Guinness Book of Records* © Guinness Publishing Limited 1988.

Illustrations by:
John Bendall 6
Manuel Benet/Bardon Press SFP 1
Peter Elson/Sarah Brown Agency 24
Elitta Fell SFP 1
Phil Gascoine 9
Robina Green 11, 24, 39
Paul Hampson/Funny Business 34
Tina Hancocks/John Martin Artists 11
Jim Hodgson 3, 14, 18
Stephen Holmes 40
Ian Kellas/Funny Business 15, 20, 21, 23, 25, 38, SFP 3
Pat Ludlow/Linda Rogers Associates 21
Rolf Mohr/Sarah Brown Agency 7
Mike Ogden SFP 4
Oxford Illustrators 8, 9, 16, 26, 31
Colin Paine 27
Joanna Quinn 37, 39
John Richardson/Funny Business 29
Chris Riddell 1, 16, 17, 28, 36
Anthony Sidwell 16
Kate Simpson 2, 13, SFP 2
Jane Smith cover
Kay Smith 19
Brian Walker 4, 33

Studio and location photographs by:
Rob Judges, Mark Mason, Franta Provaznik
Stills photography by Rob Judges